DRUG TREATMENT SYSTEMS IN AN INTERNATIONAL PERSPECTIVE

Drugs, Demons, and Delinquents

Editors

Harald Klingemann
Geoffrey Hunt

SAGE Publications
International Educational and Professional Publisher
Thousand Oaks London New Delhi

For information:

SAGE Publications, Inc.
2455 Teller Road
Thousand Oaks, California 91320
E-mail: order@sagepub.com

SAGE Publications Ltd.
6 Bonhill Street
London EC2A 4PU
United Kingdom

SAGE Publications India Pvt. Ltd.
M-32 Market
Greater Kailash I
New Delhi 110 048 India

Printed in the United States of America

Library of Congress Cataloging-in-Publication Data

Drug treatment systems in an international perspective: Drugs,
demons, and delinquents / edited by Harald Klingemann and Geoffrey Hunt.
 p. cm.
 Includes bibliographical references and index.
 ISBN 0-7619-0542-1 (cloth : acid-free paper)
 ISBN 0-7619-0543-X (pbk. : acid-free paper)
  1. Drug abuse—Prevention—Cross-cultural studies. 2. Drug
abuse—Treatment—Cross-cultural studies. 3. Narcotic
addicts—Rehabilitation—Cross-cultural studies. 4. Narcotics,
Control of—Cross-cultural studies. I. Klingemann, Harald, 1948-
II. Hunt, Geoffrey, 1947-
 HV5801 .D619 1997
 362.29'18—ddc21   98-19733

This book is printed on acid-free paper.

98 99 00 01 02 03 04 10 9 8 7 6 5 4 3 2 1

Acquiring Editor:	Jim Nageotte
Editorial Assistant:	Heidi Van Middlesworth
Production Editor:	Sanford Robinson
Editorial Assistant:	Karen Wiley
Designer/Typesetter:	Rose Tylak
Indexer:	Juniee Oneida

DRUG TREATMENT SYSTEMS IN AN INTERNATIONAL PERSPECTIVE

The editors dedicate this book
to their fathers

Contents

Acknowledgments

This publication is the outcome of the efforts of 47 authors from 20 countries. The Kettil Bruun Society for Social and Epidemiological Research on Alcohol provided the intellectual context, the professional stimulus, and an international network for the effort. Also, it conferred upon the project the society's official status, even though the book is about illicit drugs—not a prominent topic in the Society's mandate.

To coordinate a project of this type with so many different authors is an immense and complicated undertaking; it would not have been possible without the support of several research institutions and funding agencies, as well as the assistance of many people.

Financial support was provided by the Swiss Federal Office for Education and Science (Grant no. 8471106) and the Swiss Federal Office of Public Health (Grant no. 8048). We thank officials at both of these agencies for this testimony to their belief in the project.

Two research institutes—the Swiss Institute for the Prevention of Alcohol and Drug Problems, Lausanne, a World Health Organization Collaborating Centre for Substance Abuse Research, Prevention and Documentation, and the Institute for Scientific Analysis, Alameda, California—also contributed financially and hosted several editorial meetings.

Jim Nageotte, our editor at Sage Publications, Inc., has from the beginning demonstrated his belief in the project and encouraged us through its various stages. His occasional use of German in his regular e-mail communications was something our German-born editor in Switzerland found particularly appealing.

Many of our friends and colleagues gave generously of their time to review drafts of the thematic and country chapters. They include Nuño Felix da Costa, Director, Programa Nacional de Prevenção das Toxicodependencias, Lisbon; Harold Holder, Director, Prevention Research Center, Berkeley, California; Jørgen Jepsen, Director, Alcohol and Drug Research Center, University of Aarhus, Denmark; Ludek Kubicka, Research Scientist, Prague Psychiatric Center, Prague; Klaus Mäkelä, Secretary and Research Director, Finnish Foundation for Alcohol Research, Helsinki; Ron Roizen, independent researcher, Berkeley, California; and Laura Schmidt, Research Scientist, Alcohol Research Group, Berkeley, California. We wish to thank Andrea Mitchell, director of the library at the Alcohol Research Group, Berkeley, California, for keeping the editors apprised of the latest literature on drug treatment, and all the available on-line data sets.

We are particularly grateful to James Gallagher for undertaking the linguistic editing of the book and improving the quality of the English. He has given much time to revising the manuscripts, consulting with the Swiss editor, and communicating with authors to ensure the preservation of their intent.

Renée Girardet of the Swiss Institute for the Prevention of Alcohol and Drug Problems ensured the smooth and timely progress of the project, constantly applying an organizational rigor that, too often, the editors lacked. Like Dr. Gallagher, she is a veteran from the alcoholism treatment book *Cure, Care, or Control,* and perhaps unwisely, but enthusiastically, undertook the task again. She was assisted by Edith Bacher and Heidi Vaucher, whose cooperation is also highly appreciated.

Introduction

Drugs, Demons, and Delinquents:
The Result of a Cross-Cultural Research Project

As the rhetoric of the drug war developed, and with it, a growing concern about illicit drugs and the spread of HIV/AIDS, the call for more drug treatment services could be heard. Many countries with previously few specific drug treatment services have seen a rapid expansion in the past 10 years. In this book, we examine the ways in which 20 countries from around the world have chosen to cope with the spread of illicit drugs.

Although comparative cross-national studies on policy making and policy evaluation have a long tradition in addiction research, comparative analysis of the treatment response to drug problems in the wider sense has been neglected. At best, it has been dealt with in a technical and restricted way and lacks regional coverage. Information on the basic features of treatment systems presented, for example, in an overview of control policies and epidemiological data recently published by the Regional Office for Europe of the World Health Organization (Harkin, Anderson, & Goos, 1997), and the first annual report on the State of the Drugs Problem in the European Union, in 1996, from the European Monitoring Centre for Drugs and Drug Addiction (EMCDDA, 1996) is limited to European countries and does not deal with the functioning of treatment systems in general.

It is against this background that this book should be seen. Its publication provides for the first time information on the development of drug treatment from a global perspective. The 20 countries included are Austria, Canada, China, Colombia, England, Finland, France, Germany, Hungary, Italy, Japan, the Netherlands, Peru, Poland, Portugal, Spain, Sweden, Switzerland, Russia, and the United States. The need to produce a global view of drug treatment is obvious in view of such developments as the globalization of the drug industry, the international drug trade and drug consumption, and the import and export of treatment models. Regrettably, in spite of the editors' attempts to provide such a global perspective and provide information from all of the major geographical regions,

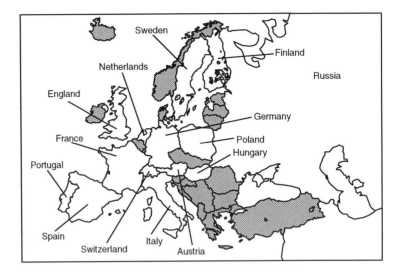

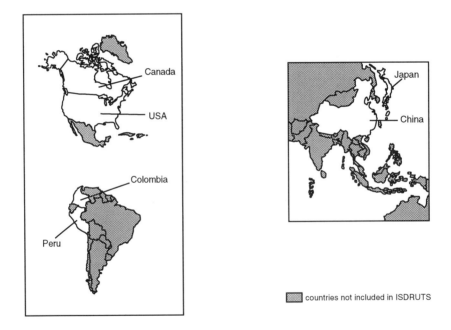

Figure I.1 International Study of the Development of Drug Treatment Systems (ISDRUTS), Geographical Coverage

certain areas, notably Africa and South Asia, are missing. Nevertheless, the wide range of countries represented here provides the reader with an excellent overview of current developments in treatment in different parts of the world.

The production of a book with information on so many countries went far beyond the normal task of individual scholars collecting and analyzing data and writing up their results. In 1993, when the initial group of researchers came together in

Toronto to begin work on the book, none realized the extent to which its production would become a fascinating cross-cultural dialogue between colleagues from 20 countries. At four workshop meetings, in Canada, Poland, Portugal, and Scotland, the country authors described and explained the development of the drug treatment systems in their different countries not only to the two editors but also to other members of the working group. The material contained in the book has been produced by 47 authors, who come not only from 20 different countries but also from a variety of different disciplines—an unusually heterogeneous research team. The product—the book—represents only the end point of complex negotiations among the project participants. The interaction of the contributors, the scientific editors, the language editor, the commentators, and the publisher was itself influenced heavily by cultural values and codes of intercultural communication. These interactions can in turn be understood as a social system in the classic sense defined by Parsons (1951):

> A social system consists in a plurality of individual actors interacting with each other in a situation which has at least a physical or environmental aspect, actors who are motivated in terms of a tendency to optimization of gratification and whose relation to their situations, including each other, is defined and mediated in terms of *a system of culturally structured and shared symbols.* (pp. 5-6; italics added)

We believe, therefore, that the information on our dealings with the project participants and the interpretations within a wider framework of cultural communication are vital for a full understanding of the book. For the reader, reference to this framework will help to avoid premature conclusions and illustrate the reality with which drug treatment has to contend in the context of various cultural value systems.

Key Features of the Book

The book is not intended as either an international handbook providing detailed descriptions of treatment modalities around the world or a manual to determine which methods work best. Pharmaceutical drugs and over-the-counter medications are not taken into consideration, even though the dividing line between illicit and licit drugs has become increasingly blurred, and tobacco, as a licit substance, at least in the United States, is fast becoming a socially unacceptable drug.

Instead, this volume develops four central features initially covered in the first book project, on alcohol treatment systems (Klingemann, Takala, & Hunt, 1992). First, the editors and country authors have adopted a system approach that provides a comprehensive overview of the main features of the treatment system in its societal context. "The word 'system' refers to those social structures and processes that have the function of drug treatment and, in a narrower sense, to the interconnection of different treatment units or agencies, chains of treatment and referral channels" (Klingemann et al., 1992, p. 4). The analytical focus is less on the "client path"—for example, entry and retention in the system and help-seeking behavior—

and more on the "community path"—for example, the coordination of services and system description (Rush, 1996). The definition of *system* proved to be more straightforward than that of *treatment*. Substitution therapy, heroin prescription programs, professional reintegration measures, and activities designed to promote recovery without paid help (self-organized natural recovery) all create difficulties in describing and analyzing the treatment response.

Second, we used a protocol/shopping list to ensure that a minimum of comparable information was supplied, while at the same time allowing each contributor to capture the specific flavor and story of his or her country. The list ensured that information on the following points would be provided: an inventory of drug treatment activities in each country; a discussion of the sociopolitical structure; trends in drug-related problems; the division between political, judicial, health, and social authorities; treatment rationales and specific methods; institutional cooperation and financing structures; and the role of self-help groups and unconventional methods and programs.

The use of an interdisciplinary approach is a third feature of the book, and the range of disciplines represented goes beyond addiction research. It includes, for example, political science, psychoanalysis, and criminology. (For details, see the list of biographical sketches). We tried also to encourage coauthorship, ideally between a public health policymaker, a drug treatment professional, and a social scientist, in order to broaden the database and stimulate an intracultural discussion on each country's story.

Finally, the editors have included a glossary, which explains key terms that may be unfamiliar to readers outside the particular country. It includes information on leading figures and institutions in the treatment fields in various countries, as well as key terms and concepts not necessarily mentioned or explained in detail in the text. An explanation of these concepts and terms deals not with standard, official, or true definitions in a scientific sense but with the treatment rationale or cultural definition of the term. For the same reason, such terms as *use, abuse,* and *dependency* may be used by country authors in different ways and consequently have not been unified or replaced in the editorial process. All glossary terms are designated by country of origin and can be read as background information by readers who have a specific interest in a given country. Readers can also find the titles of the works cited in both English and the original language, thereby easing access to information not available in English.

In addition to these features, the editors have introduced certain organizational elements that, it is hoped, will enable the reader to use the book more effectively as a truly cross-cultural reference work on drug treatment systems. Instead of producing merely a collection of largely unconnected contributions held together only symbolically by an introduction or summary, the intention has been to supply the readers with a series of intermediate reviews and topical comparative discussions throughout the book. More specifically, to strengthen the analytical and comparative power of the collection, the 20 country reports have been grouped according to overarching themes such as "experimental countries," "treatment in drug-producing countries," "drug treatment in traditional wine countries," or "treatment in countries with punitive policies." Each group of country reports is followed by a commentator's critique on the shared leitmotif of the countries discussed. In most cases, these commentators were not members of the ISDRUTS project group or, in some cases, were not even involved in addiction studies. They came to their task with fresh ideas brought from such diverse disciplines as criminology, psychoanalysis, political science, and anthropology. Readers can use their overviews to conduct their own comparative analyses.

The presentation of three thematic chapters in the last part of the book continues the comparative theme by reviewing each of the country chapters from the perspective of one particular issue. Before publication, the completed chapters were examined and approved by each author to avoid any questions of misinterpretation. All three topics, chosen from a longer list, concentrate on previously under-researched treatment system issues. The chapter on women and drug treatment examines a number of questions, such as the extent to which treatment services in different countries consider gender-specific differences, or the situation of women in mixed institutions and how access to treatment is guaranteed. The chapter on modes of financing treatment is an informative analysis of the material basis of the changing features of treatment systems, depicting the impact of funding schemes reaching out to the specificities of treatment modalities. The chapter on the relationship between the alcohol and drug treatment systems considers the extent to which the growth of a drug treatment system has blurred the dividing lines between alcohol and drug treatment. From a technical point of view, the three thematic chapters allowed the country authors to concentrate more on other issues, which in turn eased the tension between concentrating on rich regional coverage exemplified in a greater number of countries represented in the book and concentrating on the more in-depth information on the specific features of national treatment systems.

Finally, the country background information table in the appendix to the book provides data on size of population, type of political economy, surface area, degree of urbanization, gross national product, and unemployment. Readers can thus make more systematic comparisons between countries, especially in regard to their size and wealth.

Taken as a whole, the contributions contained in this volume provide access to information on drug treatment systems from a wide cross-section of 20 countries; they take into account the cultural and societal context of the organization of drug treatment. We are sure that it will enable researchers and students of addiction, health planners and administrators, and treatment professionals to place the development of their own countries' treatment systems in a wider context and to examine the extent to which that development shares common structural features with that of other countries and other cultures.

The Cultural Status of Information

In the editors' attempt to collect descriptive indicators of subdomains of treatment systems, they quickly realized that the cultural status of empirical data and their availability cannot be taken for granted. There is a danger in assuming beforehand that more familiar types of data—for example, official statistics/monitoring data and data obtained from special surveys—are superior to key informant opinions merely because the former lend themselves more easily to academic standards of referencing and reproducibility. This point is well illustrated by the reactions of the Colombian author to our request for additional material. To the request for more information about the available services, he replied:

> This is Colombia, a developing, crazy, and chaotic country, not Germany, France, or Switzerland. I cannot answer your questions. Nobody knows how many institutions there are here! In the same month, you can have 3 to 10 new ones opening and five others closing. Don't ask me to break down by type a ghostly (or amebic) body, there is no formal directory, and no official census.

On client profiles, he responded: "Patient characteristics are shared at formal and informal meetings with other institutions." Finally, on the use of treatment methods, he answered:

> No surveys are available. If you want, you can say that this is my personal opinion. My impression is that you think that we in this country have (as you probably have in Europe) an army of sociologists doing surveys on thousands of issues. This is very far from reality.

The key informant, in his roles as clinic director, research director, and policymaker, occupies a central role in many informal work-related communication networks and can therefore provide information similar to that obtained by a Delphi-type process. This information may be an even more valid basis for a prognosis of the development of the drug treatment system than the use of the VESPA reporting system adopted from the United States.

Moreover, interaction with the authors from Colombia, Peru, and Spain brought out a healthy resistance to our attempts to focus solely on treatment for the use of illicit drugs. The draft reports from the Latin American countries and Spain stressed the crucial public health importance of alcohol abuse in those countries. The Peruvian authors were equally concerned about the editors' focus on treatment at the expense of prevention. They insisted that structural measures of prevention in the form of promotion of crop substitution programs were a vitally important element of their drug treatment system.

Also, the general cultural setting influences the seemingly clear-cut division between scientific researcher and policymaker. These roles seemed to merge in the case of the Latin American countries. For example, our key informant from Peru is a scientific member of the Inter American Society of Psychology, and is, at the same time, a fieldwork coordinator for a jungle community action program in areas experiencing terrorist activities. At the Edinburgh workshop of the project group, the author presented the organizers with a vest woven in one of the jungle prevention cooperatives—a strong symbolic comment on our efforts to isolate and pin down the treatment system.

The influence of culture on the combined roles of our contributors was an important issue also in the case of the People's Republic of China. Disentangling political statements from descriptive and policy information proved difficult, and some information seemed to be very restricted and based on unclear sources. This did not signify any lack of expertise on the part of our authors, however; rather, it was due to efforts to apply Western-style thinking and writing to non-Western conditions. The Chinese way of writing and thinking, based on an Eastern philosophical tradition, favors a more holistic way of reasoning than is characteristic of the Western style of research. Also, it would be naive to overlook the enormous difficulties that our Chinese colleagues have in not merely obtaining information but also obtaining approval to use it. Finally, we need to remember the political obligations of professional scientists who have to struggle for scarce government funding and recognition.

National Treatment Systems as Global Actors

Interaction with our authors also taught us something about the question of the boundaries of treatment systems. As mentioned earlier, in the context of the European Union, the level of analysis chosen here—national political states or, in some cases, regions—may actually prove inadequate for capturing trends toward a global treatment system with elements of diffusion, exchange, and import and export. For example, the acceptance and role of the harm reduction approach in various countries are influenced not solely by political forces or the extent of drug-related problems, but also by the experiences and "model behavior" of experimental countries such as England, the Netherlands, and Switzerland. The Liverpool experiments in England have served as an important reference point for trials of heroin prescription in Switzerland, which may, in turn, provide a model for other countries, such as Australia and Germany. Other examples include the diffusion of American monitoring systems and treatment models to Latin America, and the extension by the European Union of its influence through the funding of research into treatment and prevention in central European countries such as Poland.

Our key informants were not always aware of these global exchange processes, or of the impact of the reputation of specific drug treatment experiments on other countries. For example, the senior editor in Switzerland was disappointed on discovering that an early draft of the English paper did not contain a detailed insider story of the Liverpool experiment. However, from discussions with the senior author, the editor realized that in England the experiment had only a marginal influence on the development of the treatment system. Consequently, despite its reputation abroad, it could not be made a focus of the chapter. In a different way, the Latin American authors were well aware of North American influences on their national treatment systems and even described the difficulties of applying foreign treatment modalities with cultural values in sharp opposition to those of Latin America.

Venturing Into Unknown Territory

The familiarity of the editors with the drug treatment systems in individual countries varied and depended on either the extent to which the country was represented in the scientific literature or whether they had personal contact with the addiction researchers in those countries. From this perspective, the Latin American countries and Japan and China were *terra incognita.* In these cases, the need to validate the country stories was obvious. One way of doing so was to encourage multiple authorship, thereby ensuring a broader basis of information. This was not altogether successful, however. Requests to country authors to invite the collaboration of co-researchers, from different institutes if possible, were not always welcome and in some cases even violated cultural codes of networking. For example, the editors' efforts to bring together researchers from different institutes in Japan were unsuccessful. Similar difficulties arose when they tried to build a female/male American/Finnish team, match treatment and research colleagues in Portugal, and enlist monitoring and survey experts for the Latin American contributions. In the first two cases, different research perspectives and interests were contributory factors; in the third, the editors were not sufficiently sensitive to the precarious financial and other constraints that prevented the authors from investing more time in an international book project.

Conclusion: Where Are the Demons?

The subtitle of this collection of chapters promises demons (in Greek, *daimon* = evil spirits), but readers may look for them in vain. Browsing the country reports, readers will realize that the image of drug dependency as a condition is hard to change; an individual once "possessed" either in the historical sense in the temperance period by "the devil rum" or today by the demon heroin or crack cocaine is considered hard to change. These perceptions in turn exert an important influence on what are considered appropriate treatment measures.

In reviewing the country reports, the editors have done everything possible to eliminate alarmist or moralistic statements that could be taken as problem amplification with little or no empirical foundation. In other words, the editors have chased the demons out, or at least introduced them in a "safer" divine form (see Noschis in "Dionysus Is Back" on drug treatment in wine-producing countries). Where necessary, the editors have cleansed individual country stories to ensure that scientific standards are upheld and moralistic attitudes removed. Nevertheless, the reader, in examining the development of the treatment systems in these 20 countries, should still keep in mind that the demons can reappear, as is often the case when the emotional dimension comes to dominate the public debate on drug-related policy.

References

European Monitoring Centre for Drugs and Drug Addiction (EMCDDA). (1996). *Annual report on the state of the drug problem in the European Union.* Lisbon: Author.

Harkin, A. M., Anderson, P., & Goos, C. (1997). *Smoking, drinking and drug taking in the European region.* Copenhagen: Alcohol, Drugs and Tobacco Programme, WHO Regional Office for Europe.

Klingemann, H., Takala, J. P., & Hunt, G. (Eds.). (1992). *Cure, care, or control.* Albany: State University of New York Press.

Parsons, T. (1951). *The social system.* New York: Free Press.

Rush, B. (1996). Alcohol and other drug problems and treatment systems: A framework for research and development. *Addiction, 91,* 629-642.

Harald Klingemann
Geoffrey Hunt
Lausanne and Berkeley, June 1998

Part I

Drug Prohibition and the

Abstinence Paradigm

Chapter 1

The Drug Treatment
System in the United States:
A Panacea for the Drug War?

Geoffrey Hunt
Anna Xiao Dong Sun

According to the latest U.S. National Drug Control Strategy issued from the White House, "Drug abuse has plagued America for more than a century" (Office of National Drug Control Policy, 1997, p. 5). To continue to fight this plague, President Clinton recently requested $16 billion for 1998 (an increase of approximately $1 billion from the 1997 budget).

The latest outbreak of the plague began in 1982 with President Reagan's declaration of a "War on Drugs" (Glasser & Siegel, 1997). Under this clarion cry, politicians, criminal justice officials, prevention experts, and treatment specialists have painted a bleak picture of the impact of drug abuse on the social fabric of the United States. Having agreed that there was an epidemic of drug problems, different groups argued that they held the answer, and each sought to ensure that its own particular agenda was given adequate finance. Law enforcement officials argued that increased funding was necessary to ensure not only that police officers could rid the urban scene of drug dealers but also that border patrols could be strengthened to protect U.S. citizens from the wholesale import of illegal drugs. Prevention experts, relatively new players on the scene, argued that to solve the drug problem, it was essential to introduce changes at the normative level in order to create a climate where drug use was no longer acceptable—a "drug-free" America. Finally, treatment providers argued that until the drug addict was treated and cured, the problem would never be solved. For this panacea to work, increased funding was necessary to expand treatment services.

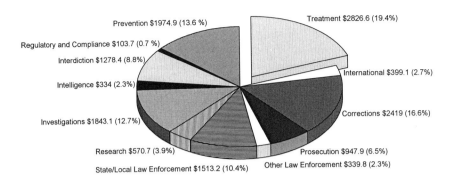

Figure 1.1 President's Federal Drug Budget Request by Detailed Function, 1996
SOURCE: National drug control strategy: Budget summary, February 1995, The White House.

Partly as a result of the conservative administrations of Presidents Reagan and Bush, and partly because every politician wished to be seen as tough on crime, the lion's share of the increased spending on drug abuse was acquired by criminal justice and law enforcement officials—a situation that has continued under President Clinton. According to figures from the White House, of the $14.5 billion requested for the 1996 federal budget for drug control, 63% was for law enforcement, 19.4% for treatment, and 13.6% for prevention (see Figure 1.1). In 1980, the total federal expenditure on drug law enforcement was approximately $1 billion. The budget for the Drug Enforcement Agency itself had grown from under $200 million at the beginning of 1980 to $857 million in 1996.

Despite having to compete with the law enforcement system, the U.S. drug treatment system is, by international standards, an enormous structure with more than a quarter of a million people employed in more than 5,000 specialty facilities. These include hospitals, residential facilities, methadone clinics, therapeutic communities, outpatient programs, and correctional institutions. They employ a wide range of treatment modalities, including pharmacological methods such as maintenance and detoxification, and behavioral methods such as verbal therapy, skill development, conditioning therapy, personal counseling, and peer support. Nevertheless, treatment experts still argue that the demand for treatment, estimated by the White House at 3.6 million chronic users (Office of National Drug Control Policy, 1997), continues to far outstrip its availability. For example, the National Association of State Alcohol and Drug Abuse Directors has estimated that only 15% to 20% of serious drug abusers receive treatment (Schlesinger & Dorwart, 1992).

This belief in treatment as a panacea for drug problems has a long and uneven history and, as Currie (1993) has pointed out, tends to ignore questions as to whether more of the same is needed or attention should be directed at expanding successful and closing unsuccessful programs. However, questions of treatment efficacy are themselves hotly debated, and there is little or no agreement on what is effective treatment, despite the plentiful funding and considerable time that has been devoted to research on treatment. To begin to understand how the treatment system, whether based on medical intervention or on behavior modification, has developed into its current structure, we must begin by recalling some of its colorful history.

First, however, two important points need to be made. The first is that the term *system* implies a coherent and organized entity, and yet as Schlesinger and Dorwart (1992) have astutely noted, "The current system is a hodgepodge of philosophies and practices . . . and is a 'system' only in the ecological sense. . . . There is virtually no collective planning or cooperation" (p. 199). Because no organized national strategy has ever been implemented, treatment services in different communities have developed at different rates, and the mix of services differs considerably from one part of the country to another. Public treatment services are organized at the state level and vary substantially from state to state. Private services are even less organized. The treatment system that has developed, therefore, is complex and disorganized, and the reader is warned against obtaining a false impression of a coherent structure of services.

Second, the authors have had to rely on the available published data, which, in comparison with those of other countries, may appear to be comprehensive. Regrettably, in many cases, the more recent data are less comprehensive and detailed than the earlier data. One reason for this decline in the quality of national survey data has been the diminishing role of the federal government in monitoring the performance of the treatment system. "Data gathering systems that previously tracked basic measures of system performance were abandoned or became out-moded" (Schlesinger & Dorwart, 1992, p. 199). Consequently, to provide a detailed overview of the treatment system, the authors have found it necessary to use the earlier data with respect to certain of its features.

A Brief History of Drug Treatment in the United States

Given the complexity of the treatment system, the most efficient way of describing its development is to compartmentalize or periodize it. Fortunately, periodizing is not a new idea, and many writers, such as Courtwright (1992), Courtwright, Joseph, and Des Jarlais (1989), and Brecher (1972), have used such an approach.

The Late 19th and Early 20th Centuries

Brecher (1972) has called this period a "dope fiend's paradise" (p. 3) because opium was on sale legally and cheaply. It was a period of minimal government intervention with virtually no effective regulation of narcotics.[1] Although several states had statutes governing the sale of opiates (and indeed, many municipalities forbade the smoking of opium), the laws against it were only sporadically enforced. Physicians prescribed opiates liberally, drugstores dispensed them to customers without prescription, and many grocery and general stores sold them. There were two distinct groups of opiate users: those addicted to opium and morphine, and opium smokers. The former, unlike the recent stereotypes of drug addicts, consisted of upper- and middle-class women (Brecher, 1972, p. 17), whereas the opium smokers were portrayed as irresponsible and wicked (Courtwright, 1982). Because of societal attitudes toward the smoking population, especially the Chinese, municipal authorities soon legislated against opium smoking and opium dens (Morgan, 1978). Early forms of treatment were of three types: maintenance—keeping patients on a prescribed dose to enable them to function normally; detoxification; and "cure" (Musto, 1973).

1909 to 1923: The Development of Federal Legislation

If Brecher is correct in characterizing the previous period as a "dope fiend's paradise," then the years 1909 to 1923 must be characterized as the period of inception of law enforcement in drug treatment, at least at the federal level. Earlier, the medical profession had dominated the rudimentary treatment available. By the end of this period, law enforcement had asserted itself as the final arbiter as to type of treatment allowed.

The Harrison Narcotics Act, passed by Congress in 1914, was the most important piece of federal legislation of this period, and it was to become the basis of much of the later legislation. It is of interest that although the Harrison Act was to have enormous and far-reaching consequences for the use of opiates and other drugs, it was passed with little or no fanfare on the part of either the legislators or the public (Musto, 1973); drug addiction attracted little interest in comparison with the increasing furor associated with legislative proposals to prohibit alcohol. The Act's key clause, which was to create havoc in the lives of most addicts, stated that a physician could prescribe opiates "in the course of his professional practice only." Law enforcement officers from the Prohibition Unit interpreted this to mean that opiates could not be prescribed to addicts to maintain addiction.

Although this decision clearly warned individual doctors against prescribing opiates to maintain an addiction, the question of what to do with addicts was left unanswered. At first, public health officials in different parts of the country created public opiate clinics, where addicts could receive free narcotics; these were to be the forerunners of methadone maintenance clinics. Although 44 opiate clinics were set up, they were short-lived, and by 1923, the Narcotic Division of the Bureau of Internal Revenue had closed down the last one (Terry & Pellens, 1970; Waldorf, Orlick, & Reinarman, 1974).

1923 to 1960: The Classic Era

With the closure of the narcotic clinics, the principal public institutions for addicts became prisons and jails. In 1917, federal prisons contained 151 prisoners convicted of narcotic violations. By 1928, this number had risen to 2,341, mostly users of heroin (Anglin & Hser, 1990), which represented 31% of the entire prison population (Dershowitz, 1973). Many in the prison system were concerned about the "demoralizing effect" of addicts on the other prisoners. Although a Judiciary House Committee in 1928 decided that the solution to the problem lay in segregation (Kane, 1973), it was not until 1935 that the first "narcotic farm" was opened at Lexington, Kentucky (Courtwright et al., 1989). The second was opened in 1938 at Fort Worth, Texas. Lexington, the larger, had 1,000 beds and 500 employees. These farms, which lasted until the early 1970s, were run by the Public Health Service under the watchful eye of the Justice Department and the newly created (1930) Federal Bureau of Narcotics.[2] Although official statements about Lexington praised its success, its treatment results were not impressive (Maddux, 1988). Nevertheless, according to a report of the Institute of Medicine (Gerstein & Harwood, 1990), the narcotic farms were important in the development of later treatment for three reasons: First, they preserved the right of addicts to admit themselves to treatment voluntarily; second, they established a precedent for federal provision for addiction treatment; and third, because of the research programs of the Public Health Service, these hospital/prisons helped develop a cadre of researchers and clinicians with experience in drug addiction.

The involvement of the criminal justice system in drug treatment continued with the commencement of the civil committal program, established first in California, in 1961, and later in New York State. These programs of the 1960s—a form of legally mandated treatment for offenders dependent on illicit drugs—were established in an atmosphere of increasing concern about the spread of addiction. California inaugurated its program with legislation establishing a new treatment facility, the California Rehabilitation Center, at Corona (Anglin, 1988; Dershowitz, 1973). New York followed in 1966, at a time of increasing political concern about drug addiction and its possible relation to crime (Waldorf, 1971).

The 1970s: A Productive Period in Federal Expansion of Treatment Services

In his address to Congress in June 1971, President Nixon had observed that drug abuse was an increasing problem and was contributing to the costly wave of urban crime (Courtwright, 1992). To counter this development, Nixon announced the creation of the Special Action Office of Drug Abuse Prevention (SAODAP), which was given overall responsibility for drug treatment and rehabilitation. One of its major functions was to provide funds to communities to reduce waiting lists at community treatment agencies. SAODAP legislation required each state government to create an administrative organization to oversee drug abuse programs within its jurisdiction. As Besteman (1992) points out, this part of the legislation allowed the states some resources to begin to organize drug treatment systems.

In 1973, the National Institute on Drug Abuse (NIDA) was established with the responsibility to oversee the national network of treatment programs, as well as to continue to fund research on drugs. In its first year, its operating budget was nearly $300 million (NIDA, 1991). At the same time, NIDA converted all of its direct contracts with treatment providers into grants, which resulted, as Gerstein and Harwood (1990) have noted, in "less federal direction and greater autonomy for the treatment programs" (p. 240). This arrangement continued until 1981, when, under the Reagan administration, the Omnibus Budget Reconciliation Act (OBRA; Pub. L. No. 977-35) transferred to the states responsibility for treatment services. All community-based funding was brought together into one unrestricted "Block Grant," which covered alcohol, drug, and mental health services. The grant was administered by NIDA's parent organization, the Alcohol, Drug Abuse and Mental Health Administration (ADAMHA). "The OBRA also implemented the government's agenda of 'privatizing' health care by de-emphasizing the role of the government or public sector" (Schmidt & Weisner, 1993, p. 371).

By the late 1960s, the vast increase in drug use by a more heterogeneous group of users had resulted in a demand for a wider range of treatment, including nonresidential treatment for nonopiate addicts and self-help groups based on Alcoholics Anonymous treatment ideology. The commencement of two treatment modalities at that time—methadone maintenance and therapeutic communities—was especially important.

Methadone Maintenance

Methadone maintenance was particularly attractive during the Nixon presidency and his "War on Crime," both because methadone was a legal drug and because it had the incidental effect of reducing drug-related criminality among addicts. However, although it was seen as a useful means of controlling social problems associated with heroin addiction, the prescription of methadone was, from its inception, subjected to an elaborate series of controls. As Rosenbaum (1995) has noted, "Clinics had to comply with a complex set of rules governing admission to treatment attendance, dose level take-homes, urinalysis and record keeping methods" (p. 146). Zweben and Payte (1990) have pointed out: "Program administrators quickly learned that survival depended more on the condition of the records than on that of the patients" (p. 594). Notwithstanding these controls, these clinics increased rapidly, and by 1977, about 80,000 people were being maintained on methadone (Gerstein & Harwood, 1990).

Therapeutic Communities

At first, the best-known therapeutic community in the United States was Synanon, established at Ocean View, California, in 1958 by Charles Dederich, a former alcoholic. Synanon combined abstinence and a family environment where the residents lived together and helped one another "through mutual reinforcement, companionship and social pressure" (Saxe & Shusterman, 1991, p. 8). According to Deitch (1973), the therapeutic communities developed at a time when there were very few successful treatment programs: "The new methods which departed from the traditional were exciting innovations and seemed to hold promise as the panaceas for treating drug addiction" (p. 172). Therapeutic communities also brought to drug treatment a new category of "specialists"—the professional ex-addict (Jaffe, 1979).

The Drug Treatment System Today

Drug Use and Drug Users

Discussions about prevalence of drug use have tended to focus on two issues: (a) the number of illicit drug users and (b) the number of people experiencing problems or causing problems for others as a result of their drug use. Estimates of the prevalence of drug use come mainly from the National Household Survey of Drug Abuse, and there is considerable controversy as to their accuracy. These probability samples have been drawn at intervals of 1 to 3 years since 1972. The 1995 survey estimated that "12.8 million Americans were current illicit drug users, meaning they had used an illicit drug in the month prior to interview" (SAMHSA, 1996b, p. 2). Also, an estimated 17.8 million had used marijuana in the previous year, and 65.5 million had tried it at least once in their lifetime; the corresponding figures for 1988 were 19.5 million and 60.8 million (SAMHSA, 1996b). Although in 1995, the estimated number of 1.9 million current cocaine users (including crack) had not changed since 1994, "it had declined from 5.7 million in 1985" (SAMHSA, 1996b, p. 17).

Although there is no simple connection between the number of illicit drug users and the number that need treatment, policy analysts have attempted to draw connections. One of the most recent attempts to estimate the need for treatment among household residents is described in the report of the Institute of Medicine (Gerstein & Harwood, 1990), in which data from the 1988 National Household Survey were used. The data were "classified to yield categories of clear, probable, possible and unlikely need for treatment" (Gerstein & Harwood, 1990, p. 79). It was estimated that of the 14.5 million individuals (7.3% of the household population over 12 years of age) who had "consumed an illicit drug at least once in the month before the survey, 1.5 million can be categorized as having a clear need for drug treatment" (Gerstein & Harwood, 1990, pp. 79-80).

In addition to the numbers in the general population, an increasing proportion of drug users are incarcerated in federal and state prisons and jails. In 1996, federal and state prisons detained 1,112,448 prisoners (93,167 and 1,019,281, respectively; Office of National Drug Control Policy, 1997). An estimated 30.5% (60% federal and 22% state) were drug offenders (General Accounting Office, 1996a, 1996b; Nadelmann, 1997). This increase in prisoners has resulted directly from the drug war and the policy of "getting tough on drugs." "The increase in drug offenders accounts for nearly three quarters of the total growth in federal prison inmates since 1980" (Office of National Drug Control Policy, 1997, p. 19). Between mid-1985 and 1990, arrests for violations of drug laws rose from an annual average of 750,000 to 1.4 million (Nadelmann, 1997). Also, federal drug sentences were lengthened by 59% between 1980 and 1989 (Nadelmann, 1997).

Treatment Clientele and Services

Data on the drug and alcohol treatment systems come from two sources: the National Drug and Alcoholism Treatment Utilization Survey (NDATUS), which is conducted at 3-year intervals and collects data on one day per year from public and private agencies; and the National Association of State Alcohol and Drug Abuse Directors (NASADAD), founded in 1983. Although the NDATUS material provides substantial data on the drug treatment system, it has a number of short-comings. According to Schlesinger, Dorwart, and Clark (1991), the most serious is that facilities are included only if "they treat alcohol and drug abuse exclusively or operate a separate unit that specializes in that treatment" (p. 26). Second, as Schmidt and Weisner (1995) point out, "Because listings are obtained in coopera-tion with state alcohol and drug administrations, coverage of public sector units is more complete than coverage of private sector units that are not under state jurisdiction" (p. 320). NASADAD collects annual data only from those programs that receive funds administered by the state alcohol or drug agency.

In 1991, there was a total of 9,057 drug and alcohol treatment units (SAMHSA, 1993), of which 10% were for drug abuse, 11% for alcohol abuse, and the rest for combined treatment. Treatment capacity—that is, the maximum number of patients who can be admitted—gives an idea of the types of service available and their location. Most by far (91%) were outpatient programs; 8.3% were rehabilita-tion/residential services. Only 290 units were devoted solely to methadone treat-ment, but 560 could administer methadone. These clinics served a total of 95,286 addicts. About two thirds were freestanding, nonresidential facilities; 10% were in community mental health centers; 7% were in hospitals; and 7% were in residential facilities or halfway houses.

By 1994, a total of 943,623 addicts were being treated for alcohol and drug addiction, 235,838 of them for drug addiction only. An estimated 87% of these were day patients receiving outpatient rehabilitation—75% in drug-free and 12% in methadone programs. The remaining 13% were in 24-hour treatment—11% in rehabilitation and 2% in detoxification (SAMHSA, 1996a). Regrettably, the more recent NDATUS data do not separate the data on patients into illicit drug and alcohol categories; consequently, it is necessary to either use NDATUS data from earlier years or look elsewhere for additional material. The NDATUS survey of 1991 (SAMHSA, 1993) provided a much more detailed statistical breakdown. Of a total of 811,819 people in drug and alcohol treatment units, 29% (237,008) attended drug-abuse-only clinics; 85% of these were in outpatient services, 11% in residential or rehabilitation units, and the remaining 4% in detoxification units; 40% received methadone maintenance treatment; 66% were male; 68% were between the ages of 25 and 44; and 23.6% were intravenous drug users. Ethnically, 49% were white, 31% were African American, and 18% were Hispanic.

The 1994 survey (NASADAD, 1996) put the number of drug users admitted for treatment in 1994 at 756,917. Of these, 63% were male, and 68% were between the ages of 25 and 44. Ethnically, although the largest proportion (44%) was white, African Americans at 38%, Hispanics at 12%, and Native Americans at 1% were overrepresented as proportions of the general population. Although heroin had long been the primary drug of abuse, by 1994 cocaine (43% of admissions) had taken its place; admissions of heroin users accounted for only 22%, and of marijuana users, 18%. Between 1989 and 1994, total admissions rose from 596,683 to 724,646; in the case of heroin users, from 122,310 to 158,353; of cocaine users, from 193,859 to 283,107; and of marijuana users, from 96,279 to 123,535.

To examine other changes in admissions for drug treatment, one must rely on figures that combine the numbers in both drug and alcohol clinics (SAMHSA, 1996a). Between 1980 and 1994, the most rapid growth was in the 35- to 44-year-old age group, whereas the under-21 and over-45 age groups had proportionately declined. The percentage of women also increased at this time, growing from 25.2% to 29.7%. As to ethnic background, there was a decline in admissions of white patients from 62.7% in 1980 to 58.9% in 1994, and a rise in the percentages of African Americans and Hispanics from 20.6% to 22.6%, and 13.4% to 14.6%, respectively.

Treatment Related to the Criminal Justice System

According to Lipton, Falkin, and Wexler (1992), there is no agreement on the percentage of prison and jail inmates being treated for drug addiction. Therefore, for an overview of drug treatment in the penal system, it is necessary to combine data from a number of sources. The NDATUS 1994 survey estimated the numbers in drug and alcohol treatment in correctional facilities (both prisons and jails) at 38,329, or 4% of all prisoners (SAMHSA, 1996a), or twice the 1980 percentage. Federal prisons had 42 treatment units, with 3,331 patients, of whom 23% were drug abusers. Variation in the availability of drug and alcohol units can be illustrated with 1991 NDATUS data. For example, whereas Ohio had the most units (28), followed by Florida (24), Texas (12), California (11), and Michigan (11), 26 states had either none or only one. Overall, penal drug treatment capacity was 9,150, or 5% of the prison population. Given the number of illicit drug users who have been arrested and imprisoned, this means that the great majority of prisoners with substance abuse problems are still not receiving treatment (Lipton & Wexler, 1988). A 1988 survey of the U.S. Department of Justice reported that only 6% of state prison inmates were receiving drug treatment, and a 1990 California survey confirmed this finding, showing that less than 3% of prisoners were in treatment (Currie, 1993). Indeed, the California Commission on Inmate Population management, which investigated drug treatment in prisons, concluded that "aside from self-help groups such as AA and other self-help programs . . . there are virtually no drug treatment programs in our adult prisons" (Currie, 1993, p. 197). In 1987, the American Jail Association, in a survey of 57% of the nation's jails (Peters & May, 1992), found that 28% of them offered drug treatment other than detoxification. Volunteers provided 33% of these services, which meant that "funded drug treatment programs were present in only 19% of jails surveyed" (Peters & May, 1992, p. 400). The patients were 66% white, 23% African American, and 8% Hispanic. The most common forms of treatment were group counseling (78%), individual counseling (78%), and drug education (76%).

Prisoners in treatment are only one section of the treatment population connected to the criminal justice system. In addition, a significant number of arrested individuals are brought into contact with treatment as part of either the court referral system or their parole. For example, in 1972, the organization Treatment Alternatives to Street Crime (TASC) initiated a program intended to divert individuals arrested for "lesser" drug offenses, such as marijuana possession, "to avoid 'clogging the justice system'" (Gerstein & Harwood, 1990, p. 114). Today, there are 133 TASC programs in more than 25 states (Swartz, 1993). They make available community-based treatment to recognized addicted offenders who have been arrested. These offenders are then encouraged to enter drug programs through such means as "deferred prosecution, creative community sentencing, and pretrial intervention" (Anglin & Hser, 1990, p. 428). Once in the program, the offenders' progress is monitored and reported on (Swartz, 1993).

Financing Structures

Since the early 1970s, not only have substantial changes taken place in the federal government's methods of funding drug abuse programs, but also the proportion of the total budget it contributes has significantly altered. In 1976, "only 5% of all revenues in treatment programs came from private sources" (Schlesinger & Dorwart, 1992, p. 205). Since then, private payments have increased dramatically, and by 1989, private sources accounted for 40% of the total expenditure. In 1991, of all treatment facilities, the federal government owned 2.6% and state or local authorities owned 14.8%; 18.4% of all treatment facilities were private-for-profit, and 63% were private-not-for-profit (SAMHSA, 1993). Moreover, the growth in federal funding since the 1970s has not been uniform. In 1969, the federal government spent $40 million on drug treatment; this grew to $300 million by 1974. Since 1986, as a result of the Anti-Drug Abuse Acts of 1986 and 1988, federal expenditure increased dramatically to the 1995 figure of $2.6 billion, and the amount requested for 1997 is $2.9 billion (General Accounting Office, 1997).

Today, drug treatment, like alcohol treatment (Weisner & Morgan, 1992), is organized in two parallel systems—one funded publicly and the other privately. The two are not merely separate but, more important, unequal. Whereas the public system experiences excess demand and "treats clients with relatively low cost interventions . . . the private system has excess capacity and emphasizes high cost residential or in patient treatment methods" (Pauly, 1991, p. 165). The public system includes relatively large multisite residential programs; methadone clinics; and small, not-for-profit outpatient clinics in approximately 2,000 different communities. According to many policy analysts, in spite of the drug war, the public system is still largely underfunded, and, indeed, parts of it are continuing to be cut back. As Currie (1993) has noted, "The public system of drug treatment . . . was inadequate to begin with and was then systematically scaled back during much of the 1980s" (p. 214). In contrast, the private system is growing rapidly and, as

Gerstein and Harwood (1990) have noted, "The total revenues received by its providers are beginning to approach the total revenues of providers in the public tier" (p. 201). The private system receives the bulk of its revenue from patients covered by private insurance. Most private health insurance is obtained through employer-sponsored health insurance plans; 21 million employees of private companies had drug treatment coverage in 1990 (Gerstein & Harwood, 1990). Patients treated by the public services are covered by government programs. Between the private and the public systems are not-for-profit institutions, which are funded from both the federal government and private insurance. Although, overall, 20% of their budget comes from private sources, in specific types of institutions, the percentage may be higher—for example, 66% of the funding of not-for-profit hospitals is private. Schmidt and Weisner (1993) have pointed out that the success of the not-for-profit category "is best explained by the unique adaptiveness of this organizational form to the exigencies of both the public and private funding systems. Nonprofits benefit from legal and tax exemptions not accorded to for-profit businesses" (p. 371).

The private and public sectors differ substantially regarding revenue per patient. Whereas the private sector "received 41% of the reported drug treatment expenditures while treating 22% of the clients, public-tier providers received 59% of total revenues and treated 78% of the clients" (Gerstein & Harwood, 1990, p. 203). Consequently, the average revenue per client for the private sector was $2,450, but for the public sector it was only $1,240. Finally, as is to be expected, the counselor-to-client ratio was also significantly different—1:7.2 in the private residential and inpatient sector and 1:9.7 in public institutions.

The two services differ also regarding their patients. In 1994, an estimated 17% of all clients in treatment were in privately funded drug and alcohol treatment, whereas in 1980 the percentage of clients was only 5%. The private sector has "reported a higher proportion of men in treatment [both drug and alcohol] than the national average, and a higher proportion of white and Hispanic clients. Conversely, they served lower proportions of women and black clients" (SAMHSA, 1996a, p. 29). Whereas the public system treats low-income patients, the private system treats patients paid for by health insurance. Those treated in publicly financed programs

> have longer histories of drug taking, are more likely to have taken more types of drugs, are less likely to be employed or engaged in other socially conventional activities . . . and are more likely to have records of criminal activity and involvement in the criminal justice system. (Gerstein & Harwood, 1990, p. 205)

Increasing concern about containment of health care costs has contributed to shifting the emphasis in treatment from inpatient to outpatient services. In 1994, 87% of all drug and alcohol patients were in outpatient treatment, compared with 84.1% in 1980. This trend was even more marked in the privately funded sector, where the percentage of outpatients increased from 80.4% in 1980 to 94% in 1994, whereas patients in rehabilitation declined from 15% to 4.6% (SAMHSA, 1996a).

Evaluation

Since the early 1970s, considerable attention has been devoted to assessing the effectiveness of drug treatment programs. In general, different methods of assessment have been used, and results have been inconsistent. Also, as Anglin and Hser (1990) have noted, the following factors have complicated the interpretation of the assessment findings: "the heterogeneous nature of the drug-dependent population, the relapsing nature of dependence, the difficulty of conducting controlled studies, non-specifiable and often intangible treatment components, and the interactions among these considerations" (p. 406).

Although the simplest goal of treatment has been to attempt to get the drug user to stop using drugs, it tends to ignore other, related issues, such as crime reduction, prison management, and the spread of AIDS. Therefore, in assessing the effectiveness of treatment, it is important to use outcome measures that take account also of related behavior. Such measures have included "cessation or decreased use of the primary drug of dependence; decreased levels of illegal activities . . .; increased employment and decreased reliance on social services agencies; improved social and family functioning; [and] improved psychological functioning" (Anglin & Hser, 1990, p. 409).

Methadone programs have been evaluated extensively, and most studies have obtained positive outcomes. Recent reviews have shown that these programs produce significant decreases in opioid use and criminality, as well as improvement in general health. However, Anglin and Hser (1990) point out that the absence of control groups makes "a strict quantification of the positive results impossible" (p. 418). Nevertheless, administrators, counselors, and clients still maintain that methadone maintenance is a controversial treatment.[3]

Evaluation studies of therapeutic communities—for example, the Drug Abuse Reporting Program (DARP) and the Treatment Outcome Prospective Study (TOPS)—have shown significant improvements in immediate and long-term outcomes (De Leon, 1984). The Institute of Medicine study cautiously concluded that "those clients who stay in TC's for at least a third or half of the planned course of treatment . . . are much closer to achieving the treatment's goals at follow-up than those that drop out earlier" (Gerstein & Harwood, 1990, p. 166).

Outpatient drug-free treatment includes a wide range of programs. The primary treatment approach uses services that rely on counseling and training in social skills. Overall, the DARP data suggest that, although these programs are less effective in retention, in longer-term outcomes they are "as effective as methadone maintenance or therapeutic communities. However, the favorable results for outpatient drug-free programs are restricted to "non-addicts, clients who used opioids less than daily" (Anglin & Hser, 1990, p. 422). Finally, despite the importance of chemical dependency treatment programs in drug treatment, there is less evaluation material on them than on other programs. Consequently, it is very difficult to evaluate their effectiveness accurately.

Discussion and Conclusion

The Development of Harm Reduction Methods

Despite widespread use of legal prevention strategies, the epidemic of HIV infection among injection drug users continues. As a result of this spread of infection and the limited success of preventive measures, needle exchange programs emerged in the mid- to late 1980s as a possible additional measure. The first such formal program began in Amsterdam in 1984, and the first in the United States, in Boston, began in 1986. The early programs were established "as explicit acts of civil disobedience to publicly test the prescription laws and to call public attention to the issue of AIDS in IDU's [IV drug users]" (Centers for Disease Control and Prevention, 1993, p. 145).

The first structured needle exchange program was begun in Tacoma, Washington, in 1988, and it was followed in the same year by two others, in San Francisco and New York City. Today, more than 60 major U.S. cities have such programs (Reinarman & Levine, 1997). Most have been established by AIDS activists, not by the treatment system. Although they were mostly illegal and privately funded at first, challenges to laws governing needle exchange and needle availability resulted gradually in many being supported, rather cautiously, by local government authorities. As yet, however, the U.S. Congress and the federal government have ignored the mounting evidence in favor of these programs and have consistently voted to ban any funding for them.

Recurring Themes

As Weisner and Morgan (1992) made clear in their discussion of the alcohol treatment system in the United States, the political and economic changes in societal concerns about alcohol shaped the course of the treatment system much more profoundly than did mere changes in drinking patterns and drinking problems. This is also true of the drug treatment system. Attitudes to illicit drugs and their use, and the corresponding increase in criminalization of drugs and drug use, have affected profoundly both the type of permitted treatment and the target groups identified. Certain themes recur in this history of treatment.

The first theme is the way in which attitudes toward the role of treatment change. In the 1920s, many of the advocates of narcotic control believed that once legislation had removed narcotics from U.S. society, the unfortunate addicts would be ultimately "cured" by treatment. In the 1970s, during the "War on Crime," treatment was seen as a way of solving the crime problem: Once addicts were treated and cured, crime rates would drop substantially. Today, treatment is often portrayed as a panacea for the "drug problem." Leaving aside the issue of whether treatment works, these beliefs in its efficacy ignore both the extent to which drug abuse may reflect wider societal ills (Currie, 1993) and, as Barker (in this book) has noted, the extent to which treatment is a misnomer for alternative forms of control (see also Conrad & Schneider, 1992).

A second theme is the connection between treatment and law enforcement. Once opium and heroin had been declared illegal, it was obvious that law enforcement officials would play a prominent role in dealing with the addict. However, what was not so obvious was the extent to which criminal justice officials would become intimately involved in both encouraging and hindering certain types of treatment. For example, the fears that emerged around the development of maintenance programs in the 1920s and the 1960s can be seen to be similar to those that are currently voiced about needle exchange programs. In the 1920s, officials from the Treasury Department were concerned that opium from the clinics was finding its way to the street drug markets, and that as a result, addiction would be further encouraged. In the 1960s, officials of the Bureau of Narcotics voiced a similar concern about methadone. Today, law enforcement officials and members of Congress argue that the distribution of needles encourages more injection of drugs (Reinarman & Levine, 1997).

A final theme in the development of the treatment system is the extent to which federal and state legislation and local ordinances have often been at variance. For example, in the 1920s, the federal government, with the assistance of the U.S. Supreme Court, was able to enforce federal regulations against the wishes of the local authorities and even the states on how best to deal with addicts. Today, the conflict between these three levels of government continues. In California, for example, despite the Republican governor's veto of the Needle Exchange Program bill, local authorities, such as San Francisco, directly challenged the veto by declaring a public health emergency, which allowed them to provide needle exchange services.

More recently, in November 1996, with the passing of Proposition 215, the people of California approved the use of medical marijuana (a specific U.S. term) as a legally available medicine. In response, the Office of National Drug Control Policy began to coordinate a campaign against the California initiative. The White House administration threatened to withdraw federal licenses to prescribe controlled substances from any doctor who prescribed marijuana; it even hinted at criminal prosecution. However, partly as a result of a ruling by a U.S. district court, and partly because of concerted action by activists and the medical establishment, the federal government has withdrawn its threats. Such conflict between different levels of government may indicate that the official establishment at least may be relenting in its drug war under increasing public dissatisfaction. Its heavily puni-tive policy has placed 300,000 American citizens behind bars and is costing more than $20 billion a year, but it has done little to solve drug problems. Even the latest White House "drug czar" (Director of the Office of National Drug Control Policy) has admitted that the metaphor of the drug war is misleading and that "a more appropriate analogy for the drug problem is cancer" (Office of National Drug Control Policy, 1997, p. 5). This shift from a war to a disease metaphor may be an indication of a future of more enlightened thinking, when treatment and prevention will be accorded the same status as law enforcement.

Notes

1. For a critique of Brecher's perspective, see Baumohl (1992).
2. The Federal Bureau of Narcotics was established in 1930; its first director was Harry Anslinger. For an extended discussion of the Bureau and its previous association with liquor law enforcement, see Musto (1973).
3. See Hunt and Rosenbaum (1997) for a fuller discussion of clients' perceptions of methadone treatment.

References

Anglin, M. D. (1988). The efficacy of civil commitment in treating narcotic addiction. In C. G. Keukfeld & F. M. Tims (Eds.), *Compulsory treatment of drug abuse: Research and clinical practice, Vol. 86* (NIDA Research Monograph, pp. 8-34). Rockville, MD: National Institute on Drug Abuse.

Anglin, M. D., & Hser, Y-I. (1990). Treatment of drug abuse. In M. Tonry & J. Q. Wilson (Eds.), *Drugs and crime, Vol. 13* (pp. 393-460). Chicago: University of Chicago Press.

Baumohl, J. (1992). The dope fiend's paradise revisited. *The Surveyor, No. 24.*

Besteman, K. J. (1992). Federal leadership in building the national drug treatment system. In *Drug abuse services research series: Extent and adequacy of insurance coverage for substance abuse services. Institute of Medicine report: Treating drug problems, Vol. 2* (pp. 41-58). Washington, DC: U.S. Department of Health and Human Services.

Brecher, E. M. (1972). *Licit and illicit drugs.* Boston: Little, Brown.

Centers for Disease Control and Prevention. (1993). *The public health impact of needle exchange programs in the United States and abroad, Vol. 1.* San Francisco: Author.

Conrad, P., & Schneider, J. (1992). *Deviance and medicalization: From badness to sickness.* Philadelphia: Temple University Press.

Courtwright, D. (1982). *Dark paradise: Opiate addiction in America before 1940.* Cambridge, MA: Harvard University Press.

Courtwright, D. (1992). A century of American narcotic policy. In *Drug abuse services research series: Extent and adequacy of insurance coverage for substance abuse services. Institute of Medicine report: Treating drug problems, Vol. 2.* Washington, DC: U.S. Department of Health and Human Services.

Courtwright, D., Joseph, H., & Des Jarlais, D. (1989). *Addicts who survived: An oral history of narcotic use in America, 1923-1965.* Knoxville: University of Tennessee Press.

Currie, E. (1993). *Reckoning: Drugs, the cities, and the American culture.* New York: Hill and Wang.

Deitch, D. (1973). Treatment of drug abuse in the therapeutic community: Historical influences, current considerations and future outlook. In *Drug use in America: Problem in perspective. The technical papers of the second report of the National Commission on Marihuana and Drug Abuse, Appendix Vol. 4: Treatment and rehabilitation* (pp. 158-175). Washington, DC: Government Printing Office.

De Leon, G. (1984). Program based evaluation research in therapeutic communities. In F. Tims & J. Ludford (Eds.), *Drug abuse treatment evaluation: Strategies, progress and prospects, Vol. 51* (NIDA Research Monograph, pp. 69-87). Rockville, MD: National Institute on Drug Abuse.

Dershowitz, A. M. (1973). Constitutional dimensions of civil commitment. In *Drug use in America: Problem in perspective. The technical papers of the second report of the National Commission on Marihuana and Drug Abuse, Appendix Vol. 4: Treatment and rehabilitation* (pp. 397-449). Washington, DC: Government Printing Office.

General Accounting Office. (1996a). *Drug and alcohol abuse: Billions spent annually for treatment and prevention activities.* Washington, DC: Author.

General Accounting Office. (1996b). *Federal and state prisons: Inmate populations, costs, and projection models.* Washington, DC: Author.

General Accounting Office. (1997). *Drug control: Observations on elements of the federal drug control strategy.* Washington, DC: Author.

Gerstein, D. R., & Harwood, H. (1990). *Treating drug problems: Vol. 1. A study of the evolution, effectiveness and financing of public and private drug treatment systems* (Committee for the

Substance Abuse Coverage Study Division of Health Care Services, Institute of Medicine). Washington, DC: National Academy Press.

Glasser, I., & Siegel, L. (1997). When constitutional rights seem too extravagant to endure: The crack scare's impact on civil rights and liberties. In C. Reinarman & H. Levine (Eds.), *Crack in America: Demon drugs and social justice* (pp. 229-248). Berkeley: University of California Press.

Hunt, G., & Rosenbaum, M. (1997). "Hustling" within the clinic: Consumer perspectives on methadone maintenance treatment. In J. A. Inciardi (Ed.), *Heroin in the age of crack-cocaine*, pp. 188-214. Thousand Oaks, CA: Sage.

Jaffe, J. H. (1979). The swinging pendulum: The treatment of drug users in America. In R. L. Dupont, A. Goldstein, & J. O'Donnell (Eds.), *Handbook on drug abuse* (pp. 3-16). Rockville, MD: National Institute on Drug Abuse.

Kane, J. A. (1973). *A legal history of the Narcotic Addict Rehabilitation Act of 1966: Vol. 4. Treatment and rehabilitation* (pp. 485-515). Washington, DC: Government Printing Office.

Lipton, D. S., Falkin, G. P., & Wexler, H. K. (1992). Correctional drug abuse treatment in the United States: An overview. In C. G. Leukefeld & F. M. Tims (Eds.), *Drug abuse treatment in prisons and jails, Vol. 118* (NIDA Research Monograph, pp. 8-30). Rockville, MD: National Institute on Drug Abuse.

Lipton, D. S., & Wexler, H. (1988). *The drug crime connection invests correctional rehabilitation with new life*. New York: Narcotic and Drug Research.

Maddux, J. (1988). Clinical experience with civil commitment. *Journal of Drug Issues, 18,* 575-594.

Morgan, P. (1978). The legislation of drug law: Economic crisis and social control. *Journal of Drug Issues, 8,* 53-62.

Musto, D. (1973). *The American disease: Origins of narcotic control*. New Haven, CT and London: Yale University Press.

Nadelmann, E. (1997). Drug prohibition in the U.S.: Costs, consequences, and alternatives. In C. Reinarman & H. Levine (Eds.), *Crack in America: Demon drugs and social justice* (pp. 288-316). Berkeley: University of California Press.

NASADAD (National Association of State Alcohol and Drug Abuse Directors). (1996). *An analysis of state alcohol and drug abuse profile data: Fiscal year 1994*. Washington, DC: Author.

National Institute on Drug Abuse (NIDA). (1991). History of NIDA. *NIDA Notes, 5*(5).

Office of National Drug Control Policy. (1997). *The national drug control strategy, 1997*. Washington, DC: White House.

Pauly, M. (1991). Financing treatment for substance abuse. In W. Cartwright & J. Kaple (Eds.), *Economic costs, cost-effectiveness, financing, and community based drug treatment, Vol. 113* (NIDA Research Monograph, pp. 165-175). Rockville, MD: National Institute on Drug Abuse.

Peters, R., & May, R. (1992). Drug treatment services in jails. In C. Leukefeld & F. Tims (Eds.), *Drug abuse treatment in prisons and jails, Vol. 118* (NIDA Research Monograph, pp. 000-000). Rockville, MD: National Institute on Drug Abuse.

Reinarman, C., & Levine, H. (1997). *Crack in America: Demon drugs and social justice*. Berkeley: University of California Press.

Rosenbaum, M. (1995). The de-medicalization of methadone maintenance. *Journal of Psychoactive Drugs, 27,* 145-149.

SAMHSA (Substance Abuse and Mental Health Services Administration Office of Applied Studies). (1993). *National drug and alcoholism treatment unit survey (NDATUS): 1991 main findings report*. Washington, DC: U.S. Department of Health and Human Services.

SAMHSA (Substance Abuse and Mental Health Services Administration Office of Applied Studies). (1996a). *National drug and alcoholism treatment unit survey (NDATUS): Data for 1994 and 1980-1994*. Washington, DC: U.S. Department of Health and Human Services.

SAMHSA (Substance Abuse and Mental Health Services Administration Office of Applied Studies). (1996b). *National household survey on drug abuse*. Washington, DC: U.S. Department of Health and Human Services.

Saxe, L., & Shusterman, G. (1991). *Drug treatment modalities: A taxonomy to aid development of services research*. Rockville, MD: National Institute on Drug Abuse.

Schlesinger, M., & Dorwart, R. (1992). Falling between the cracks: Failing national strategies for the treatment of substance abuse. *Daedalus, 121,* 195-237.

Schlesinger, M., Dorwart, R., & Clark, R. (1991). Treatment capacity for drug problems in the United States: Public policy in a fragmented service system. In *Background papers on drug abuse financing and services research: Drug abuse services research series, No. 1* (pp. 16-57). Rockville, MD: NIDA.

Schmidt, L., & Weisner, C. (1993). Developments in alcoholism treatment: A ten year review. In M. Galanter (Ed.), *Recent developments in alcoholism, Vol. 11* (pp. 369-396). New York: Plenum.

Schmidt, L., & Weisner, C. (1995). The emergence of problem-drinking women as a special population in need of treatment. In M. Galanter (Ed.), *Recent developments in alcoholism, Vol. 12* (pp. 309-326). New York: Plenum.

Swartz, J. (1993). TASC—The next 20 years: Extending, refining, and assessing the model. In J. A. Inciardi (Ed.), *Drug treatment and criminal justice* (pp. 127-148). Newbury Park, CA: Sage.

Terry, C., & Pellens, M. (1970). *The opium problem.* Montclair, NJ: Patterson Smith.

Waldorf, D. (1971). Compulsory treatment in New York's candy coated jails. *Drug Forum, 1,* 21-35.

Waldorf, D., Orlick, M., & Reinarman, C. (1974). *Morphine maintenance: The Shreveport clinic, 1919-1923.* Washington, DC: The Drug Abuse Council.

Weisner, C., & Morgan, D. (1992). Rapid growth and bifurcation: Public and private alcohol treatment in the United States. In H. Klingemann, J. P. Takala, & G. Hunt (Eds.), *Cure, care, or control: Alcoholism treatment in sixteen countries* (pp. 223-252). Albany: State University of New York Press.

Zweben, J., & Payte, J. (1990). Methadone maintenance in the treatment of opiate dependence: A current perspective. *Western Journal of Medicine, 152,* 588-599.

Chapter 2

The Treatment of Drug-Related Problems in Canada: Controlling, Caring, and Curing

Alan C. Ogborne
Reginald G. Smart
Brian R. Rush

Before the arrival of Europeans, the indigenous peoples of Canada made no use of psychoactive substances (Smart, 1983). Even the tobacco smoked by many Indian tribes had a low nicotine content. Alcohol use was also unknown. This contrasts with parts of the United States and with South America, where indigenous peoples used alcohol and a variety of drugs long before the arrival of Europeans.

European explorers and early settlers were very familiar with alcohol and with medicines containing cannabis or opium. In 1606, Champlain's apothecary cultivated cannabis in Nova Scotia (Le Dain, 1973), and it has since been grown in most other parts of the country.

Medicines containing opium, and later morphine and cocaine, were initially imported in large quantities from Europe and the United States, but after the provinces were united in 1867, large numbers of patent-medicine factories were established, especially in Ontario and Quebec (Smart, 1983). Medicines containing morphine or cocaine were extremely popular during the 19th century, and many could be obtained without prescription. Opiates could also be purchased from some general stores or ordered by mail. Physicians prescribed opiates for pain, cough,

AUTHORS' NOTE: The views expressed in this chapter are those of the authors and do not necessarily represent the views of the Addiction Research Foundation, London, Ontario.

diarrhea, and a host of other conditions, and morphine was even used to treat alcoholism (Brecher et al., 1972). It is therefore certain that many people were dependent on drugs to some degree. The aristocratic vice of opium eating and the degeneracy associated with excessive opium use were widely recognized. Dependence on opium, morphine, chloral hydrate, cocaine, and laudanum—a mixture of opium and alcohol—was also common among patients admitted to private sanatoria, especially women and people with easy access to these drugs (e.g., physicians, nurses, pharmacists).

During the 19th century, opium smoking was largely confined to Chinese immigrant workers living on the West Coast, who had brought the smoking habit from China. Some actors, artists, and prostitutes frequented "opium dens," and this added to middle-class suspiciousness of the otherwise relatively contained and "foreign" habit of opium smoking.

The use of opium for recreation and self-medication became illegal after the passage in 1908 of the first Opium Act, which limited its import and use to medical purposes. In the same year, the first Patent Medicines Act set limits on the use of opiates in over-the-counter medicines. It is of interest that neither act was specifically intended to deal with addiction or related problems. The Opium Act, which was passed with little discussion, owed much to the moral indignation of the middle class and especially of its chief architect, William Lyon Mackenzie King. The Patent Medicines Act, which was rigorously debated, was designed partly to limit the exaggerated or blatantly false claims of effectiveness made by some manufacturers and salespeople; it was also intended to address the concern of temperance workers and tax collectors about products containing alcohol.

The Opium Act was rigorously enforced, and its principal victims were Chinese immigrants. Many were deported over the next decade. Physicians were also targeted, especially after 1925, when the Act was amended to prohibit the prescription of opiates for the relief of addiction. The amendment, which remained in effect until 1961, was not challenged by the medical profession, and the federal police sometimes used decoy patients to entrap physicians; many physicians were successfully prosecuted, but the profession did not challenge even this practice.

After the passage of the Opium and the Patent Medicines Acts, some addicts turned to heroin and morphine—drugs that are easier to conceal, yet more potent and usable by injection. This occurred especially in British Columbia, which to this day has the highest prevalence of addiction to opiates. However, the nonmedical use of opiates and other drugs did not become widespread until the late 1960s. By this time, the Opium Act had been replaced by the Narcotic Control Act, which, among other provisions, set a minimum sentence of 7 years in prison for importing narcotics (including cannabis).

From 1914 to 1924, the annual number of convictions under the Opium Act (later the Opium and Drug Act) ranged from 770 to 1,866. There was then a steady decrease until the 1930s and an increase after World War II, but until the mid-1960s there were fewer than 600 in any year.

Drug Use in Canada

Cannabis was the first illicit drug with wide appeal in Canada (Smart, 1983). During the late 1960s and the 1970s, cannabis use among high school students (Grades 9 to 13) in Toronto increased from 7% to 23%. Use of other drugs, such as barbiturates, speed, and LSD, also increased during that time, but these were less popular than cannabis.

Surveys indicate that most types of drug use among Canadian students peaked around 1979, and cocaine use slightly later. Despite a slight upward trend in 1993, rates of reported drug use have declined sharply since 1979, and cannabis use declined by as much as 50% (Adlaf, Smart, & Walsh, 1993). Although overall drug use has declined among students, there remains a small proportion of heavy users that has fluctuated in number but shows no real decline. In 1993, in the province of Ontario, 12.7% of students in Grades 7 to 13 reported using cannabis at least once in the previous 12 months; the corresponding rates for use of LSD, heroin, and cocaine were 6.9%, 1.2%, and 1.5%, respectively.

Population surveys show a decrease in use of drugs also among adults—tranquilizers by more than 50% from a peak in the 1970s, and stimulants and sleeping pills in the late 1980s. Cannabis use also has declined in Ontario from its peak in 1984 (11.2% to 6.8%), but in the case of cocaine there has been little change from 1984, when the first trend studies of use were made in the province (Adlaf et al., 1993).

Smart and Adlaf (1990) found that cocaine-related admissions to a large treatment center in Toronto had increased significantly since about 1980. In recent years, these have included an increasing proportion of women and young people. Cannabis-related admissions declined during the same period. In the past few years, cocaine admissions have peaked and begun to decline, although cocaine is still the most commonly used drug after alcohol among treatment populations receiving treatment services (see below).

Although drug use appears to be declining in the Canadian population, there are still reasons for concern. Heroin deaths have increased in two cities, Vancouver (British Columbia) and Toronto, in the past 2 years, apparently in association with global increases in the availability of inexpensive and relatively pure heroin (Metro Toronto Research Group on Drug Use, 1994). Also, drug use among Ontario students increased in 1993 after a long series of declines; LSD use showed an especially large increase. Drug use is also very high in certain groups. For example, a study in Toronto showed that 86% of street youth had alcohol or drug problems (Smart, Adlaf, Walsh, & Zdanowicz, 1992), and most did not receive treatment for them.

Drug use is also a significant problem in many native communities and among native high school students. Apart from alcohol, native people tend to use a wide range of other drugs, including cannabis, narcotics, stimulants, and, especially, inhalants (Scott, 1992).

The rate of HIV infection among injection drug users has been low (4% to 7%), and, to June 1993, only 478 people with AIDS (6% of all AIDS cases) had injection drug use as a risk factor. However, there are reports of high rates of HIV infection among drug users in prisons (Thorn, 1992) and of a recent sharp increase in drug-related HIV infection among addicts in Montreal (Riley, 1995).

Treatment of Drug Abuse in Canada

Treatment of drug abuse in Canada defies simple characterization. Largely a provincial responsibility, it varies among and within the provinces and territories, and it has complex, mostly unresearched relationships with local patterns of drug use and sociopolitical conditions. In many places, drug users are treated within the general health and social services, and specialized services are provided mostly by agencies concerned with both drugs and alcohol. Thus, the drug treatment system in Canada does not have clear boundaries, and drug users with similar characteristics may be treated quite differently in different circumstances.

However, drug treatment across the country has certain common features. For example, all treatment takes place against a backdrop of a strong prohibitionist, law-and-order approach to nonmedical drug use, and many users in treatment are involved with the criminal justice system. At the same time, provincial and federal ministries of health, social service, and justice have supported the development of professional treatment services based on disease or on complex biopsychosocial models of addiction. There is also evidence of growing commitment to program evaluation, and the future of drug treatment may be increasingly tied to the results of studies of cost-effectiveness. Each of these features is now examined in more detail.

The Law-and-Order Context of Drug Treatment

Canada is a signatory to the United Nations Single Convention on Narcotic Drugs and has an official policy of prohibiting the nonmedical use of narcotic drugs, including cannabis. Compared with most countries of the Middle East and East Asia, Canada is relatively benign in its treatment of drug users, but far less so than the Netherlands and some other European countries. For example, Canada has no heroin maintenance clinics, and until recently there were only a few, rather rigidly run methadone programs. Long prison terms are given to those who attempt to import drugs, and the possession of cannabis can lead to a stiff fine or even imprisonment. From 1986 to 1991, the police have become more active in their pursuit of drug users, and this has resulted in an increase in drug convictions, especially those involving small amounts of cannabis (Erickson, 1992). Although Canada's drug strategy is very different in tone from the United States' "war on drugs," it continues to give high priority to reduction in supply by means of police surveillance and enforcement. Harm reduction, although supported by many professionals and evidenced by the growth of needle exchange programs, has yet to be declared a priority by the federal government or by provincial governments (Riley, 1995).

Canada's drug control priorities have affected the treatment of drug users in several ways. Until 1961, physicians were legally prevented from prescribing drugs for the treatment of addiction, and addicts were forced to use drugs obtained on the black market or through fraud and deception. Although physicians now have the right to prescribe methadone for addicts, rules governing this practice have prevented most general practitioners from doing so until recently. Heroin can be prescribed only for pain, although few physicians choose it over other narcotics, such as morphine.

In the past, prohibitionist priorities supported compulsory treatment programs, and they continue to propel many drug users toward treatment both within and outside the justice system. Until the 1960s, most publicly supported treatment was based in prisons, and attendance was required for incarcerated addicts. Compulsory detention for treatment of addiction is still technically permitted under the Narcotic Control Act, and a proposed omnibus drug bill would increase judges' discretion to order treatment as an alternative to a criminal penalty. The courts have discretion to order treatment as part of a sentence in the case of addicts arrested for drug-related or other offenses. Offenders have the right to refuse court-ordered treatment, but those who agree to treatment may be given lighter sentences, and drug users charged with offenses often enter treatment programs to impress judges and to make a case for leniency.

Treatment Within the Justice System

Treatment services in the justice system have been influenced by developments in the broader treatment system, and much of the justice system's official line on treatment is the same as others'. Provincial systems of justice provide an addiction assessment and counseling service to prisoners and offenders on probation, and the Federal Ministry of Correctional Services has recently introduced at all federal inmate reception centers a self-administered, computerized assessment of lifestyle. This is intended to assess the nature and severity of the substance use and to facilitate the planning of individualized treatment. The justice system also contracts with general addiction services (also for alcoholics and other addicts) for treatment of individuals on probation and parole.

The justice system commonly refers cases to specialized addiction treatment services. Data from the province of Saskatchewan for 1991 show that 46% of all clients of its specialized services for addiction were involved with the legal system, and at least 25% had court orders requiring them to have treatment. In a sample of youth treated at a Toronto addiction service, 18% had such court orders, and another 31% were involved with the law in some way (Ogborne, unpublished analysis).

Although the beliefs and practices of the Canadian justice system with respect to the treatment of addiction merit further research, the system appears to be both paternalistic and pragmatic. Addicts are seen as having chronic, relapsing problems needing long-term professional help. Judges, lawyers, and especially probation officers express concern about the welfare of addicts in the justice system and regard treatment ordered by a court as being in the best interests of addicts. At the same time, the justice system shows a commitment to the evaluation of its policies and programs, including the new federal initiatives in assessment and treatment (Fabiano, 1993). This is in line with a tradition of criminal justice studies on treatment of addiction. Examples are experimental studies of innovative milieux (Murphy, 1970) and group treatment (Annis, 1979), and uncontrolled follow-up studies of cases treated within the correctional system (Beech & Gregorson, 1964; Richman, 1966).

Those who provide treatment services tend to be ambivalent about referrals from the criminal justice system. They recognize that many clients have external motivations, and they try to use motivational interviewing techniques to engage them in a process of change (Rush, Ellis, Allen, & Schmidt, 1995). However, they tend to regard those referred from the correctional system as less interested in change and less reliable than others. Also, interviews conducted for this chapter showed that some agencies are unwilling to accept addicts referred from courts or with court cases pending.

Treatment in Other Nonspecialized Settings and Systems

Many drug users receive counseling from school and youth counselors, social workers, family counselors, nurses, general practitioners, psychiatrists, and clergy. Drug users are also treated for dependence or drug-related illnesses in general hospitals as well as in specialized addiction programs in hospitals. A recent report from Saskatchewan showed that over a 1-year period, 56% of cases given a diagnosis of substance abuse were seen by community physicians in hospitals or at mental health centers rather than in specialized addiction programs.

Except for hospital data, there are no national data on drug users treated in either specialized or nonspecialized services. Even national data for hospitals do not distinguish between admissions to specialized addiction programs and others. Hospitals in the Yukon and Northwest Territories are excluded from national hospital statistics. Across all other hospitals, there were 1,340 discharges with a diagnosis of drug psychosis in the fiscal year 1989-1990: a rate of 5.1 per 100,000. In the same year, there were 4,216 discharges with a diagnosis of drug dependence (16.1 per 100,000) and 1,767 discharges with a diagnosis of nondependent use of drugs (6.7 per 100,000). These figures total to 7,323 (27.9 per 100,000). These discharges mean that patients had been admitted for those conditions and eventually discharged—cured or uncured. No information is available on the specific drugs used.

Across Canada, Narcotics Anonymous groups meet in most large cities and are considered an integral part of the treatment system; their total number or that of their members is not known.

Specialized Services for
the Treatment of Addiction

History and Recent Trends

The development of Canada's drug treatment programs has been closely linked
with that of programs for alcoholics. This reflects the influence of provincial
alcoholism foundations or commissions, which were well established when the
need for more drug treatment services first arose (Rush & Ogborne, 1992). Only
in British Columbia were separate drug and alcohol commissions established, and
they were merged in 1973. Other provincial governments, because of increasing
drug problems, authorized provincially funded alcoholism foundations or commissions to provide or establish drug treatment services.

The "rush to combine" alcohol and drug programs, which had been criticized
elsewhere (Pitman, 1967), was favored in Canada, where they were readily accom-
modated within the public health frameworks established by Canadian foundations
and commissions (Popham & Schmidt, 1968).

Government funds contributed to a remarkable growth in the number of specialized drug and alcohol services from the mid-1960s through the 1980s. Thus, of
340 specialized services operating in 1976, two thirds had been established since
1970, and treatment service budgets had increased from Can. $14 million to Can.
$70 million (Reid, 1981). This growth occurred in provinces that continued to fund
treatment through commissions, as well as in Quebec, where commissions had
been dissolved, and Ontario, where they no longer funded treatment services.

Many types of addiction programs were established, mostly for alcoholics, but
during the 1970s they were established for users of other drugs as well, including
methadone programs and therapeutic communities for narcotic users, and a few
special programs for users of other drugs (cocaine, inhalants). Federal funding for
treatment increased through the late 1980s, when a national drug strategy was
announced. Since 1988, such funding has amounted to almost Can. $500 million
in cost-sharing arrangements with the provinces for new programs for women,
adolescents, and federal offenders. Priority is given to multidisciplinary, community-
based programs.

The provinces have also continued to support specialized addiction services, and
new services are still being established in some regions. However, some provinces
have been hampered by fiscal restraints, and some have been unable to find the
required matching funds to qualify for assistance under the national drug strategy.

After the war, specialized addiction treatment services were provided primarily
by medical and paramedical professionals, but from the 1960s psychologists, social
workers, and mental health counselors became more prominent. In addition, some
treatment agencies, special detoxification centers, and residential treatment centers
have always employed recovered, or recovering, alcoholics as counselors.

Current Financing and Organization
of Addiction Treatment Services

Outside the justice system, drug treatment services have been funded from a variety of sources but mostly from provincial ministries of health. These ministries receive local tax revenue and health insurance funds as well as federal transfer payments under the Canada Health Act and other federal programs. The act, in force since 1965, guarantees every citizen access to necessary health services regardless of ability to pay. The federal government matches all provincial funding, provided the provinces have uniform, publicly administered health insurance programs that offer universal, comprehensive, and transferable benefits. The provincial share is made up directly from treasury funds or from premiums paid by employers and employees. Public assistance is provided to those not otherwise covered and unable to pay.

Most provinces have a small private sector that charges fees for services. Quebec has the largest number of private service programs, but their overall significance is not known. A few private hospitals still operate, and some treat substance abusers, but these hospitals have not been researched. Some treatment centers charge for room and board when patients can afford to pay, but the contribution of such payments is negligible across the national treatment system.

The estimated total cost of specialized services is Can. $350 million to $400 million (about Can. $15 per capita). Estimates of the costs of services provided by nonspecialized hospitals, physicians, and others are not available, but they are very high.

Common Treatment Approaches and Services

There is no national database of treatment services in Canada, and no national studies have been undertaken since 1976. Lists of services available in different provinces are published, but not all use the same classification schemes. We shall therefore present mainly a qualitative overview of the Canadian treatment system, drawing on our general knowledge, interviews with key informants conducted especially for this chapter, and similar interviews for a chapter on treatment of alcoholism in a companion volume (Rush & Ogborne, 1992).

A systems approach to treatment is common across the country. It comprises a range of different services along a continuum of care, matching cases to treatment programs. Particularly influential have been the writings of Glaser and his colleagues (Glaser, Greenberg, & Barrett, 1978) and Pattison (1982), as well as the report of the U.S. Institute of Medicine (1990) titled *Broadening the Base of Alcohol Treatment*. Other features of drug treatment across the country are multifunctional services and an emphasis on coordination and case management. In general, community-based, nonresidential programs are favored over hospital-based or residential programs. Some hospital-based programs continue, but how many there are is unknown. Ontario has only six, but their services are largely nonmedical and community oriented (Ellis & Rush, 1993).

Both within and among regions, providers of specialized services hold divergent views on the nature of addiction. Whereas many subscribe to a social learning model of addiction, others accept a disease model, and there is no clear national consensus. Where a disease model prevails, services are medically oriented and residential. Where the social learning model is the more influential, services are mostly nonmedical and nonresidential, and behavioral therapy is the rule. Programs for native people increasingly incorporate native cultural and spiritual values and practices.

There is general interest across the country in integrating addiction services with other services, and providers of addiction services everywhere are trying to involve other agencies in case finding, case management, and referral. Some provinces have special programs to encourage or train medical and other professionals to offer brief interventions to clients with substance abuse problems. Client advocates are seeking to ensure that alcohol and drug users receive the other services they need from other agencies, and also encouraging them to use health and social services appropriate to their needs.

Except for those agencies that provide services for native people, most Canadian addiction treatment agencies serve a diverse population and do not restrict services to particular age groups, or to males or females, or to users of specific drugs. However, some provide a range of specialized services in response to demand and the needs of the population. Where there are only a few agencies, they tend to offer services for the general population. In some provinces, treatment settings and modalities are becoming highly diversified, with special provision for youth, women, the elderly, or other population groups (e.g., specific cultural groups, the physically disabled).

Most provinces have a variety of programs, including detoxification centers, outpatient and residential programs, assessment/referral services (Ogborne & Rush, 1990), and methadone programs.

Therapeutic communities were more popular in Canada during the 1970s than they are today, and many have closed down. Some provinces now have none, and others have only one or two.

Methadone Programs

Under the 1961 Narcotic Control Act and its amendments, physicians may prescribe methadone to addicts (Peachy & Franklin, 1988), but the requirements for close monitoring of patients, urine testing, and counseling have, in effect, excluded most general practitioners from doing so. Methadone is prescribed mostly by physicians in special clinics. However, several provinces are exploring a broader, more community-based approach to methadone treatment, with a larger role for general practitioners and community pharmacies. In this approach, the specialized treatment center stabilizes the narcotic user; contracts with the user the terms of a longer-term treatment plan; and manages the case, arranging with a community physician and pharmacy to provide methadone prescriptions and support. An evaluation of one such community model found some evidence of improved outcome, but professional opinion about the implementation of the program and its cost-saving potential has been mixed (James, Mayberry, & Moran, 1994).

Methadone clinics generally provide low-threshold doses of methadone (50 mg to 100 mg) for short periods (up to 6 months). However, in 1993, 34% of cases had been in treatment for more than 5 years and 20% for more than 10 years. The total number in treatment (2,373) was double that of 7 years earlier and 3.5 times that in the early 1980s. The increase reflects the establishment of new methadone programs as much as an increase in narcotic addiction.

Needle Exchange Programs

Owing to the efforts of public health professionals, several large Canadian cities have had needle exchange programs since the late 1980s. They supply condoms, as well as bleach kits to clean syringes. The spread of AIDS among intravenous drug users has been a major reason for the needle exchange programs. They have been credited with reducing needle sharing among street youth (Hankins, Gendron, & Rouah, 1994). Their number across the country is unknown. Ontario is reported to have 12 to 14 such programs, but there are no aggregate data on their operation or clients.

Common Concerns and Possible Future
Directions of Treatment of Drug Abuse in Canada

Large fiscal deficits and a sluggish economy are motivating Canadian governments to trim all forms of spending. Severe restraints or cutbacks have been imposed in many sectors and especially in the health sector, where some hospitals have closed and waiting lists have lengthened. In this climate, funds for drug addiction services are very unlikely to be increased, and there have been instances of large cuts for addiction services. Planners and providers of addiction services have responded to the economic stringency by maximizing the efficiency of services. Most provinces are emphasizing less costly outpatient services and restricting more costly inpatient services to those in greatest need. There is a widespread and growing effort at early case finding and at coordinating addiction services with other health and social services.

Accountability is being promoted by the use of information systems that generate routine reports on clients, services, and costs, and many individual programs have undertaken process and outcome evaluation. There is a demand to study the cost-effectiveness of different treatment approaches and to rethink traditional abstinence-oriented approaches. A pragmatic, empirical approach to treatment may thus characterize the future.

New ways to engage clients in treatment and to prevent drop-out are being explored in several provinces. It is common for some types of cases to drop out. For example, a recent study of youth in selected outpatient treatment programs in Ontario showed that 33% of cases had dropped out after one or two visits, and that 28% left residential programs on or before the tenth day, few of them with staff approval. Across all treatment programs in Ontario, drop-out rates were estimated at 17% to 35%. Some agencies reported that none of their clients completed treatment (Ellis & Rush, 1993).

The absorption of most addiction foundations or commissions into government departments has been criticized by those who wish to maintain a strong identity for addiction services and those who seek national consensus on key issues. In some provinces, it is no longer clear who speaks for addiction services or where information can be obtained about them. Communication has thus become more difficult both across and within provinces.

There is a general effort to increase access to services by women, youth, and ethnocultural minorities; if funding permits, this will continue, and it is expected that services will become more specialized or individualized, as well as more flexible in the form of outreach, day or evening services, and services that make maximum use of community resources and self-help materials.

Resources permitting, it is likely that there will be more programs for cases with both mental health and drug addiction problems and closer ties between mental health and addiction services, as there are already with respect to people with mental health and alcohol problems.

AIDS cases are relatively rare in most addiction programs, but this may change. Some key informants knew of addiction services that showed a profound insensitivity to people with AIDS. AIDS awareness programs for addiction workers have been developed and are likely to both continue and expand.

Needle exchange and other harm reduction programs are gaining wider acceptance, but harm reduction is not included in Ontario's Substance Abuse Strategy (Ontario Ministry of Health, 1993). However, there are high-level discussions on a harm reduction approach to heroin addiction in British Columbia (Riley, 1995). A recent spate of deaths has focused attention on the inadequacies of present approaches, and one federal minister has suggested that the decriminalization of heroin should be considered. However, it is not clear what this would mean in practice.

Addiction treatment benefits in many ways from the commitment and activities of professionals. The professionals have successfully maintained the profiles of alcohol and tobacco as the substances of greatest concern and ensured attention to them in both national and provincial drug strategies. They have lobbied successfully against the adoption of a hard-line, war-on-drugs attitude and promoted a harm reduction approach to drug-related problems. They have also limited the influence of ideologues in addiction treatment and fostered a commitment to evaluation. There are few enthusiastic advocates of specific cures, and claims for the success of specific programs are typically modest and qualified (a very Canadian characteristic). It is of interest that the criminal justice system is also committed to evaluation and paying attention to accountability and the efficient use of resources.

Drug abuse is treated, however, in the context of a strong law-and-order approach to its prevention. Canada's drug laws are quite severe, and the Royal Canadian Mounted Police continue to have a great deal of influence at the highest levels of policy. A proposed new "omnibus" drug bill has provision for new punitive measures, and there is talk in some quarters of the need for compulsory treatment of drug addicts, though not of alcoholics or smokers. Thus, although drug users have access to state-funded treatment programs with medical and psycho-social care, they are also being pursued by the police and brought to court to be fined or sentenced to prison. Addicts in treatment are often in trouble with the law, and the courts may require treatment as a condition of probation. Of course, this happens in most countries and especially in the United States, where powerful political forces oppose all liberal reforms and demand intensification of the war on drugs. Canada's drug problem is not so serious or politicized as in the United States, and the potential for rational reform is thus greater. However, because drug problems are not high on the public agenda, significant reforms are unlikely in the short term, and money for new programs is limited. Because alcohol and drug programs in Canada have few champions and limited prestige, they can expect little total expansion in the near future. Of course, new approaches are still possible as older approaches are discarded and the need for improved coordination and integration of services becomes more apparent.

References

Adlaf, E. M., Smart, R. G., & Walsh, G. W. (1993). Trend highlights from the Ontario student drug use survey, 1977-1991. *Canadian Journal of Public Health, 84*(1), 64-65.

Annis, H. M. (1979). Group treatment of incarcerated offenders with alcohol and drug problems: A controlled trial. *Canadian Journal of Criminology, 21,* 3-15.

Beech, C. E., & Gregorson, A. I. (1964). Three year follow-up study—Drug addiction clinic, Mimico. *Canadian Journal of Corrections, 6,* 211-224.

Brecher, E. M., & Editors of Consumer Reports. (1972). *Licit and illicit drugs.* Mount Vernon, NY: Consumers Union.

Ellis, K., & Rush, B. R. (1993). *Alcohol and other drug services in Ontario: Results of a provincial survey, 1992.* Toronto: Addiction Research Foundation.

Erickson, P. G. (1992). Recent trends in Canadian drug policy: The decline and resurgence of prohibitionism. *Daedalus, 121,* 239-267.

Fabiano, E. (1993). *Developing a model for the provision of substance abuse treatment.* Ottawa: Correctional Services of Canada.

Glaser, F. B., Greenberg, S. W., & Barrett, M. (1978). *A systems approach to alcohol treatment.* Toronto: Addiction Research Foundation.

Hankins, C., Gendron, S., & Rouah, F. (1994, March). *The role of specialized centres for HIV prevention among injection drug users.* Paper presented at a conference on harm reduction, Toronto.

James, D., Mayberry, C., & Moran, J. (1994). *AADAC's opiate dependency program: Evaluation of the enhanced program component.* Edmonton: Alberta Alcohol and Drug Commission.

Le Dain, G. C. (1973). *Final report of the commission of inquiry into the non-medical use of drugs.* Ottawa: Information Canada.

Metro Toronto Research Group on Drug Use. (1994). *Drug use in metropolitan Toronto.* Toronto: Department of Public Health.

Murphy, B. C. (1970). *A quantitative test of the effectiveness of an experimental treatment for delinquent opiate addicts.* Abbotsford, BC: Canadian Penitentiary Service.

Ogborne, A. C., & Rush, B. R. (1990). Specialized addiction assessment/referral services in Ontario: A review of their characteristics and roles in the addiction treatment system. *British Journal of Addiction, 85*(2), 197-204.

Ontario Ministry of Health. (1993). *Partners in action: Ontario's substance abuse strategy.* Toronto: Queen's Printer for Ontario.

Pattison, E. M. (1982). A systems approach to alcoholism treatment. In E. M. Pattison & E. Kaufman (Eds.), *Encyclopedic handbook of alcoholism* (pp. 1089-1108). New York: Gardner.

Peachy, J. E., & Franklin, T. (1988). Methadone treatment in Canada: The clinical question continues. *Canadian Medical Association Journal, 138,* 17-19.

Pitman, D. (1967). The rush to combine: Sociological dissimilarities of alcoholism and drug abuse. *British Journal of Addiction, 62,* 337-342.

Popham, R., & Schmidt, W. (1968). Some comments on the "rush to combine." *British Journal of Addiction, 63,* 25-27.

Reid, A. (1981). Alcoholism treatment in Canada: A review of current programs and policy issues. *International Journal of the Addictions, 16,* 647-681.

Richman, A. (1966). A follow-up of criminal narcotic addicts. *Canadian Journal of Psychiatry, 11,* 107-115.

Riley, D. (1995, January). *Harm-reduction approaches.* Presentation to Ontario's Health Recovery Steering Committee.

Rush, B. R., Ellis, K., Allen, B., & Schmidt, G. (1995). *Assessment and referral agencies in Ontario: Results of a descriptive survey.* Toronto: Addiction Research Foundation.

Rush, B. R., & Ogborne, A. C. (1992). Alcoholism treatment in Canada: History, current status and emerging issues. In H. Klingemann, J. P. Takala, & G. Hunt (Eds.), *Cure, care, or control: Alcoholism treatment in sixteen countries* (pp. 253-269). Albany: State University of New York Press.

Scott, K. (1992). Substance use among indigenous Canadians. In D. McKenzie (Ed.), *Aboriginal substance use: Research issues* (pp. 9-41). Toronto: Canadian Centre on Substance Abuse and National Native Alcohol and Drug Abuse Program.

Smart, R. G. (1983). *Forbidden highs: The nature, treatment and prevention of illicit drug abuse.* Toronto: Addiction Research Foundation.

Smart, R. G., & Adlaf, E. M. (1990). Trends in treatment admissions for cocaine and other drug abusers. *Canadian Journal of Psychiatry, 35,* 621-623.

Smart, R. G., Adlaf, E. M., Walsh, G. W., & Zdanowicz, Y. M. (1992). *Drifting and doing: Changes in drug use among Toronto street youth, 1990-1992.* Toronto: Addiction Research Foundation.

Thorn, S. (1992). Education the main weapon as prison officials defend against AIDS threat. *Canadian Medical Association Journal, 146,* 573-580.

Institute of Medicine. (1990). *Broadening the base of alcohol treatment.* Washington, DC: National Academy of Science Press.

Chapter 3

Expansion and Implosion: The Story of Drug Treatment in Sweden

Anders Bergmark

The beginning of the present epidemic of drug problems in Sweden can be connected to the onset of the general drug epidemic in Western Europe and the United States in the 1960s. Earlier instances of drug problems in Swedish society have been described by Olsson (1994) and Lindgren (1993). Stensmo (1979) designated the late 1960s as a period of investigation of the present Swedish drug problem. Between 1967 and 1969, four government commissions published reports on drug abuse and measures to deal with it; the reports had, as a central theme, the development and expansion of treatment resources. A 10-item manifesto adopted by the government in 1968 covered the same ground. Thus, the development of the present Swedish drug treatment system began about the end of the 1960s with an expansion of resources for drug treatment and, more important, a shift from a system—the psychiatric care system—to a loose arrangement largely lacking in either organization or cohesion, and not under the control of the authorities, that we call the field of drug treatment. It began to expand in the late 1960s, grew progressively until the end of the 1980s, and, at the beginning of the 1990s, imploded into the alcohol treatment system, disappearing as a distinct entity. This field and the story of its rise and fall is the subject of this chapter.

Reported prevalence rates of illicit drug use can be of questionable value as a basis for evaluating changes over time within a country in the use of illicit drugs. Comparative research may easily misinterpret available data. For example, Reuter, Falco, and MacCoun (1993) estimated the prevalence of heroin addicts in Sweden to be 150 per 100,000 population around 1990. However, these figures are based on a misinterpretation of a 1979 case-finding study that reported 12,000 (i.e., 150 per 100,000 population) "heavy drug abusers," but of whom only about 1,000 could be called classic heroin addicts; the remaining 11,000 were mainly users of amphetamines and cannabis. Such inconsistencies in reported prevalence rates can seriously invalidate comparative international analysis. With these reservations, we use reported prevalence rates to outline the extent in general and the distinctive characteristics of the Swedish drug abuse problem.

In 1979, a nationwide case-finding study of illicit drug use estimated the number of heavy drug abusers at 10,000 to 14,000 (Socialdepartementet, 1980). Heavy drug abuse was defined as any intravenous use of illicit drugs, or any daily or almost daily use of illicit drugs. The number of intravenous users was estimated at 7,500 to 10,000, of whom 1,500 to 2,000 were injecting daily; about 70% of the intravenous users took mainly amphetamines. Of the daily or almost daily injectors, 750 to 1,000 were using opiates. The noninjectors were mainly daily users of cannabis or a combination of cannabis and amphetamines.

A similar study in 1992, on a population largely comparable to that of 1979, showed an increase in the number of heavy abusers to an estimated 14,000 to 20,000, up about 5,000 since 1979. Although more drug abusers were taking opiates as their main drug, amphetamines were still the most used (Olsson, Byqvist, & Gomer, 1993). One major difference between 1979 and 1992 was in age distribution. The 1992 population (Figure 3.1) suggests a fall in the number of new drug abusers during the 1980s, probably in the early or middle 1980s, according to Skog (1993), and associated with the growing public awareness of AIDS.

In Sweden, as in most countries, AIDS and HIV infection are an important part of the drug problem, but their incidence is relatively low (Figure 3.2). At the beginning of 1993, there were 633 HIV-infected drug users, of whom 89 were later diagnosed with AIDS. Most of the cases of HIV infection were in the Stockholm area, where almost 80% of HIV prevalence is found (SCB, 1994). It is estimated that between 80% and 90% of all intravenous drug users have been tested for HIV infection.

The Beginning—"Surfaces of Emergence"[1]

Because drug-related problems before the 1960s were treated within psychiatry, as though they were a mental disease, one can hardly talk of drug treatment as such in this period. Rather, the psychiatric system developed certain ways of managing drug treatment, which contributed to the formation of a drug treatment field. Thus, a number of psychiatric hospitals established specific drug units in which treatment was often organized in line with the concept of "therapeutic community" as it had been developed at Henderson Hospital in England (Jones, 1979). These specialized units represented both a response to the growing numbers of young and "different" drug addicts and a break with conventional psychiatry. This treatment ideology inspired a new type of residential drug treatment, based on small units, with about five to seven personnel and 10 to 15 beds, that adopted the Swedish version of the democratic therapeutic community ideology. These changes were the first signs of a drift away from psychiatry and medicine and toward becoming part of, or at least

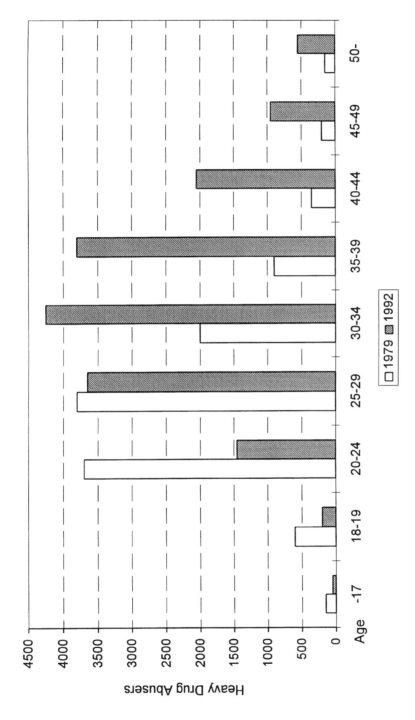

Figure 3.1 The Age Distribution for Heavy Drug Abusers in 1979 ($N = 12,000$) and 1992 ($N = 17,000$)
SOURCE: Skog (1993).

NOTE: The term *heavy drug abuse* refers to any intravenous use of illicit drugs, or any daily/almost daily use of illicit drugs.

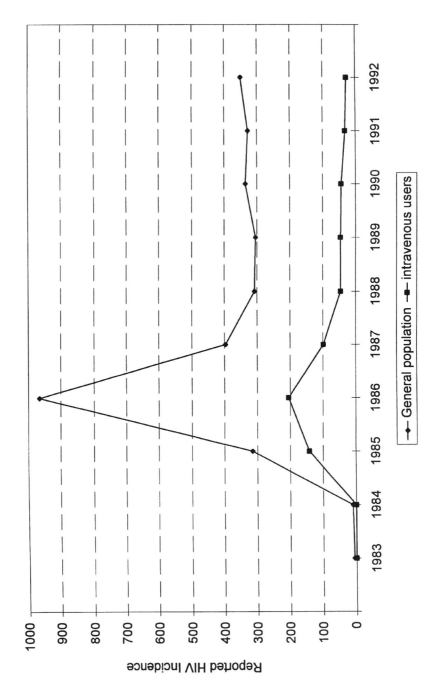

Figure 3.2 Reported Incidence of HIV Infection Between 1982 and 1992 Among Intravenous Drug Users and the General Population
SOURCE: SCB (1994).

36

closely associated with, the social services. They reflected also the general change in the social perception of the drug problem during the 1960s, which gradually eroded the position of psychiatry and led to the creation of the new field of nonmedical drug treatment.

In an analysis of the Swedish drug debate of the 1960s, Lindgren (1993) identified an undermining of the position of experts as an essential characteristic, closely connected to the appearance of a new type of activist, the socially committed layperson, who not only criticized the general management of the drug problem but also questioned the legitimacy of experts. Lindgren connects this trend with the "care and reform strategy," which transposed the drug problem from the domain of psychiatry and psychopathology to that of youth culture and general social criticism. The drug problem became, like many other problems in the late 1960s, a subject of general criticism on the part of the New Left, which was establishing itself at that time and represented the drug problem as one of the consequences of capitalism in Swedish society.

The fact that alcohol treatment in Sweden was largely nonmedical influenced considerably the form that the drug treatment field was to take. Being a social service, alcohol treatment could legitimize the assignation of treatment responsibility to a field that was not controlled by the medical profession; drug treatment was comparable to alcohol treatment, which provided an acceptable conceptual model. In some respects, however, the alcohol treatment system was not considered a model to be imitated. Some of the founding texts of drug treatment accused the alcohol treatment system of being ineffective and unable to help its clients in any substantial way (Socialdepartementet, 1969), and the future of drug treatment was to take a different direction.

Institutions designated as general reformatory institutions for juvenile delinquents have had a significant influence on drug treatment. In the early 1970s, some of them undertook treatment, and as they grew in numbers and influence, they became an important, if informal, part of the field. It is notable that the first and most famous of these institutions developed an ideology that was designated not as treatment but as "socialistic fosterage"—of which a central tenet was the need for coercion to rehabilitate the drug addict. Over the past two decades, its reputation for success combined with its emphasis on coercion has kept this ideology at the center of an intense and often heated debate about coercion in general in the social services.

The Professional and Economic Context

Although today's drug treatment in Sweden originated in psychiatry, it was connected from the beginning with the social services sector, but it was not until 1982, when the Social Services Act came into force, that it was officially assigned as a responsibility of that sector. At the same time, it has remained largely unaffected by the profession that dominates the social services sector in general, namely, social work.

We have noted that the relative ease with which drug treatment could be established outside the sphere of medicine in Sweden was related to its close similarity to the organization of alcohol treatment, which had earlier become a largely nonmedical domain. However, again, Swedish social workers had neither special training nor any clinical experience for the task and could not direct the development of the field. Thus, it may be said that through a concurrence of government funding, official reports, legislation, and the general public discourse on the drug problem, a "professional field without professionals" was created. This expression is not intended to denote a factual situation in the sense that such a professional field actually exists; instead, it is a designation of an illusion that drug treatment constitutes a professional field—it is a territory of imaginary knowledge and skills. This "illusory" domain is institutionalized in the sense that it is present in legislation, commission reports, administrative routines, and mass media debate. It is a domain whose existence, by and large, can be said to be de jure rather than de facto.

In 1978, a government report stated:

> Specific treatment for drug abuse has existed for a little more than ten years. Within the drug treatment system there is a lot of knowledge and experience. It is now urgent to collect this knowledge and to transmit it to the new personnel of the treatment system. (Socialdepartementet, 1978, p. 64; author's translation)

This referred to the early and middle 1970s. Six years later, another government report stated that treatment methods during the same period had been based on an esprit de corps rather than on knowledge, and that a "fosterage approach"—rather than the therapy approach of the 1970s—was the most appropriate treatment ideology (Socialdepartementet, 1984). Such inconsistency in government recommendations has been the rule in the short history of Swedish drug treatment; the position taken at any particular time is most likely to represent retrospective support for the dominant treatment ideology of the previous 1 or 2 years. This may be attributable to the lack of a professional body that could guard the gate against different treatment entrepreneurs.

It is not by chance that treatment units in general prefer to recruit staff on the basis of "life experience" rather than formal education, and that most staff have no special training in drug treatment (Bergmark & Oscarsson, 1988). Indeed, there is hardly any such special training. There has been no profession entitled to act and speak for the field of drug treatment over the past two decades, a time during which the drug treatment field has been lavishly funded and nongovernmental entrepreneurs have been able to operate in the drug treatment market in the favorable conditions of the welfare state. This fueled the general expansion of drug treatment during the 1970s and 1980s.

The Swedish drug treatment market is unusual (Bergmark & Oscarsson, 1994). Many drug addict "treatment users" are not the true purchasers of the treatment. Even when treatment appears to be voluntary, the drug addict has most likely felt coerced to enter treatment, perhaps by threats of withdrawal of economic benefits (e.g., public assistance), or because of a provision in the law for explicit coercive treatment (Socialdepartementet, 1987). Thus, although the Social Services Act represents treatment as a "social right," the actual customer in the market of drug treatment is generally not the drug addict but the social worker in the social welfare agency. And until recently, this type of purchaser had no real concern about the cost of purchasing treatment.

Sweden probably spends more on publicly funded treatment for drug abuse than most countries. The Nordic welfare states in general spend a lot on treatment for alcohol and drug abuse (e.g., see Klingemann, Takala, & Hunt, 1992), and among them, Sweden spends most. During the 1970s and the 1980s, there were virtually no economic restraints on treatment for drug abuse. Only recently, with the economic recession of the 1990s, did expansion slow down.

Although some local communities have always tended to limit expenditure on drug treatment, this has had little effect in view of the liberal subsidies provided by the central government for almost 20 years, amounting to 75% to 100% of the expenditure of the local communities. The result of the combination of guaranteed funding and the absence of a profession to act and speak for the drug treatment field has been that the government authorities have never been able to control it. Without experts or professionals, there can be no legitimate knowledge, and therefore no stable development of the field. The attempt in the mid-1980s to establish coercion as the appropriate treatment ideology was a typical instance of the use of the retrospective strategy, which was the only basis on which the authorities could express a point of view of some substance. Characteristically, it also occurred at a time when the influence of the coercion ideology had begun to diminish.

The Evolution of the Treatment System

For a long time, until the mid-1980s, inpatient treatment predominated. It was not that there was no outpatient treatment; rather, most of the treatment authorities did not consider outpatient treatment sufficient (e.g., see Socialdepartementet, 1984, p. 62). In 1978, 10 years after the institution of the new field of drug treatment, there was a reasonable balance of inpatient and outpatient resources— 23 and 17 units, respectively.[2] For the period 1978 to the mid-1980s, Figure 3.3 shows a greater increase in inpatient than in outpatient capacity. This trend ended in 1986/1987 with a steep increase in outpatient resources and a slight fall in the number of inpatient units, followed after 1988 by a steep decline in both. The remarkable expansion of inpatient resources up to the mid-1980s can be related to two main factors: how the Swedish society perceived the drug abuse problem, and the incentive provided by government subsidies for inpatient units. The public regarded the drug addict as a "drug-controlled criminality machine" (Bergmark & Oscarsson, 1988, p. 175), for which outpatient treatment was inadequate; out-patient facilities were seen as a means of getting drug addicts into inpatient treatment. And up until 1986, the government subsidies favored inpatient over outpatient treatment.

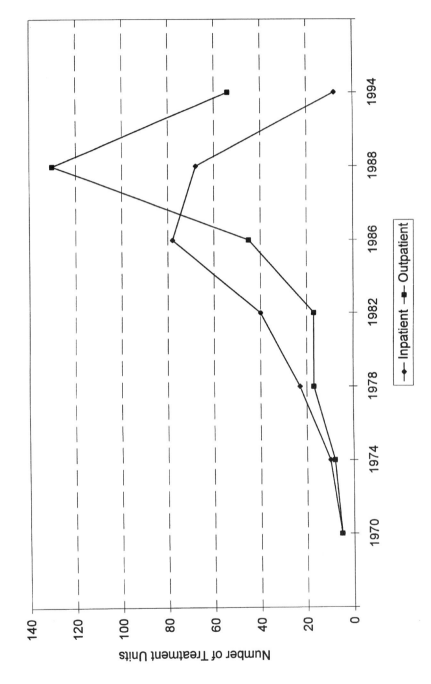

Figure 3.3 The Development of Inpatient Units Between 1968 and 1994

SOURCE: Bergmark and Oscarsson (1993, 1994); Socialdepartementet (1978; 1984, p. 11; 1987); Socialstyrelsen (1993).

The strong increase in outpatient resources in 1986/1987 (Figure 3.3) came about after the general public and the authorities learned that some drug users had become infected with HIV, and that intravenous use was an important factor in the epidemiology of HIV infection. The Swedish government adopted a policy of reaching all intravenous users with detoxification and treatment, and it directed a substantial part of the resources it had reserved for AIDS to the establishment of new outpatient units in order to reach all drug users with an offer of treatment (Socialstyrelsen, 1993).

Despite the remarkable expansion of outpatient resources at this time, the National Board of Health and Welfare (Socialstyrelsen, 1993) was hardly justified in claiming that the efforts of the latter part of the 1980s had no precedent in the history of drug treatment in Sweden, at least as regards genuine results. The expansion brought no new treatment methods and lacked sufficient stability (as shown in Figure 3.3) to maintain funding beyond the limits of that provided by the government (Riksrevisionsverket, 1993). Notwithstanding certain claims to the contrary, there has been hardly any expansion of inpatient treatment since 1986 (see Socialstyrelsen, 1993). The extreme decline in the number of inpatient units at the end of the 1980s (Figure 3.3) was not part of any general decline in inpatient treatment. According to the National Board of Health and Welfare (Socialstyrelsen, 1993), the number of institutions that the County Government Boards designated as "treatment or residential homes for adult abusers," and that comprised both alcohol and drug units, increased progressively through the 1980s and the early 1990s. However, the extent of the expansion of inpatient treatment in general has been put in doubt by Bergmark and Oscarsson (1994). The changes in the numbers of individuals (cross-sectional data) in inpatient treatment for problems classified as drug abuse do not reflect the decrease in inpatient institutions for drug treatment (Table 3.1).

It can only be concluded that the boundaries between alcohol and drug treatment systems had been changed in some way. This is considered in the final section of this chapter.

Treatment Content—Settings and Ideologies

The principles that underlie the form and content of drug treatment in Sweden were laid down largely by the 1982 Social Services Act, which clearly states that treatment for alcohol and drug abuse should be voluntary. Nevertheless, drug users are commonly brought into and held in coercive treatment. In 1994, roughly 10% of all treatment episodes in the social service sector were compulsory. In the 1990s, there have been 200 to 400 such treatment episodes per year with respect to individuals with an identified drug abuse or combined alcohol and drug abuse problem (SCB, 1994). The legal basis for compulsory treatment of drug users is contained in two laws enacted in association with the Social Services Act (1982): the Care of Alcoholics and Drug Abusers Act, and the Act on Child Care; the latter, although designed for the general protection of children, provides also for com-

Table 3.1   Voluntary Inpatient Treatment Population on 31 December, by Type of Abuse
(in percentages)

Type of Abuse	1988	1989	1990	1991	1992
Alcohol	69	62	62	57	53
Drugs	14	13	12	15	15
Alcohol and drugs	14	20	22	23	27
Other	3	5	4	5	5
Total	100	100	100	100	100
N	3,660	4,291	3,794	4,168	3,397

SOURCE: SCB (1994).

pulsory treatment of young drug abusers (under 20 years of age). The Care of
Alcoholics and Drug Abusers Act had an antecedent in the 1954 Temperance Act,
which had provision for compulsory treatment of alcoholics. Before 1982, such
treatment for a drug abuser required committal to a psychiatric institution.

In 1989, an amendment to the Care of Alcoholics and Drug Abusers Act
extended the criteria for compulsory treatment from a threat to the life of a drug
abuser to a situation in which a drug abuser "was irresponsibly running the risk of
destroying his future life." In practice, this meant that any intravenous drug abuser
could be compelled to take treatment.

The 1989 amendment also made it possible to extend the time in treatment from
2 months (with a possible extension of 2 months) to 6 months. This was done
explicitly in the belief that an extended period of compulsory treatment was needed
to motivate the alcoholic or the drug abuser to seek further treatment voluntarily.
However, it had little effect; from 1982 to 1994, roughly 80% of those in compulsory treatment have not continued with voluntary treatment, and of the remaining
20%, there is no information on how many completed their treatment (SCB, 1994).
Nevertheless, among the Nordic countries, Sweden is exceptional in its belief in,
and practice of, compulsory treatment (Lehto, 1994), based on the paternalistic
rationale that it is acceptable to constrain freedom in the interest of the individual's
well-being.

Although drug treatment has been a task of the social services since the early
1970s, there are still two other domains of concern in it, namely, psychiatry and
the reformatory institutions for young people. Psychiatry, which, as we have seen,
lost its preeminent role in drug treatment in the mid-1960s, retained two specific
tasks—detoxification and methadone maintenance. Of these, detoxification is the
more substantial. For more than 20 years, the number of inpatient psychiatric
treatment episodes for a primary diagnosis of drug addiction has remained fairly
stable at about 3,000 per year (Socialdepartementet, 1987; Riksrevisionsverket,
1993). Mostly, these episodes have not exceeded a week, which corresponds with
the standard procedure of detoxification in the psychiatric units specialized in this
procedure.

Because the main thrust of Swedish drug policy, in addition to the "care and
reform strategy" mentioned at the beginning of this chapter, has always been to

eliminate the illicit drug, it has played down harm reduction programs. The responsible administration has opposed methadone maintenance during the past two decades. At the end of the 1960s, the exception was Ulleråker Hospital in Uppsala, which was permitted to undertake a program for up to 150 patients. It soon developed a reputation for excellent management, and over time, it was able to increase its capacity to 450 patients. However, until 1987, it was the only one of its kind and was often referred to as an experiment. Then, as HIV infection and AIDS began to be associated with drug use, methadone treatment became more acceptable, and in 1987, a new program, with a capacity for 250 clients, was established in Stockholm.

Needle exchange is probably the most controversial harm reduction strategy, and the government has always been strongly against the idea. Nevertheless, there are two pilot exchange programs in southern Sweden.

The reformatory institutions for young people have played an important part in modern drug treatment in Sweden. Juvenile delinquents have been for a long time a charge of the social services. We have seen that in the 1970s some of these institutions for juvenile delinquents undertook drug treatment. By the mid-1980s, there were 18 such units with a total of 260 places, and they had become more a part of the drug treatment field than of any other system.

The methods of the first drug treatment units were inspired mainly by the concept of the therapeutic community, in its somewhat nonspecific, "democratic, non-hierarchical" version. This approach was often supplemented with ideas from different psychotherapeutic schools, such as transactional analysis, gestalt therapy, psychoanalysis, and existential therapy. In general, however, staff had had no formal training in these methods, and it is doubtful whether they were put into practice.

One effect of the coercive ideology in the reformatory units was to polarize ideologies in the drug treatment field. The proponents of "coercive socialistic fosterage" criticized other forms of treatment as being "liberal" and based on "fuzzy psychology" rather than on a "necessary" political analysis of the drug problem. Their advocacy reinforced the nonprofessional character of the drug treatment field: Not only did they lack any formal professional credentials, but they also openly opposed a professional approach, seeing it as conflicting with a political mission.

At the beginning of the 1980s, the coercive ideology had become quite influential. About half of the institutions providing voluntary treatment of adult users were applying it (Bergmark et al., 1989) through an emphasis on work, social training, and restrictions on personal freedom. However, the influence of this ideology began to wane when the government authorities adopted it as their own. The modified Care of Alcoholics and Drug Abusers Act, when it became law in 1989, constituted the official zenith of the coercion ideology. By then, however, this ideology had more or less vanished from the practical field of drug treatment (Bergmark & Oscarsson, 1993). A possible explanation for this development may be that the political and antiprofessional character of the original coercive ideology was transformed by the official approval and promotion to a practice model for drug treatment, and thus lost its possibilities of reproduction as a political ideology rather than a professional one. But through such a transformation, the authenticity of the ideology was lost, and thus also the possibilities for the staff and the patients to share a mutual vision of the world in a more fundamental sense. As a result, some of the therapeutic impact was also lost (cf. Frank, 1961).

By the end of the 1980s, various psychological theories had recaptured much of the ground they had lost. The more comprehensive were, in effect, modern versions of psychoanalytic theory. Although this has occurred in a field that still has no professional practitioners, it may nevertheless herald a second era for psychiatry and a solution to the lack of professionals. Also pointing in this direction are recent claims—although mostly unsubstantiated—that most drug abusers are also mentally disturbed.

The treatment ideologies discussed above have referred to inpatient treatment. Outpatient treatment ideologies are less well documented, at least with regard to the period before the expansion of outpatient resources in 1986, but they were much more stable than those that underlie inpatient treatment; psychological theories in general and psychoanalytical theories in particular have always played an important part in outpatient practice, 25 years ago as well as today. Some of the inpatient methods are impractical in outpatient treatment.

A Rush to Combine?

Schmidt and Weisner (1993) have characterized the trend toward combined treatment as the most significant organizational change in American treatment systems during the 1980s. To what extent this may have been true of Sweden as well is now discussed; we ask whether the marked decline in inpatient drug treatment facilities, as shown in Figure 3.3, can be explained by an increase in combined treatment.

A preliminary answer has to be "maybe." Although some surveys (Socialstyrelsen, 1993) indicate such an increase, others suggest that at least in part it was no more than a change in name. For this reason, one should consider the criteria for classifying treatment programs according to the categories of drug, alcohol, or combined treatment.

The most common ground for such classification has been what treatment practitioners call their own practice. This appears as a reasonable basis for classification if there is reason to believe that there generally exists a congruence between such labels and the types of clients that receive treatment. However, this is not always the case. In a 1992 study, the National Board of Health and Welfare (Socialstyrelsen, 1993) concluded that only 8% of inpatient facilities could be called drug treatment units, and only 15% of alcohol treatment units, whereas up to 66% of treatment units treated substance abuse of all types. However, a study of Statistics Sweden (referred to in Socialstyrelsen, 1993) indicates that classifying treatment units with reference to their predominant category of clients gives a different picture: 20% would then be designated as drug treatment units, 30% as alcohol treatment units, and 39% as treatment units for substance abuse of all types. Bergmark and Oscarsson (1994) found that about one third of all inpatient units could be designated as drug treatment units; this classification was based upon stricter criteria and a more sophisticated basis for categorizing than in previous studies.

If the problems of the clients are taken as the basis for classifying treatment units, another classification problem arises, namely, that of deciding whether a given individual ought to be described as having problems (or a major problem) with drugs, or with alcohol, or possibly with both and other substances.

Treatment personnel, researchers, and administrators have long known that many drug abusers also take alcohol in such quantities as to constitute a problem in itself (Bergmark et al., 1989; Socialdepartementet, 1978, 1987). This may well be the key factor in the recent change in the description of treatment types—in particular, the emergence of combined treatment as the most frequent treatment type—with respect to both drugs and alcohol. But because the finding of alcohol problems among drug users is not recent, some other factors may have triggered a new use of this association. Two such factors are discussed here.

The 1980s were not only a decade with opportunities for stockbrokers, but also a time when many treatment entrepreneurs tried to establish themselves in the field of inpatient alcohol treatment (Bergmark & Oscarsson, 1994). Because of the economic recession of the early 1990s, many treatment units came under economic pressure. For the first time, treatment entrepreneurs experienced a characteristic element of a market economy, namely, competition because of overproduction and falling demand, and this may have led them to take action to expand the market, such as broadening the criteria for admission to treatment units.

The second factor represents a reversal of some of the arguments that connect the growth of combined treatment with a general erosion of the boundary between drug treatment and alcohol treatment, as expressed, for example, by advocates of chemical dependency treatment or drug legalization. It is clear from Figure 3.1 that a substantial proportion of heavy drug abusers are now more than 40 years old. Many of them may now have mainly alcohol rather than drug problems. But, having once been labeled as heavy drug abusers, they may continue to be classified as such, rather than under their actual category of alcohol abusers—the association with drugs can be hard to shed. Thus, the persistence of the distinction between drug treatment and alcohol treatment institutions may result in a category of treatment called combined treatment.

Notes

1. The term "surfaces of emergence" is taken from Foucault (1972), who uses this term in a chapter that deals with the question of "the formation of objects."

2. The data on inpatient units have been collected from different sources (Bergmark & Oscarsson, 1993, 1994; Socialdepartementet, 1978; 1984, p. 11; 1987; Socialstyrelsen, 1993) and should, therefore, be interpreted with caution. Before the new Social Service Act was passed in 1982, most sources included only the inpatient units in receipt of government funding. Afterward, all statistics are related

to the list of "care and residential homes," which is kept by the National Board of Health and Welfare. In this chapter, I have tried to adjust for these difficulties. The data on the outpatient facilities are also flawed; there are elements of incompatibility between certain concepts to which the data refer. The outpatient data have also been assembled from the same sources but must be interpreted with even more care, because their conceptual as well as their legal contexts are liable to be more biased than those of inpatient treatment.

References

Bergmark, A., Björling, B., Grönbladh, L., Olsson, B., Oscarsson, L., & Segraeus, V. (1989). *Klienter i institutionell narkomanvård* [Clients in residential treatment]. Uppsala: Uppsala universitet.

Bergmark, A., & Oscarsson, L. (1988). *Drug abuse and treatment—A study of social conditions and contextual strategies.* Stockholm: Almqvist & Wiksell International.

Bergmark, A., & Oscarsson, L. (1993). *Den socialtjänstbaserade missbrukarvården* [Alcohol and drug treatment within the social service sector]. Stockholm: Centrum för utvärdering av socialt arbete [Center for the Evaluation of Social Work].

Bergmark, A., & Oscarsson, L. (1994). Swedish alcohol treatment in transition? Facts and fiction. *Nordic Alcohol Studies, 11,* 43-54.

Foucault, M. (1972). *The archeology of knowledge.* London: Tavistock.

Frank, J. (1961). *Persuasion and healing: A comparative study of psychotherapy.* Baltimore: Johns Hopkins University Press.

Jones, M. (1979). Democratic therapeutic communities or programmatic therapeutic communities or both? In G. De Leon & J. T. Ziegenfuss (Eds.), *Therapeutic communities for addictions* (pp. 19-28). Springfield, IL: Charles C Thomas.

Klingemann, H., Takala, J. P., & Hunt, G. (Eds.). (1992). *Cure, care, or control—Alcoholism treatment in sixteen countries.* Albany: State University of New York Press.

Lehto, J. (1994). Involuntary treatment of people with substance related problems in the Nordic countries. In M. Järvinen & A. Skretting (Eds.), *Missbruk och Tvångsvård* [Coercion and alcohol and drug abuse]. Helsingfors: Nordiska nämnden för alkohol- och drogforskning [Nordic Council for Alcohol and Drug Research].

Lindgren, S. Å. (1993). *Den hotfulla njutningen* [The menacing pleasure]. Stockholm: Symposium Graduale.

Olsson, B. (1994). *Narkotikaproblemets bakgrund* [The background of the drug problem]. Stockholm: Centralförbundet för alkohol- och narkotikaupplysning [Swedish Council for Information on Alcohol and Other Drugs].

Olsson, O., Byqvist, S., & Gomer, G. (1993). *Det tunga narkotikamissbrukets omfattning i Sverige 1992* [The prevalence of heavy drug abuse in Sweden 1992]. Stockholm: Centralförbundet för alkohol- och narkotikaupplysning [Swedish Council for Information on Alcohol and Other Drugs].

Reuter, P., Falco, M., & MacCoun, R. (1993). *Comparing Western European and North American drug policies.* Santa Monica, CA: RAND.

Riksrevisionsverket [National Audit Bureau]. (1993). *Narkomanvården* [Drug abuse treatment]. Stockholm: Author.

SCB [Statistics Sweden]. (1994). *Statistiska meddelanden 1989-1994* [Statistic messages, 1989-1994]. Stockholm: Author.

Schmidt, L., & Weisner, C. (1993). Developments in alcohol treatment systems: A ten-year review. In M. Galanter (Ed.), *Recent developments in alcoholism: Vol. 11. Ten years of progress* (pp. 369-396). New York: Plenum.

Skog, O. J. (1993). Narkotikamissbrukets utvikling i Sverige 1979-1992. In O. Olsson, S. Byqvist, & G. Gomer (Eds.), *Det tunga narkotikamissbrukets omfattning i Sverige 1992* [The prevalence of heavy drug abuse in Sweden 1992]. Stockholm: Centralförbundet för alkohol- och narkotikaupplysning [Swedish Council for Information on Alcohol and Other Drugs].

Socialdepartementet [Department of social affairs]. (1969). *Narkotikaproblemet* [The drug problem]. Stockholm: Author.

Socialdepartementet [Department of social affairs]. (1978). *Åtgärder mot narkotikamissbruk* [Actions against drug abuse]. Stockholm: Author.

Socialdepartementet [Department of social affairs]. (1980). *Tungt Narkotikamissbruk—En totalun-dersökning 1979* [Heavy drug abuse—A nationwide study 1979]. Stockholm: Author.

Socialdepartementet [Department of social affairs]. (1984). *Offensiv narkomanvård* [Offensive drug treatment]. Stockholm: Author.

Socialdepartementet [Department of social affairs]. (1987). *Missbrukarna, socialtjänsten, tvånget* [Alcohol and drug abusers, the social services, and coercive treatment]. Stockholm: Author.

Socialstyrelsen [National Board of Health and Welfare]. (1993). *Missbrukarvård till rätt pris?* [The right price for alcohol and drug treatment?]. Stockholm: Author.

Stensmo, C. (1979). *Kollektivet Trollängen* [The therapeutic community "Trollängen"]. Uppsala: Acta universitatis Upsaliensis.

Chapter 4

Finland: Drug
Treatment at the Margins

Aarne Kinnunen
Juhani Lehto

It is difficult to distinguish any particular system of drug treatment in Finland. There are at least three main reasons why Finland may differ from most other Western European countries with regard to drug treatment. First, the country is considered to have less drug use and fewer problems with drugs than most Western countries. The use of heroin, which is the main drug of concern in many other countries, has been particularly uncommon. Second, in drug policy, drug use has been regarded as a problem of either juvenile delinquency, in the early 1970s, or professional crime, in the 1990s. Mostly, the public has not distinguished between drug use and drug dependence, or between "soft" drugs and "hard" drugs, and therefore the treatment needs and rights of addicted users have not received due consideration. Third, there is an extensive system for the treatment of alcohol dependence, and it has been the practice since the beginning of the 1970s to assign drug treatment to that system.

Although there has never been a distinct system of drug treatment, there have been efforts during the past 30 years to treat drug users in separate units—within the alcohol treatment system, the public psychiatric care system, the private health care system by private physicians, or the prison service. However, after the initial surge of political support and publicity, the treatment units have often had difficulty defending their position at the margins of these systems.

In this chapter, these themes are developed, and different phases of drug treatment in Finland are elaborated.

Epidemiology of Drug Use
and Drug-Related Problems

The abuse of opiates and amphetamines was first noticed in the 1930s among the upper social classes and health care personnel. Although a prevalence of 200 to 400 cases of problem drug use was not considered a social problem, Finland received several reminders of its exceptionally high consumption of heroin from the Permanent Control Opium Board (Rosenqvist, 1974). The high level of consumption was due partly to extensive use of cough medicines containing heroin. During World War II, Finnish soldiers used considerable amounts of amphetamines; large amounts of morphine and heroin were used as well for relief of pain. As a result, a few hundred former soldiers had become addicted to these substances and were treated in psychiatric hospitals. After the war, the use of opiates spread among a small, distinctive group, mostly workers with criminal backgrounds (Westling & Riippa, 1956). There was a remarkable change during the 1960s. The use of new drugs, especially hashish among young people and amphetamines among criminal subcultures, increased, and the use of opiates decreased.

Surveys on Drug Use

Drug use has been studied by surveys of military conscripts. During the period 1980 to 1987, about 10% of conscripts had taken drugs at least once. Mostly, they had smoked hashish. About 1% had taken drugs more than 10 times (Kontula, 1995). The surveys of 1992 and 1993 showed a considerable increase in lifetime prevalence of drug use—17.2% in 1992 and 13.6% in 1993. However, no respondent reported intravenous use of heroin or morphine (Jormanainen, Lehesjoki, Seppälä, Peitso, & Koskenvuo, 1994; Kansanterveys, 1996).

In a survey carried out every second year, young people 14 to 18 years of age have been asked whether they knew of others among their acquaintances who had taken drugs. Between 1981 and 1995, the proportion of those who said they did more than doubled, from 15% to about 40%. In 1995, the most commonly used drugs in this respect were licit psychoactive medicines and cannabis. About 5% stated that someone they knew had taken heroin or amphetamines at least once (Rimpelä, Pohjanpää, Terho, Pienmäki-Jylhä, & Poikajärvi, 1995).

Two fairly recent (1992) nationwide surveys showed that 1% of the population had used cannabis during the previous year (Kontula, 1995; Partanen, 1994). The lifetime prevalence of cannabis use for the total population was 4.6%, considerably lower than in many Western European countries (Partanen, 1994). These surveys revealed so few users of hard drugs that it was difficult to determine their prevalence in the population. Cannabis use was highest among young single adults in the Helsinki metropolitan area, and all age groups, including the elderly, were using licit psychoactive medicines and alcohol (Kontula, 1995).

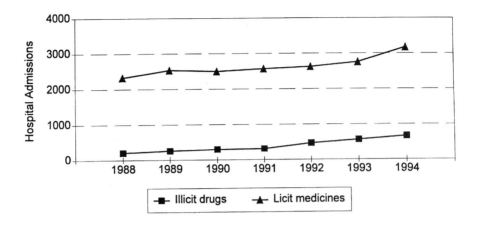

Figure 4.1 Hospital Admissions for Drug Dependence, Intoxication, or Poisoning by
Illicit Drugs or Licit Psychoactive Medicines as the Main Diagnosis, 1988-1994
SOURCE: STAKES (1988-1994).
NOTE: The figures for licit medicines are based on the classes 3041A and 3054A of the Classification of Diseases:
anxiolytica, sedativa et hypnotica.

Treatment Data

The 1990s have seen a significant increase in demand for inpatient hospital
treatment for drug dependence. In about two thirds of such cases, the drugs
involved are licit psychoactive medicines (Figure 4.1). Of the illicit drugs, amphetamines have shown the most notable increase regarding treatment episodes
(Figure 4.2; Hein, 1996).

A rough estimate of the number of drug-user clients in social and health services
has been obtained from a 1-day case count undertaken in all of these service units
on one day in every fifth year. The most recent such count recorded 9,300 cases
of substance abuse, of which about 23% related to licit psychoactive drugs, 9% to
cannabis, and 7% to other illicit drugs. About 90% of those who were using drugs
were also taking alcohol; only 10% were using drugs only. On the basis of this
study and the statistics available from the social and health services, Kaukonen
and Haavisto (1996) have estimated that the numbers of drug users with whom the
social and health services deal annually are the following: 80,000 for alcohol;
15,000 to 20,000 for licit psychoactive drugs; 5,000 for surrogate alcohol, solvents,
or inhalants; 5,000 to 8,000 for cannabis; and significantly fewer for hard drugs.

Drug-Related Deaths and Health Problems

Mainly licit medicines, but also illicit drugs, cause accidental intoxication and
death of nondependent people. In 1994, there were 151 such deaths, as well as 113
from a combination of medicines or drugs and alcohol. Those due to drugs have
not been distinguished from those due to licit medicines. Deaths of drug-dependent

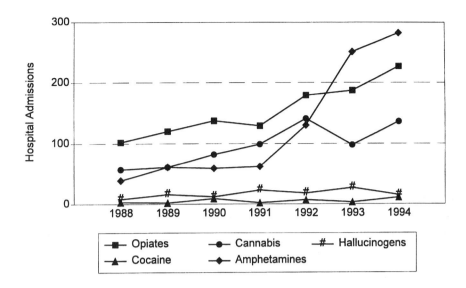

Figure 4.2 Trends in Numbers of Hospital Admissions for Illicit Drug Use
SOURCE: STAKES (1988-1994).

users from classical drug poisoning have been rare in Finland—17 were recorded in 1993 and 13 in 1994.

In recent years, systematic studies of causes of death of men aged 15 to 34 years carried out in the Department of Forensic Medicine of the University of Helsinki found drugs—especially cannabis, amphetamines, and opiates—in increasing numbers of victims of homicide and traffic accidents (Vuori & Ojanperä, 1994); in 1994, illicit drugs were found in 66 cases.

AIDS and HIV infection are not an important part of the drug problem in Finland. By the end of 1995, of a total of 725 cases of HIV infection, only 3.6% were intravenous drug users (Kansanterveys, 1996). According to prison administration data, in the past 6 years, of 800 to 1,000 HIV tests carried out in Finnish prisons annually, only four revealed HIV infection.

Recently, hepatitis B and C associated with intravenous drug use have been found quite frequently among drug-dependent clients of some specialized treatment institutions for substance abusers.

Summarizing the Data

Drug abuse had already been recorded in Finland in the 1930s and after World War II. In the late 1960s, new types of drug use appeared among young Finns, and experimentation with cannabis was almost at the average level for Western Europe. During the past 25 years, there has been no more than scattered use of heroin or cocaine. Cannabis has been the most popular illicit drug, and amphetamines the most popular hard drug. Personnel of the social and health services see more cases of abuse of licit psychoactive medicines than of illicit drugs.

Many data sources indicate a comparatively low level of dependence on so-called hard drugs. These sources include data on fatal overdoses, prevalence of AIDS and HIV infection among injecting drug users, and drug treatment, as well as data from the criminal justice system. However, available data indicate a quite clear increase in drug use and treatment needs in the 1990s. The supply of many drugs has increased, and prices have fallen (Kinnunen, 1996). Abuse of licit medicines mixed with alcohol still seems to be the country's most serious drug problem.

Drug Legislation and Enforcement

With Norway and Sweden, Finland tends to be a hard-liner in drug policy (Christie & Bruun, 1985). All three have maintained repressive policies toward drug use in any form and strict police action directed at users and user-dealers. Although Norway and Sweden have extensive networks of health and social services concerned with prevention and treatment of disease, drug policy in all three countries has a criminal justice rather than a medical orientation (Hartnoll, 1993).

In Finland, a 1966 decree made the use of drugs a criminal offense, as soon as it had been noticed that use of hashish had spread among young people. The Drugs Act of 1972 confirmed the illicit nature of the use of drugs. In 1994, the parliament enacted new narcotics legislation that did little to alter the existing laws. It set the maximum prison sentence for drug offenses at 10 years. The use of drugs can still incur, at most, a 2-year prison sentence, but usually a fine is considered the proper penalty for use or possession of small amounts of narcotics.

In 1994, there were more than 2,500 convictions for drug offenses. Of 3,200 prisoners on a given day in 1995, 8% had been sentenced for drug offenses (Kansanterveys, 1996). Studies in prisons have indicated that 12% of the prisoners are drug addicts, and 45% are alcoholics (Joukamaa, 1991; Kansanterveys, 1996).

Development of Drug Treatment

Finnish drug treatment has developed since the 1960s in four phases:

1. A psychiatry phase, in the late 1960s
2. A social therapy phase, in the early 1970s
3. A phase of decline of drug treatment as a separate health care entity, between 1975 and 1986
4. A "let a thousand flowers bloom" phase, since 1986

The Psychiatry Phase

The increasing needs for treatment related to the new wave of drug use in the late 1960s were first met by the psychiatric hospitals. At the beginning of the

1970s, annual admissions of drug users for inpatient treatment reached about 900, but soon they dropped to fewer than 300.

Treatment of alcohol-dependent patients followed a parallel trend. They were among the first to be excluded from psychiatric hospitals, in line with a policy of "deinstitutionalization" of psychiatric care, introduced in the 1970s (Takala & Lehto, 1992). In both cases, the compensatory outpatient services were instituted within the social services system, not within psychiatry—an instance of demedicalization or depsychiatrization of substance abuse treatment.

The Social Therapy Phase

A government committee that considered the future of drug treatment in 1969 and 1971 (Komiteanmietintö, 1969, 1971) recommended a basic model borrowed from the modernization plans and processes of the alcohol treatment system, and it adopted principles that have since influenced the drug treatment system. These principles were that the new system for alcohol treatment also met drug users' need for treatment, and that there was no need for a specialized drug treatment system; that treatment primarily should be on a voluntary outpatient basis, and not residential; and that the alcohol care system should undertake drug treatment in the framework of social welfare rather than psychiatry.

The committee's recommendations and principles were implemented by the establishment of a system of youth centers attached to the new, specialized outpatient units for alcohol treatment—the A-clinics—in the major cities, and by the designation of two inpatient institutions for alcohol treatment, Järvenpää Addiction Hospital and Mikkeli A-koti, to undertake as a particular responsibility the treatment of drug abusers. Until 1984, the specialized substance abuse treatment institutions received a major part of their income from the central government in the form of an earmarked subsidy. Thus, the central authorities could use a significant financial incentive to ensure that the committee's suggestions were implemented.

Drug treatment was thus attached to the social therapy part of the alcohol treatment system of the early 1970s. It was mainly voluntary and used many kinds of discussion therapy, most often led by social workers with a therapeutic orientation (Takala & Lehto, 1992). This was considered at the time the most modern and humane part of the alcohol treatment system. It contrasted with the traditional inpatient institutions, which still provided involuntary treatment, with strong emphasis on manual work in the treatment programs. The new youth centers and the designation of two inpatient institutions for drug treatment also provided a distinct identity for the new social therapy.

The Phase of Decline of Drug Treatment as a Separate System

Rather soon, it became evident that the youth centers and the two inpatient institutions would not survive by treating only or predominantly drug users. Most of the clients of the youth centers had alcohol abuse as their primary substance abuse problem. Many had experimented with drugs, mainly with cannabis, but most did not regard drug dependence as their major problem. Also, Järvenpää Addiction Hospital and Mikkeli A-koti admitted individuals whose major problem substance was alcohol.

The preparations for new legislation on the cure and care of alcohol and drug abusers began in the mid-1970s and were completed in 1986 (Misuser Act of 1986). In accordance with the committees that dealt with drug treatment in 1969 and 1971, the preparations were based on the principle of similarity between alcohol and drug problems as well as between alcohol and drug treatment. The new law uses the concept of "problem use of intoxicating substances" and makes no distinction between alcohol and drugs in any aspect of treatment or prevention. In contrast to the earlier laws and committee reports, it emphasizes the role of primary medical care and general social services in the care and cure of people with problem use of intoxicating substances. The implication is that only the most difficult problems of substance abuse should be treated in the specialized system (Lehto, 1992).

In 1984, a change in the state financing of all health and social services also affected drug treatment. Previously, it was possible to give higher state subsidies to favored sectors of the social services, such as drug treatment. After 1984, all sectors obtained the same percentage of their costs from the state, and it was no longer possible to compensate, for instance, for the lack of clients in drug treatment.

Three key factors, therefore, weakened the separate identity of drug treatment between 1975 and 1986: the lack of distinct drug treatment clients; the strategy adopted in the preparations for the new law on services for alcohol and drug abusers; and the change in the state subsidy system. Although the two inpatient units and the youth centers of the A-clinics continued through this phase, their particular approach to drug abusers weakened significantly.

The "Let a Thousand Flowers Bloom" Phase

At about the same time as the Misuser Act came into force, there was a reaction on the part of advocates of a distinct drug treatment system. This was confirmed when the nondifferentiating principle of the previous phase was approved by the parliament in 1986. Several factors contributed to this change:

1. New groups were successfully entering into the public debates on drug policy. Particularly successful in attracting public attention were the newly formed organizations of parents of drug users. Their message emphasized the need to target action on young drug users, as well as the need for compulsory treatment, but it also argued the case for treatment rather than punishment. They claim that alcohol treatment institutions cannot deal adequately with drug treatment.

2. International influences, such as the United States' "war on drugs" and increased cooperation in drug policy among Western European countries, also resulted in greater prominence for drug policy on the Finnish political agenda. Drug use and associated criminality are increasingly seen as a threat to society, a threat that should be combated

on all fronts. Without specialized drug treatment, Finland seemed to have fallen below international standards.

3. The drug issue as an argument for reforms of criminal justice policy, and the competition of the drug police for new resources, could not be convincing without an acknowledgment that drug problems create treatment needs. Thus, the hard-liners of drug policy debates often tried to soften their public image by criticizing the absence of a system of specialized drug treatment.

4. The advocates of a distinct drug treatment system and of more resources often needed an increase in drug use to justify their claims. Also, they took advantage of the difficulties in determining accurately and unquestionably the prevalence of drug use to assert that it was increasing progressively. Public opinion, influenced by the constant message of the drug police and the media that drug use and drug problems were increasing, was also a factor in emphasizing a need for reform. The expansion of specialized drug treatment institutions was thus based more on perceptions derived from media messages than on expressed or ascertained treatment needs of clients.

A new wave of distinct, specialized drug treatment began. Most of the new institutions were run by private organizations with public funding. In Finland's universal and comprehensive health care system, municipalities provide treatment for their residents by agreeing to pay for expenses. Three institutions were established in the Helsinki metropolitan area: an outpatient clinic and a small withdrawal unit at the University Central Hospital of Helsinki; the Hietalinna community, which offers nonmedical, nonresidential, and residential therapy; and the Kisko Institution, which offers long-term inpatient treatment. They were instituted in the mid-1980s as a result of high-level agreements between the central state authorities, the municipalities of the region, and the service providers. The Hietalinna and Kisko units were financed from earmarked funds of the Ministry of Social Welfare and Health. The specialized services include also a nongovernmental organization running a reception and guidance home for drug abusers. Soon, the services were extended by a new, medically oriented, outpatient A-clinic (Kettutie) that was given particular responsibility for treating drug abusers. It receives special funding arranged by the Slot Machine Association and administered by the Ministry.

Drug treatment also has been the subject of the reform of the Mental Health Act and the Criminal Law in the 1990s. The reform of the Mental Health Act provided for compulsory treatment of drug abusers under 18 years of age, but this provision has been invoked only rarely. The Criminal Law reform permits waiving of prosecution or penalty in cases where the offender agrees to treatment by the social and health authorities, and the offense (e.g., the use or possession of a small amount of narcotics) is not a serious breach of the law.

Many of the drug treatment units met financial difficulties during the deep economic recession after 1991. Municipalities have become more and more reluctant to pay for treatment. Also for economic reasons, treatment periods have become shorter (Hakkarainen & Kuussaari, 1996). About one third of the treatment institutions for substance abuse (alcohol and drugs) have had to close, and almost 20% of the staff of the social therapy services have become unemployed. There has been a tendency to increase the use of outpatient care and reduce inpatient

Table 4.1   The Distribution of Cases of Recognized Abuse of Licit Drugs, Cannabis, and
Hard Drugs Among the Clients Who Had Contact With the Public Social and
Health Services on October 10, 1995 (in percentages)

Unit	Licit Drugs	Cannabis	Other Drugs
Social welfare office	14	7	8
A-clinic, outpatient	13	16	13
Specialized inpatient treatment	12	22	22
Service housing for substance abusers	17	15	13
Day activity center for substance abusers	7	8	7
Primary health care, outpatient	8	2	3
Primary health care, inpatient	2	1	2
General hospital, outpatient	4	4	5
General hospital, inpatient	2	1	2
Psychiatric services, outpatient	6	6	7
Psychiatric services, inpatient	15	17	18
Total	100	100	100
N	2,174	861	901

treatment, especially in the psychiatric services, but without a corresponding
increase in resources for outpatient care. Thus, the future of the specialized drug
treatment units is in some doubt, but some institutions are looking to drug treatment
to compensate for a declining demand for alcohol treatment (Hakkarainen &
Kuussaari, 1996).

The available data indicate that drug use has increased in the 1990s, and there
has been a corresponding increase in demand for treatment services. The future
planning of drug treatment is likely to be based more on ascertained needs than on
unsubstantiated ideas about the nature and extent of the drug problem.

The Nondifferentiated
Substance Abuse Services

The National Board for Social Welfare and Health made an assessment of all
the substance abusers who had contact with the social and health services on
October 10, 1995 (Kaukonen & Haavisto, 1996; see Table 4.1).

Most of the cases were found at nondifferentiated services for substance abusers,
and many also at social welfare offices or general health services, such as primary
health care centers and general psychiatric services. Common characteristics were
loneliness, inadequate housing or outright homelessness, and low social standing.
Up to 60% were unemployed. Most were under 40 years of age, with an average
age of around 30. The proportion of women was highest in psychiatric services
and A-clinics, but they were a clear minority in all groups, accounting for about
23% of all drug users. Although the greatest concentration of drug users was in the
Helsinki metropolitan area, cases were found in all parts of the country. It is notable
that about 90% were users of multiple drugs (mainly licit drugs or cannabis) and
alcohol, and therefore, it is not possible to determine from the total number of

clients the number of drug addicts or, especially, the number of hard-drug addicts receiving treatment in the Finnish social and health service system.

Nongovernmental organizations also have a recognized role in drug treatment. They include the parent organizations, six or seven Narcotics Anonymous groups, some religious organizations, and a few groups that organize outreach activities for young substance abusers in the larger cities. These organizations often receive small grants from the municipalities or from the system of state support for nongovernmental organizations.

Private medical practitioners are known to treat drug users. In Finland, most health care is provided by the municipalities and is funded partly by state subsidies, but some patients attend private practitioners. The Medical Control Board forbids the prescription of psychoactive drugs to drug users, but there have been instances of physicians found by the Board to be contravening the professional regulations in this respect. At the beginning of the 1990s, some physicians were found to be using buprenorphin (Temgesic®), an opioid similar to morphine, for these patients. The Medical Control Board regarded such "opioid maintenance" as a contravention of the regulations and forbade the practice. It may be concluded from other cases coming to the attention of the Board that at least tens of hard-drug addicts are being treated by private practitioners.

Substitution Treatment and AIDS Prevention

The Hesperia psychiatric hospital in Helsinki has had a small methadone maintenance program for several years. In the mid-1990s, it had only seven clients. Finland has had no special needle exchange programs, but pharmacies sell needles and syringes quite cheaply to intravenous drug users.

Two expert committees (*Narkomaanien*, 1991; *Opioidiriippuvaisten*, 1993) have studied the need for instituting substitution treatment in Finland. Both concluded that there was a small number of drug addicts who could benefit from methadone maintenance and suggested an experimental phase, to be strictly controlled by the country's leading psychiatric units, after a thorough study of treatment needs. However, no such "high-threshold" substitution treatment program has yet been implemented.

The authorities have argued against special harm reduction programs on the grounds that there is relatively little intravenous drug use (particularly of heroin), that drug users have a low prevalence of AIDS and HIV infection, and that they have easy access to needles and syringes without special programs. Also, the idea of maintenance treatment or of withdrawing an addict with medicine has not found acceptance in the drug treatment system. Maintaining an addiction has been seen as inconsistent with treatment; curing addiction with medicine leads to another addiction and in this way legitimizes the continuous use of drugs. However, the expert committee reports can be considered as legitimization in principle of change in the future.

Discussion

The Finnish drug treatment system, if one can speak of a system, has had several developmental phases since the 1960s. The first was in the psychiatric services. Then followed the nonmedical model of alcohol treatment, which became almost totally integrated with the much stronger alcohol treatment structure. During the past 10 years, there have been attempts, again, to institute specialized drug treatment that follows a number of different models. The nonmedical, social therapy model is one of these. However, many of these attempts have run into difficulties after obtaining initial financial and political support. Many seem to depend on particular earmarked funding by the central authorities. Because such funding is an exception in the Finnish social and health services, which are managed by the municipalities without earmarked funding for different client groups or functions of the services, this dependence has posed a permanent threat to the continuity of drug treatment units.

Also, many of the drug treatment efforts represented responses to perceptions of drug problems derived from the media rather than from ascertained or expressed treatment needs. Drug issues have been colored by the prohibitionist nature of the Finnish narcotics control policy (Hakkarainen, 1990, 1992, 1994). To Finnish social scientists, the "real" drug has been alcohol, which has dominated the drug market with a deep symbolic significance and with which "narcotics brought in from an alien culture cannot compete" (Kontula, 1987, p. 64). It is not surprising that most of the research into addiction or substance abuse in Finland has concerned alcohol, a field in which rigorous analyses of the social consequences of drinking have been offered (e.g., see Mäkelä, Österberg, & Sulkunen, 1981). Clearly, in these circumstances, the drug problems for which drug treatment and drug treatment units had been conceived and designed were not those prevalent among their clients. Their addictions were to alcohol and licit drugs, and often, they were older than the clients for which the services had been planned. At the same time, many of the severely addicted and marginalized drug users have been using the general social and health services or private medical practitioners. The criminal justice system has remained the main social response to drug problems.

Three factors are likely to influence the development of Finnish drug treatment in the late 1990s. The first is a deep economic recession that has resulted in a crisis in public finances and a sharp tightening of funding for the social and health services, including drug treatment. Drug treatment experiments are unlikely to be specifically funded, and there will be pressure to integrate drug treatment with the stronger institutions of the social and health services.

The second factor is increased European cooperation, underlined by Finland's accession to the European Union in 1995. In the international community, drug issues are high on the political agenda, and this keeps them high also on the national agenda. Until now, international examples, pressures, and conventions have been arguments for increased activity on the part of the criminal justice system and for reforms in the provision of drug treatment. Prevention and treatment services for drug users may become more standardized throughout all European countries, because the principle of free movement within the European Union now applies to drug users as it does to the population in general (Dorn & White, 1994). Although HIV infection does not appear to be a serious public health hazard, this could change. In particular, the nearness of the Baltic countries and the St. Petersburg region, and the growth of their national drug problems, could influence the supply and distribution of drugs in Finland (Simpura & Tigerstedt, 1992).

The third factor is that the drug picture has changed during the 1990s. Increasing use of illicit drugs, especially in urban areas, is seen as a difficult social problem, already evident in the demands made on the treatment services (Holopainen, 1992). In future, the planning of drug treatment could be based more on actual needs for drug treatment than on general perceptions of the drug problem.

Thus, there are trends, such as an increase in drug use and closer international links, that suggest that in the future, the drug problem, drug policy, and the drug treatment system in Finland will be more in line with those of the other countries of the European Union. However, because the European Union has no single model of drug policy, Finland seems to have more than one choice. Also, although there is clear evidence of an increase in the use of illicit hard drugs in Finland, the scene is still dominated by licit psychoactive drug abuse and mixing heavy drinking and drug taking. It is therefore likely that the particular features of drug abuse and the drug treatment system in Finland will persist well into the next century.

References

Christie, N., & Bruun, K. (1985). *Den gode fiende* [The good enemy]. Oslo: Norwegian University Press.

Dorn, N., & White, S. (1994). European free movement, drug users and access to health services. *International Journal of Drug Policy, 5*(4), 226-234.

Hakkarainen, P. (1990, September). *The formation of prohibitionist drug policy in Finland: Political, moral and professional aspects in the legislative process of the Finnish Narcotics Act 1972.* Paper presented to the international conference on Drug Use and Drug Policy: A European Perspective, Cologne, Germany.

Hakkarainen, P. (1992). *Suomalainen huumekysymys. Huumausaineiden yhteiskunnallinen paikka Suomessa toisen maailmansodan jälkeen* [The Finnish drug issue. The social status of drugs in Finland after the second World War]. Helsinki: Alkoholitutkimussäätiö julkaisuja No 42.

Hakkarainen, P. (1994, December). *Construction of the drug problem in Finland.* Paper presented at a COST A 6 workshop, Warzaw.

Hakkarainen, P., & Kuussaari, K. (1996). Erikoistunut huumehoito: palvelurakenne ja huumehoidon järjestelmä [Specialized drug treatment in Finland: Service structure and treatment system]. *Alkoholipolitiikka, 61,* 30-41.

Hartnoll, R. (1993). *Multi-city study of drug misuse: Drug misuse trends in thirteen European cities.* Co-operation Group to Combat Drug Abuse and Illicit Trafficking in Drugs (Pompidou Group). Strasbourg: Council of Europe, Direction of Social and Economic Affairs.

Hein, R. (1996). *Alkoholi ja huumeet 1995—kulutus, käyttö ja haitat. Tilastotiedote* [Alcohol and drugs 1995—Consumption, use and harms. Statistical notice]. Helsinki: STAKES.

Holopainen, A. (1992). *The medical project for addiction treatment services in Finland.* Helsinki: A-Clinic Foundation.

Jormanainen, V., Lehesjoki, M., Seppälä, T., Peitso, A., & Koskenvuo, K. (1994). Huumeita kokeilleet varusmiehet syksyllä 1992 [The experiences of drug use among conscripts in autumn 1992]. *Suomen Lääkärilehti, 49*(33), 3483-3489.

Joukamaa, M. (1991). *Suomalaisten vankien terveys* [The health of Finnish prisoners]. Turku, Finland: Kansanterveystieteen julkaisuja M 107/91.

Kansanterveys. (1996). *Kansanterveyslaitoksen tiedotuslehti* [National Public Health Bulletin] 2.

Kaukonen, O., & Haavisto, K. (1996). Päihdetapauslaskenta vuonna 1995 [Assessment of intoxicant-related cases in 1995]. *Alkoholipolitiikka, 61,* 130-138.

Kinnunen, A. (1996). *Isännät, rengit ja pokat. Huumemarkkinat ja oheisrikollisuus Helsingissä* [Drug markets and drug related crime in Helsinki]. Helsinki: Oikeuspoliittisen tutkimuslaitoksen julkaisuja 133.

Komiteanmietintö. (1969). *Huumausainekomitean mietintö 1969: B 53* [The report of narcotics committee]. Helsinki: Author.

Komiteanmietintö. (1971). *Huumausaineneuvottelukunnan mietintö No 1. Ehdotus huumaus-ja lääkeaineiden väärinkäyttäjien hoitoorganisaation kehittämiseksi 1971: B 39* [The report of narcotics advisory committee No. 1. The proposal for developing a treatment organization for abusers of illicit and licit drugs]. Helsinki: Author.

Kontula, O. (1987). Special features of narcotics control and the narcotics situation in Finland. In P. Stangeland (Ed.), *Drugs and drugs control: Scandinavian studies in criminology* (Vol. 8, pp. 53-66). Oslo: Norwegian University Press.

Kontula, O. (1995). The prevalence of drug use with reference to problem use in Finland. *International Journal of the Addictions, 30,* 1053-1066.

Lehto, J. (1992). Huumeongelmien hoito [The treatment of drug problems]. *Sosiaalinen aikakauskirja, 86*(4), 20-22.

Mäkelä, K., Österberg, E., & Sulkunen, P. (1981). Drink in Finland: Increasing alcohol availability in a monopoly state. In E. Single, P. Morgan, & J. de Lint (Eds.), *Alcohol, society and the state: The social history of control policy in seven countries* (pp. 31-60). Toronto: Addiction Research Foundation, in collaboration with the WHO Regional Office in Europe.

Narkomaanien hoidon järjestäminen Helsingissä [The arrangements for treatment of drug addicted in Helsinki]. (1991). Työryhmän raportti. Helsingin kaupungin terveysviraston raportteja. Sarja B. Raportti 55/91.

Opioidiriippuvaisten narkomaanien lääkehoitotyöryhmän muistio [Memorandum of working group for arranging medical treatment for opiate addicts]. (1993). Helsinki: STAKES. Aiheita 13/93.

Partanen, J. (1994). Märkä pilvi [Wet high]. *Alkoholipolitiikka, 59,* 397-411.

Rimpelä, M., Pohjanpää, K., Terho, P., Pienmäki-Jylhä, P., & Poikajärvi, K. (1995). Huumeet nuorten arjessa [Drugs in everyday life of the youth]. Helsinki: STAKES, Aiheita 28/95.

Rosenqvist, P. (1974). Inställningen till de internationella narkotikakonventionerna i Finland under 1920- och 1930-talen [Adaptation to the International Narcotics Agreements in Finland in the 1920s and 1930s]. *Alkoholpolitik, 1,* 13-20.

Simpura, J., & Tigerstedt, C. (Eds.). (1992). *Alcohol, drugs and social problems around the Baltic Sea* (NAD Publication No. 21). Helsinki: Nordic Council for Alcohol and Drug Research.

STAKES [National Research and Development Centre for Welfare and Health]. (1988-1994). *The hospital treatment register.* Helsinki: Author.

Takala, J. P., & Lehto, J. (1992). Finland: The non-medical model reconsidered. In H. Klingemann, J. P. Takala, & G. Hunt (Eds.), *Cure, care, or control: Alcoholism treatment in sixteen countries* (pp. 87-110). Albany: State University of New York Press.

Vuori, E., & Ojanperä, I. (1994). Myrkytyskuolemat ja niiden oikeuskemiallinen tutkiminen [Fatal poisonings and their forensic toxicological investigation]. *Kemia-Kemi, 20,* 302-306.

Westling, A., & Riippa, J. (1956). Pre-war and post-war narcomania in Finland. *Annales Medicinae Internae Fenniae, 45,* 151-174.

Chapter 5

Thunder and Silence in Drug Treatment: Four Nations in Moral Concert

Judith C. Barker

Comment on Part 1

This collection of papers on drug treatment approaches in Canada, Finland, Sweden, and the United States is remarkable for the clarity with which it both reveals and conceals common cultural and societal values that underpin their approach to drug treatment. These nations are in concert. Revealed in these chapters is a vigilance and loud furor over drugs and drug-related activities that are deemed illicit. So-called hard drugs, such as heroin and cocaine, are the major focus of government policy and treatment regimens, but soft drugs, such as marijuana, come under intense scrutiny as well. The latter are often presented as "gateway" drugs, demons enticing users into deeper and deeper depths of addiction, despair, and depravity. Because the authors were explicitly instructed to focus on illegal drugs, these chapters tacitly acknowledge the existence, but do not directly address the size or scope, of problems associated with the use and abuse of licit drugs such as tranquilizers or painkillers—the acceptable addictions of the silent but moral majority.

One notable exception to this generalization is alcohol, a legal drug that constitutes a major focus of government regulation and treatment activity in all four nations. Indeed, a predominant theme throughout these chapters is the extent to which alcohol treatment modalities serve as templates for the development of drug treatment efforts. Alcohol and drug treatment services are often conjoint, as

Ogborne, Smart, and Rush note for Canada, Bergmark for Sweden, and Kinnunen and Lehto for Finland. Hunt and Dong Sun's chapter shows that only in the United States are drug treatment services, independent of alcohol-related services, extensively available.

Tobacco, too, is often alleged to act as a "gateway" to other drugs. Especially in the United States, tobacco is rapidly becoming another legal drug that is acquiring or reacquiring the moral ambiguity and contradictory regulation that has surrounded alcohol for decades.

The vigilance and furor over drugs and drug treatment results in a deafening clamor over certain aspects, such as the psychopharmacology and pathology of addiction, or funding priorities for prevention and eradication versus control and treatment. This is accompanied by silence over other equally salient but less well investigated aspects of drug use—for example, the social, political, and economic conditions that conspire to demonize or exorcise the moral status of certain substances; the demographic distribution of drug use in the population (why, in all these countries, is it mainly young male adults who use drugs?); or the long-term outcomes of drug treatment (what differentiates those whose treatment is successful from those whose drug treatment does not wean them from reliance on or use of addictive substances?). Ironically, these latter aspects are central to the development of successful drug policy and treatment strategies, but often, it would seem, attention to these issues is unheard, drowned out by louder noises.

Public perception of the growth of a drug problem, and the development of particular constituencies, along with the vocal advocacy of such special interest groups (e.g., parents of drug-addicted youth), have been central to the formation of recent drug policies in these countries. The media, too, have played a key role in influencing, even creating, public and governmental opinion. Reports from the international arena, notably the United States and its War on Drugs, have had major impacts. Writing about the development of the drug treatment system in Finland, for example, Kinnunen and Lehto note that the "expansion of specialized drug treatment institutions was . . . based more on perceptions derived from media messages than on expressed or ascertained treatment needs of clients" (p. 55).

Thunderously evident in these pieces is each country's moral condemnation and criminalization of the drug addict. This is most evident with respect to Finland, where, Kinnunen and Lehto state, drug use is regarded as a problem of delinquency or professional crime. Drug policy in Canada, Sweden, and the United States is predicated on less openly asserted but nevertheless actual assumptions about the chronic and deliberate antisocial nature of drug use. Quietly present in all of these chapters is a discussion that reveals that over several decades, drug policy has tended to shift away from medical or psychiatric treatment of users or addicts in community settings toward strategies that provide essentially little or no treatment in settings of incarceration. "Treatment" is arguably a misnomer, for what is being offered is more clearly punishment, with little rehabilitative effort or effect. Treatment for drug use is presented as being somewhat infrequently and often unwillingly sought by users themselves; hence the existence of coercive drug treatment services, especially in conjunction with the justice system. Ogborne,

Smart, and Rush refer to the importance of court-ordered treatment in Canada; Kinnunen and Lehto discuss a rarely invoked but nevertheless extant law requiring compulsory treatment for juvenile offenders in Finland; and Bergmark discusses the coercive ideology of reform that underpins drug treatment in Sweden. With respect to the United States, Hunt and Dong Sun note that although drug treatment services are supposedly available, the vast majority of imprisoned substance users receive no treatment—they are merely incarcerated criminals. In other words, "treatment" has exacerbated, even enforced, the marginal position and deviant nature of drug users and the impropriety of their activities.

Rather than hand over to medicine, or even share with medicine, the social control aspects of drug use, the legal system in each of these four nations has retained its status as the premier enforcer of the production of a well-regulated, disciplined, and docile citizenry. Conrad and Schneider (1992) remind us that

> medical social control does not preclude the simultaneous or even coordinated operation of legal controls. . . . Drug addiction . . . [offers an] . . . opportunity to examine the conditions under which medicalization receives support or has to compete with alternative moral paradigms for ownership and control of problem behavior. (p. 283)

Medical dominance is thus a social and political, not a scientific, achievement. In the main, however, there has been silence about the specific social and political mechanisms, the claims and counterclaims, whereby the medical and legal establishments vie for the right to define and control drug treatment. Why has medicine been unable—or reluctant, or unwilling—to claim drug treatment for itself alone? Perhaps the moral paradigms underpinning law and medicine in these nations overlap so much that a vibrant contestation and resistance with respect to drugs and drug treatment cannot yet be created or sustained.

Drug treatment stands in marked contrast to the continuing medicalization (even attempted normalization) of many other "social problems" over the same time period in these countries. Formerly regarded as social problems but now more likely to be seen as disease based are such issues as juvenile delinquency, epilepsy, and even alcoholism. Many people now challenge the social deviance model of alcoholism and have successfully advocated its being viewed as a curable or manageable medical condition. What is unclear is why the moral opprobrium attached to drug use, and thus to drug treatment, should be so entrenched, so resistant to change, at a time when other morally dubious states, such as being mentally ill, could be successfully redefined "from badness to sickness." Is this but another example of the production of deviants best suited to specific societal circumstances?

Several of these authors allude to the new development whereby addicts or recovered addicts are employed in drug treatment. Bergmark notes about Sweden that "through a concurrence of government funding, official reports, legislation, and the general public discussion on the drug problem, a 'professional field without professionals' was created . . . [an] 'illusory' domain" is institutionalized. Why has medicine not vigorously contested the development of paraprofessionals, drug treatment counselors, social workers, and others whose occupations, although specifically devoted to drug treatment, often require little formal training in relation to drugs, medicine, or human services? Moreover, drug treatment is an occupation into which many former addicts or drug users are drawn (Klingemann, 1997). Is there something about drugs (and, for that matter, alcohol) that demands a special rapport or affinity between those receiving and those providing treatment? This is, of course, a powerful means whereby drugs and drug use remain the focus of life for former addicts but now in a fashion acceptable to the dominant class. Are rehabilitated drug users unable to find—or subtly excluded from—other kinds of meaningful work? Is the lack of protest on the part of the medical, legal, or social work professions about the development and use of paraprofessionals a subtle way of ensuring that drug treatment is a discreditable human services modality, one that remains thereby therapeutically ineffectual, politically impotent, and socially insecure, but economically lucrative?

Social theorists have long equated the shape and form of contemporary society with the rise and eventual dominance of the capitalist economy (Gordon, 1988; Hahn, 1995; Hutton, 1988). Individual disciplined and docile citizen-bodies in industrial society derive their utility—and hence their moral status—from central social values, identified as independence and self-control, productivity and rationality. Drug users violate these principles. They are not in control of illicit substances; rather, they are highly dependent upon them. They cannot sustain work in mainstream occupations but are alleged to turn instead to criminal activity to support an expensive and detrimental habit. (Habit, it should be noted, is a concept that implies both volition and ability to change.) They are irrational and may espouse ludicrous ideas or engage in bizarre or unpredictable behavior. Moral treatment and withdrawal of all addictive drugs are often touted as the only means of rehabilitating a drug user. Moral treatment, involving the inculcation of alternative values (usually derived from urban, Western, bourgeois, middle-class life), and the exercise of self-control will turn drug addicts into not merely rational but also productive, independent individuals. Regrettably, the only moral treatment provided to many drug users in Canada, Finland, Sweden, and the United States is that available in the prison system, well known for its informal social order based on an ideology and moral stance that contrast very strongly with those of the dominant ruling class.

Ironically, there is a treatment option that can achieve the desired changes for addicts, but it is distinctly nonmoral in form. Methadone, another addictive substance, has interesting, even paradoxical, properties. It can not only reduce the physical health consequences associated with addiction to hard drugs but also enable a drug-addicted individual to become a self-controlled, productive, and useful member of society. Yet in these four countries, methadone maintenance and harm reduction are not the most prominent modes of drug treatment, and they are often only reluctantly accepted. Social, medical, and legal policy and practice make treatment by methadone maintenance difficult to provide and monitor. For example, Ogborne, Smart, and Rush report in their chapter that in Canada, "physicians may prescribe methadone to addicts . . . but the requirements for close monitoring of patients, urine testing, and counseling have, in effect, excluded most general practitioners from doing so. Methadone is prescribed mostly by physicians in special clinics" (p. 28).

Methadone maintenance is expensive; this reduces its availability to some addicts who seek treatment and accounts in part for high drop-out rates. Also contributing to the high drop-out rates is the humiliation often associated with it: Addicts must conform to clinic rules and regulations, even when these undermine the very goals of such treatment, namely, the addict's lawful employment, financial independence, dignity, and self-esteem (Hunt & Rosenbaum, 1998). This is yet another way in which the moral message about drugs and the social worth, or worthlessness, of drug addicts is delivered to those seeking treatment and release from their demons. In the chapter on the United States, Hunt and Dong Sun note that attitudes toward illicit drugs and illicit drug use and the corresponding increase in criminalization of drugs and drug use have had a profound effect on both the type of treatment that has been allowed and the target groups that have been identified. What is it about drugs and drug use that makes the moral taint so usefully indelible?

Being waged to various degrees in Canada, Finland, and Sweden, and most prominently in the United States, is a declared "war" on drugs. Over the past decades, enormous increases have occurred in the resources deployed to counter illicit drugs. Vast sums of money are expended and very large numbers of staff employed in the pursuit and control of a very small proportion of the population involved in the untaxed and unregulated commercial exchange or use of substances deemed to be illegal. To be sure, many outcomes of drug use are undesirable for addicts, their families, and society. Drug use leads to extensive morbidity, premature mortality, criminal activity, and the creation of an underclass profiting from the illegal production, distribution, and consumption of drugs. But there are benefits, too. Addicts keep their physiological and psychological cravings quiescent and, in general, physically harm only themselves. Benefiting also, but less clearly, is the underclass, a group of people often otherwise systematically excluded from legitimate social opportunities and rewards. Benefiting perhaps most of all, however, is the ruling class, which obtains jobs, income, political power, attributions of moral worthiness, and incentives to further pursue the war on deviant behavior manifested by illicit drug use.

Could it be that focusing so hard on drugs, and on very specific but rather limited aspects of drugs and drug use at that, distracts attention from other pressing but politically sensitive topics requiring far more radical agendas for change? Drugs and their consequences might fade into mere background noise, into a problem of less exaggerated proportions, if, in general, more attention was given to understanding the creation, source, and deployment of concepts and mechanisms of social control, as well as to examining and creating means of redistributing wealth and social opportunity more equitably among gender, age, class, and ethnic groups.

Granted, Canada, Finland, and Sweden are among the more successful of the Western nations attempting to reduce social inequities through progressive legislation and reform. Canada's approach to immigrant and ethnic diversity has produced successful models other than those of the "melting pot." Finland has an admirable record of promoting women to positions of political power, and Sweden's welfare state is a model that many nations aspire to follow. Although less successful, perhaps because it is not only far larger in scale but also more heterogeneous, the United States is nevertheless still actively grappling with issues of discrimination and barriers to economic and social advantage. All of these nations share a strong commitment to an ideology of equality. It is a mythic equality, however, often fondly assumed to result in a classless society, divided more by the outcome of individual choices and actions and by aptitude than by the inherent strictures and constraints of a ranked society. In the context of the equally strong sociocultural emphasis on independence and self-control, this ideology of classlessness quickly leads to an emphasis not on equality of social or economic opportunity or access to such opportunity, but on conformity—a conformity derived not so much from religious or political values as from individual behavior. In these egalitarian societies, a relatively narrow range of behavior is acceptable or tolerable, and the lifestyle typical of many drug addicts, especially those using hard drugs, falls outside this range. Drug addicts are nonconformists in need of moral treatment. With this view, these nations are truly in concert.

References

Conrad, P., & Schneider, J. W. (1992). *Deviance and medicalization: From badness to sickness* (Expanded ed.). Philadelphia: Temple University Press.

Gordon, D. R. (1988). Tenacious assumptions in Western medicine. In M. Lock & D. R. Gordon (Eds.), *Biomedicine examined* (pp. 19-56). Dordrecht: Kluwer.

Hahn, R. A. (1995). *Sickness and healing: An anthropological perspective.* New Haven, CT: Yale University Press.

Hunt, G. P., & Rosenbaum, M. (1998). "Hustling" within the clinic: Consumer perspective on methadone maintenance treatment. In J. Inciardi & H. Harrison (Eds.), *Heroin in the age of crack cocaine* (pp. 188-214). Thousand Oaks, CA: Sage.

Hutton, P. H. (1988). Foucault, Freud, and the technologies of the self. In L. H. Martin, H. Gutman, & P. H. Hutton (Eds.), *Technologies of the self: A seminar with Michel Foucault* (pp. 121-144). Amherst: University of Massachusetts Press.

Klingemann, H. (1997, June). *Addiction careers and careers in addiction.* Paper presented at the 23rd annual Alcohol Epidemiology Symposium of the Kettil Bruun Society, Reykjavik, Iceland.

Part II

The Experimental Countries

Chapter 6

The English Drug Treatment System: Experimentation or Pragmatism?

Susanne MacGregor
Lynne Smith

reatment works!" was the main conclusion of an independent review carried out by a task force on drug treatment services in England and published in May 1996 (Task Force, 1996). Because of stress on evidence-based medicine in the British National Health Service (NHS), the Task Force commissioned a series of investigations to inform its deliberations. In addition, it received submissions and took evidence from a range of interested parties and made visits to services.

Although the investigations have so far shown little that is new—and the largest of them, the National Treatment Outcomes Research Study (NTORS),[1] is still in its early stages—the Task Force was persuaded that treatment works. It limited its intervention in policy to issuing guidance on treatment to the medical profession and health care funding agencies. More standardization and regulation of practice can be expected. Providers of treatment will be pressed to collect routine monitoring information to help funding agencies evaluate services.

The establishment of the Task Force had coincided with a substantial shake-up in the health and social services, resulting from the restructuring of the health services and the introduction of community care to reduce the role of institutional care (National Health Service and Community Care Act, 1990). It was feared that the report of the Task Force would result in further cuts in services, as well as greater standardization and central control, and that particular views on appropriate treatment and care would predominate. However, the consequences were much less restrictive than had been feared, and the treatment and care services continued to function in the cold climate of fiscal austerity that characterizes the social services in the post-welfare-state era.

Other social trends also are influencing drug treatment services in England. A report from researchers in Manchester has argued that drug use has become an integral part of youth culture and a significant part of the lives of even schoolchildren (Parker, Measham, & Aldridge, 1995; see also Leitner, Shapland, & Wiles, 1993). Most surveys taken together indicate that between one fourth and one third of young people have tried solvents or illicit drugs by the age of 20. Cannabis figures prominently; possibly one fourth of young adults have tried it. In the 1990s, the most marked development has been the integration of LSD and Ecstasy into mass youth culture, complementing the established use of amphetamines. Heroin and cocaine use, however, remains at very low levels, at around 1% or less of the young adult age group (Baker & Marsden, 1994). Patterns of use of heroin and other hard drugs are highly variable; location and setting are important intervening factors (Matthews & Trickey, 1996). The heroin problem in particular is now highly scattered and localized. Some towns and cities are more affected than others, and use is often concentrated in neighborhoods. New heroin users are now more likely to be from poor, working-class neighborhoods (Pearson, 1987).

How did England (and Britain) get to this state of affairs? How are the drug treatment services coping with the increased scale of demand and the changing patterns of use?

A Short History of Drug Policy in England

A central argument here is that different contexts produce different responses. Developments can be viewed as falling into distinct phases or periods. In each period, the balance between treatment and care, on the one hand, and control and punishment, on the other, is the key variable. Objectives of treatment have varied from helping people become drug-free to concentrating on stabilization, risk reduction, or harm minimization.

In reviewing the evolution of approaches to drug treatment and care throughout the 20th century, key questions are, Which drugs have been viewed as illicit? and What has been thought to count as a problem—for whom and why?

A characteristic of the British system is that it has been and remains pragmatic (Grant, 1994). Over time, it has developed by trial and error, step-by-step experimentation, and avoidance of extremes. This remains the case in spite of some shifts in the general political and ideological climate since the 1980s. A second constant feature has been the tension between the specialist and the generalist (Glanz, 1994). The third has been the separation between the debate conducted in public and that conducted in policy networks. There is a certain fear that too much public involvement in discussions might inhibit intelligent policy making.

The conflicts generated by the tensions within these three features explain the shifts between periods that mark the story of drug treatment in England. These shifts are marked by change in the prevalence and character of drug use, some increased public attention to the problem, and possibly new legislation or regulations, followed by a settling down into a new phase characterized by new approaches and the involvement of a broader spectrum of professional and semi-professional groups.

British policy on drugs can be said to have had four phases (Berridge, 1984), and a fifth is under way.

Phases One and Two (1800s-1920s/1920s-1960s): Increasing Professional Control and the Development of the British System

Key events in this development include the 1920 Dangerous Drugs Act, which represented a penal reaction to a perceived cocaine epidemic. The Rolleston Report of 1926 reasserted the disease model of addiction. It reaffirmed the doctor's freedom to prescribe, especially to prescribe maintenance doses of opiate drugs as a form of treatment. The principles of clinical freedom and the relative independence of the medical profession from the state were important aspects of this arrangement (Berridge, 1984). A system of medical control operated within a penal framework of national and international controls. This system lasted until the late 1960s. It has often been remarked that the British system worked because there was no drug problem (Edwards, 1969).

Phase Three (1960-1980): Establishing Clinics

Drugs as a social order issue arrived with youth culture and the growing generation gap (Young, 1971). Drug use was mainly London-based, involving students and rebellious, countercultural youth. Cannabis was the main drug used, but heroin use increased as well among small groups, mainly young men. Treatment of addiction was to be concentrated in new clinics (drug dependency units) based in hospitals. Thus, medical professional independence, so jealously guarded since the 1920s, was eroded. But some relative independence was retained: The medical profession would decide on the composition of treatment regimens. A short period of competitive prescribing soon gave way to an emphasis on methadone, especially its oral form. Maintenance increasingly gave way to reduction, which meant short-term prescribing or no prescribing of methadone. The amount of heroin prescribed fell by 40% from 1971 to 1978, mostly in the early 1970s. From a fairly early stage, the clinics accepted few new patients for long-term prescription of heroin. Those that remained were a few early, long-term patients who were allowed to remain on maintenance treatment (Stimson & Oppenheim, 1982).

Short-term treatment, a 3-month detoxification regimen based on withdrawal, had become the dominant form. However, the clinics were seeing only a small proportion of all drug users—the rather special group of heroin users; they were not seeing the most common type of drug misuser, the multiple-drug users, who were difficult, sometimes violent, and led erratic and unstable lives. There were, in any case, very few clinics outside of London. Barbiturates figured among the drugs misused, and the effects of barbiturate dependence and the dangers of sudden withdrawal were important aspects of the drug scene (Jamieson, Glanz, & MacGregor, 1984). As professional social workers and voluntary-sector drug workers grappled with this problem, their voices were increasingly heard in the policy world, especially through the channel of the Standing Conference on Drug Abuse (SCODA), the national coordinating and representative body for drug services and those working with drug misusers. Social models of care began to influence thinking more generally in social psychiatry and in drug policy. This gave rise to the notion of the problem drug user, which for a time displaced that of the drug addict or drug dependent. Drug misusers were seen as experiencing problems— social, psychological, physical, and legal—connected to their drug use, especially to frequent and excessive use. They began to be treated by a social-psychological approach based on social learning models and theories.

Phase Four (the 1980s): The Expansion of Community-Based Services

Ironically, just as this approach had gained some ascendance, a new wave of heroin use hit the country and restored the concept of drug misuse as a mainly physiological matter—an illness rather than a result of problems in living. Prescribing of heroin became an important issue again. In this phase, general medical practitioners were seeing more drug users among their patients, but mostly they were not interested in providing long-term care and preferred to pass these patients on to specialists (Glanz, 1994).

Attempts to maintain some control over the increase in prescribing were instituted in 1984; the Department of Social Security issued guidelines on good clinical practice, fearing that the problems of the early 1960s might be repeated on a larger scale. At this point, however, the main source of heroin was not leakage from the health services but the vastly increased supply on the illicit market. In 1975, 3,425 addicts were notified to the Home Office (the Government Ministry responsible for the justice system); this figure had risen to 12,000 in 1984. In the next 10 years, there would be a further two- to threefold increase. The numbers notified were generally recognized to be only the tip of the iceberg. The 1980s saw an increasingly punitive approach to drug use as it became closely associated in the public eye with crime and social disorder (and with the poorer and more working-class population groups). Government policy expressed in a 1985 policy document, *Tackling Drugs Misuse,* was aimed at reducing supplies from abroad, making enforcement even more effective, maintaining effective deterrents and tight domestic controls, developing prevention, and improving treatment and rehabilitation. The two sides of policy—treatment and the criminal justice system—began to converge. The size and nature of the problem meant that treatment and rehabilitation practitioners could no longer remain separate. Probation officers, for example, began to play a greater role in the network of services. The Drugs Trafficking Offences Act of 1986 indicated a further shift to a more punitive response, symbolizing the decline of a primarily medical and specialist approach to drug treatment. There were countervailing trends, however. The Department of Health made a major effort to develop community-based services with central funding (MacGregor, Ettorre, Coomber, Crosier, & Lodge, 1991), especially outside London. In this array of new services, community psychiatric nurses grew in influence as members of community drug teams. The aim was at first to use these teams as catalysts to encourage greater involvement by general medical practitioners and other generalists, such as public health nurses and health educators, but in the end they were to become simply yet another new layer of specialist services.

Influenced partly by ideas from the United States and the increasingly moral tone of social debate, some people were placing increased stress on abstinence as the goal of treatment. A division appeared between them and the advocates of harm minimization—a new name for what had tended to be the practice in parts of the voluntary sector in the 1970s. The timing of the arrival of AIDS was significant in influencing the outcome of this dispute. It halted the slide toward a more punitive response and changed the public's perception of the drug misuser. The fear of the spread of HIV infection to the general population became more important than the desire to cure the addict. Containment, monitoring, and surveillance became the main themes of policy and provision. The term *harm minimization* was adopted for a policy designed primarily to attract drug users to services and maintain their contact with the services.

Phase Five (the 1990s): Community Partnership

The rationale of community partnership is that drug misuse reflects failures of socialization and community disorganization. The young drug user, especially in deprived areas, is seen as the principal social problem. The often local concentration of styles of life determines the logic for devising local solutions to local problems. The central level urges improved coordination between key state agencies such as the Home Office, the Department of Health, the Department of Education and Employment, and Customs and Excise. Underlying this is awareness that with the growth of the problem and continuing fiscal austerity, treatment must become cheaper (or more cost-effective). The system of expensive clinics and rehabilitation houses is too costly to maintain. Paradoxically, however, cost does not seem to be a consideration with regard to imprisonment. The increased stress on the assertion that "prison works" and on mandatory and longer sentences for dealing and trafficking in drugs has brought an increase in the prison population, a relatively expensive form of containment. This explains why the Task Force's report draws attention to the savings likely to accrue from transferring criminally active drug users to the treatment and care system, where they have less inclination or less opportunity to commit crimes.[2]

In the early 1990s, community care reforms gave greater responsibility to local authorities for the financing of care and rehabilitation services. The Department of Social Security was determined to reduce expenditure on residential care. As the financing of services became more difficult, it became convenient for the government to delegate responsibility to lower levels of administration of health and social services, thus diffusing the political problem.

The effect was to increase the influence of the Home Office, which throughout had retained responsibility for prevention. Although a penal response continues to dominate, judges, police officers, and civil servants are increasingly advocating prevention. Practical common sense derived from firsthand experience influences these views.

The publication in 1995 of the policy document *Tackling Drugs Together* was an important event in the development of drug treatment in England. It further stressed prevention and the involvement of the wider community. Some borrowing of ideas from the United States is evident in the ascendancy of ideas of community in social policy. The aim to involve the generalist—medicine, social work, and nursing—appears once again, but it remains doubtful whether this can be carried through. General medical practitioners are demanding extra pay for the treatment of drug misusers. Care in the community, like other forms of deinstitutionalization, can be expensive in providing small group houses or day centers. Prevention campaigns directed at a larger proportion of the population can also be costly. Policy at the local level is designed to associate local authorities, responsible for housing, social services, education, and planning, and police with psychiatrists and other drug specialists to implement coordinated local strategies.

The English approach to treatment is therefore likely to continue to manifest much variety and local freedom, more than that of many other countries. This acknowledges the differences between drug users and their needs in different parts of the country and in different services. *Tackling Drugs Together* is a strategy designed to last until 1998. It is designed to

> take effective action by vigorous law enforcement, accessible treatment and a new emphasis on education and prevention to increase the safety of communities from drug related crime, reduce the acceptability and availability of drugs to young people and reduce the health risks and other damage related to drug misuse. (p. vii)

This coherent approach, which calls for the combined action of agencies from central and local government, the criminal justice system and the National Health Service, and statutory and independent sectors, is both ambitious and pragmatic. It remains to be seen how it will work out in practice.

Current Models of Treatment: Settings and Ideologies

The treatment services in England are closely linked to care and support, as well as to punishment, and most drug misusers have experienced a variety of such services. In response to the new contract culture in the marketized health and community care services, the independent sector (previously known as the voluntary sector) has altered the package of services it offers. In general, there has been a move to offer integrated packages of care, serving defined target groups of clients. Similar developments can be observed in the health services. The drug treatment services in England are, in rough order of specialization: residential rehabilitation, drug dependency units or clinics, inpatient treatment and detoxification in public hospitals or private clinics, community-based drug treatment centers, community drug teams, drug counseling and advice centers, needle or syringe exchange schemes, general medical practitioners, and self-help groups.

In addition, there is a range of related services, such as outreach activities, telephone help lines, projects for people dependent on tranquilizers or other prescribed drugs, and projects on specific problems related to AIDS and HIV infection.

A rapid review of drug services in August 1994 (see Figures 6.1-6.4) revealed 1,042 separate treatment services (MacGregor, Smith, & Flory, 1994). There were also more than 1,000 syringe exchange schemes; in addition, more than 1,200 pharmacies were participating in the needle exchange schemes of their local areas. Also, many more services had some role in the treatment and care of drug misusers: advice services, telephone help lines, administrative offices, training and education schemes/projects, self-help groups, and tranquilizer projects, as well as housing projects, general practice, general psychiatry, general hospital medicine, and nursing and social services. Other services that connect with drug misusers include specific projects for young people and adolescents—from general youth projects to those concerned with disadvantaged groups—as well as the probation service and, an important feature, the prisons, especially the prison medical service.

From these 1,042 services, 567 could be categorized as dedicated drug treatment services. Of these, 194—more than one third—were so large in size and extensive in scope, performing a number of activities closely linked so as to form an integrated service for a particular geographical area, that they could be regarded as an integrated system of services operating at a local level. This represented a growing trend for local services to amalgamate—or for offshoots of one service to remain linked to the mother-service (e.g., where a clinic formed a community drug team, which in turn established an outreach project). The divisions between services are not straightforward. It is not a simple matter merely to arrive at a count of services—much depends on how services are categorized and where the line is drawn between treatment and care. Services vary greatly in size and in their range of activities and interventions.

The main point to note overall in reviewing English drug treatment services is their variety and diversity and the increasing influence of locale and local culture on the character of the services offered. The North Thames region, for example, has a range of well-established facilities, reflecting its early involvement in providing treatment and care for drug users. Large multidisciplinary teams follow a pragmatic approach, with special attention to HIV-positive patients. A complex range of services covers needle exchange, inpatient care, outpatient clinics, methadone clinics, central assessment units, and community drug teams. Similarly, south of the river Thames in London, services are well established. Heroin and opiate use dominates use of services, but crack is causing growing concern (as it is also in north London and the Midlands). This area has several residential rehabilitation services. Harm reduction is the objective of most services. Although abstinence and progression toward a drug-free (and crime-free) life are the ultimate goals, it is recognized that some people will continue to misuse drugs for the foreseeable

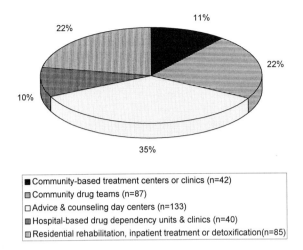

Figure 6.1 Main Drug Treatment Services in England
SOURCE: MacGregor et al. (1994).
NOTE: "Main drug treatment services" refers to those services that are dedicated, or specialized, drug services. They include those units that have as their main purpose the treatment of individuals affected by the use of illegal drugs. They do not include more mainstream services, such as general medical practitioners, accident and emergency units, and mental health services, which have a role in providing treatment but not as their mainstream function.

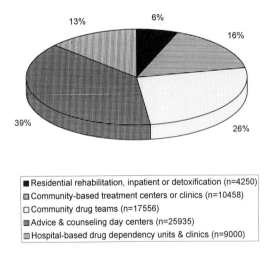

Figure 6.2 Distribution of Client/Patient Population Among Different Types of Service: Estimate of Number Seen per Month (August 1994)
SOURCE: MacGregor et al. (1994).
NOTE: The number seen per month is a figure derived from a survey conducted in August 1994. The inpatient data refer to those in contact with inpatient services and thus reflect the number in the month who were in attendance, or receiving treatment, on a residential basis.

future; harm reduction seeks to minimize the harm they do to themselves, others, and the community (Plymouth Community Drug Service, 1994, p. 5).

Methadone is the most commonly prescribed drug, usually taken orally but in some cases injected. The main aim of prescribing is reported to be stabilization and detoxification, but it also brings improved health and a reduction in crime. In

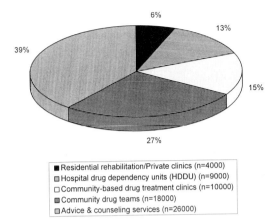

Figure 6.3 Numbers of Cases in Contact With Drug Treatment Services in England
(August 1994 estimates)
SOURCE: MacGregor et al. (1994).
NOTE: Some clients may be in contact with more than one service. The figures reflect multiagency contact, and duplicate counting is avoided as far as possible. Contact may be of various kinds and includes all those who sought some help at whatever level.

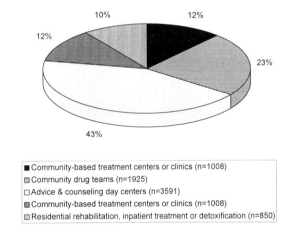

Figure 6.4 Estimate of Number of New Cases Seen in August 1994 in Different Types
of Service
SOURCE: MacGregor et al. (1994).
NOTE: New cases are those seeking a first contact with the service in question. Admission is not a reliable guide to many of the services offered, because "admission" may not be available or warranted. Some services offer "drop in"-type contact, which imposes few formal admission requirements.

recent years, methadone prescribing as part of a program of controlled withdrawal has become a dominant feature of drug treatment in the English health services, either by consultant psychiatrists in hospital services or by general practitioners (sometimes together with community drug teams—so-called shared care). It may be short-term—for 6 weeks—or continue for longer periods, depending on clinical judgment of the needs of the patient. More recently still, on an experimental basis, patients have been admitted to hospital for rapid detoxification with a cocktail of drugs under general anesthesia.

At the other end of the spectrum of prescribing policies are those best known internationally as building on the work of John Marks at Widnes in Liverpool, in the Merseyside region, and of others who have prescribed heroin, sometimes in the form of reefers. Here, the aims are to separate the drug users from the criminal underworld into which they are otherwise drawn to obtain supplies, and to control the quality and quantity of the drug being used. The Liverpool scheme has served as a model for Switzerland and has influenced the debate in other countries, such as Australia.

Between 1989 and 1991, for example, two drug dependency units in Merseyside prescribed smokable methadone or heroin to opiate injectors to encourage them to give up injecting. Smokable cocaine or amphetamine has also been prescribed. Smoking is said to simulate the "rush" experienced from injecting and may be suitable for injectors unwilling to settle for the milder effects of oral use (Marks, Palombella, & Newcombe, 1991). It has proved especially attractive as a means of reducing the risk of HIV infection from injecting. Another aim has been to draw into services the estimated 80% of addicts who are not in treatment because they are deterred by the rigid regimens of conventional services but find sniffing and smoking more acceptable.

The reefers were produced by a local pharmaceutical firm and distributed to local pharmacies, which usually dispensed weekly sufficient for two to six cigarettes a day. They cost slightly more than oral, but less than injectable, methadone. Patients suitable for this regimen were long-term opiate injectors who wished to stop injecting.

Psychiatrists split over this approach to prescribing. Critics of the Marks approach claimed that the prescribing of smokable substances brought psychiatry into disrepute but more often argued that it was pragmatic not to follow this route because it would antagonize the proponents of abstinence and might lead to draconian controls on the medical profession. The call for harmonization from Europe, which tends to threaten the more liberal regimens of the United Kingdom and the Netherlands, is seen as a danger, and experts try to avoid the issues and keep their practices out of the public eye. The prescribing of reefers and the publicity that Marks and others tended to attract through the media were seen as a threat to the more circumspect practices of those who conformed with central policy. They fear that the privileged autonomy of the medical profession to prescribe might be lost if it were used excessively. The opponents of this view argue that results are encouraging with respect to the reduction of intravenous use. The patients cope well, their health improves, their relationships are more stable, and worries about intravenous drug use are reduced.

There is growing criticism of what now seems excessive use of methadone. Partly, the difference reflects the extent to which the social-psychological aspects of drug dependence are recognized: Dependence is not purely on the drug itself but just as much on the experiences and customary practices associated with drug use.

Evidence points to considerable use of other services: The more chronic or incapacitated drug users—those who eventually end up as inpatients—have attended accident and emergency departments and most other services at some time. There is a substantial amount of sharing of patients and clients among services, and this complicates attempts to measure the effectiveness of any one treatment or service. Care is an important aspect of treatment and inseparable from it in affecting the final outcome.

Conclusion

In spite of the sea changes in organization and in underlying social conditions, pragmatism continues to characterize the English approach to drug treatment. Whatever the rhetoric in the media or in Parliament, those charged with looking after people and delivering services practice moderation and avoidance of excess, and compromise and consensus remain distinctive features of policy and practice. Treatment as a whole is clearly linked now to punishment and compulsion at one extreme and to prevention at the other. Paradoxically, in increasingly fragmented and constantly changing health and social services, partnership is being emphasized as the solution to most problems. It is the new mode of regulation, suited to the postindustrial and post-welfare-state society. However, alongside this benign development goes an increasingly tough response to those who refuse to be incorporated. The hard core of the unemployed and the deviant, who include drug misusers, may expect harsher treatment or exclusion from treatment if they fail to play the game. Certainly, they cannot expect scarce public sector funds to be expended on their treatment and care. Oddly, however, as drug use has become more extensive and drug misuse endemic, and suppliers and dealers are more severely punished, there is increasing use of caution for those caught in possession of small amounts for personal use. The system could not cope with attempting to process the numbers of those who break the rules.

So far, English treatment services have survived a series of tests by being resilient and able to adapt, and by the basic commitment of their staff to deliver good services and show concern for a relatively unpopular client group. Their commitment and underlying values should not be overlooked. The services, while becoming larger and more diverse, retain a coherence and an integration that distinguish them from those of other sectors. This allows them to remain a relatively successful and powerful pressure group, able to influence decision making at the center through representation in key forums. The survival of the drug treatment services will depend on their ability to replicate this degree of coherence, organization, and influence at the local levels, to which powers have been increasingly devolved.

Notes

1. The National Treatment Outcomes Research Study (NTORS) is the largest study of treatment outcome of drug misusers ever conducted in the United Kingdom. It was commissioned by the Task Force and is to be funded by the Department of Health to the year 2000. It provides detailed information about the drug-related social, psychological, and health problems of people commencing treatment across England, and it studies the structure and content of services provided. It aims to provide a detailed account of the impact of treatment on drug-related problems, health, and social functioning. Dr. Michael Gossop is director of the NTORS Project, which is run from the National Addiction Centre at the Maudsley Hospital in London.

2. The Task Force presented evidence to show that the 1,100 drug misusers included in the NTORS study had committed 70,000 crimes in the 3 months before they entered treatment. Had these crimes been committed at the same rate over a 2-year period, it was argued, it would have cost their victims £34 million (about US$53 million), owing mainly to shoplifting, burglary, and car theft, the most common kinds of crime committed by this cohort. The press gave great prominence to these statistics, not surprisingly, because they appeared in the first paragraph of the Task Force's Executive Summary.

References

Baker, O., & Marsden, J. (1994). *Drug misuse in Great Britain*. London: Institute for the Study of Drug Dependence.

Berridge, V. (1984). Drugs and social policy: The establishment of drug control in Britain 1900-1930. *British Journal of Addiction, 79*, 17-29.

Department of Health. (1995). *Tackling drugs together: A strategy for England 1995-1998*. London: ITMSO.

Edwards, G. (1969). The British approach to the treatment of heroin addiction. *Lancet, 1*, 768-772.

Glanz, A. (1994). The fall and rise of the general practitioner. In J. Strang & M. Gossop (Eds.), *Heroin addiction and drug policy: The British system* (pp. 151-166). Oxford, UK: Oxford University Press.

Grant, M. (1994). What is so special about the British system? In J. Strang & M. Gossop (Eds.), *Heroin addiction and drug policy: The British system* (pp. v-vi). Oxford, UK: Oxford University Press.

Jamieson, A., Glanz, A., & MacGregor, S. (1984). *Dealing with drug misuse: Crisis intervention in the city*. London: Tavistock.

Leitner, M., Shapland, J., & Wiles, P. (1993). *Drug usage and drugs prevention: The views and habits of the general public*. London: Home Office Drugs Prevention Initiative.

MacGregor, S., Ettorre, B., Coomber, R., Crosier, A., & Lodge, H. (1991). *Drugs services in England and the impact of the central funding initiative* (ISDD Research Monograph Series No. 1). London: Institute for the Study of Drug Dependence.

MacGregor, S., Smith, L., & Flory, P. (1994). *The English drugs treatment services report to the Department of Health*. Enfield, UK: Middlesex University.

Marks, J., Palombella, A., & Newcombe, R. (1991). The smoking option. *Druglink, 6*(3), 10-11.

Matthews, R., & Trickey, J. (1996). *Drugs and young people*. Leicester, UK: Leicester University Centre for the Study of Public Order.

National Health Service and Community Care Act. (1990). London: HMSO Books.

Parker, H., Measham, F., & Aldridge, J. (1995). *Drugs futures: Changing patterns of drug use amongst English youth*. London: Institute for the Study of Drug Dependence.

Pearson, G. (1987). *The new heroin users*. London: Basil Blackwell.

Plymouth Community Drug Service. (1994). *Development of services for drug misusers in Plymouth*. Unpublished report.

Stimson, G., & Oppenheim, E. (1982). *Heroin addiction: Treatment and control in Britain*. London: Tavistock.

Task Force (The Task Force to Review Services for Drug Misusers). (1996). *Report of an independent review of drug treatment services in England*. London: Department of Health.

Young, J. (1971). *The drugtakers*. London: Paladin.

Chapter 7

Integrating Care, Cure, and Control: The Drug Treatment System in the Netherlands

Jack T. M. Derks
Marten J. Hoekstra
Charles D. Kaplan

The Sociopolitical Structure of
Health Care and Drug-Related Trends

Unlike most countries in their approach to drug control, the Netherlands has chosen the course of experimentation rather than prohibition (Kaplan, 1984). Medical (including social-psychiatric or public health) experiments have become an integral part of the country's response to drug problems. Many visitors to Amsterdam are intrigued at being able to walk into so-called coffee shops and buy cannabis. They often see this as free distribution of cannabis and do not recognize it as a grand social and public health experiment to test the strategy of "separation of markets" for preventing high-risk youth from stepping up to the next level of hard drugs. Visitors may also observe one of the modern mobile clinics for dispensing oral methadone (methadone buses). They may also think that methadone is given freely to anyone who walks in, which is not the case. Also, with some help from an Amsterdam addict or a drug counselor or researcher, they can find the places where injectable morphine, injectable methadone, or oral dextromoramide is dispensed. All of these unique practices are examples of institutionalized experiments (Hoekstra & Derks, 1993).

The distinction between soft and hard drugs, first made in the new Opium Act of 1976, is the cornerstone of the Dutch definition of drug problems. The basis of this distinction is the social acceptability of the risk associated with the use of a given drug. Only cannabis has been defined as a soft drug. For the most part, the use of soft drugs has not been considered a problem for many years, but it is being reevaluated. Current concern is about abuse in the coffee-house system, and there are new programs that focus on the potentially harmful effects of excessive use of cannabis by young people.

The legal distinction between hard and soft drugs is also the basis of official tolerance of small-scale cannabis trade, in contrast with the considerable efforts made to suppress the large-scale trade. Until the mid-1990s, there was no special policy on the small- and medium-scale trade in soft drugs, and it developed without hindrance. This has changed. In 1991, the Amsterdam City Council announced that measures were being prepared to restrict the nuisance (from "noise and other annoyance") caused by coffee shops in the city, and to restrict their proliferation. There are an estimated 400 to 500 in Amsterdam alone ("De schaamte," 1994; Sociaal en Cultureel Planbureau, 1993). The total for the Netherlands as a whole was estimated at 1,200 to 1,500 in 1991. In addition, there were between 700 and 2,200 cannabis dealers in private houses and 500 to 1,000 in community centers (Kuipers, 1991). Thus, in all, there were between 2,400 and 4,700 cannabis outlets, or between 1 per 2,600 and 1 per 5,200 of the population over 15 years of age. Recent official figures are much lower: 1,100 to 1,200 coffee shops and some 900 other outlets (Government Paper, 1995). The system is run by dealers in the shady transitional sphere between legal and illegal business. Partly because the European Court does not allow the Dutch Ministry of Finance to impose purchase tax on the coffee shops, they make very good profits (recently estimated by the Police Information Service to be 325 million Dutch guilders, or US$170 million per year).

There is discussion on whether this policy on cannabis has led to an increase in its use. A small but growing proportion of the clients who use the system of specialized outpatient treatment services (Consultation Bureaus for Alcohol and Drugs—CADs) have had problems with cannabis. Almost half of these took cannabis as the primary drug. For the other half, cannabis plays a role in their dependency behavior with regard to other drugs, alcohol, or gambling (IVV, 1996).

Apart from cannabis, criminality and AIDS have become key policy concerns in relation to hard drugs. Hard drug addicts in Dutch jails constituted 10% of all prisoners in 1970 but 50% or more in 1995 (Bovens, 1996). The national registration of CAD clients shows that about half of the drug addicts are prosecuted for property offenses. Prosecutions of CAD clients for drug dealing have dropped from more than 30% in 1989 to 13% in 1995. There is now fear of a rise in "professionalization" of the small- and medium-scale trade in hard drugs. For several years, the Amsterdam police have been reporting declining general criminality figures (20% since 1993), due mainly to a decrease in street robbery, housebreaking, theft of and from cars, and pickpocketing ("Criminaliteit," 1996).

Of the AIDS cases diagnosed in 1990, 9.8% were intravenous drug users. In 1994, this figure rose to 12.5% (de Zwart & Mensink, 1996). An estimated 30% of hard drug addicts in Amsterdam are seropositive (van den Hoek, 1990). They were infected in the early years of the 1980s, before syringe exchange programs were begun. In Amsterdam, the Municipal Public Health Service considers the AIDS-drug epidemic to be past its zenith (GG & GD, 1996). For the rest of the country, the estimates and data from research tend to be much lower. Recent data indicate that in Rotterdam 12% of users who ever injected drugs are seropositive for HIV, compared with 1.5% of the nonintravenous users. In the south of the Netherlands, these figures were 10% and 0%, respectively (Wiessink, 1995). Prevention of HIV infection is regarded as of the utmost importance. The efficacy of needle exchange as it relates to HIV prevention policies and drug prostitution policies has been evaluated, with generally positive results (Grund, Stern, Kaplan, Adriaans, & Drucker, 1992; van Ameijden, 1994).

Historical Survey

The Dutch definition of drug problems is characteristically not dominated by moral overtones. This does not necessarily mean that morality has not played a part in the historical development of definitions and responses to certain substances. In the mid-19th century, the Netherlands' fight against the "evils" of alcohol was comparable to that of other European countries. There is some continuity between mid-19th-century definitions of alcohol and late-20th-century drug definitions, in that a peaceful regulation of the problem was preferred to war. Policies based on creating fear of the dangers of drugs (as well as alcohol), and forcing drug users into illegality or incarcerating them, have been considered in the Netherlands as counterproductive, costly, and bad policies that are immoral in their consequences.

It was not until the beginning of the 1970s that the Netherlands was faced with a socially significant drug problem. Until 1970, small quantities of heroin, cocaine, or amphetamines were used in a few artistic circles. In Chinese communities in the bigger cities, opium was used in "opium kits" that were tolerated by the law and controlled by the police. Around 1970, the use of amphetamines became popular among small groups of young people in Amsterdam, and at about the same time, small quantities of opium "leaked" from the Amsterdam Chinese community to the "modern youth" (hippies). Soon after that, the import and street sale of heroin began. The substance at first was regarded very suspiciously by the Amsterdam drug users. From its introduction in the autumn of 1972, the increase continued in the number of users of hard drugs as well as the number of drug problems. In the same year, the Baan Commission report (Werkgroep verdovende middelen, 1972), prepared at a time when there were virtually no hard drug problems, recommended the legal distinction between hard and soft drugs.

The treatment system originated at the beginning of the 20th century from the initiatives of alcohol activists. Psychiatric hospitals with specialized residential treatment clinics were established. The ambulatory system of the CADs was founded in the 1920s, consisting of social-medical centers for alcohol dependents. They functioned as probation institutes subsidized by the Ministry of Justice. In 1969, at the instigation of the Netherlands Lower House and against the wishes of the government, the CADs were given tasks in drug counseling. In the 1970s, the Outpatient Mental Health Services were set up as a new entity in health care. The CADs retained their independence and continue to do so. A new state subsidy scheme came into being for CADs in 1979. Because the Ministry of Justice cut the probation budgets in the 1980s (to less than 30% of the total CAD budget), CADs had to leave posts unfilled and carry out a radical reorganization of probation care.

The paths of the subsidizing Ministries of Justice and of Health are diverging more and more. In 1988, the government separated the financing of the CADs into two streams; since then, it has been gradually withdrawing its subsidies. Decentralization has become the policy keyword. At the suggestion of the Association of Netherlands Municipalities, the CADs were placed under the authority of the local city councils. In 1994, against strong opposition from the CADs, the financing of the entire outpatient system was rearranged on a temporary basis with no special provision for addiction facilities. The financial future of outpatient drug care is still unclear.

Drugs in Society

The prevalence of cannabis use seems to follow the development of the semilegal supply infrastructure. Although the subject is under discussion, the figures more and more tell a plain story. At the end of the 1980s, a small increase (5%) was reported in the subpopulation using cannabis (Driessen, van Dam, & Olson, 1989). However, de Zwart (1989) reported the opposite: A number of surveys had indicated a drop between 1983 and 1987. Some years later, a national survey of 11,000 pupils by the Netherlands Institute on Alcohol and Drugs found large increases in cannabis use in school-age groups (de Zwart, Mensink, & Kuipers, 1993; Kuipers, Mensink, & de Zwart, 1993). Recent publications report an increase in cannabis use in both its lifetime and past-month prevalence in the general population and a twofold increase from 1984 to 1992 in students between the ages of 12 and 18 years (de Zwart & Mensink, 1996).

The Netherlands resembles other European countries in the nature and extent of hard drug use. For some years, rough estimates have been made of the number of users of hard drugs (heroin, cocaine, and amphetamines). From memoranda issued by the city council and drug services, Leuw (1984) estimated for Amsterdam that there were 1,500 hard drug users in 1973, 5,000 in 1974, and 8,000 to 10,000 in 1984. The 1984 estimate was the highest ever reached. Since 1987, the Amsterdam figures have tended to fall. Buning (1990) put them at 5,800 to 7,500 for 1989. Recently, new and better estimation methods have shown a reduction for the period 1983 to 1990 (Reijneveld, 1991). The Amsterdam Municipal Public Health Service reports ever-decreasing numbers and recently referred to the drug problem as vanishing (GG & GD, 1996).

The estimates of hard drug users for the whole of the Netherlands were stable for some years, at 15,000 to 20,000 from the mid-1980s (de Zwart, 1989), but they increased to about 24,000 in 1990 (Driessen, 1990), and to 27,000 in 1995 (Bieleman, Snippe, & de Bie, 1995; Government Paper, 1995), in striking contrast to the Amsterdam figures. Cocaine use and abuse as well as the abuse of multiple drugs have been rising in the past 15 years.

Treatment Institutions

The Netherlands has an extensive network of specialized institutions for dependency care ("categorical dependency care"), either exclusively outpatient or inpatient, or mixed. They treat alcohol, drugs, and gambling dependency, and they preserve a separate approach and orientation from those of general mental health services. However, there is a trend toward their increasing integration with those services. The Dutch Association of Addiction Treatment and Care Centers (NeVIV), the national umbrella organization for addiction treatment and care, merged with a national Mental Health Association in 1997.

In 1990, the categorical sector consisted of a total of about 100 institutions: 16 CADs at 90 locations, 20 residential dependency clinics, 50 social-care-oriented facilities for drug counseling and 6 methadone projects of municipal health authorities, with about 250 branches. In 1995, these 100 institutions were integrated into 45 institutions. There has always been much contact between the services, but this has not always resulted in effective cooperation. Overt and covert competition occurred. Numerous attempts to coordinate the admission and counseling of clients failed because of ideological differences. This ideological competition has been decreasing in recent years.

Besides the professional institutions, a number of self-help organizations play a role. Alcoholics Anonymous (AA) has been active in the Netherlands for more than 50 years, and AA-style groups for drug addicts (Narcotics Anonymous) have been formed. The National Foundation for Parents of Drug Addicts and the National Point of Support for Drug Users also operate throughout the country, with self-help and policy advocacy as their objectives. Also, associations of former clients of therapeutic communities provide after-care services as well as support for the communities' programs. Relations between self-help groups and the professional institutions are good. The latter often provide meeting rooms and secretarial assistance to the groups. The groups play a role in stimulating the professional institutions to try out innovations.

The Legal Division of Labor

Since the beginning of this century, the CADs have provided probation services for addicted criminals. They inform and advise them about legal matters, assist those detained in police stations, draft reports accompanying addicts to court, and counsel them about aid available in prisons. Prisons provide an increasing number of drug-free departments, from 11 with 240 cells (beds) in 1993, to 15 with more than 440 beds by 1995. CAD staff function in these departments as group counselors, ensure continuity of care by referring detainees to services outside the prison (NeVIV, 1991), and operate "alternative punishments" (e.g., community service).

In 1993, the government set up intervention programs to diminish drug-related nuisance and crime: Addicted offenders can choose between strict punishment and treatment; "drug-free departments" are being established in most prisons, and more places are being provided for criminal clients in the residential treatment system. In general, there has been extensive functional integration of different types of addiction treatment and care and organizational clustering of providers of addiction care.

Treatment Rationales

The government memorandum *Drug Policy in Motion* (ISAD, 1985) laid down "normalizing" as a policy basis for the management of hard-drug use. The primary consequences of hard drug use (i.e., health damage) are regarded as less serious than the secondary consequences of the prohibition of drugs. Because legalization is not a realistic option, owing to international treaties and the unpredictability of the consequences, the government has chosen to normalize the drug problem. This policy promotes a vigorous attempt by society toward the social and cultural integration of the consequences of the abuse of drugs and a decrease of criminalization and stigma attached to drug users. The relevant terms are "harm reduction," "risk reduction," and "harm minimization."

The rationale is that it is acceptable to apply some pressure on addicts to use the services but that compulsion is not suitable. Dutch law forbids compulsion (Government Memorandum, 1988, 1994). Policy is designed to make dependency bearable for large numbers of addicts by supplying them with methadone on a maintenance basis. Dutch experiments and experiences with the care of addicts are part of the practice of social psychiatry. The core of this health policy was best stated by the former head of the Department of Social Psychiatry of the Amsterdam Municipal Public Health Service, Dr. Wijnand Mulder (1981): "If cure is not possible, not doing harm is the next target" (p. 2). On the supply side, the government wants to obtain and maintain a grip on the drug trade by implementing a tougher investigation and prosecution policy. Normalization policy strives for the equal treatment of illicit drug users and users of socially accepted drugs, such as tobacco, alcohol, and caffeine.

The recent government memorandum *Drug Policy in the Netherlands: Continuity and Change* (Government Paper, 1995) states,

> Given the relatively good results which have been achieved, we do not believe that there is any reason for a fundamental re-examination of drugs policy in the Netherlands, which is primarily geared to controlling the harm done to people's health. (p. 15)

However, there has been a shift in policy from cure, treatment, and care to containment, public health, and the reduction of social consequences of addiction (petty crime, nuisance, and inner-city turmoil).

The Dutch "multiple functional" method of drug treatment includes inpatient treatment under the supervision of psychiatrists. More prominent, however, are numerous and varied extramural programs. They include methadone provision; "street corner" work; relief work; crisis intervention; counseling; prevention work; day and open-door centers; and study, work, and housing projects. A number of projects are aimed at specific ethnic groups, such as Moroccans and Surinamese, and at certain categories of clients, such as heroin prostitutes or children of addicted mothers. These functions are implemented in very different combinations, according to local circumstances and priorities. The current integration of institutions combines most of these functions into regional and multifunctional services.

Treatment Capacity, Needs, and Offers

The Organization Information Systems on Addiction Care and Treatment (IVV, 1990-1996) provides national statistics. Admissions for all forms of dependence (alcohol, drugs, gambling) to the 16 CADs increased from 45,000 in 1988 to some 54,000 in 1993, and slightly more than 55,000 in 1995. Admissions for illicit drug dependence increased from almost 17,000 in 1988 to 22,500 in 1993 and almost 26,000 in 1995. Consistently over the years, about 40% of the clients of CADs have drug problems. The absolute number of drug clients has increased by more than 50% since 1988. For the past several years, about 20% of the drug-dependent patients have been referred by the criminal system. The outpatient services are staffed with a total of 1,650 full-time equivalents, and in 1994 they cost DFL 137 million (US$71 million) per year.

An interesting feature has been an increase in cannabis users seeking treatment at the CADs, from 3.4% of all drug-dependent clients in 1988 to 7.8% in 1993 and 9.6% in 1995 (IVV, 1994-1996). The total number of regular users of cannabis is estimated at 675,000, which indicates that 0.5% of the population seeks help from the outpatient addiction treatment services. Admissions for cocaine dependence have also increased, from only 5.5% in 1988 to almost 10% in 1993 and 14% in 1995.

In the residential treatment services, admissions almost doubled between 1980 and 1990 (Derks, 1993) and since then have further increased by one third. De Zwart and Mensink (1996) counted 4,400 admissions of drug patients to residential treatment in 1994 (about one third of all admissions of addicted patients). The residential services in the Netherlands employ 850 full-time staff and cost DFL 134 million (US$70 million) per year.

Methadone programs are widespread in the Netherlands. Individual methadone treatment began in 1979 and in less than 10 years developed into a nationwide methadone dispensing system. In 1988, the low-threshold national dispensing system had more than 65 dispensing points. Its growth continued in the first half of the 1990s, when 12,500 to 15,000 people were receiving methadone. The numbers dropped to 11,000 in 1995—the equivalent of 40% to 45% of the country's opiate addicts. Most receive fairly low doses; the mean dosage is 35 mg to 40 mg. About three fourths of methadone clients participate in maintenance programs, of which the primary aim is not to stop the dependency but to reduce its negative effects and normalize the functioning of the patient. The clients of maintenance programs are generally older than those of the reduction programs, which use methadone as a tool for long-term detoxification.

In keeping with the harm reduction rationale, methadone maintenance is designed to reduce secondary effects of drug abuse, such as AIDS or violence. The longitudinal, in-depth study of Swierstra (1990) of 91 heroin addicts indicates that the normalization policy has been effective in diverting heroin addicts from criminal to conventional lifestyles but less effective in getting them clean. A national research project on client satisfaction found that a majority (two thirds) of the surveyed addicts in methadone programs were generally content with the methadone provision, and a larger proportion (three fourths) of clients of ambulatory counseling and rehabilitation programs were generally content with their treatment and care (Jongerius, Hull, & Derks, 1994). This finding reflects the widespread experience in the Netherlands that to be effective, methadone or other substitution treatment must be flanked by counseling and additional care and rehabilitation (Derks, 1990a; van de Wijngaart, 1990).

In residential clinics, treatment consists of detoxification (a brief stay of several weeks), a short stay (of up to 3 months), or a longer stay, and it is followed by after-care at an outpatient department. Eleven independent residential services and nine departments of general psychiatric hospitals specialize in dependency care. The total of 900 treatment places for the country is not larger than the capacity of one large psychiatric hospital. As a rule, long-term treatment takes place in drug-free therapeutic communities. They use a treatment model that places the clients in a phased and intensive program, with complete abstinence as the rule (i.e., no methadone). Ongoing clinical program evaluation, concentrating on outcomes, retention of patients, and comorbidity in drug addicts in treatment services is yielding results that help to improve the care system (Hendriks, 1990; Kooyman, 1992; van Limbeek, Wouters, Kaplan, Geerlings, & van Alem, 1992).

"Off the Mainstream" and Institutional Experiments

Since the first half of the 1970s, when the legal basis for a policy aimed at separating markets for soft and hard drugs was laid down, numerous ideas and proposals have been advanced to "solve" the drug problem, which until very recently was defined almost exclusively as a hard drug problem. Many of these ideas and proposals led to some variant of social or medical experimentation. Besides the medical dispensing of opiates and opioids, experimentation included the toleration of a "heroin house dealer" at a day center for addicts, the establishment of "heroin cafes," and the installation and toleration of a "free zone" for addicts in downtown Amsterdam.

Not surprisingly, the most radical proposals were never implemented. In 1984, the Amsterdam department of the Dutch left-liberal party (D'66) proposed the legalization of all substances that could be used for pleasure, including hard drugs such as heroin and cocaine. Hard drugs would be dispensed to anyone who asked for them and who had been resident in Amsterdam for more than a year. In this view, the medical dispensing of hard drugs is accepted as a transitional stage toward full legalization. At that time also, the Amsterdam municipal government suggested an experimental heroin-dispensing program under medical supervision for some 300 addicts that was designed to improve their health *and* reduce drug-related criminality. After months of vehement public and official discussion, the central government coalition of Christian Democrats and Socialists and also the Dutch Royal Society of Medicine categorically rejected the proposal.

Some of the Dutch proposals for experimentation did not get stuck at the planning stage because they simply were *not* planned. In the mid-1970s, an experimental project was undertaken at an Amsterdam day center for heroin and amphetamine addicts (the so-called HUK). The staff reasoned that it was better to have one well-known hard drug dealer around than numerous unknown dealers. To avoid trouble with the law, the staff did not call the dealer a "house dealer." But in a municipal memorandum, the situation was described as "a protected illegal market where heroin is dispensed under supervision of the staff." Mostly, the heroin was of good quality, indeed the best in Amsterdam. Clients could buy small quantities, and the supply was stable. Entrance to the center was restricted to registered addicts. For more than 5 years, HUK operated in this way. In 1982, the municipal government terminated the experiment because the situation had become more and more uncontrollable. The local community increasingly protested against the expanding heroin market, which operated round the clock. Addicts from other European countries came to the center to buy heroin, and the clients of the program served as runners. Moreover, the physical and psychological condition of the clients deteriorated progressively (Haverkamp, 1984).

In 1979, a social crisis caused by the squatting of about 1,000 addicts of Surinamese origin in a theater building in the heart of Amsterdam led to another experimental project. (There is a large subpopulation from Surinam, a former Dutch colony.) To regulate this problem, six heroin cafes were established in different parts of the city. The municipality took the responsibility for their management. After 2 years, the policy was judged to be a catastrophe (Fabius, 1983). Local communities had protested furiously. The dealing in drugs in the cafes repeatedly induced violence, and two cafes burned down. Adequate management of the cafes turned out to be impossible. Only one cafe had merely minor problems, but this was due to a lack of interest of the customers.

Other experiments were scrupulously planned and carefully set up, such as the Amsterdam Morphine-Dispensing Program, which dispensed injectable morphine on top of a dose of oral methadone to 38 "extremely problematic drug addicts." The program was implemented in the second half of the 1980s by the Municipal Public Health Service and the Amsterdam Foundation for Drugs Care (SDA), and it was evaluated continuously (Daansen & Derks, 1994; Derks, 1990a, 1990b; Derks & Daansen, 1986a, 1986b). Its rationale was to provide addicts with a legal hard drug on the basis of medical indication to help them overcome their illicit drug dependency problems. The emphasis was on the regulation and stabilization of addiction and on structuring the time freed by the cessation of dependent behavior. The program was designed to lessen self-inflicted harm and to change the addicts' lifestyles, not to produce abstinence. The conclusion of the evaluation was that the program had *limited but positive* results. In general, it performed better with psychiatric than with physical problems.

Recently, after a change of government (the cabinet is a coalition of Social Democrats and Liberals—including the left-wing liberals), and after a positive recommendation in 1995 by the Dutch Health Council, a number of heroin-dispensing experiments have been planned in which injectable as well as oral heroin (smokable heroin) is to be dispensed. The first of these experiments, a pilot with 50 addicts, began in March 1998. For full execution of the experiments, the involvement of 750 addicts is intended. The implementation of the experiments according to the plans will need continuous political support. Interestingly, in the national survey on client satisfaction mentioned before, 65% of the surveyed clients of methadone programs did not opt for the dispensing of substances other than methadone. Of the 35% of those who chose other substances, 73% mentioned benzodiazepines (sleepers and tranquilizers) as preferred substances, and only 17% wanted hard drugs (heroin and amphetamines) dispensed (Jongerius et al., 1994).

Discussion

The Dutch treatment system has become increasingly decentralized. The opponents of decentralization fear further fragmentation and isolation from other mental health services and a diminution of the quality of care. They foresee additional problems in the residential treatment services and in the interplay of the principal funders of the system, the Ministries of Justice and Health. Dependency care, they say, should be available to all citizens, like other health services; its provision should not depend on local welfare policies. The supporters of decentralization point to the advantages of dependency care being managed by local councils, which they say are best placed to ascertain local needs for services.

The National Council for Public Health (NRV) issued recommendations in 1989 and 1990 on the position, organization, and financing of dependency care. They reflected predominantly the perspectives of organized mental health care. Dependency care should be interdisciplinary (health care, mental health care, judicial guidance and counseling, and social services) to the extent that funding from plural sources permits. The Council favors close cooperation between the institutions in health regions by their further integration or by federation and coordination of the policies of the funding organizations.

What will the Dutch treatment system look like after the year 2001? Policy trends point to discrepancies between long-term policies on treatment and on financing. The government is withdrawing from funding and leaving policy making more and more to the funders: the insurers (residential care), local councils (outpatient care), and the probation services (CAD probation). Expansion of government services was mainly in the fields of reducing drug-related nuisance and inner-city turmoil. The clustering of provisions is left largely to the treatment institutions and their funders. The government will not adopt a specific policy for eliminating the structural barriers to efficient treatment; therefore, they are likely to remain, and even to increase. The service providers have accepted this uncertain situation more and more and are adopting entrepreneurial positions vis-à-vis a retreating government. A fruitful relation between treatment policy and provisions policies can be achieved along two roads that are not necessarily exclusive: the implementation of the functional approach laid down by the National Council for Public Health, and the development by the government of a policy on quality of care.

It remains to be seen how the continuous uncertainty will affect the quality of dependency care. The Dutch treatment system by the year 2001 will undoubtedly have pioneered bold new treatment options, ranging from experimentation with new pharmacological products targeting underlying neurobiological mechanisms to behavioral interventions such as work programs and social network integration. One thing is certain: The Netherlands will continue to be a source of innovative treatment modalities that other countries without a tradition of normative pluralism and experimentation with treatment will find unthinkable and difficult to comprehend.

References

Bieleman, B., Snippe, J., & de Bie, E. (1995). *Drugs binnen de grenzen, harddrugs en criminaliteit in Nederland; schattingen van de omvang* [Estimates of hard drugs and criminality in the Netherlands]. Groningen/Rotterdam: Stichting Intraval.

Bovens, R. (Ed). (1996). *Justitie en Zorg* [Justice and care]. Utrecht: Nederlandse Vereniging van Instellingen voor Verslavingszorg (NeVIV) [Dutch Association of Addiction Treatment and Care Centres].

Buning, E. C. (1990). *De GG & GD en het drugprobleem in cijfers. Deel IV* [Quantitative data on the municipal public health service and the drug problem. Part IV]. Amsterdam: Municipal Public Health Service (GG & GD).

Criminaliteit blijft afnemen in Amsterdam [Criminality drop in Amsterdam continues]. (1996, 23 December). *Het Parool,* p. 1.

Daansen, P., & Derks, J. (1994). Heroin, kein Allheilmittel, aber brauchbar [Heroin, no wonder drug, but useful]. *Sucht, 40,* 334-339.

Derks, J. (1990a). *Het Amsterdamse Morfine-verstrekkingsprogramma. Een longitudinaal onderzoek onder extreem problematische druggebruikers* [The Amsterdam morphine dispensing programme. A longitudinal study of extremely problematic drug addicts in an experimental public health programme]. Utrecht: Nederlands centrum Geestelijke volksgezondheid.

Derks, J. (1990b). The efficacy of the Amsterdam morphine dispensing programme. In A. H. Ghodse & C. D. Kaplan (Eds.), *Drug misuse and dependence: The British and Dutch response* (pp. 85-108). London: Parthenon.

Derks, J. (1993). Verslavingsziekten [Addiction diseases]. In D. Ruwaard & P. G. N. Kramers (Eds.), *Volksgezondheid Toekomst Verkenning. De gezondheidstoestand van de Nederlandse bevolking in de periode 1950-2010* [Public health future scenarios. The health status of the Dutch population in the period 1950-2010] (pp. 334-342). The Hague: SDU.

Derks, J., & Daansen, P. (1986a). Hilfe für Altfixer: Mit dosiertem Morphium gegen Heroin [Care for long-term injectors: With an adequate dose of morphine against heroin]. *Psychologie Heute, 13*(3), 67-69.

Derks, J., & Daansen, P. (1986b). Injizierbare Opiatverabreichung zur Behandlung chronischer Drogen-abhängiger, das Amsterdamer Morphiumexperiment [The dispensing of injectable opiates in the care of long-term injectors. The Amsterdam morphine programme]. *Kriminologisches Journal, 18*(1), 39-49.

De schaamte van de coffeeshop [Disgrace of the Coffee Shop System]. (1994, 31 January). *Volkskrant,* p. 13.

de Zwart, W. M. (1989). *Alcohol, tabak en drugs in cijfers* [Quantative data on alcohol, tobacco and drugs]. Utrecht: Nederlands Instituut voor Alcohol en Drugs (NIAD) [Netherlands Institute of Alcohol and Drugs].

de Zwart, W. M., & Mensink, C. (1996). *Jaarboek verslaving 1995* [Addiction Year Report 1995]. Utrecht/Houten: NIAD/Bohn Stafleu Van Lochum.

de Zwart, W. M., Mensink, C., & Kuipers, S. B. M. (1993). *Kerngegevens roken, drinken, druggebruik en gokken onder scholieren vanaf 10 jaar* [Core data on smoking, alcohol and drug use, and gambling among school children of 10 years and older]. Utrecht: Nederlands Instituut voor Alcohol en Drugs (NIAD) [Netherlands Institute of Alcohol and Drugs].

Driessen, F. M. H. M. (1990). *Methadonverstrekking in Nederland* [Methadone distribution in the Netherlands]. Rijswijk/Utrecht: Bureau Driessen.

Driessen, F. M. H. M., van Dam, G., & Olson, B. (1989). De ontwikkeling van het cannabisgebruik in Nederland, enkele Europese landen en de VS sinds 1969 [Development of cannabis use in the Netherlands, several other European countries and the USA since 1969]. *Tijdschrift voor Alcohol, Drugs en andere Psychotrope stoffen, 15,* 2-14.

Fabius, G. (1983). *Tekst, uitgesproken op PAO-cursus drugsbeleid op 7 oktober 1983* [Paper post-academic university education, 7 October 1983]. Amsterdam: Municipality of Amsterdam, Department: Vgz/lh, 2 October 1983.

GG & GD (Municipal Public Health Service). (1996). *Dovend vuur. Jaarbericht Drugsafdeling 1994-1995* [Extinguishing fire. Year report drugs department 1994-1995]. Amsterdam: Author.

Government Memorandum. (1988). *Dwang en drang bij de hulpverlening aan verslaafden* [Coercion and persuasion in giving assistance to addicts]. Rijswijk/The Hague: Ministerie van WVC en Ministerie van Justitie [Ministries of Health and Justice].

Government Memorandum. (1994). *Overlastbestrijding*[Fight against nuisance]. Rijswijk/The Hague: Ministerie van WVC en Ministerie van Justitie [Ministries of Health and Justice].

Government Paper. (1995). *Drugs policy in the Netherlands: Continuity and change.* Rijswijk: Ministry of Foreign Affairs/Ministry of Health, Welfare and Sport/Ministry of Justice and Ministry of the Interior.

Grund, J.-P. C., Stern, L. S., Kaplan, C. D., Adriaans, N. F. P., & Drucker, E. (1992). Drug use contexts and HIV-consequences: The effect of drug policy on patterns of everyday drug use in Rotterdam and the Bronx. *British Journal of Addiction, 87,* 381-392.

Haverkamp, G. (1984). Carrière- en scenevorming onder autochtone heroïnegebruikers [Development of careers and scenes in Dutch heroin addicts]. *Tijdschrift voor Criminologie, 26,* 136-148.

Hendriks, V. M. (1990). *Addiction and psychopathology: A multidimensional approach to clinical practice.* Unpublished doctoral dissertation, Erasmus University, Rotterdam.

Hoekstra, M. J., & Derks, J. T. M. (1993). Verslaving en verslavingszorg in Nederland [Addiction and addiction care in the Netherlands. In *Handboek Verslaving, hoofdwerk* [Handbook of Addiction, Main Volume] (pp. A 2000 1-A 2000 22). Alphen aan den Rijn: Bohn, Stafleu & Van Lochum.

ISAD (Interdepartementale Stuurgroep Alcohol- en Drugbeleid) [Interdepartmental Steering Group on Alcohol and Drug Policy]. (1985). *Drugbeleid in beweging, naar een normalisering van de drugproblematiek* [Drug policy in motion, toward the normalization of drug problems]. Leidschendam: Ministry of Health.

IVV (1990, 1991, 1992, 1993, 1994, 1995, 1996). Stichting Informatievoorziening verslavingszorg [Organization information systems on addiction care and treatment]. In *Landelijk Alcohol en Drugs Informatie Systeem/National Alcohol and Drugs Information System (LADIS/ADDICTIS).* Utrecht: Stichting Informatievoorziening Verslavingszorg (IVV) [Organization Information Systems on Addiction Care and Treatment].

Jongerius, J., Hull, H., & Derks, J. (1994). *Hoe scoort de verslavingszorg? Kwaliteitsbeoordeling door cliënten: een landelijk onderzoek* [Addiction care: Judgments by clients on outcome and quality. A nation-wide research project]. Utrecht: Nederlands centrum Geestelijke volksgezondheid.

Kaplan, C. D. (1984). The uneasy consensus: Prohibitionist and experimentalist expectancies behind the international narcotics control system. *Tijdschrift voor Criminologie, 26,* 98-109.

Kooyman, M. (1992). *The therapeutic community for addicts: Intimacy, parent involvement and treatment success.* Amsterdam/Lisse: Swets & Zeitlinger.

Kuipers, H. (1991). *Inventarisatie cannabis-verkooppunten in werkgebieden van korpsen rijks- en gemeentepolitie* [Survey of cannabis sales outlets in National and Municipal Police Regions].

Utrecht: Nederlands Instituut voor Alcohol en Drugs (NIAD) [Netherlands Institute of Alcohol and Drugs].

Kuipers, S. B. M., Mensink, C., & de Zwart, W. M. (1993). *Jeugd en riskant gedrag* [Youth and risk behavior]. Utrecht: Nederlands Instituut voor Alcohol en Drugs (NIAD) [Netherlands Institute of Alcohol and Drugs].

Leuw, E. (1984). Door schade en schande: de geschiedenis van drughulpverlening als sociaal beleid in Amsterdam [Learning by bitter experience: History of social policy on assistance to drug users in Amsterdam]. *Tijdschrift voor Criminologie, 26,* 151-152.

Mulder, W. G. (1981). *Drugsbeleid in Amsterdam* [Drug policy in Amsterdam]. Amsterdam: Gemeente Amsterdam, afdeling Voorlichting [Municipality of Amsterdam; Department of Public Relations].

NeVIV (Nederlandse Vereniging CADs). (1991, September). *Raamnota Verslavingsreclassering* [Framework memorandum on probational rehabilitation for addicts]. Utrecht, the Netherlands.

Reijneveld, S. A. (1991). *Methadonverstrekking in Amsterdam in 1990. Jaaroverzicht van de Centrale Methadon Registratie* [Methadone distribution in Amsterdam in 1990. Annual review of the central methadone register]. Amsterdam: GG & GD Municipal Public Health Service; Stafbureau for Epidemiology and Documentation.

Sociaal en Cultureel Planbureau. (1993). *Het Nederlandse softdrugbeleid; een verkenning van de grenzen* [The Dutch soft drug policy; An exploration of the boundaries]. Rijswijk: Author.

Swierstra, K. (1990). *Drugscarrières; van crimineel tot conventioneel* [Drug careers; From criminal to conventional]. Unpublished doctoral dissertation, University of Groningen, Groningen, the Netherlands.

van Ameijden, E. (1994). *Evaluation of AIDS-prevention measures among drug users: The Amsterdam experience.* Unpublished doctoral dissertation, University of Amsterdam, the Netherlands.

van den Hoek, A. (1990). *Epidemiology of HIV infection among drug users in Amsterdam.* Amsterdam: Rodopi.

van de Wijngaart, G. F. (1990). *Competing perpectives on drug use. The Dutch experience.* Unpublished doctoral dissertation, State University Utrecht, Utrecht, the Netherlands.

van Limbeek, J., Wouters, L., Kaplan, C. D., Geerlings, P. J., & van Alem, V. (1992). Prevalence of psychopathology in drug addicted Dutch. *Journal of Substance Abuse Treatment, 9,* 43-52.

Werkgroep verdovende middelen. (1972). *Achtergronden en risico's van druggebruik* [Backgrounds and risks of drug use] (Baan Report). The Hague: Staatsuitgeverij.

Wiessink, L. e.a. (1995). *Prevalentie van HIV-infecties onder druggebruikers in Rotterdam en Zuid-Limburg* [Prevalence of HIV in drug users in Rotterdam and Southern-Limburg). Bilthoven: RIVM [National Institute of Public Health and Environmental Protection].

Chapter 8

Harm Reduction and Abstinence: Swiss Drug Policy at a Time of Transition

Harald Klingemann

Unlike the political inertia in Switzerland in many other respects, and in contrast to the gradual historical development of alcohol policy and treatment, fueled by a strong temperance movement (Tecklenburg, 1986), Swiss drug politics and the Swiss drug treatment system have undergone rapid change since the mid-1980s. The reasons can be understood only in the context of cultural traditions of problem solving and the evaluation and perception of epidemiological trends on the parts of politicians, professionals, and the public. This chapter begins with a brief outline of this context and continues with a historical overview of drug policies and changing concepts of treatment. The second part describes the outpatient and inpatient treatment sector. The final section considers methadone substitution programs and heroin prescription trials as the most prominent, but controversial, features of the "Swiss model," and refers to the outcome of the September 1997 vote on the popular initiative opposing the increasing acceptance of the harm reduction approach.

Switzerland: Drugs and Social Problems

The Swiss Confederation, with its 7 million inhabitants in four linguistic regions, can be considered a corporate consensus democracy with an almost all-party government and proportional representation of corporate interest groups, languages, cantons, and political parties at all levels of policy making (Tschäni, 1983). The country's strong federal structure attributes power in health matters mainly to the 26 cantons (states). This long-standing system of interest balancing, together with the highest per capita GNP among the European countries of the Organization for Economic Cooperation and Development (OECD; Bundesamt für Statistik, 1996, p. 144), has contributed to the general impression of a rich, conservative country with few social problems and a very low level of societal conflict. Rates of crime are indeed low (Clinard, 1978). Thus, the homicide rate of 1.32 per 100,000 population, like Australia's of 1.86, contrasts with 9.93 for the United States (United Nations Office, 1997); and Switzerland—like Japan—is one of the few countries where crime rates *declined* between 1960 and 1990 (see also Killias, 1990, and Bundesamt für Statistik, 1994). The harmonious nature of labor-employer relations, originating in a historic peace agreement in 1937, are typical of a culture of low-key conflict resolution in a general sense. At the same time, often unknown abroad, Switzerland has high rates of AIDS and of self-destructive behavior, such as suicide and the abuse of alcohol, tobacco, and illicit drugs.

The strong cultural embeddedness of alcohol consumption and the concentration of wine growers among the francophone minority of the population influences the societal response to illicit drugs, which, users of licit drugs assert, are foreign to Swiss culture and therefore unacceptable. With a per capita consumption of 9.4 liters of pure alcohol in 1995, Switzerland—together with Germany, France, Portugal, and Spain—belongs to the "wet" countries, ranking tenth worldwide, higher than Australia at 7.6 liters and the United States at 6.8 liters (Produktschaap voor Gestilleerde Dranken, 1996).

Switzerland also has high rates of tobacco use, ranking with an annual per capita consumption of 2,910 cigarettes (1990-1992), fourth after Poland and Greece in the European Region of the World Health Organization (Harkin, Anderson, & Goos, 1997, p. 5); 700,000 Swiss smoke more than 20 cigarettes a day, more than in all neighboring countries (Meyer & Gmel, 1997, pp. 30, 31).

The number of users of heroin or cocaine is estimated to have risen from 29,500 in 1990 to 44,000 in 1993. New estimates, however, indicate fewer heroin users since 1994. The number of opiate dependents has most likely leveled off at about 30,000 (Gmel, 1997a, p. 57).

A representative survey of the population in 1992-1993 found that more than one in every five males, and one in every ten females, between the ages of 15 and 39 years had used illicit drugs at least once. Most by far had used cannabis. Among the males, 2.4% had used heroin at least once, and 3.1% had used cocaine. The rates for females were 1.1% for heroin and 1.5% for cocaine (Gmel, 1997b, p. 37, Tables B2 and B3).

The most prominent indicator of drug problems, according to the media and the public—apart from their preoccupation with open drug scenes—is drug-related deaths. Such deaths, mainly from overdose, rose sharply, from 202 in 1988 to 419 in 1992, before dropping with some fluctuation to 311 in 1996 (Schweizerische Fachstelle für Alkohol- und andere Drogenprobleme, 1997, p. 64). By international comparison, Switzerland has a high rate of suicide and self-inflicted injury at 20.4 per 100,000 population (1993). Only the newly independent states of Eastern

Europe, as well as Hungary, Finland, Denmark, and Austria, have higher rates. The corresponding rates for the United States and Australia are 12.2 and 11.1, respectively (World Health Organization, in press).

A comparison of the AIDS cases and incidence rates (per million population) by country in Europe shows Switzerland, with a rate of 103.2 (adapted for reporting delays, year of diagnosis 1992), in second place after Spain (121.9), and followed by France (86.7; European Centre for the Epidemiological Monitoring of AIDS, 1995, p. 13, Table 2). Since the early 1990s, however, HIV seropositivity has decreased considerably among drug users as a function of the year when they began injecting (see overview for the WHO European Region in Harkin et al., 1997, p. 132). Current estimates put the annual number of new HIV infections at about 1,000. Thanks to prevention measures such as the distribution of sterile injection utensils, the rate of new infections attributed to intravenous drug use (10%) is lower than that attributed to homosexual (29%) or heterosexual (43%) contacts. In the period 1984 to 1995, new cases of HIV infection among drug users fell from more than 75% to 19% (Gebhardt, 1996). It is still not clear whether the number of HIV/AIDS diagnoses has decreased since 1993, because of delays in reporting new cases and different methods of making estimations (Office fédéral de la santé publique, 1996).

Switzerland: Setting the Scene for the Development of Drug Treatment—An Overview

Illicit drugs did not become an issue in Switzerland until the "wild sixties" and the onset of the hippie movement, as in many other countries. In 1969, about 500 users of cannabis were notified but very few of opiates. The first death related to illicit drugs occurred in the city of Zürich in 1972; a very few cases of cocaine use appeared first in 1974. The second revision of the national illicit drug laws took place in 1975, and the following years saw a steady rise in the number of notified drug users and drug traffickers. The early 1980s were marked by the Zürich youth revolution, triggered by a public vote on subsidies for the Zürich opera house and subsequent campaigns for an alternative cultural scene, the establishment of an autonomous youth center, and expressions of student solidarity with marginal groups, including drug users. In the early 1980s, the drug scene was infiltrated by the international drug mafia, and after the spread of the open drug scene throughout the city of Zürich, it finally settled in 1986 at the Platzspitz "needle park," which was to become notorious worldwide. At that time, there were an estimated 3,000 heroin users in the Zürich region alone. In the open drug scene, the conditions of the drug users deteriorated rapidly.

The year 1986 was a turning point in drug policy and in the prevention and treatment of drug use. Especially under the threat of HIV/AIDS, drug policy shifted first to a harm reduction approach, with a certain tolerance of open drug scenes. In February 1991, the federal government passed a package of measures to make drug policy more effective. It rested on four pillars ("*Vier-Säulen-Modell*") of equal importance: repression, prevention, treatment, and harm reduction or aid for survival. As to the fourth pillar, in a landmark decision in May 1992, the government authorized pilot prescription programs with a small number of chronic drug users, to be conducted over 3 years and scientifically evaluated. Although this decision sparked a public controversy about the conditions and the scale of these trials and led to a political countermovement, public attention was clearly focused on the dramatic developments around the open drug scenes—which had so far been half-heartedly tolerated—in the larger cities of Zürich and Bern. In the spring of 1992, under public pressure, the tolerance of open drug scenes became exhausted, and the police closed the Zürich Platzspitz (for a more detailed discussion, see Grob, 1993, and Klingemann, 1996) and the Bern Kocherpark. Decentralization of treatment and coercion became the order of the day. Police activities increased again considerably from 1990 to 1994. As a result of this new, strict approach, the number of police arrests for the use of illicit drugs almost tripled, from 12,936 to 32,032 (Bundesamt für Polizeiwesen, 1997). However, this first attempt to eliminate the open drug scene failed; it moved to the Letten site, a closed-down train station in Zürich, and soon became a core group of 250 to 300 heavy users and up to 2,500 "passing clients," much as at the Platzspitz. Under the pressure of increasing violence, gang wars, and public protest, communal and cantonal representatives met with the federal government in August 1994 for the first national drug summit. With the support of a national program organization, a three-stage action plan for closing down the Letten site—avoiding the mistakes made with the Platzspitz—was presented by the end of the year and put into effect in early 1995. The municipal and cantonal police stepped up raids on dealers, the treatment services were decentralized to avoid attracting addicts to the cities of Zürich and Bern, and the federal government approved the extension of the heroin prescription programs (see Klingemann, 1996). During the "post-Letten era," the public/media interest in the (now hidden) drug scenes dropped considerably and shifted to the discussion of the heroin prescription trials and political initiatives (Boller & Coray, 1997, pp. 45, 174). Mainly as a reaction to the public discussion of prescription programs, the "Youth Without Drugs" initiative had been launched in December 1992 by a committee representing mainly right-wing parties and comprising many well-known sportsmen. It was designed to oblige the government to pursue a drug policy based on abstinence only. The proposed changes to the Constitution (Article 68) would further exclude controlled prescription experiments, as well as long-term, low-threshold methadone maintenance programs; end attempts to differentiate between soft and hard drugs; and focus prevention programs on deterrence only.

Another popular initiative, launched in May 1993, was called "For a reasonable drug policy—tabula rasa with the drug mafia"; it came from the opposite side of the political spectrum and proposed the legalization of use of all drugs and a state drug monopoly, like the existing alcohol monopoly for spirits. It proposed the addition to the Constitution of a new article stating that "the consumption, production, possession and purchase of narcotics for individual use only is not prohibited," complemented by provisions for prevention, product information, age limits for drug use, and advertising restrictions (Art. 32 [new] of the Constitution). The initiative, launched by the Association for the Legalization of Drugs (*Droleg*), was backed by the Social Democrats and the Green Party and by numerous health-related organizations, such as the Association of Parents of Drug Dependent Youths. On March 21, 1997, both chambers of parliament recommended the rejection of both popular initiatives and emphasized once again the government's policy of the *four pillars,* formally stated on September 7, 1994. The vote for "Youth Without Drugs" was set for September 28, 1997, and that for the opposing initiative for the end of 1998. The revision of the Federal Law on Narcotics, which had progressed with the submission of a report by the "Schild expert commission" on February 19, 1996, as well as the continuation of the heroin trial programs, were postponed until after the vote. In May 1997, the second national drug report was presented, including for the first time a comprehensive appraisal of public health problems related to tobacco and alcohol as well as to illicit drugs (Müller, Meyer, & Gmel, 1997).

An Overview of Drug Therapy

The developments in inpatient care tend to be heterogeneous and characterized by structural modification and crises in adaptation. Outpatient therapy, on the other hand, follows an upward trend (see Klingemann, 1995, p. 103). The survival assistance projects, as well as the substitution and maintenance programs, are prominent on the policy agenda of the cantons: 16 new cantonal survival assistance projects were reported for 1996 alone, according to a survey of cantonal experts. Also, there are more low-threshold substitution programs offering a variety of substances. Thus, the concept of harm reduction (see Marlatt, 1996, and Uchtenhagen, 1995) has clearly become a more stable element in the general strategy of drug policy and therapy (see Table 8.1).

Means of achieving harm reduction and survival assistance include the distribution of syringes and condoms (see Simmel, 1997, pp. 130, 131), *Gassenzimmer* (public rooms for drug users) with or without injection facilities, easily available basic medical and nutritional care as well as hygiene, and aid in finding employment or housing (Moeckli, 1997).

Inpatient treatment is extremely varied as to type of ownership. Private organizations, covering a wide spectrum of worldviews and ideologies, provide a substantial share of it. Treatment modalities are accordingly varied. However, typical of most therapeutic communities is a 12-month stepwise model that first offers the drug user the protective isolation of the group and then aims at social reintegration.

In the outpatient sector, substitution treatment and its variations, linked to the program of medically prescribed heroin, have been the center of attention. Discussion on inpatient treatment has focused on the falling number of admissions, the closing of centers, and the need to adapt treatment concepts to changing needs. Although certain inpatient subsectors were characterized as areas of expansion in

Table 8.1   Treatment Facilities for Illicit Drug Users (Cantonal Survey 1996 and other estimations)

Inpatient	Cantonal Survey 1996[a]	86 facilities, 997 places
	SIPA Telephone Survey, summer 1996	78 facilities, 1,456 places/late 1995
Outpatient[b]	SAMBAD/Swiss Industry and Business Register for 1994	188 sites categorized as follows: 50 specialized drug counseling agencies 47 addiction counseling agencies 91 multipurpose agencies (including social services)
Survival assistance	Cantonal Survey 1996	116 services offered as follows: 23 "Gassenzimmer" (public rooms for drug users)/care on a day-to day basis (8 cantons) 93 housing and employment projects (13 cantons)
Substitution treatment[c]	Cantonal Survey 1996	10 cantons only with methadone 10 cantons with additional substances (e.g., heroin, codeine; including Bern and Zurich)
	PROVE reports (figures as of July 1996)	19 sites in eight cantons (including Bern and Zurich) with 913 project participants getting the following substances: 800 heroin (IV or smoked) 124 morphine (IV and oral) 50 methadone (IV)

a. The information provided by the cantonal experts for this up-to-date inventory on treatment available was quite incomplete. What was given for the outpatient sector could not be used at all, and for the other sectors, only by supplementing with figures from other sources. Therefore, the information on the canton of Bern for the inpatient sector and survival assistance was supplemented largely by referring to the Index of Facilities for Addiction Assistance (BAG 10/1996), and certain points that were unclear in various reports from the canton of Zurich on the inpatient sector were corrected in a similar manner.
b. The three categories of drug, addiction, and multipurpose counseling agencies comply with the divisions set up in the survey of the institutions as to their names and informal knowledge, if available. *Drug counseling* indicates an orientation toward problems with illicit substances, whereas the more general term *addiction* is used for assistance with problems stemming from psychotropic substances, irrespective of their legal status. Multipurpose agencies include general social services as well as social-psychiatric facilities.
c. The following cantons did not provide any information for the Cantonal Survey: Basel-Land, Freiburg, the Grisons, Jura, Solothurn, and Tessin; the canton of Glarus provided information only on substitution treatment.

1993, and only an adaptation to particular categories of addicts (women, adolescents, foreigners) was deemed necessary, the trend now appears to have turned.

Outpatient Care in Transition: Substitution Programs Put to the Test

Only since 1994 have statistics been compiled on outpatient treatment and care in the alcohol and drug sectors (SAMBAD). A breakdown by institution type reveals that, of the 278 counseling agencies listed in the Swiss Industrial and Business Register in 1993, only 45% specialized solely in illicit drugs (52) or in alcohol (73). The remaining agencies were listed under addiction agencies (52) and agencies offering multiple services, including general social services, polyclinics, and outpatient psychiatric services (94). According to the April 1994

Institution Survey, the drug counseling agencies have a more medical and inter-disciplinary orientation than do their counterparts in the alcohol sector; the addic-tion and alcohol counseling agencies are strongly oriented toward social work (Voll & Gauthier, 1997, p. 9).

The treatment network for approximately 30,000 drug users, compared with the counseling and care services available to more than eight times that number of alcohol dependents, is disproportionately well developed and differentiated: The specialized alcohol-counseling agencies outnumber the drug-counseling agencies by only 21 (73 vs. 52)! As to the variety of therapies offered, there is increasing evidence of a development toward an integrated counseling system and an inte-grated perception of addiction (see also chapter 3 by Bergmark in this book).

Methadone Treatment: Switzerland as the International Forerunner

Although substitute treatment with methadone was already available in Switzer-land in the early 1970s (see the historical overview by Eichenberger, 1997), only since 1987 has there been a sharp increase in its use—from 1,804 in 1987 to about 14,000 in 1994 (Swiss Federal Office of Public Health & Addiction Research Foundation, 1996, p. 48). With 2,000 methadone patients per million residents, Switzerland (followed by Hong Kong, with 1,818 per million) tops the list of a 24-country survey by Health Canada in 1995, with respect to not only the numbers treated but also the progressive deregulation of the distribution of methadone in 1995 (Methadone World Watch, 1997, p. 5). The United States, where large-scale methadone programs were introduced in the 1970s, trails far behind, with 441 patients per million residents. At the same time, the methadone population has also increased in all countries. In most, methadone treatment is contingent on such conditions as urine tests, authorizing procedures, central registration, fixed dos-ages, and limited take-home quantities. In Switzerland, however, it has become easier to obtain methadone treatment, and the objective of achieving opiate abstinence is being pursued more flexibly. Since the 1970s, the treatment policy indications have undergone changes ranging from "liberal/regulation-free" to "restrictive/application of strict indications" to the present "liberal/individualized indications." The changes can be attributed to the high incidence of HIV/AIDS and the practice of harm reduction since the mid-1980s.

Before the revision of the narcotics law (Betäubungsmittelgesetzes BetmG) in 1975, medical practitioners were given free rein as to what they prescribed. In view of the rising number of heroin users, the revised law introduced tighter controls on methadone treatment administered by the cantons. It could be prescribed only by a physician authorized by a cantonal agency and was subjected to numerous restrictions. It was designed to achieve abstinence from opiates within 2 or 3 years. Faced with the increase in HIV infection and with the open drug scene, many of the affected cantons adopted a more flexible policy on methadone treatment. Regulations were relaxed in the late 1980s in the large cantons of Zürich, Bern, and Basel, and the number of patients increased (see Bardeleben, Stohler, Petitjean, &

Ladewig, 1994; Olgiati, Dobler-Mikola, & Uchtenhagen, 1994); most of the other cantons then followed this policy (Klingemann, 1997, pp. 107, 108). New regulations of the compulsory health insurance, which came into effect in January 1997, modified the conditions for obtaining treatment: They reduced the minimum age from 20 to 18 years and abolished the need to prove that the dosage had been reduced or that other therapeutic efforts had failed. At present, it is sufficient to have been dependent on an opiate for at least a year and to have a medical certificate that attests to the unlikelihood of successful withdrawal or detoxification (Krankenpflege-Leistungsverordnung, KLV, 1996, p. 25).

The Swiss Program for the
Medical Prescription of Narcotics

Background and Objectives

Regional experiments in England, such as the programs of the Cheltenham drug service and the Widnes clinic, directed by Dr. John Marks, who began with heroin prescription in 1988 (see MacGregor and Smith in this volume), strongly influenced the debate in Switzerland at the time, when even unconventional measures to combat the increasing incidence of AIDS became acceptable. By a landmark decision of the federal government in 1992, the medical prescription of narcotics other than methadone was authorized as a component of its comprehensive package of measures to reduce drug problems; this is probably the most prominent feature of the national drug strategy. Discussions followed on specific drugs and numbers of subjects. At first, only morphine and not heroin was to be prescribed, and only for a very few subjects. After a controversial debate, the government compromised, offering those in favor of large programs at least extended pilot projects, with up to 700 subjects. These trials were set up to gain experience with the prescription of buprenorphin, morphine, and intravenous methadone and heroin. They had to be reviewed and approved by the National Ethics Committee of the Swiss Academy of Medical Sciences. They were designed to study the proposed treatment as a first step on the way to abstinence from drugs, to improve the addicts' physical and psychological health and their social integration, and to foster their sense of responsibility when faced with the risk of HIV infection.

The trials of medical prescription of narcotics are, above all, an attempt to reach those addicts not reached satisfactorily by conventional treatment programs. They draw upon experience gained with methadone treatment programs as well as other experiments with the prescription of narcotics.

The pilot projects were to be carried out under medical supervision, and strict criteria were established for the admission of participants. They had to be at least 20 years old and addicted to heroin for at least 2 years; in addition, two attempts at treatment had to have failed, and besides social problems there had to be visible damage to their health. Because participation was voluntary, subjects had to sign a consent form in advance. The first projects were launched in the city of Zürich at the beginning of 1994. In all, seven projects with 361 participants were carried out as the first trial series in 1994. Approval was then granted to increase the number of participants from 750 to 1,000 (with 800 heroin addicts at most), and adjustments were made to the experimental conditions and the assignment of participants to the study groups because of unfavorable experiences with intravenous morphine and methadone. In 1995, eight projects were added as a second trial series (502 participants). A day count on July 1, 1996, showed that 913 subjects were being treated and that 1,139 had been registered since the trial had begun at 18 sites in 15 Swiss cities.

Results

The Swiss Federal Office of Public Health commissioned a scientific analysis or process evaluation of these trials. They ended officially on January 1, 1997; new patients were no longer admitted, and transitional regulations for those remaining in the trials were adopted. The process evaluation is being carried out by a research team of the Institute of Social and Preventive Medicine at the University of Zürich. The results of the clinical trials, strictly limited to 3 years (1994-1996), were presented in two interim reports (1995, 1996) and a final report in July 1997. The conclusions, based on the evaluation of data of 1,146 participants from 18 sites (including one prison), are mainly positive. The final report concludes that "a continuation of the restrictive heroin maintenance treatment for the target group as defined can be recommended. Further, it should be carried out in duly equipped and controlled polyclinics, which comply with the stipulated general program conditions" (Uchtenhagen, 1997b, p. 12). The complex analyses of the 6-, 12-, and 18-month trials that underpin this general recommendation can be summarized here only briefly (for a detailed overview and discussion of the initial trial phase, see Keller, 1995).

The first interim report of the research team (Uchtenhagen, Gutzwiller, Dobler-Mikola, & Blättler, 1995; see also Uchtenhagen, Gutzwiller, & Dobler-Mikola, 1996a) evaluated the progress of 366 participants in seven projects over a 6-month observation period (1994/1995). The projects had been designed above all to reach seriously affected, long-term drug users. This was fully achieved. Participants, on average, were 30 years of age and had been addicted to heroin for 10 years, 82% had been unemployed, 86% had been sentenced in a penal court, and the majority had had both inpatient and outpatient treatment. The success of the program in this group was remarkable: 82% stayed in treatment at least 6 months, a finding that contrasts positively with the drop-out rates of other forms of treatment. It should be noted that 49% of those who did drop out switched to other treatment modalities. Of the 366 subjects who entered the program in 1994, 259 remained at least 6 months and were then interviewed a second time. Their social living conditions had improved in such areas as unemployment, homelessness, and delinquency. Many had been able to sever ties with the drug scene and become resocialized.

The second interim report (Uchtenhagen, Gutzwiller, & Dobler-Mikola, 1996b), based on 206 interviews covering the first 12 months of treatment and conducted between the 12th and 15th months of treatment with entrants from 1994, supported and largely supplemented the initial findings.

Finally, an analysis of the discharges and treatment transfers during the first year of treatment (104 in the reference year 1994) showed that they consisted mostly of individuals in poor health who were HIV positive or had a long-standing career of heroin use. Participants with shorter drug careers and fewer contacts with the drug scene, and who were less well integrated in the workforce, tended to stay in the program; 54% of those discharged changed to a different treatment program (9% abstinence oriented, and 45% methadone substitution).

In the final report in July 1997, the cohort analysis of 237 participants, who had remained in the trials at least 18 months, provided the following portrait: Their illicit use of heroin and cocaine had decreased significantly, their physical and psychological state had improved, and they had become more stable socially, as indicated by a rise in steady employment from 14% to 32% and a fall in unemployment from 44% to 20%. Their involvement with the drug scene and their use of illegal or semilegal activities, such as prostitution, to obtain money had decreased markedly (Uchtenhagen, 1997a, pp. 74-82). The retention rate, 69% (for the 18-month trial), was high in comparison with that of conventional treatment programs, and as against 89% for the 6-month trial (Uchtenhagen, 1997a, p. 58). The mortality rate among the participants was 1% (Uchtenhagen, 1997a, p. 90), which is lower than that of untreated drug users. The economic benefit of heroin maintenance treatment is considerable, particularly because of fewer criminal prosecutions and prison sentences and consequent less expense, and because of less need of medical treatment (Uchtenhagen, 1997a, pp. 114-117).

Results related to the project organization revealed that the second series of trials had fewer difficulties than the first, that neighborhood disturbances seldom occurred, that it was possible to solve security problems, and that precautions for patients with high consumption of other drugs proved effective in preventing fatalities from overdose. As to the substances tested, morphine and methadone injection and heroin cigarettes proved of limited use; because heroin has few side effects, it has proved the most suitable substance for medical prescription. In short, the feasibility of such programs has been demonstrated (Uchtenhagen, 1997a, pp. 9, 10).

Discussion

In the emotional debate and with a tight political schedule, the extremely high expectations from the project evaluation could not be fully met. The observation period was too short to predict the future development of the treatment cohorts. Besides, whether these trials are more efficient than other treatment programs is not yet clear and needs further investigation. Keller (1995, pp. 34, 35) points out that more data are needed on participants' treatment preferences in order to determine whether there was a bias in the selection of the trial participants. At the same time, he rightly warns against a naive empiricism, pointing out that political and ethical considerations will be crucial when a final decision is made on the conditions under which programs may be established and possibly extended.

Inpatient Drug Therapy: Current Trends
in Development—Continued Pressure to Adapt

With the increasing acceptance of the concept of harm reduction and the increase in outpatient counseling agencies—in particular, for various forms of low-threshold survival assistance—inpatient drug treatment experienced a crisis in the late 1980s: There was a sharp reduction in the number of occupied beds, and certain groups of addicts, including HIV-positive drug users, clearly found inpatient treatment unattractive (Kurz, 1990). Nevertheless, between 1989 and 1993, services expanded again, and numerous new facilities were opened. Figures from the canton of Zürich showed an increase of 67% in long-term treatment and 51% in detoxification patients (see Direktion des Gesundheitswesens des Kantons Zürich, 1992). This cantonal trend was reflected also in the first national survey on the state of inpatient detoxification and inpatient drug rehabilitation ("REHA2000"). A count on a fixed day in May 1993 in 131 facilities showed a high degree of capacity utilization; in particular, inpatient detoxification was found to be an expanding area, available places having increased by about 70% in 5 years, and half of the new facilities having opened between 1988 and 1993 (Mühle, 1994, pp. 14, 16). More treatment slots were called for, as well as a better match between patients and types of treatment. On October 4, 1994, the Federal Parliament drew consequences from the REHA2000 study and announced emergency measures to expand both the quality and quantity of inpatient care, improve national collaboration and coordination of treatment offered, reconsider the modalities for financing treatment, and improve monitoring. Since then, however, there have been increasing indications of a reversal of the trend in the inpatient sector. Professional circles have been speculating that the demand for treatment slots was indeed falling and that in some places, only 50% to 70% of capacity was being used. The Swiss Institute for the Prevention of Alcoholism and Other Drug Problems (SIPA) carried out a national telephone survey between June and September 1996 on this topic, in which 78 facilities (i.e., 94% of the 83 facilities contacted) in 19 of the 26 cantons took part. The information on admissions and the capacity of the facilities for the years 1993, 1994, and 1995 indicated a relatively stable situation, contrary to expectations. The absolute total of admissions had even increased from 1,538 (1993) to 1,914 (1994) to 2,017 (1995). However, this trend, at least for 1993 to 1994, can be partially attributed to missing data or differences in numbers of facilities reporting data for a given year.

After 1993, the annual average capacity reported for inpatient treatment fell slightly for the surveyed facilities on the whole, from 88% to 83% (1995); in the urban canton of Zürich, with a particularly high number of treatment slots (see above), the trend was somewhat stronger: In 1995, average occupancy fell to only 77% from 83% in previous years; five facilities reported annual average occupancy rates of only 30% to 67%. Nevertheless, this picture does not apply across the board. Although 11 facilities cut down on personnel, 19 showed an increase in 1995. The first results of the government's emergency measures in favor of the inpatient sector are apparent here.

In view of a relatively stable supply of treatment on the whole, it would be incorrect to speak of a general collapse in the demand for inpatient treatment for the period 1993 to 1996. Possibly only certain subsectors of the inpatient sector are under pressure to adapt. To what extent facilities offering abstinence-oriented, long-term treatment, or private or public treatment facilities, have been affected must still be examined more carefully. In general, however, there are indications that the inpatient sector is being gradually downsized and structurally modified. The following section analyses this process as reflected in the opinions of treatment professionals.

The Assessment of Treatment Needs and Necessary Changes by Cantonal Policymakers and Treatment Professionals

The 1996 Cantonal Survey provides important clues pertaining to cantonal willingness to increase expenditure on drug treatment. Economic considerations are increasingly influencing the setting of priorities for treatment. Above all, the cantons stress the need to expand survival assistance, particularly to the employment sector; in times of growing unemployment among young adults, this means the creation or maintenance of protected and steady jobs, even for those not willing to become abstinent (according to information from nine cantons). Seven cantons not only have discovered gaps in early detection but also stress the need for differentiated and targeted expansion in the inpatient sector. As to the latter point, a desire has been expressed for more flexible duration of treatment, better adapted to various target groups (double diagnoses, women, youth, foreigners, etc.). The complementary measures mentioned by a few cantons are signs of the "new public management." They are aimed at increased coordination and networking of facilities, more cantonal guidance and concentration of facilities, a simplification of the ownership structures and regionalization, the introduction of financial controlling, and improved collaboration between the licit and illicit drug sectors.

The above-mentioned SIPA telephone survey in 1996—1 year before the popular initiative on "Youth Without Drugs"—found that almost half of the inpatient facilities are concerned about increasing financial problems and cost pressures, and they expect drug policy to affect their work increasingly.

One fourth of all the problems foreseen for the future involve pessimistic speculations about treatment motivation on the part of prospective clients and an expected fall in occupancy rates. Consequently, 29 facilities (37%) plan conceptual changes: More specifically, this means more flexible duration of treatment, and treatment adapted more to the individual patient. This follows changes observed in patient profiles on the part of 40% of the facilities. It is noteworthy that 13 of these 31 facilities mention problems with double diagnoses—an increase in patients with serious mental disorders in addition to addiction. This has become a relevant topic, particularly in psychiatry and addiction research (e.g., Moggi et al., 1996; Verheul, Brink, & Hartgers, 1995).

On the whole, there is remarkable consensus between cantonal public health policymakers and inpatient treatment professionals about the assessment of the situation (although not necessarily about possible solutions), possibly because a broad array of specialists was consulted on establishing standards of quality of care. Although this consultation was motivated by financial policy interests, it also fostered value clarification and an exchange among administrators, managers, and treatment specialists.

Future Perspectives

The unexpectedly high vote against the popular initiative on "Youth Without Drugs" on September 28, 1997, by 70.6% of the voters (voter participation, 40.1%) and by all cantons has paved the way for a more stable and predictable future course in both drug policy and the development of the treatment system. This result strongly endorsed the federal government's four-pillar policy. What this means for the drug treatment system is that especially the fourth pillar, the application of the harm reduction principle, including the medical prescription of heroin, is politically secure. What has been excluded at the same time is a costly expansion of the inpatient sector to accommodate forced withdrawals, an exclusive fixation on abstinence as the goal of treatment, a significant reduction of needle distribution programs as part of AIDS prevention, and the reintroduction of severe restrictions on methadone treatment. The way has been cleared for a further harmonization of legal, organizational, and political efforts, which had been blocked pending the popular initiative.

The director of the Swiss Federal Office of Public Health announced in the summer of 1997 that if the popular initiative on "Youth Without Drugs" were rejected, he would propose to the federal government the continuation of the prescription of heroin as a complementary form of treatment, maintaining the prevailing strict conditions and considered as "a last-chance therapy." Between 2,000 and 3,000 hard-core addicts could benefit if they were willing to comply with the restrictive conditions of the program (*Neue Zürcher Zeitung*, 1997, p. 13). This would obviously be linked to a revision of the narcotics laws, as the Schild Commission proposed in 1996, which, as expected, would extensively legalize drug use and introduce severe measures against the drug trade (see Bundesamt für Gesundheitswesen, 1996; Fahrenkrug, 1997, pp. 201, 202).

At the same time, the basic principles underlying the package of measures on drug policy, which have proven successful over the past 6 years, are being maintained.

In the treatment sector, the orientation toward promotion of pilot projects and coordination-information/documentation will be continued. Examples are an Internet treatment slot market and the collection of statistics on addiction (see

Gervasoni et al., 1996, p. 44). The pressure for quality control in both public and private addiction services is very likely to increase.

At the political level, only a national coordination of preventive, therapeutic, and repressive measures—together with the setting aside of federal sensitivities and differences of opinion on drug policy—made it possible to get rid of the open drug scene for good. This success must have influenced voter decisions ultimately.

Cooperation on a national level has been promoted by national conferences on drugs (1995) and the creation in April 1996 of the interministerial "Coordination and Service Platform Switzerland," which includes the National Drug Board (Nationalen Drogenausschusses), with six members each from the federation, the cantons, and the municipalities (see Figure 8.1).

It should be noted that the initially critical French-speaking areas were also included (indicative was the participation of Geneva and Fribourg cantons in the heroin prescription programs).

These efforts toward national concerted action can be perceived as falling back on the tried and tested "Helvetian (Swiss) concept" of achieving a gradual, encompassing balance of interests. They have been the key to the progress made in drug policy and in the coherent and needs-oriented organization of the treatment system. Therefore, the international interest in Switzerland as a special case on drug policy is hardly surprising: This *Sonderfall* was put to the test under the particularly complicated conditions of a political culture characterized by a federal democracy of consensus, and under much pressure to find a solution to the drug problem. A literally clean, low-cost, and medically controlled approach to drug problems, rendering them invisible to the public, is surely secondary in the view of those in charge of the heroin prescription programs. However, such a response to the drug problem may not so much reflect Swiss keenness to experiment as it appeals to latent Swiss conservative values.

Finally, despite the progress in consolidation, a prognosis of the development of the Swiss drug treatment system has to take account of the uncertainty factors that are already emerging. First, the vote is still to be held on the legalization initiative (*Droleg*) pending, planned for late 1998. Its approval would mean a broad expansion of the heroin prescription programs and the establishment of a state drug monopoly. Second, there is the revision of the narcotics laws (see overview in the first part of this chapter), on which the political debate issue is still open. Moreover, such a revision could be opposed by political groups launching a popular referendum against it, thus allowing the proponents of "Youth Without Drugs" to resume their campaign for a drug-free society from a new angle.

Finally, the international influence exerted on the national drug policy should not be underestimated, particularly that of the United Nations Narcotics Control Board, which has already expressed some criticism of Swiss policies (International Narcotics Control Board, 1997, p. 57, no. 320). The WHO international expert report on the Swiss prescription trials, expected in 1998, and the Swiss position on the ratification of the UN 1988 Convention Against Illicit Traffic in Narcotic Drugs and Psychotropic Substances (which will first be decided after the vote on the *Droleg* initiative, scheduled for 1998), may play a role at the supranational level

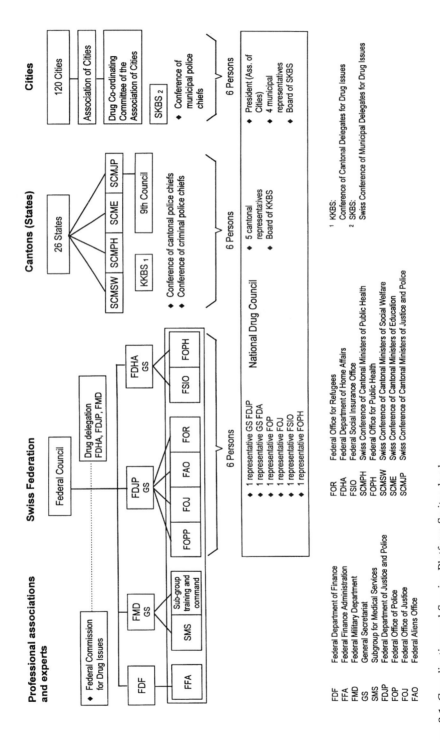

Figure 8.1 Coordination and Service Platform Switzerland

as well. Ultimately, the extent to which Switzerland moves closer to, or joins, the European Union may restrict its room for maneuver on drug policy.

References

Bardeleben, U. V., Stohler, R., Petitjean, S., & Ladewig, D. (1994). Substitutionsbehandlungen mit Methadon in Basel-Stadt [Substitution treatment with methadone in Basel-Stadt]. In D. Ladewig (Ed.), *Drogen und Alkohol* [Drugs and alcohol] (Vol. 7, pp. 55-72). Lausanne: ISPA Press.

Boller, B., & Coray, R. (1997). Der Drogendiskurs der Schweizer Presse. Dreijahresbericht 1993-1995 [The discourse on drugs in the Swiss press. A three-year report 1993-1995]. *Cahiers de recherches et de documentation—Institut universitaire de médecine sociale et préventive, 111*(9).

Bundesamt für Gesundheitswesen. (1996). *Bericht der Expertenkommission für die Revision des Betäubungsmittelgesetzes vom 3. Oktober 1951* [Report of the specialist commission on the revision of the Narcotics Law, 3rd October 1951]. Bern: Author.

Bundesamt für Polizeiwesen. (1997). *Schweizerische Betäubungsmittelstatistik 1996* [Swiss federal statistics on narcotics 1996]. Bern: Author.

Bundesamt für Statistik. (1994). *Statistisches Jahrbuch der Schweiz 1995* [Swiss statistical yearbook 1995]. Zürich: Verlag Neue Zürcher Zeitung.

Bundesamt für Statistik. (1996). *Statistisches Jahrbuch der Schweiz 1997* [Swiss statistical yearbook 1997]. Zürich: Verlag Neue Zürcher Zeitung.

Clinard, M. B. (1978). *Cities with little crime: The case of Switzerland.* Cambridge, UK: Cambridge University Press.

Direktion des Gesundheitswesens des Kantons Zürich. (1992). *Lagebericht und Gesamtkonzept für Massnahmen im Bereich des Suchtmittelkonsums* [Report on the current situation in the area of drug use and presentation of a package of measures]. Zürich: Kantonale Kommission für Drogenfragen.

Eichenberger, G. (1997). Méthadone: De l'histoire des traitements aux enjeux éthiques [Methadone: The history of treatment and ethical issues]. *Dépendances, 1,* 8-16.

European Centre for the Epidemiological Monitoring of AIDS. (1995). *AIDS surveillance in Europe* (Quarterly report 47, 30). Saint-Maurice cedex, France: Author.

Fahrenkrug, H. (1997). Politik—Illegale Drogen [Policy—Illicit drugs]. In R. Müller, M. Meyer, & G. Gmel (Eds.), *Alkohol, Tabak und illegale Drogen in der Schweiz 1994-1996* [Alcohol, tobacco and illicit drugs in Switzerland 1994-1996] (pp. 194-203). Lausanne: Schweizerische Fachstelle für Alkohol- und andere Drogenprobleme.

Gebhardt, M. (1996). *Aids und HIV in der Schweiz. Epidemiologische Situation Ende 1995* [AIDS and HIV in Switzerland. The epidemiological situation at the end of 1995]. Bern: Bundesamt für Gesundheit.

Gervasoni, J.-P., Dubois-Arber, F., Benninghoff, F., Spencer, B., Devos, T., & Paccaud, F. (1996). *Evaluation der Massnahmen des Bundes zur Verminderung der Drogenprobleme. Zweiter zusammenfassender Bericht 1990-1996. Kurzfassung* [An evaluation of the federal measures to reduce drug problems. Second summary report 1990-1996. Short version]. Lausanne: Institut universitaire de médecine sociale et préventive.

Gmel, G. (1997b). Abhängigkeit [Dependence]. In R. Müller, M. Meyer, & G. Gmel (Eds.), *Alkohol, Tabak und illegale Drogen in der Schweiz 1994-1996* [Alcohol, tobacco, and illicit drugs in Switzerland 1994-1996] (pp. 49-57). Lausanne: Schweizerische Fachstelle für Alkohol- und andere Drogenprobleme.

Gmel, G. (1997a). Konsum—Illegale Drogen [Consumption—illicit drugs]. In R. Müller, M. Meyer, & G. Gmel (Eds.), *Alkohol, Tabak und illegale Drogen in der Schweiz 1994-1996* [Alcohol, tobacco, and illicit drugs in Switzerland 1994-1996] (pp. 36-48). Lausanne: Schweizerische Fachstelle für Alkohol- und andere Drogenprobleme.

Grob, P. J. (1993). The needle park in Zürich: The story and the lessons to be learned. *European Journal on Criminal Policy and Research, 1,* 48-61.

Harkin, A. M., Anderson, P., & Goos, C. (1997). *Smoking, drinking and drug taking in the European region.* Copenhagen: Alcohol, Drugs and Tobacco Programme, WHO Regional Office for Europe.

International Narcotics Control Board. (1997). *Report of the International Narcotics Control Board for 1996.* New York: United Nations.

Keller, R. (1995). Diversifizierte Drogenabgabe. Erfahrungen im Ausland und Pilotversuche in der Schweiz [Diversified drug distribution. Experience abroad and pilot trials in Switzerland]. *Kriminologisches Bulletin, 1,* 7-45.

Killias, M. (1990). Gun ownership and violent crime: The Swiss experience in international perspective. *Security Journal, 1,* 169-174.

Klingemann, H. (1995). Therapie und Betreuung [Therapy and care]. In Schweizerische Fachstelle für Alkohol- und andere Drogenprobleme (Ed.), *Illegale Drogen in der Schweiz 1990-1993. Die Situation in den Kantonen und der Schweiz* [Illicit drugs in Switzerland 1990-1993. The situation in the cantons and in Switzerland] (pp. 91-138). Zürich: Seismo Verlag.

Klingemann, H. (1996). Drug treatment in Switzerland: Harm reduction, decentralization and community response. *Addiction, 91,* 723-736.

Klingemann, H. (1997). Illegale Drogen [Illicit drugs]. In R. Müller, M. Meyer, & G. Gmel (Eds.), *Alkohol, Tabak und illegale Drogen in der Schweiz 1994-1996* [Alcohol, tobacco and illicit drugs in Switzerland 1994-1996] (pp. 103-123). Lausanne: Schweizerische Fachstelle für Alkohol- und andere Drogenprobleme.

Krankenpflege-Leistungsverordnung, KLV. (1996). *Verordnung über Leistungen in der obligatorischen Krankenpflegeversicherung. Änderung vom 13. Dezember 1996.* [Decree concerning the provisions for mandatory health insurance. Legal revision nof 13 December 1996.] Bern: Swiss Federal Office of the Interior.

Kurz, T. (1990). Die stationären Drogentherapien im Frühjahr 1989 [Inpatient drug therapies in spring, 1989]. *Drogalkohol, 2,* 132-139.

Marlatt, G. A. (1996). Harm reduction: Come as you are. *Addictive Behaviors, 21,* 779-788.

Methadone World Watch. (1997). Survey reports on MMT trends. *Forum, 6*(2), 5, 8.

Meyer, M., & Gmel, G. (1997). Konsum—Tabak [Consumption—tobacco]. In R. Müller, M. Meyer, & G. Gmel (Eds.), *Alkohol, Tabak und illegale Drogen in der Schweiz 1994-1996* [Alcohol, tobacco and illicit drugs in Switzerland 1994-1996] (pp. 30-35). Lausanne: Schweizerische Fachstelle für Alkohol- und andere Drogenprobleme.

Moeckli, C. (1997). Arbeit und Wohnen [Work and housing]. In R. Müller, M. Meyer, & G. Gmel (Eds.), *Alkohol, Tabak und illegale Drogen in der Schweiz 1994-1996* [Alcohol, tobacco and illicit drugs in Switzerland 1994-1996] (pp. 124-128). Lausanne: Schweizerische Fachstelle für Alkohol- und andere Drogenprobleme.

Moggi, F., Hirsbrunner, H.-P., Wittig, R., Donati, R., Brodbeck, J., & Bachmann, K. M. (1996). Stationäre Behandlung von Patienten mit Doppeldiagnosen [Inpatient treatment of patients with double diagnoses]. *Verhaltenstherapie, 6,* 201-209.

Mühle, U. (1994). *REHA 2000—Gesamtschweizerische Planungsgrundlagen für die Weiterentwicklung der stationären Drogentherapie* [Foundations for the planning and development of inpatient drug therapy in Switzerland]. Im Auftrag des Bundesamtes für Gesundheitswesen. Urs Mühle Fachstelle für Sozialarbeit im Gesundheitswesen.

Müller, R., Meyer, M., & Gmel, G. (Eds.). (1997). *Alkohol, Tabak und illegale Drogen in der Schweiz 1994-1996* [Alcohol, tobacco and illicit drugs in Switzerland 1994-1996]. Lausanne: Schweizerische Fachstelle für Alkohol- und andere Drogenprobleme.

Neue Zürcher Zeitung. (1997, 11 July). Heroinabgabe als therapeutische Ergänzung. Positive Erfahrungen mit der ärztlichen Verschreibung [Heroin distribution as a therapeutic supplement. Positive experiences with medical prescription], *158,* p. 13.

Office fédéral de la santé publique. (1996). Sida information [AIDS information]. *Bulletin, 12,* 5.

Olgiati, M., Dobler-Mikola, A., & Uchtenhagen, A. (1994). Die methadonunterstützte Behandlung im Kanton Zürich [Methadone-supported treatment in the canton of Zürich]. In D. Ladewig (Ed.), *Drogen und Alkohol* [Drugs and alcohol] (Vol. 7, pp. 73-103). Lausanne: ISPA Press.

Produktschaap voor Gedistilleerde Dranken. (1996). *World drink trends 1996: International beverage consumption and production trends.* Guildford/King's Lynn, UK: Biddles Ltd.

Schweizerische Fachstelle für Alkohol- und andere Drogenprobleme. (1997). *Zahlen und Fakten zu Alkohol und anderen Drogen* [Facts and figures on alcohol and other drugs]. Lausanne: Author.

Simmel, U. (1997). Schadensbegrenzung/Schadensverminde [Harm reduction]. In R. Müller, M. Meyer, & G. Gmel (Eds.), *Alkohol, Tabak und illegale Drogen in der Schweiz 1994-1996* [Alcohol, tobacco, and illicit drugs in Switzerland 1994-1996] (pp. 129-131). Lausanne: Schweizerische Fachstelle für Alkohol- und andere Drogenprobleme.

Swiss Federal Office of Public Health & Addiction Research Foundation. (1996). *Swiss methadone report: Narcotic substitution in the treatment of heroin addicts in Switzerland.* Bern/Toronto: Author.

Tecklenburg, U. (1986). The present-day alcohol treatment system in Switzerland: A historical perspective. *Contemporary Drug Problems, 13,* 555-583.

Tschäni, H. (1983). *Wer regiert die Schweiz?—Der Einfluss von Lobby und Verbänden* [Who governs Switzerland?—The influence of lobbies and associations]. Zürich: Orell Füssli Verlag.

Uchtenhagen, A. (1995). Harm reduction: The case of Switzerland. *European Addiction Research, 1*(3), 86-91.

Uchtenhagen, A. (1997a). Synthesebericht [Summary report]. *Versuche für eine ärztliche Verschreibung von Betäubungsmitteln. Abschlussbericht der Forschungsbeauftragten* [Trials of medically prescribed narcotics. Final report of the research team]. Zürich: Institut für Suchtforschung/Institut für Sozial- und Präventivmedizin der Universität.

Uchtenhagen, A. (1997b). Zusammenfassung des Syntheseberichts [Short version of the summary report]. *Versuche für eine ärztliche Verschreibung von Betäubungsmitteln. Abschlussbericht der Forschungsbeauftragten* [Trials of medically prescribed narcotics. Final report of the research team]. Zürich: Institut für Suchtforschung/Institut für Sozial- und Präventivmedizin der Universität.

Uchtenhagen, A., Gutzwiller, F., & Dobler-Mikola, A. (1996a). Medical prescription of narcotics. Background and intermediate results of a Swiss National Project. *European Addiction Research, 2,* 201-207.

Uchtenhagen, A., Gutzwiller, F., & Dobler-Mikola, A. (1996b). *Versuche für eine ärztliche Verschreibung von Betäubungsmitteln. Zweiter Zwischenbericht der Forschungsbeauftragten* [Trials of medically prescribed narcotics. Second interim report of the research team]. Zürich: Institut für Suchtforschung/Institut für Sozial- und Präventivmedizin der Universität.

Uchtenhagen, A., Gutzwiller, F., Dobler-Mikola, A., & Blättler, R. (1995). *Versuche für eine ärztliche Verschreibung von Betäubungsmitteln. Zwischenbericht der Forschungsbeauftragten* [Trials of medically prescribed narcotics. Interim report of the research team]. Zürich: Institut für Suchtforschung/Institut für Sozial- und Präventivmedizin der Universität.

United Nations Office—Crime Prevention and Criminal Justice Division. (1997, April 27). *United Nations International Survey on Firearms Regulations (UNSFR).* Draft version presented in Vienna.

Verheul, R., Brink, W. v.d., & Hartgers, C. (1995). Prevalence of personality disorders among alcoholics and drug addicts: An overview. *European Addiction Research, 1*(4), 166-177.

Voll, P., & Gauthier, J. A. (1997). *Ambulante Suchtberatung 1994. Statistik der ambulanten Behandlung und Betreuung im Alkohol- und Drogenbereich (SAMBAD). Pilotbericht zu den Ergebnissen des 1. Halbjahres* [Outpatient addiction counselling 1994. Statistics on outpatient treatment and care for alcohol and drugs (SAMBAD). Pilot report on the results for the first six months]. Lausanne: Schweizerische Fachstelle für Alkohol- und andere Drogenprobleme.

World Health Organization. (in press). *World health statistics annual 1995.* Geneva: Author.

Chapter 9

Tailoring Drug Treatment to Changing Times

Gabriele Bammer

Comment on Part 2

D rug treatment and other harm reduction strategies often seem to sit uncomfortably within the prohibitionist approach to psychoactive drug use. To a greater extent than prevention and law enforcement, changes to or innovations in drug treatment tend to be subject to heated debate. Furthermore, the efficacy of drug treatment, particularly methadone maintenance treatment, is continually subject to scrutiny. This is not to disparage the need for evaluation; indeed, it could be argued that a comparable emphasis on evaluation is needed for prevention and law enforcement activities. The challenge is to institute drug treatment and broader policy where evidence of effectiveness carries more weight than does politics.

Evaluation is a political as well as a scientific activity. On the one hand, the act of evaluation can give an activity recognition and legitimacy. This is particularly the case when the activity is new or on the fringes of political acceptability; the evaluators are a well-respected research organization; and there is an independent, particularly public, source of funding. New and fringe activities welcome evaluation for this very reason, and denying an activity an independent evaluation can condemn it. On the other hand, with entrenched activities, suggesting that evaluation is needed can be a signal that the activity is falling out of favor and that funding cuts will be instituted. The high political and community acceptance of law enforcement and prevention as a public good most probably explain the lack of evaluation of these activities, even though expenditure on them is high and effectiveness could undoubtedly be increased.

Politically, the act of evaluation is often more important than the results of the evaluation. For the new or fringe activity, the fact that an independent and respectable evaluation is occurring can be used to expand, gather support for, and entrench the activity. Then, even negative results can be written off by saying that during the time of the evaluation, the activity has markedly changed (which may or may not be true). For an entrenched activity, the signal that it is falling out of favor may activate opponents, who can successfully mobilize against the activity. At that point, a positive evaluation may be too late to save it.

The current scrutiny of drug treatment, particularly methadone maintenance treatment, suggests that the supporting and opposing forces are both strong. In the case of methadone maintenance treatment, the main opponents are those favoring treatment that emphasizes abstinence rather than stabilization.

The three chapters in this section focus on countries that have sought to improve drug treatment even if this has gone against world trends and international political pressures.

The Netherlands has a long history of innovative approaches to drug treatment and drug policy generally and has recently been joined by Switzerland, which has embarked on an ambitious series of trials of a range of new treatment options. England stands out not so much for its innovation but for continuing an approach that emphasizes clinical freedom, especially in the prescription of substitution therapies and the continued availability of the medical use of psychoactive drugs banned in other countries. An example of the latter is the availability of diacetylmorphine (pharmaceutical heroin) for the treatment of chronic pain. Australia could also be added to these three experimental countries.

Although political forces certainly operate in each of these countries, it can be argued that they provide models of how to meet the challenge of giving increased weight to evidence of effectiveness and to rationality. Two examples illustrate this point. The first is how the countries respond when desired outcomes are not achieved or when there are unexpected negative consequences. There is not a return to the status quo; instead, lessons are learned, and the negative consequences are used to develop modified or different approaches. Examples include the Dutch and Swiss reactions to the formation of open drug scenes and to the immigration of dependent users from surrounding countries, as well as the Dutch responses to problems arising from the toleration of heroin house dealers and heroin cafes.

The second example relates to the prescription of diacetylmorphine to dependent heroin users. As indicated earlier, England stands out for never having prevented such prescription. The Swiss trials of diacetylmorphine prescription from 1994 to 1996 illustrate the science as well as the politics of evaluation. Ironically, the releasing of interim results by the Swiss has been criticized as politically motivated, but this has, in fact, kept outcomes in high profile. In addition, both successes and failures have been even-handedly reported. The proposals for trials in the Netherlands and Australia also emphasize evaluation of outcomes.

The prescription of diacetylmorphine in England also illustrates some of the points about the politics of evaluation made earlier. Despite the fact that there has been prescription of diacetylmorphine to dependent users for more than 30 years, there is little evidence concerning its efficacy because there has been little independent evaluation. Diacetylmorphine prescription has been a fringe activity since the early 1970s, and the lack of evaluation may well have contributed to its marginalization. It is noteworthy that the reasons for the move of diacetylmorphine prescribing from a mainstream to a fringe activity are highly contested. It is clear, however, that restrictions on the ability to prescribe, and the policy and funding changes that curtailed the practice, were generally introduced in the absence of rigorous evaluation.

As well as providing a rational basis for decision making, an added benefit of experimentation and evaluation is the exposure to illicit drug users, which in itself begins to dispel stereotypes. Australia is at the forefront in the formation of advocacy groups, first of illicit drug users and, more recently, of families of illicit drug users. They have been very effective in combating misinformation about illicit drug use and users, which has helped in the development of more realistic policies.

Most debate about drug policy has focused on abandonment of a prohibitionist stance. There has been little examination of whether prohibitionist policy should be modified rather than abandoned, and how this could best be done. England, the Netherlands, Switzerland, and Australia have all shown that innovation and experimentation can be conducted without undermining the basis of prohibition. Nevertheless, advocates of prohibition generally feel threatened by such changes, because they usually are not the instigators. Like all social policy, prohibition must adapt to changing times. The examples in this chapter have shown the direction of some of those changes in the area of drug treatment, but there is a need for more experimentation, debate, and careful evaluation.

Part III

Social Change and

Drug Treatment in

Central Europe and Russia

Chapter 10

The Drug Treatment System in Russia: Past and Present, Problems and Prospects

Yakov Gilinskiy
Vladimir Zobnev

The Social Situation in Russia

Deviant human behavior, including drug abuse, is related to social, economic, and political processes, especially at times of intense social change (E. Durkheim, R. Merton, etc.). Issues of drug abuse and its prevalence cannot be understood without an analysis of their social context.

The regime of the former Union of Soviet Socialist Republics (USSR) depended on control by the State of all spheres of social life, regulation of all forms of human conduct, an all-embracing control over the carrying out of orders, compulsory and absolute uniformity and unanimous approval of all actions of "the Party and government," and an array of harsh penalties for noncompliance. The Soviet experiment to establish a social Utopia (the slogan on the gate of the Solovki camp read: "Happiness for Everyone Through Violence") led eventually to catastrophe—the disintegration of production and of the economy in general; the loss of trade skills; the proletarianization and marginalization of the population; the absence of a middle class; a severe deterioration of the social infrastructure with respect inter alia to health care, education, culture, and communication; several political crises; a crisis of moral and spiritual values; and the growth of mafia-type organized crime (Zaslavskaja, 1995; Zaslavskaja & Arutjunjan, 1994).

Although Gorbachev's reforms were radical (glasnost; the multiparty system; the liberation of the Baltic States—Latvia, Lithuania, and Estonia—which Stalin had annexed; the lifting of the Iron Curtain; and the right to hold private property), many of their consequences were far from beneficial, and many of the problems of the previous period persisted. Power is still in the hands of a ruling elite; corruption, always common in Russia, is rampant; interethnic conflicts have caused many deaths; and nationalism, anti-Semitism, and neofascism have been promoted with little or no resistance. Consequently, there is a host of social problems, of which organized crime, especially drug trafficking, is particularly troubling. Government police have been ineffective against crime, and many of the police, instead of suppressing trafficking, have themselves become either users or distributors of drugs. The extent of the drug trade can be assessed only by means of indirect indicators, including the successes of the police and the customs service and the extent of the drug distribution trade throughout the Russian territory. (For a more detailed account, see Dolgova & Djakov, 1996, pp. 68-70.) Action against the drug trade is further hampered by corruption in the police force and, indeed, throughout the criminal justice system. The State's relations with drug-exporting countries, including Azerbaijan, Chechnia, and many Middle Asian countries, further complicate attempts to control the burgeoning drug trade. One of its most serious consequences has been the increase in drug-related crime. Official figures indicate a more than sixfold increase from 1988 to 1995, but given the unreliability of official statistics, the actual increase is certainly higher.

The Epidemiology of Drug Abuse

The number of registered users of narcotic substances increased from 25.7 per 100,000 population in 1985 to 60.6 per 100,000 in 1994 (Crime and Delinquency, 1992, 1994; Smirnov, 1990). Drug use is most prominent in the Primorskiy, Krasnodar, Krasnoyarsk, and Stavropol territories; in the Rostov, Novosibirsk, Samara, and Uliyanovsk regions; and in St. Petersburg and Moscow. The number of drug users in St. Petersburg during the 1990s is estimated at 0.06% of the city's population. A survey has found that 7% of secondary or high school students, 26% of vocational school students, and 39% of teenagers in police custody in a reception/distribution center had tried illicit drugs. Surveys of St. Petersburg adults in 1993 revealed that about 10% had used some drug at least once. Similar surveys in Moscow during the 1980s and 1990s have given similar results (11% of teenagers and 10% of adults).

Narcotics specialists in St. Petersburg have estimated that between 100,000 and 300,000 of the city's residents (3% to 6% of the city population) are drug users. The pattern of drug use in St. Petersburg has varied over time. For example, since the early 1980s, the consumption of drugs containing medical substances (omnopon, morphine, codeine) has decreased, whereas that of opium and psychostimulators has increased. In the early 1960s, opiates and barbiturates were the most popular substances, and in the 1980s it was psychostimulators. Since the late 1980s, the use of hallucinogenic substances has increased, in both synthetic form (phencyclidine) and natural form (the "liberty cap," a small mushroom found in the local forests). Use of cocaine is increasing slowly, and the use of hashish, rapidly. In the mid-1990s, ecstasy made its appearance, but opiates are still the most popular. Although the main sources of narcotics are within the country, outside supplies come from former USSR territories—Uzbekistan, Tadzhikistan, Turkmeniya, Kazakhstan, and Kirgizya.

According to 1990 data on drug users from the Russian Ministry of Health, 90% of them were male, nearly 80% of them lived in town, and 62% are between the ages of 18 and 29. Teenagers account for 7%, and the over-30 age group accounts for 30.5%. The majority (62%) could be classified as blue-collar workers. About 15% were unemployed, and 18% had had either previous convictions or compulsory treatment.

The percentage of opiate users has fluctuated between 44% and 52% of all drug users, hashish users between 21% and 31% of all drug users, and polydrug users between 12% and 21% of all drug users. In different parts of Russia, different drugs dominate. For instance, in the Far Eastern region, hashish is the most popular substance; in the Volga regions, opium dominates (65%); and in St. Petersburg, opium and ephedron (ephedrine) are the most commonly used (51.9% and 24.2%). The sociodemographic composition of drug users for the whole of Russia is significantly different from that of large cities. For instance, according to the Health Ministry's national data, 26 of every 100,000 Russians are drug addicts, but in St. Petersburg the figure is 48 per 100,000. The rate of female addicts in St. Petersburg is four times as high as that for Russia as a whole (25 and 6.3 per 100,000, respectively).

Owing to the size of the country and of its population, and to the deterioration of its health services, it has been impossible to determine accurately the number of cases of HIV infection or AIDS. According to the available data (though unreliable), the total number of AIDS cases in Russia increased gradually from 23 in 1989 to 863 in 1994. As of January 1, 1995, Moscow had the most cases (182), followed by the Rostov region (113), Kalmyikiya (100), St. Petersburg (83), and the Volgograd region (63; Chaika, 1995, p. 5).

The Development of the Treatment System

A 1974 order, "On Intensification of the Combat Against Drug Addiction," made it compulsory for addicts to accept treatment and for drug users to submit to medical observation. In Russia, as in other republics of the former USSR, the support system for drug addicts consisted of outpatient services (local dispensaries and medical points at workplaces), voluntary inpatient treatment (narcological hospitals and narcological departments in general or psychiatric hospitals), forced treatment in prophylactic labor treatment centers, and prison hospitals for those convicted of crimes or who refused treatment at their local dispensaries. Addicts were forbidden to travel to other countries, hold a driving license, study at an institution of higher learning, or hold a license for a hunting rifle. The effect of such restrictions was to discourage addicts from seeking treatment.

The ideological aim of treating drug users and addicts as offenders was retained. This made them criminals in the eyes of the law and affirmed the punitive approach of psychiatry as well as the negative attitude of the population toward them.

The Legal Basis of Treatment

Between 1972 and 1988, the government of the USSR issued a series of decrees, resolutions, and orders to regulate the treatment of drug addicts in areas such as compulsory treatment, reeducation, and medical observation; the prohibition of cultivating the oil-bearing poppy; and the detection and registration of addicts. These were intended to protect the people against addicts. Instead of trying to neutralize drug addiction as a social phenomenon, the State adopted a policy of neutralizing particular people who used drugs and medicaments without a medical prescription. Diagnosed drug addicts were compulsorily registered with the police and confined to hospital for treatment for at least 60 to 90 days. An addict who did not consent to the prescribed therapy was sent to a treatment center for 1 to 2 years.

Drug consumers and distributors are liable to arrest and conviction for the purchase of drugs with intent to sell (Article 44 of the Code on Administrative Offenses); for the production, purchase, storage, transport, or distribution of drugs without intent to sell (Article 224); and for intent to sell (Article 224).

The police prefer to arrest drug users rather than drug distributors because it is easier to do so. For the same reason, they prefer to detain and transfer to the courts mostly cases of addiction to narcotics, not the distributors of narcotics. In June 1993, the Parliament of the Russian Federation approved an official declaration titled "The Concept of State Policy for Drugs Control in the Russian Federation." This did not alter the legal status of drug addicts, but later the Parliament abolished the labor treatment centers, effective July 1, 1994. Thus, at present, there is no legal basis for compulsory treatment of addicts, but rehabilitation centers are likely to be set up before long to replace the former labor centers. However, the criminal code still provides for compulsory treatment for drug addiction on the basis of a court ruling with respect to a drug addict who commits a crime under Article 62 of the criminal code.

Treatment Facilities

The system of state and municipal narcological services consists of dispensaries and hospitals. They treat all addicts regardless of the substances they use. Opiate users are the largest group because others are either afraid or unwilling to enter an abstinence program. Addicts of psychostimulators, hashish, sleeping pills, and hallucinogens rarely apply for treatment.

Drug addicts are commonly treated in hospitals that admit alcoholics. If they have an infectious disease, they are put in isolation wards. Attitudes toward drug addicts on the parts of staff and other patients are very often unfriendly and negative. This was confirmed, for instance, by the 1991 monitoring of the City Narcological Health Center's doctors and psychologists in St. Petersburg. There are no methadone maintenance programs.

Most instructional and educational pamphlets are based on pharmacotherapy, and there is little psychotherapy or sociotherapy. The dominance of pharmacotherapy and the shortages of professional psychologists, psychotherapists, and social workers in the treatment system hinder improvements in treatment. There is virtually no group therapy or education directed at overcoming the addicts' uncritical attitude to their condition and encouraging abstinence and a positive view of treatment.

Medical facilities vary in their approaches to treatment. If conditions of health and hygiene permit, men and women are treated together, but patients are most often grouped by sex and age (addicts up to 16 years are treated in children's hospitals or the children's wings of general hospitals). Typical drug addict treatment wings consist of several wards for 4 to 12 patients, with 45 to 60 beds in all and an average caseload of 45.

In hospitals, addicts must be examined for AIDS and other infectious diseases, and cases of infection are transferred to a specialized infectious diseases hospital. All of the drug-dependent patients registered at their place of permanent residence are entitled to free treatment, but those who wish to be treated anonymously have to pay.

The state institutions are financed from the federal budget, and the municipal institutions from local or regional budgets. The funds allocated for treatment cover only food and board, minimal supplies of medicines, and staff salaries.

Studies of the effectiveness of state treatment are of a formal nature and provide merely an official perspective rather than an accurate assessment. Occasionally, independent research is carried out, but its findings are rarely published and are available only to specialists.

There are virtually no programs of social and psychological rehabilitation. The few experiments that are carried out take place in scientific research institutes in departments of enthusiastic professionals and with former addicts.

Medical programs developed for alcoholics in the past decade have simply been assigned to the drug treatment service. Attempts to establish new treatment programs based on group and family therapy and therapeutic communities, and on addicts' self-help programs, have been held up by economic difficulties, lack of specially trained rehabilitation staff, and unwillingness of the Russian state health service to change its structure.

Several private drug treatment facilities have been opened in which treatment consists of psychotherapy and the social rehabilitation of addicts who have overcome their dependence, but they are too few and insufficiently experienced in treatment. The patients or their relatives pay the entire cost of treatment. Community treatment centers or religious organizations usually do not charge fees but accept contributions or donations from their patients.

Various alternative, nonconventional methods of treating addiction are used, such as confronting the patient with negative consequences of drug use, the use of charms or exorcism, or working with "bio-fields" (including the patient's photograph, "haemo-sorption," and placebo therapy). Many of these methods are used with little or no research into their effects or consequences. Moreover, there is little evidence that they are more effective than more conventional practices.

In the past few years, the treatment system has experienced strong competition from private medical companies (both cooperatives and treatment centers) and private services. The popular media advertise new programs that not only offer fast treatment but also "guarantee" a complete recovery. Such advertising induces addicts to place their hope in treatment, laying the entire responsibility for recovery in doctors' hands. Often, the doctors are employed in state-run hospitals but practice in private facilities in their spare time.

There are practically no informal support networks for addicts, apart from a few community organizations, such as groups of parents of drug users (usually mothers), and some telephone help-line services. St. Petersburg has several social organizations, such as Drug Addicts Anonymous, Return, or Pilgrims; these are officially registered and do serious work in rehabilitating difficult addicts.

Conclusion

The extremely radical and rapid social changes under way in Russia today give rise to deep pessimism and lack of hope for the future. Such apathy and social depression provide an environment in which the use of illicit drugs is attractive. The criminal justice system and the medical establishment remain punitive and aggressive in their attitudes toward drug users. This, together with the backwardness of the medical and social infrastructure, results in ineffective aid to drug users.

The break-up of the state monopoly of services for drug addicts has had two consequences: one positive (the provision of alternative aid on a commercial basis) and one negative (a lack of control over the quality of medical care, with ineffective treatment practices and the activities of medical charlatans).

As drug use has increased, the age of initiation has fallen and the number of female addicts is growing. The ready availability of alcoholic spirits and the prevalence of drinking among older generations make the use of illicit drugs as forbidden fruit increasingly enticing to young people. Drug prevention measures are poorly organized and inefficient. The mass media make a positive contribution to informing the public about the problems of drug addiction, but at the same time they not infrequently present the use of drugs in an enticing way, alluring and attractive to youth.

We believe that people have the right to impair their health if they so desire, whether with alcohol, tobacco, or narcotics, and that it would be counterproductive to resort to force, whether of a medical or a legal nature, to stop them from doing so. The historical experience in Russia has been that repressive and prohibitive methods have never been effective in solving social problems; consequently, we believe that it is only by the legalization of narcotics (under certain conditions and with certain limitations) that the problems will be overcome and the market in illicit drugs controlled.

References

Chaika, N. (1995). *Recent data on the HIV/AIDS epidemic in Eastern Europe.* St. Petersburg: Pasteur Institute. (in Russian)

Crime and Delinquency. (1992). *Statistical review (1993).* Moscow: MVD [Ministry of Internal Affairs] RF [Russian Federation], MJ [Ministry of Justice] RF, Statistical Committee of the Commonwealth of Independent States (CIS). (in Russian)

Crime and Delinquency. (1994). *Statistical review (1995).* Moscow: MVD [Ministry of Internal Affairs] RF [Russian Federation], MJ [Ministry of Justice] RF, Statistical Committee of the Commonwealth of Independent States (CIS). (in Russian)

Dolgova, A., & Djakov, S. (Eds.). (1996). *Organised crime—3.* Moscow: Criminological Association.

Smirnov, A. (Ed.). (1990). *Crime and delinquency in the USSR in 1989: Statistical review.* Moscow: Juridical literatura. (in Russian)

Zaslavskaja, T. (Ed.). (1995). *Where is Russia going? The alternatives of social development.* Moscow: Aspect Press. (in Russian)

Zaslavskaja, T., & Arutjunjan, L. (Eds.). (1994). *Where is Russia going? Alternatives of social development I.* Moscow: Intercentre. (in Russian)

Chapter 11

Therapeutic Communities as a Major Response to Drug Abuse in Poland

Grażyna Świątkiewicz
Jacek Moskalewicz
Janusz Sierosławski

The Social Epidemiology of Drug Abuse in Postwar Poland

Until the late 1960s, drug abuse in Poland was considered mainly an individual medical problem, affecting only a few people. National statistics showed only about 100 to 150 drug-dependent patients annually. Most cases were iatrogenic: Dependence occurred because of extended medical treatment with psychoactive drugs, such as morphine. Others were health professionals with easy access to drugs (Bielewicz, 1984; Łęczycka & Steffen-Kuszt, 1984), but there are no statistics on this group; the problem was not considered a threat to law and order.

Drug abuse began to increase at the end of the 1960s. In the spring of 1968, students in Warsaw, Kraków, and other university towns organized demonstrations and strikes and, like young people in other countries, questioned the foundations of the political and social organization of the society (Bratkowski, 1985; Malinowska, 1985). Those who came of age in the late 1960s were eventually defined as a group that represented a threat to the existing order. To discredit their aspirations and public image, their leaders were accused of parasitism, luxurious consumption, and drug abuse. In 1968, for the first time, police statistics contained separate data on drug addicts, which implied that drug abuse was beginning to be redefined as a social problem rather than a medical condition (Raport MO, 1981). At that time,

> young people abused various kinds of licit drugs, both opiate derivatives and synthetic pain-killers of morphine-like action, as well as sedatives and hypnotics, and stimulants, including atropinizing drugs and volatile substances. The majority of young drug-users consumed psychoactive drugs orally. The drugs were obtained illicitly (by

theft, burglary of pharmacies, forging prescriptions, etc.). (Sikorska, Moskalewicz, Sierosławski, & Zamecki, 1990, p. 1)

This first wave of drug abuse lasted several years before being arrested by restrictions on the availability of licit drugs. Some psychoactive pharmaceuticals were withdrawn from the market, special prescriptions were introduced for narcotic drugs, and pharmacies were better protected against theft. Drug abuse temporarily stabilized. Drugs previously obtainable licitly were difficult to replace by foreign products because of strict border controls and limited tourism, and currency exchange rates made all imports very expensive. However, a policy that sought to control availability without curbing demand could not be effective in the long run.

The "Poppy Period"

Political and economic reforms introduced in the early 1970s raised people's material aspirations and levels of consumption, but prosperity was short-lived; by the mid-1970s, the renascent aspirations could no longer be satisfied. It was then, in response to the continuing demand, that a technology of home production of opiates was invented. The raw material was readily available from poppy plants cultivated all over the country without any legal restrictions. Poppies had been grown in Poland for centuries, not for their psychoactive properties but mainly for seeds used in traditional cuisine (Christmas noodles, poppy cakes). Drug users "discovered" their psychoactive properties partly because of the restrictions that had been imposed on licit psychoactive drugs. At first, they used poppy milk and drank a poppy tea infused from poppy straw. Later, they extracted from poppy straw an injectable mixture of opiates, known as "Polish heroin" or "kompot." Soon, homemade opiates became the drug of choice of Polish addicts (Moskalewicz & Sierosławski, 1991).

This second wave of drug abuse was reflected in hospital statistics that showed a surge in admissions toward the end of the 1970s. Despite clear epidemiological evidence, the mass media did not report the increase in drug abuse. Articles and reports on the domestic drug scene were censored. Drug abuse was a problem of capitalist societies; it was even caused by capitalism. As a social problem of socialist society, it was not officially recognized (Świątkiewicz & Moskalewicz, 1995).

Drug Abuse as a Public Issue:
Social Problems and Political Changes

The economic crisis exploded in a wave of strikes in the summer of 1980. For the first time since the war, the working class and the intelligentsia joined in common social protest. Solidarity that crossed class boundaries became a symbol. Economic problems found their expression in political agitation. Independent trade unions represented the political interests of the society. For almost 2 years, Poland witnessed conflict between the government and the first independent trade union, Solidarity. The economy continued its slump. The public heatedly debated all political and social problems, including drug abuse. Media coverage of drug abuse was higher than ever before. According to Frieske and Sobiech (1987),

> In the first ten months of 1981 Polish newspapers published close to 300 articles, of which 200 covered topics from the Polish drug scene. This number of publications . . . was higher than the total number of all articles (on drug abuse) that had appeared during the whole post-war period. (p. 192)

In the early 1980s, hospital admissions for drug dependence tripled, from about 1,000 in 1980 to more than 3,000 in 1984, and there was a corresponding increase in the number of addicts known to the police and of school pupils seen to be taking drugs (Łuczak, 1989). Drug abuse was now recognized as a social problem. A wide public debate was followed by expanded voluntary action and finally by legislation on prevention of drug abuse, enacted by the Parliament in January 1985 (Dziennik Ustaw, 1985). The new legislation laid the foundations of a comprehensive and liberal policy on drug abuse. It was designed to control availability and provided for severe penalties for production and distribution, but it did not penalize either use or possession of drugs. Despite concern that such a liberal approach might worsen the problem, the years that followed saw a decline in drug abuse as measured by medical and law enforcement statistics.

Spread of Drug Use in the 1990s

The political and economic changes of the early 1990s brought new social problems and exacerbated many others, but not drug abuse as much as others. In 1990, admissions to residential treatment and rehabilitation increased for the first time in 6 years—by 14% over 1989, for instance, and in 1991 by a further 26%. Then, in the next 3 years, the annual rate of increase dropped to an average of 6%. The estimated total numbers in specialized drug treatment, including residential services and outpatient clinics, did not exceed 7,000 (Moskalewicz & Sierosławski, 1992).

Notwithstanding the high rate of growth of hospital admissions for abuse of inhalants and stimulants, patients dependent on homemade opiates, mostly intravenously injected, still formed the bulk of inpatients. According to Sierosławski (in press), their share among all drug-dependent patients decreased slightly, from 80% in 1990 to 75% in 1995. Some used opiates only; others took other drugs besides opiates, mostly sedatives and hypnotics, and progressively more often, amphetamines. Of the rest, the most numerous were those dependent on inhalants (6.3%). The distribution of diagnoses varied randomly.

The police reported a cumulative total of about 18,000 drug abusers in 1995. Police records show an increasing trend since 1991, a year later than indicated in inpatient hospital records. Long-term trends in police and health care records are similar. Marijuana consumption is also increasing, and there are plentiful supplies of amphetamines and hallucinogens. Poland produces large quantities of illicit amphetamines. In general, experimental use of illicit drugs has been on the rise. National surveys of students of the last class of postprimary schools in 1992 to 1994 found that the proportions who had used drugs in the year preceding each survey had increased from 5% to 10% each year (CBOS, 1994; Zieliński, 1992).

The Evolution of the Treatment System

The foundations of the specialized drug treatment system were laid at the beginning of the 1980s. The previous practice of treating drug dependents in mental hospitals and clinics or in alcohol treatment clinics was seen to be inappropriate to the new culture of drug abuse among youth and to its nonmedical character.

Charismatic Leaders and Political Recognition

As early as 1972, a group of psychology students founded a club where teenage hippies on drugs could obtain psychological help. These young people had not completed their schooling, and the idea of "a school of sociotherapy" was born. First, a special class at a secondary school enrolled about 20 students with drug and other problems, and, in 1977, 16 completed secondary education, and six began university. This was an unquestionable success for Jacek Jakubowski—a former student of psychology who was headmaster of this experimental class. Until the end of the 1970s, about 70 "difficult" teenagers who had not been accepted in normal schools because of drug use took part in this experiment (Jakubowski, 1982). Also in 1972, a psychiatrist, Ewa Andrzejewska, director of a neuro-psychiatric sanitarium, established a small unit to admit young addicts and personally took part in their psychotherapy, making it a priority of the sanitarium (Andrzejewska, 1982). The head of the unit was another charismatic individual, a psychologist, Marek Kotański, who later established the first long-term rehabilitation center for drug users. Fascinated by the Synanon model, Kotański introduced to drug treatment a concept of therapeutic community with a hierarchy and strict rules (Kotański, 1982). Until the end of the 1970s, these were the country's only centers offering specialized treatment, and they could serve only a minute proportion of those in need of help. The rest had to seek treatment in mental hospitals, which could not meet their expectations and labeled them "psychiatric cases."

A more professionalized drug treatment system began in 1980 to 1981. It was a result of political changes associated with and manifested by Solidarity, which had opened public discussion on many social problems that had not previously been treated as public issues (Siemieński, 1985). Prominent activists in the debate had already been engaged in drug treatment. On a high tide of political tension, they were able to increase social visibility of drug abuse and obtain funds for its treatment and prevention, as well as strengthen their own social and professional position. Already in 1981, after only several months of public debate, they gained official recognition and were in a position to expand the activities they had initiated on a very small scale in the previous decade. Jacek Jakubowski fulfilled his original dream of a "school of sociotherapy" with its own building and staff, and Ewa Andrzejewska founded a voluntary organization called the Society for Prevention of Drug Abuse. The most spectacular achievement, however, was that of Marek Kotański, who succeeded in establishing his *Monar*—the Youth Movement for Prevention of Drug Abuse (Siczek, 1987).

The Monar Saga, or the "Polish Synanon"

Monar set about developing its own treatment system, which consisted of counseling and rehabilitation centers, as well as projecting its public image and increasing its visibility. Its crucial feature was residential rehabilitation. Its counseling role was confined to building motivation, referring people to rehabilitation centers and detoxification units, and counseling parents. It did not provide treatment as such, but its preventive activities included early case finding of addicts and referral for treatment. It offered long-term residential rehabilitation, up to 2 years, in several periods, graded by increasing freedom and responsibility. Patients were normally expected to do manual work—everything needed to keep a center going. Education could be continued; drugs, alcohol, and sexual relations were prohibited; and anyone who broke these rules had to give up rehabilitation and leave the center (Kotański, 1984).

This new approach attracted many clients. A major attraction was its separation from mental health services—clients were no longer stigmatized as mad, they dressed in ordinary clothes, and they lived among other young people who shared their problems and culture. The staff were young psychotherapists who could understand and accept the different culture and lifestyle. Moreover, according to the rules of a psychotherapeutic community, clients shared in decision making and felt responsible for their community.

In under 3 years, Monar set up a network of counseling and rehabilitation services for drug addicts; it then included 14 residential rehabilitation centers, mostly in rural areas, in old, dilapidated manor houses or farmhouses. First, clients had to renovate them, which added to their satisfaction and strengthened their identification with the movement. In its pioneering period, Monar enjoyed a good reputation among addicts. Waiting lists for admission were long. After some time, its internal rules were made more restrictive; smoking was banned, and other rules were more strictly enforced.

Monar and the Public Treatment
Sector: Integration and Competition

After several years of enthusiastic activity, Monar had produced many people strongly committed to its Synanon-inspired ideology. However, some of its staff came to consider its rules too restrictive and its methods humiliating, and they left to work in new rehabilitation centers organized by the national health service. The new centers deviated very little from Monar but claimed to offer a more humane approach for clients who were disappointed with its orthodox form of rehabilitation.

A 1985 law on prevention of drug abuse integrated into one system various forms of specialized drug treatment that had been developing since the early 1980s. It made drug treatment and rehabilitation free of charge and established the principle of voluntary treatment; only a family court could compel minors to take treatment. It provided for a variety of treatment institutions, such as day care units and hostels, and encouraged voluntary initiatives. However, the law's potential was not fully exploited. The specialized drug treatment system was limited to outpatient clinics, detoxification units, and rehabilitation centers.

Outpatient care was designed to be an entrance to the system. Outpatient clinics were intended mainly for treatment, rehabilitation, and prevention. In practice, they referred clients to residential detoxification or directly to inpatient treatment or rehabilitation. The system had about 30 specialized drug treatment clinics; and nongovernmental organizations ran 25 counseling centers, 20 of them in the Monar system.

Several detoxification centers were established, mostly as separate units at mental hospitals, and provided more than 100 beds in all. There was practically no outpatient detoxification. The process took about 3 weeks on average. It was meant to precede long-term rehabilitation, but most patients submitted to detoxification only to interrupt intensive drug use and to reduce tolerance.

Rehabilitation was assigned to the public health service and voluntary organizations (mostly Monar). More than 30 centers were established, with accommodation for more than 900 clients. The Monar inpatient rehabilitation model, which was the one adopted, provided for a 2-year program, but most clients stayed only from a few days to several weeks; fewer than 10% completed the course successfully.

The law on prevention of drug abuse endorsed the system that had been evolving since 1981. In principle, it adopted concepts pioneered by Monar but reserved detoxification strictly for medical services. Detoxification was the last medical fortress in an area dominated by nongovernmental organizations and nonmedical professions. The law endorsed the claim of medicine that without its competence, this serious social problem could not be solved.

In general, although conceptually similar, the public health system of outpatient clinics and rehabilitation centers was in competition with Monar. Many addicts took advantage of these new opportunities and sought help in the public health rehabilitation centers. Monar no longer had a problem of waiting lists but of empty beds, and the problem increased with declining trends in drug abuse, which lasted until the end of the 1980s. At the time, Monar devised new preventive approaches, with less attention to its former clients, the addicts. In 1985, it initiated the National Movement of Pure Hearts to inspire young people to help others and to promote a lifestyle free of psychoactive substances (Schmidt & Kalicki, 1987).

Drug Treatment in the Era
of HIV Infection and Transition

The epidemic of HIV infection, which affected intravenous drug users in Poland in the late 1980s, brought further change in the treatment system. The media gave full, often hysterical, coverage to the rapid spread of the epidemic. The public associated AIDS with drug abuse, and fear of AIDS increased intolerance of drug abuse. Many seropositive addicts could no longer live in their families or communities because of discrimination and repulsion, and increasing numbers eventually found accommodation in Monar centers. In response to this new demand, Monar modified its therapeutic regimens and even adopted harm reduction approaches: When the first case of HIV infection among addicts was recorded in the summer of 1988, it began free distribution of syringes and needles.

From the beginning of 1989, the Minister of Health and Social Welfare permitted regional chief medical officers to finance syringe exchange programs. Addicts welcomed this new initiative and attended the programs in increasing numbers, where, as well as syringe exchange, many received treatment and were educated about HIV infection. It appears that the relatively early use of syringe exchange slowed the spread of the HIV epidemic, after 2 years of rapid growth. By the end of 1995, 7 years after the onset of the epidemic in Poland, infected addicts numbered about 2,500 and constituted 10% to 20% of all intravenous drug users.

The spread of HIV infection reopened a discussion on methadone replacement therapy. Its advocates had new arguments in its favor, and some former opponents changed their position on the question. Nevertheless, opposition to it remains strong because it is considered to conflict with the principle of drug prohibition and drug-free treatment. The first methadone program was launched in 1992 by the Institute of Psychiatry and Neurology. To facilitate the project, it was given research status. The crucial question was whether methadone was an appropriate substitution for "Polish heroin" (Baran-Furga & Chmielewska, 1994). The program was at first limited to 6 months and was designed to achieve full abstinence. As well as methadone, clients were offered psychotherapy for 1.5 hours per week (Bury & Rokicka, 1994). About 10% successfully completed the 6-month program, about 50% were expelled, and the rest continued with methadone maintenance. At about the same time, a special program was initiated for HIV carriers only, in a hospital of the Warsaw Medical Academy. However, methadone maintenance is not yet an approved treatment in Poland.

The Present Debate on Drugs

Since the beginning of the 1990s, the drug debate in Poland has been concerned mainly with crime and the penalization of drug possession, but also, though only marginally, with treatment. Efforts were begun in 1992 to introduce new legislation to penalize drug possession, but these efforts raised political controversy. Repeated revisions have been drafted, rejected, and redrafted. The legislation of

1985 is still in force as of 1997. Nevertheless, under economic pressure, there have been concrete proposals to reduce treatment costs. In 1993, the National Program of Drug-Abuse Prevention proposed that only 40% of the long-term rehabilitation centers (with 2-year programs) be maintained and the remainder changed into short-term centers, providing rehabilitation for up to 1 year. However, in 1997, two thirds of all those centers retained the 2-year rehabilitation approach. Nevertheless, efforts have been made to expand outpatient and counseling services, outreach work is under way, and almost half of the staff of outpatient services have been trained in the appropriate treatment methods.

There is resistance to the reform of drug treatment. The system, with its roots reaching back to the early enthusiastic period of Solidarity, is inflexible and difficult to change. It is more open to adapting new ideas to existing structures than to replacing some of the traditional model with new ideas. The issue now is whether the resistance is due to the "normal" inertia of the system or to the conservatism of its founders.

References

Andrzejewska, E. (1982, October). *Dóswiadczenia w prowadzeniu leczenia i resocjalizacji młodzieży uzależnionej na podstawie pracy oddziałów odwykowych w Stołecznym Zespole Neuropsychiatrycznej Opieki Zdrowotnej dla Dzieci i Młodzieży w Zagórzu k. Warszawy* [Treatment and resocialization for drug dependent youth, experiences from Neuropsychiatric hospital for children and youth in Zagórze]. Paper presented at the Symposium on Drug Abuse in Poland, Częstochowa.

Baran-Furga, H., & Chmielewska, K. (1994). Terapia metadonem [Methadon therapy]. *Alkoholizm i Narkomania, 1*(15), 25-43.

Bielewicz, A. (1984). Rozpowszechnienie nadużywania leków w Polsce [Prevalence of drug misuse in Poland]. In A. Śliwowski & W. Górecki (Eds.), *Medycyna Srodowiskowa. Cześć IV. Problemy diagnostyki i Terapii* [Environmental medicine. Part IV. Diagnostic and therapeutic problems] (pp. 9-19). Warsaw: CMKP.

Bratkowski, P. (1985). Subkultura [Subculture]. *Magazyn Monar, 85,* 38-39.

Bury, L., & Rokicka, M. (1994). Psychoterapia grupowa w programie metadonowym [Group psychotherapy in methadon programs]. *Alkoholizm i Narkomania, 1*(15), 65-70.

CBOS. (1994). *Młodziez iuz ywki* [Youth and psychoactive substances]. Warsaw: Centrum Badania Opinii Publicznej.

Dziennik Ustaw PRL [Official gazette announcing current legislation of the Polish People's Republic]. (1985). *Ustawa o zapobieganiu narkomanii z dnia 31 stycznia 1985* [Law of January 31, 1985, on preventing drug abuse]. Nr 4, poz. 15.

Frieske, K., & Sobiech, R. (1987). *Narkomania: Interpretacja problemu społecznego* [Drug abuse: Interpretation of a social problem]. Warsaw: Institut Wydawniczy Zwiazkóv.

Jakubowski, J. (1982). *Zintegrowany system wychowawczy dla młodzieży nieprzystosowanej, z uzależnieniem lekowym—koncepcja i program społeczno-pedagogiczny. Szkolny Ośrodek Socjoterapii* [Integrated upbringing system for drug-dependent young people—concept of socio-pedagogical program. Sociotherapeutic School Center] (Typescript). Warsaw: Polskie Towarzystwo Psychologiczne [Polish Psychological Society].

Kotański, M. (1982, October). *Program organizacji profilaktyki, lecznictwa i resocjalizacji narkomanów w Polsce na podstawie koncepcji merytorycznej Stowarzyszenia "Monar"* [Program on prevention, treatment and resocialization for drug addicts in Poland on the basis of the "Monar" concept]. Paper presented at the Symposium on Drug Abuse in Poland, Częstochowa.

Kotański, M. (1984). *Ty zaraziłes ich narkomanią* [You infected them with drug abuse]. Warsaw: Państwowy Zakład Wydawnictw Lekarskich.

Łęczycka, K., & Steffen-Kuszt, T. (1984, December). Analiza rozwoju narkomanii na podstawie obserwacji w oddziale odwykowym w Pruszkowie [An analysis of drug abuse development on the basis of observations of the inpatient clinic in Pruszków]. In T. Chruściel & B. Hołyst (Eds.), *Zeszyty Problemowe Narkomanii. Materiały Sympozjum 10-12.12.1984* [Fascicles of drug-abuse-related problems. Proceedings of the Symposium 10-12.12.1984] (pp. 173-184). Warsaw: Państwowy Zaklad Wydawnictw Lekarskich.

Łuczak, E. (1989). Zjawisko uzależnień wśród młodzieży w Polsce [Drug abuse among Polish youth]. In *Problemy zagrożenia młodzieży uzależnieniem* [Problems of risks of drug abuse among young people] (pp. 5-42). Warsaw: Ministerstwo Edukacji Narodowej.

Malinowska, M. (1985). Okiem socjologa. Kim są polscy narkomani [From the sociologist's perspective. Who are Polish drug addicts]. *Magazyn Monar, 85,* 26-28.

Moskalewicz, J., & Sierosławski, J. (1991). Style życia narkomanów. Raport z badań [Drug addicts' life styles. Research report]. Warsaw: Institute of Psychiatry and Neurology.

Moskalewicz, J., & Sierosławski, J. (1992). Umieralność wśód osób uzależnionych od substancji psychoaktywnych [Mortality among drug addicts]. *Alkoholizm i Narkomania, 9,* 105-115.

Raport MO. (1981). *Zespól do Walki z Narkomania Komendy Stołecznej lecznej Milicji Obywatelskiej* [Team for Combating Drug Abuse at the Warsaw Civic Headquarters]. Unpublished report.

Schmidt, G., & Kalicki, R. (1987). Powstaje Centrum Czystych Serc [Center of Pure Hearts is emerging] (Leaflet of the Center).

Siczek, J. (1987). *Zmartwychwstali* [The resuscitators]. Warsaw: Krajowa Agencja Wydawnicza.

Siemieński, M. (1985). *Po tej stronie granicy* [On this side of the border]. Warsaw: Wydawnictwo Radia i TV.

Sierosławski, J. (in press). Rospowszechnienie uzależnień od środków odurzajacych i psychotropowych w 1995 [Prevalence of drug dependence in 1995]. *Serwis Informacyjny Narkomania.*

Sikorska, C., Moskalewicz, J., Sierosławski, J., & Zamecki, K. (1990). *Polish summary on drug abuse* (Paper prepared for World Health Organization Regional Office for Europe). Warsaw: Institute of Psychiatry and Neurology.

Świątkiewicz, G., & Moskalewicz, J. (1995). Changing definitions of the drug problem: An analysis of Polish newspapers in 1985 and 1990-93 period. In M. Lagerspetz (Ed.), *Social problems in newspapers: Studies around the Baltic Sea* (pp. 71-82). Helsinki: NAD.

Zieliński, A. (1992). Badania rozprzestrzenienia środków psychoaktywnych w szkołach ponadpodstawowych Ochoty i Śródmieścia [Study on the prevalence of drugs in post-primary schools]. *Alkoholizm i Narkomania, 9,* 63-81.

Chapter 12

Drug Users as
Scapegoats in Hungary?

Zsuzsanna Elekes
Éva Katona
Borbála Paksi

In 1985, at the 13th Congress of the Hungarian Socialist Workers Party, the existence of a drug problem in Hungary was acknowledged officially for the first time. Previously, little was known or acknowledged about drug consumption. A few professional publications on the topic had appeared at the beginning of the 1970s, but it was not until the 1980s that a significant change in the official perception of the problem began to appear. It was marked by a short-lived attempt to establish a hospital drug treatment program and an extensive drug prevention publicity campaign on both radio and television that portrayed the seriousness of the problem and made drug consumption the main focus of attention. Given the country's other, more substantial social problems, such as its economic condition, it is possible to argue that the drug issue allowed the authorities to distract public attention from more intractable problems to a relatively simpler issue. The effects of the campaign were reflected in a public opinion poll conducted in 1985 by the Communications Research Institute, which ranked the growing danger of drug problems second in severity as a social concern after worries about falling living standards (Nagy, 1985).

At that time, there were few therapeutic institutions where drug users could receive long-term residential treatment, and official policy was directed toward criminalizing all drug consumption and portraying it in a highly negative way. Books for professionals in the field published between 1985 and 1990 depicted drug users as criminals and as seriously "ill and guilty" (Rácz, 1990, p. 34). Newspaper stories tended to sensationalize the issue and used expressions such as "the plague of our age," "terrible age," and "the great enemy" (Kara, 1993). According to a 1990 survey, a representative sample of the adult population considered drug consumption very dangerous and believed that first-time use led automatically to severe addiction, which could be arrested only by skilled help. A majority, although believing it appropriate to tackle drug problems with penalties, felt that punishment was not the solution and that treatment within the health care system was the best way to reduce the use of drugs.

Since 1989, when the former opposition group came to power, deviant behavior has ceased to occupy the center of public and political attention. The spread of liberal ideologies has emphasized individual freedom, including the rights to consume excessive amounts of alcohol, commit suicide, and take drugs. Police policy toward drugs has been strongly influenced by the political changes, as well as by internal, structural changes within the police, making them more a civilian force and less a political instrument. There has been increasing uncertainty about the role of the police in the new political system. The secret service, which was part of the police system, has been dissolved, as has the Youth and Family Protection Division of the police force, which had some responsibility for drug control enforcement activities.

These changes have been reflected also in press coverage. Although newspaper articles and discussions about drugs are still strongly negative, their tone is less hostile toward drug users and less sensational. Attitudes toward drug use have become more tolerant, and the 1980s view of the drug user as a "criminal junkie" has given way to that of a "sick person" (Ács & Tóth, 1994). A 1992 study among secondary school students also indicated a softening of attitudes toward drugs and more moderate opinions on the dangers of drugs than in 1990.

Legislation on drugs has also changed. A new 1993 law (BTK 1993/§282.A) penalizes drug trafficking and production more severely than before but declares drug addiction to be a health problem. Although some legal questions are still not clear (e.g., What quantity of drugs kept can be regarded as illegal? and What types of treatment can replace punishment?), the 1993 law emphasizes the restriction of supply. Its liberal provisions have produced some seemingly contradictory effects. Recently, antidrug activities of the police and the border guards have increased significantly as a result of substantial funding from European Union and other international projects to restrict the flow of illicit drugs, and this has resulted in increased drug confiscations. At the same time, however, the law permits medical treatment as an option instead of imprisonment for drug users caught in possession of a small amount of illicit drugs for personal use.

Drug-Related Data

Data on drug users began to be collected only toward the end of the 1960s, and systematic epidemiological studies began in the late 1980s. Regrettably, these studies were not comparable and suffered from serious methodological flaws (Gerevich & Bácskai, 1995). The first officially registered drug-related death

Table 12.1 Confiscation of Drugs Between 1990 and 1994

Drugs	1990	1991	1992	1993	1994
Heroin (kg)	4.0	7.6	160.0	427.3	812.3
Morphine (kg)	3.0	—	—	1.6	—
Opium (kg)	0.2	—	—	1.0	—
Marijuana (kg)	0.6	6.8	34.3	10.0	9.9
Hashish (kg)	—	—	2.4	253.5	24.4
Cocaine (kg)	—	8.9	5.0	3.4	26.5
LSD (stamp/pieces)	—	29	163	64	665
Amphetamines (kg)	—	—	—	0.3	27.4
Cannabis (kg)	—	—	96	10	1,808
Cannabis plantation	—	—	4	1	21
Illegal amphetamine laboratory	—	—	—	1	2

SOURCE: Unpublished 1995 data from National Police Headquarters. Discussed in *Multi-city study of drug misuse, National Report of Hungary, Budapest report 1994.* Dr. Éva Katona. Manuscript, Council of Europe.

occurred in 1969. Police records put the number of such deaths at 61 between 1973 and 1989. However, much of this information is unreliable because it was only in 1995 that "drug-related death" was clearly defined; for instance, in 1994, the police reported 5 deaths, and the treatment system reported 28.

Criminal data on drugs are also not reliable. The police compile such data under the heading of "main crimes." For example, the burglary of a pharmacy is a main crime, and stealing opiates a secondary crime. The main crime carries the more severe penalty. Drug-related crimes are registered only if they are connected with one of the main crimes. Recorded cases of drug confiscation numbered only 43 in 1992, 63 in 1993, and 92 in 1994 (see Table 12.1).

Epidemiological surveys have provided more reliable information on drug-related trends. The first genuine data on drug consumption in Hungary date from 1974, when two secondary schools in Budapest were surveyed; 5% of the students sampled had used some form of drug. A 1985 survey of secondary schools in Budapest revealed that 6% of those questioned had tried glue sniffing, and 10% had tried an illicit drug (Elekes, 1986). A similar survey in 1992 (sample size 4,700), also in Budapest, found that 12% of the students had tried an illicit drug at least once in their lives; marijuana was the most frequently used drug (lifetime prevalence rate 6%); the prevalence rates for opiates, amphetamines, and glue sniffing were 3%; and 17% of the students admitted using sedatives at least once (Elekes & Paksi, 1994). Finally, the 1995 European School Survey Project on Alcohol and Drugs, which surveyed a national representative sample of 16-year-old students, found the lifetime prevalence of illicit drug use to be 10%; that of inhalants was 5.3%, and of marijuana and hashish, 4.8% (Elekes & Paksi, 1996).

There is little reliable information on drug consumption by adults. A representative survey in 1990 revealed that 5.5% of the adults questioned had already tried an illicit drug (Elekes, 1993). It also confirmed that the abuse of certain drugs, especially marijuana, began in the second half of the 1970s (marijuana appeared for the first time then in the lifetime prevalence of those under 30 years of age), and that it was only in the few years previous to the survey that the use of most of the illicit drugs had become common in the younger age groups.

Treatment Institutions

The Hungarian health care system provides almost all methods and types of medical treatment for drug addicts, but, like the data on drug use, the available information is sketchy at best. The services are almost equally divided between prevention, medical care, and rehabilitation. Professional institutions dominate. There are four main groups of professional health centers for drug addicts: detoxification centers, wards for alcoholics, psychiatric wards, and outpatient drug clinics.

Seven regional clinics serve outpatients, and there are four specialized inpatient units, with 100 to 150 beds throughout the country. In most treatment facilities, drug addicts are treated along with alcoholics. Special wards for alcoholics provide about 3,000 beds.

A national network of educational guidance centers provides basic medical services for outpatient drug addicts under the age of 18 years, as well as advisory services for social problems; from these centers, drug users can be sent to a children's or adults' neurological clinic if their addiction has become established. These clinics are required to provide data on numbers of patients and types of drug. However, because of the inadequacy of the registration and coding system, the data are somewhat inadequate and tend to refer to licit rather than illicit drugs.

Relatively few drug users have been treated for addiction in neurological clinics for either children or youth, but much larger numbers have had inpatient treatment in adult psychiatric clinics (see Table 12.2): In December 1992, for instance, 84 were under medical treatment—79 for drug addiction and abuse, and 5 for psychosis caused by drugs—and 250 opiate users were receiving medical care in 1993.

For a number of reasons, it is difficult to analyze data from non-drug-specific health institutions. Patients on admission may be registered for a medical condition other than drug addiction. Also, the subsequent diagnosis, if it is shown on the case sheet at all, depends on many factors. In most cases, to avoid the consequences of criminal responsibility for addiction, drug addicts are not registered as such. Also, physicians, including psychiatrists, and other health workers often refuse to register drug addiction to avoid stigmatization of patients. Some hospitals register drug addicts officially because of their positive reputation with regard to drug addicts. Even then, however, diagnoses may not always be reliable, because staff are not well trained in the diagnosis of drug problems, nor are diagnostic systems oriented toward drug problems (Elekes & Paksi, 1993).

Although the data from outpatient drug centers and from psychiatric clinics specializing in drug problems are generally more reliable, outpatient drug centers have not been required to provide regular information. Moreover, treatment staff sometimes distrust researchers. More specifically, five out of nine drug outpatient centers reported the following client loads for 1993 ($N = 396$ cases with at least

Table 12.2 Number of Drug Patients Registered in Psychiatric Clinics Between 1986 and
        1996

	1986	1988	1990	1992	1993	1994	1995	1996
Mental disorders caused by drugs/ICD-IX: 292/	154	196	1,641	203	198	228	70	212
Drug addiction and abuse/ ICD-IX: 304, 305.1.9/	1,155	1,064	1,179	1,215	1,208	977	74	488

SOURCE: Yearbook of Public Health (1997).
NOTE: Data on alcohol not included. These are primary diagnoses that refer to the total number of patients registered in the given year.

one contact in 1993) according to primary drug use: 63% opiates, 25% glue/
solvents, 6% cocaine, 6% cannabis/marijuana.

Epidemiological data do not indicate that lower socioeconomic groups are
particularly affected by drug problems, but they are disproportionately represented
in treatment centers (Pálvölgyi, 1992). The reasons are unclear. One reason may
be that the treatment centers, which are part of the state health care system, are not
considered suitable for drug users in the higher socioeconomic groups. Also, there
are indications that drug users from the lower socioeconomic groups prefer medical
and professional treatment (Kolozsi, 1992).

Overall, treatment and rehabilitation predominate over prevention, which has
tended to be neglected. It is carried out by nonprofessional organizations at various
clubs and street work sites, and it focuses on youth. Also, schools give drug
education.

Conclusion

The available data show that the spread of illicit drug use and the resulting drug
addiction are not very extensive. Although a significant number of people experiment with drugs, the estimated number of serious drug addicts is low, especially
in comparison with the number of those affected by alcohol problems and mental
illness. Also, deaths from drugs are fewer than from suicide. However, the issue
of drug use has provoked extreme reactions from the public and the concerned
professions. The political and economic changes have not advanced the democratization of the country, and the new market economy has made the people poorer
and brought more social problems. Society has become less tolerant and looks for
scapegoats, finding them in minorities, immigrants, and anyone who is seen to be
"different." The criminal justice system has dominated the drug scene and has
tended to inflate the problem, with the result that the general public believes that
drug problems are far more serious than the prevalence of drug use would indicate.
In general, the public disapproves of drugs more than alcohol and stigmatizes drug
users more than alcoholics, suicides, or homosexuals.

Hungary's drug policy has paid little attention to the treatment of drug addicts,
and there are only a few drug-specific institutions, owned and managed mainly by

churches and religious bodies. The state health care system has no facilities for long-term treatment; its hospitals have no beds for drug addicts and its outpatient clinics no staff, and there are few specialists in addiction. Doctors wish to protect their "normal" patients from drug addicts, whom they often refuse to treat. Specialist clinics for addicts lack sufficient resources, and this affects the amount and quality of treatment. Even in psychiatric units, treating drug addicts attracts little esteem. The private system has not compensated for the inadequacy of the state health care system, and there are few, if any, alternative facilities or even self-help groups. (There is only one self-help group for drug users, and there are two for "problem" youth.) Consequently, and owing also to the stigmatization of drug addicts and their fear and distrust of health care institutions, they are less and less likely to get the help they need.

References

Ács, I., & Tóth, L. (1994). *Drogal kapcsolatos attitüdök a sajtóban* [Drug-related attitudes in the press]. Unpublished doctoral dissertation, Budapest University of Economic Sciences, Budapest.

Elekes, Z. (1986). 14-18 éves fiatalok ivási szokásai [Drinking habits of 14-to-18-year-old youths]. *Alkohológia, 17*(1), 12-13.

Elekes, Z. (1993). *Magyarországi droghelyzet a kutatások tükrében* [The Hungarian drug situation in the mirror of research]. Budapest: Országos Alkohologiai Intézet [National Institute of Alcohol].

Elekes, Z., & Paksi, B. (1993). Adalékok a hazai drogprobléma jellegének elemzéséhez [Additional analysis of the Hungarian drug problem]. *Esély, 6,* 24-35.

Elekes, Z., & Paksi, B. (1994). Adalékok a magyarországi drogfogyasztás alakulásához [New developments in drug consumption in Hungary]. In I. Münnich & F. Moksony (Eds.), *Devianciák Magyarországon* [Deviance in Hungary] (pp. 308-322). Budapest: Közélet.

Elekes, Z., & Paksi, B. (1996). *A magyarországi középiskolások alkohol és drogfogyasztása* [The alcohol and drug consumption of Hungarian secondary-school students] (ESPAD Hungarian Country report). Budapest: Népjóléti Minisztérium.

Gerevich, J., & Bácskai, E. (1995) Drug use in Hungary: An overview. *International Journal of the Addictions, 30,* 291-303.

Kara, J. (1993). *Drogpolitika a magyar sajtóban* [Drug politics in the Hungarian press]. Unpublished doctoral dissertation, Budapest University of Economic Sciences, Budapest.

Kolozsi, B. (1992). A magyar népesséf empátia készlete [Empathy of the Hungarian population]. In J. Gerevich & A. Veér (Eds.), *A kábítószer kihívása* [The drug challenge] (pp. 140-175). Budapest: Gondolat.

Nagy, L. G. (1985). Aggodalmak és várakozások [Worries and expectations]. *Alkohológia, 16*(4), 68-75.

Pálvölgyi, M. (1992, October). *Kórházban kezelt drogfüggők* [Drug addicts treated in hospitals]. Paper presented at the symposium on "Deviant Behaviour in Hungary," Pilisszentkereszt, Hungary.

Rácz, J. (1990). A drogfogyasztás sémájának társadalmi konstrukciója Magíarorszáhon [Social distribution of drug consumption patterns in Hungary]. *Alkohológia, 21*(1), 28-35.

Yearbook of Public Health. (1997). Népjóléti Minisztérium [Ministry of Welfare].

Chapter 13

From Ideology to Social Reality: Drug Use in Postcommunist Society

Hans-Dieter Klingemann

Comment on Part 3

The introduction of democratic political institutions, such as competitive elections, after the revolutions in the communist countries in the early 1990s fundamentally changed the process of policy formation in Central and Eastern Europe, including that of drug policies. The problems associated with drug addiction, and its treatment and prevention, are now part of the public agenda and discussed freely by those concerned—the medical profession, legislators, the police, politicians, and citizens. An open debate on drug abuse as a social problem was not possible at all in the dark years of Stalinism. It was regarded as a problem that should simply not occur in a communist society. Nevertheless, if it occurred, it must have been caused by sickness, criminal disposition, or the class enemy. For this reason, there was almost no empirical research into drug abuse, and what was known at all—for example, from army records—was kept secret from the public.

Transition to democratic politics in the 1990s brought drug problems into the open. However, the change had already set in during the post-totalitarian phase. Social causes of drug abuse were no longer denied, and empirical data were gradually generated and made available for discussion, at least among the *nomenklatura*. In Russia, slowing economic growth and an erosion of ideological and moral values gave rise to the reforms of Mikhail Gorbachev. His policies of perestroika and glasnost set a path toward liberalization *without* democratization, which finally failed because the people of the former Soviet Union wanted liberalization *with* democratization. However, there is no doubt that since the 1970s, and particularly after the Gorbachev reforms, it has been possible to discuss policy issues, including drug policies, more freely and broadly, and on a better basis of empirical data and research. Poland was probably the most "liberal" country of the so-called Eastern Bloc; even in Stalinist times, the regime there was more authoritarian than totalitarian. Societal pluralism was upheld in these and subsequent years primarily by the Catholic Church, which was always strong enough to preserve a measure of autonomy. At the least, it could ensure that its voice was heard on social and educational matters, which helped to guarantee pluralism vis-à-vis the communist state. Thus, there is reason to expect that nonstate social initiatives would also play a prominent role in influencing drug policy and structuring the drug treatment sector both during the authoritarian phase and after the democratic transition. In Hungary, the moderates in the regime and the moderates in the democratic opposition had the upper hand in preparing and steering the course of transition in the late posttotalitarian phase. Negotiation was the preferred mode of interaction. The elites of the former Hungarian communist regime have collectively decided to tolerate some of the nonofficial organizations in order to initiate the transition process. It must be remembered, however, that since World War II, Hungary has had a very checkered history. From 1948 to 1953, Hungarians had to suffer through an extremely harsh totalitarian phase, which was followed by a reform period (1953 to 1956) and a communist counterrevolution (1956 to 1962). After 1962, liberalization took root in many policy areas (e.g., the New Economic Mechanism) and gave rise also to efforts to shed more light on drug abuse and its social correlates.

In cross-section surveys, Russian, Polish, and Hungarian citizens have rated their general state of health poorer than that of all other countries treated in this volume (and for which comparative data are available). In the 1990 World Values Survey, 29% of Hungarians rated their state of health as poor or very poor; 18% of Russians and 17% of Poles held similar opinions (see Table 13.1).

For Russia, new data from the 1995/97 World Values Survey are available (1997: 23% in Russia and 21% in Poland). They indicate that the subjective evaluation of state of health has further deteriorated.

A similar tendency emerges from the more specific reports of Gilinskiy and Zobnev; Elekes, Katona, and Paksi; and Świątkiewicz, Moskalewicz, and Sieroslawski in this volume. In the former Soviet Union, Gabiani and associates took the lead in investigating drug abuse in Georgia during 1967 to 1972. Although results of this study have carried the "For special use only" stamp, this was no longer true of the consecutive surveys in Latvia, Primorskiy, Stavropol, Novosibirsk, Lvov, Moscow, and Tashkent. After these, many more surveys were undertaken, in particular by the Department of Deviant Behavior of the Institute of Sociology of St. Petersburg University. Their overall results seem to indicate that drug abuse has increased in Russia since the revolution of the 1990s. A similar tendency is reported from research in Poland. Here, a national survey of high school students (1992 to 1994) showed an increase of 5% to 19% among those who

Table 13.1 Postcommunist Countries in Perspective: Evaluation of State of Health, Readiness to Engage in Social Welfare Services, and Attitudes Toward Drug Addicts and Drugs in 20 Countries

Country	State of Health[a] %	Heavy Drinkers and/or Drug Addicts % Unwanted Neighbors[b]	N
Italy	3.2	71.4	2,018
Switzerland	3.3	41.2	1,400
Sweden	3.4	68.7	1,047
Finland	3.6	75	588
Netherlands	4.1	80.8	1,017
Canada	4.6	74	1,730
United States	5.2	84.1	1,839
China	5.2	83.9	1,000
France	6.4	64.1	1,002
Great Britain[c]	6.6	74.7	1,484
Japan	9.0	92.6	1,011
Spain	10.1	63	4,147
East Germany	11.8	83.3	1,336
West Germany	12.9	79.1	2,101
Portugal	14.9	71.6	1,185
Poland	*16.8*	*—*	*938*
Russia	*17.8*	*93.5*	*1,961*
Hungary	*29.1*	*93.7*	*999*
Brazil[d]	3.3	66.7	1,782
Mexico[d]	3.7	76.6	1,531
Chile[d]	5.8	67.1	1,500
Mean	8.6	71.6	1,505

SOURCE: World Values Survey 1990.
NOTE: The *World Values Survey 1990* combines the efforts of more than 80 principal investigators who carried out the World Values Survey in 43 societies. It builds on the 1981 European Values Systems Survey directed by Jan Kerkhofs, Ruud de Moor, Juan Linz, Elisabeth Noelle-Neumann, Jacques-René Rabier, and Hélène Riffault. The data set is available for academic use from all major data archives. The *World Values Survey 1995/97* is now being conducted in countries of all continents. It is coordinated by Ronald Inglehart. The data will be released to the academic community in 1999.
a. "All in all, how would you describe your state of health these days? Would you say it is very good, good, fair, poor, or very poor?" (percentage reported above is poor and very poor).
b. "On this list are various groups of people. Could you please sort out any that you would not like to have as neighbors?" "Heavy drinkers"; "Drug addicts" (percentage reported is heavy drinkers and/or drug addicts sorted out).
c. Data are unavailable for England alone.
d. Not included in this volume.

had taken drugs. In Hungary, reliable data have been available since at least 1974. A comparison with data generated in the 1990s shows that drug use has about doubled. Reports also indicate that social groups have played an important part in setting up drug treatment systems in Poland especially, which is well in line with a more differentiated view of that country's posttotalitarian development.

Most of the findings of the available studies indicate that in former communist countries, drug use has increased in their posttotalitarian phase and after transition to democratic rule. The population is very well aware of this. Together with Japan, the Eastern European countries tolerate alcoholics and drug addicts the least—compared with other countries. As Table 13.1 shows, only 6.3% of the Hungarians would accept these deviants in the neighborhood (compared to 6.5% of Russians and 7.4% of Japanese). Why is this so? What are the likely causes of this development? The evidence is too scarce to draw any firm conclusions. However, access to drugs has become easier, which may be particularly tempting for the young, who want to satisfy their curiosity. Drugs may also be attractive to those people who suffer most from the hardships of an unprecedented political, economic, and social change. If this is the case, drug use may be expected to decrease to a level of so-called normal pathology of modern society. Further research is needed to proceed from speculation to sound knowledge.

For the present volume, Klingemann and Hunt have made a commendable effort to include former communist countries in their worldwide analyses. Many more of the former communist countries have been omitted, however. Like those discussed here, all are striving to set up liberal democratic institutions. However, also like those discussed here, they differ in their posttotalitarian trajectories. Thus, detailed analyses are required in order to do justice to, and to understand pathways of drug policies in, all of the postcommunist countries of Central and Eastern Europe.

Part IV

From Moral Crusades to

Cost-Efficient Pragmatism

Chapter 14

Illicit Drugs in Germany and the Emergence of the Modern Drug Treatment System

Irmgard Vogt
Martin Schmid

Germany Today

With the end of World War II, Germany was divided into four zones, which in 1949 became two separate states, the Federal Republic of Germany, commonly known as West Germany, and the German Democratic Republic, or East Germany. After the collapse of the Eastern bloc in 1989, the two were reunited in 1990 as one country, Germany (Bundesrepublik Deutschland), with a population of almost 80 million. Germany is now a federal state, with 16 constituent *Länder* ("states"); each *Land* has its own government, with responsibility for many spheres of political action.

Although East and West Germany differed in many respects, they resembled each other in some. They were largely alike in relation to tobacco and alcohol, but they differed markedly regarding the production, import, and consumption of psychoactive substances such as cannabis, hallucinogens, heroin, and cocaine. It was only in West Germany that it became fashionable, in the late 1960s, to experiment with these substances. East Germany's borders were so well sealed that illicit drugs did not enter it, from either the West or the East. Therefore, it is West Germany that has a postwar history of psychoactive substance use and abuse of the type mentioned above. Therefore, the following review of the history of illicit drug use, the reaction of society to it, and the development of treatment systems is based necessarily on data from the former Federal Republic of Germany.

Drug Laws and the Emergence of
the Modern Drug Treatment System

Drug Laws

With the constitution of the Federal Republic of Germany in 1949, a number of laws that had been enacted during the German Empire (1870 to 1919) or the Weimar Republic (1919 to 1933) were restored. They included those regulating the market for consumer goods such as alcoholic beverages (cf. Vogt, 1989) and tobacco, and for over-the-counter and prescription drugs, including preparations of opiates and cocaine for medical use. The so-called Opium Law, enacted in 1929, restricted the production and marketing of a number of psychoactive substances and provided for the prosecution of offenders under the criminal laws. It was concerned mainly with heroin and cocaine and their equivalents, as well as with cannabis products. It was a first step toward the prohibition of substances that previously had been legally produced and marketed by the pharmaceutical industry.

In the postwar period and early 1950s, annual convictions for offenses against the Opium Law numbered around 1,500; most were of middle-aged health care professionals. This figure declined steadily in the late 1950s and early 1960s, then began a slow increase, and rose steeply between 1968 and 1971. First, it was hashish and hallucinogens, such as LSD and mescaline, that began to flood the market, followed soon by opium derivatives and heroin.

Society reacted strongly to the drug crisis of the late 1960s and 1970s; in short, it adopted American policies of prohibition and repression. The Opium Law was revised and renamed the Narcotics Law (Betäubungsmittelgesetz) in 1971-1972, increasing the severity of court sentences for drug offenses. In 1981-1982, it was again revised to reinforce the repression of dealers but also to enable addicts to be transferred into abstinence therapy. To enforce the law, new branches of police forces (Rauschgiftdezernate) were set up in the Länder; they included a monitoring police squad attached to the Federal Criminal Police Office (Bundeskriminalamt, BKA).

The narcotics laws of the 1970s and 1980s had two quite different main effects. First, they influenced greatly how the public as well as the medical profession perceived drug addiction, which came to be seen as a serious social problem or scourge. Medical professionals, especially psychiatrists, have played a leading part in forming the repressive drug policy of the past 25 years, thus setting standards for the profession. Most doctors favor abstinence treatment, and until 1990, they strongly opposed even drug substitution.

Second, the laws unintentionally helped create illicit drug markets, with their own subcultures of criminalized drug dealers, drug users, addicts, and a specialized economic system (Scheerer, 1989; Vogt, 1996). There is little to show for 25 years of ever more costly campaigns against illicit drugs and their use. In the shadows of a generally prosperous society, black markets for drugs thrive, and the drug subculture finds its places in which to live; this provokes ever new discussions on drug policies.

The Emergence of the Modern Drug Treatment System

The country was not prepared for the drug crisis of the late 1960s and 1970s; neither the medical sector nor social institutions had developed action plans for dealing with the new subculture of drug users and addicts. Since the beginning of the century, psychiatric hospitals had treated alcohol addicts, not addicts of opiates or other psychoactive substances. But in the early 1970s, a few psychiatrists set up separate wards for young drug addicts (Bschor, 1979, 1987); however, most of the psychiatric hospitals did not follow their example. Psychiatrists contributed to the establishment of drug policies as scientific experts (Wanke & Täschner, 1985), and also as practitioners, because all addicts willing to enter inpatient therapy first had to have detoxification in a psychiatric hospital. Detoxification programs played a key role in the treatment sector, and for many years psychiatrists directed them.

In 1970-1971, the first "release communities" were set up. Influenced by similar projects in the United Kingdom, drug policy activists—mainly former drug users, students, left-wing social workers, and psychologists—opened up counseling facilities and living accommodation for users of hard drugs. Strongly linked with the protest movement of the late 1960s and in touch with the community drug scenes, the "release movement" reached more drug users than any other service at the time. In a few cities it was very successful, and its success motivated city councils and Länder governments to grant it funds for its projects (Heuer et al., 1971).

The "release movement" and its projects can be seen as the beginning of the system of modern drug treatment in the former West Germany. However, it was a chaotic beginning. The founders constantly argued about how to understand and interpret illicit drug use and addiction; some saw it as a sign of social pathology, and others saw it as personal weakness and failure. Those who saw addiction as social pathology blamed society, and it was society that had to change or revolutionize to overcome addiction, along with other social ills. Others asserted that it was the individual who was sick and needed help—within release communities, for instance. Some of these communities later became professional therapeutic communities. After some years the movement broke down for a variety of structural and operational reasons.

In the autumn of 1970, the federal government decided to launch a federal action program against illicit drugs and agreed to fund 118 different outpatient and inpatient projects for drug addicts all over the country. The program established the first generation of nonprofit institutions dedicated exclusively to counseling and therapy for drug problems; these institutions had close links to the large, nongovernmental charitable and welfare organizations (*Wohlfahrtsverbände*), such as Caritas, Diakonisches Werk, and Deutscher Paritätischer Wohlfahrtsverband. The projects were run by a new generation of social workers who were like their clients in a number of respects, such as age, experience with various illicit drugs, and political orientation. Soon, however, the social workers began to change their views on drug problems and drug policies, from a social toward an individual and therapeutic perspective. They no longer saw addiction as a personal reaction to social pathology but as an individual problem, a personal failure in dealing with conflict and frustration.

For residential institutions, it was the beginning of a new phase: New facilities sprang up that had little in common with conventional psychiatric wards (Raschke & Schliehe, 1985). American institutions such as Phoenix House and Daytop served as models for all therapeutic communities: drug users had to "rebuild their personalities." Treatment institutions adopted phased concepts that merged psychiatric concepts of addiction and addicts with educational concepts and ideas from behavior therapy (cf. Heckmann, 1982). Typical of the time were cruel initiation rites of admission to therapeutic communities, such as aggressive in-depth interviews to document clients' motivation for abstinence, or giving up personal styles of dress and ornamentation, including cutting long hair or shaving the head. Group confrontation was a dominant feature of treatment, based on often vaguely defined sets of rules and sanctions (Kampe & Kunz, 1983). The therapists defined what was "good" and "bad" and expected total submission of the inmates (for a critique, see Vogt, 1995).

In the 1970s and 1980s, criticism of the system was rare, and alternative forms of treatment were not discussed, even though evaluation of the counseling and treatment programs did not show high rates of success. Indeed, the counseling facilities found it increasingly difficult to maintain communication with drug addicts, and the treatment institutions reported ever-increasing numbers of dropouts and long-term failures.

In 1979, the Fachverband Drogen und Rauschmittel (FDR—an association of social workers concerned with drugs and narcotics) established itself as the professional association for social workers in the field. It helped form social workers' professional views on drug problems, addiction, and drug policies. In the 1980s, the association favored criminalization of drug users and addicts unwilling to undergo residential treatment in therapeutic communities. In accordance with the representatives of the Deutsche Hauptstelle gegen die Suchtgefahren (DHS— German Council on Addiction Problems) and other important opinion leaders in the field, the FDR supported quite conservative positions. In the 1970s and 1980s, it and the DHS strongly opposed all substitution projects, declaring it unethical to treat addicts with substitutes. They denounced advocates of substitution as negligent criminals who, in offering addicts opiate-like substances, prolonged their suffering as addicts and made them "chemical slaves." Against all evidence from the United States and other countries that had long since introduced methadone maintenance therapy, they contended that the unwanted side effects were much more negative than its main effect, the satisfaction of the drug craving of addicts (DHS, 1993; Franke, 1992). Over the years, the gap between the helping professions and the addicts widened considerably, and the addicts felt more and more abandoned and alienated.

As a consequence, in the second half of the 1980s, the discussion on how best to help drug addicts intensified, and new groups of social workers expressed themselves in favor of low-threshold centers and outreach work. In 1989, a new organization, Akzept e.V., was founded for professionals who advocated the new trends. At the same time, the demand for methadone programs increased, especially when it became obvious that intravenous drug users ran a high risk of contracting and spreading HIV infection and, later, hepatitis-C infection. Finally, in 1991, the prescription of methadone was permitted by a decision of the German Supreme Court. Gradually, the dominance of the high-threshold treatment system faded. In increasing numbers, German drug counselors and physicians acquainted themselves with the treatment system in the Netherlands and Switzerland, with their different approaches to policy and treatment, which promised partial success. Even before 1991, some doctors had already begun to substitute medicaments containing codeine for the opiates that their addicted patients craved, but they went in for substitution much more after 1991, when it became easier to prescribe methadone. Today, methadone treatment is well established for ever-increasing numbers of addicts.

It was not only the treatment sector that promoted new ideas and action plans. New organizations such as the Deutsche Aids-Hilfe e.V. (DAH—German Help with AIDS) fueled the development with its political activities. It is concerned primarily with HIV infection and AIDS. At the community level, together with other pioneers, DAH organizations began to open "low-threshold centers" for intravenous users, offering them needle-exchange services, condoms, and emergency medical care. At first, those who offered low-threshold services were sometimes accused of offenses against the drug laws, especially in connection with needle-exchange programs. However, they were acquitted of all offenses and credited with setting standards for courageous projects.

With the commencement of low-threshold services and methadone programs, the 20-year-old abstinence rationale of drug treatment broke down (cf. Schmid, 1994). The FDR, Caritas (Schmidtobreick, 1994), and even the DHS renounced their abstinence ideologies or at least suspended their convictions on the subject. In the 1990s, the drug treatment field began to reorganize itself. As a side effect of the introduction of the substitution programs, physicians (Gölz, 1994), especially psychiatrists, increased not only their influence on drug treatment but also their commitment to it (Schwoon & Krausz, 1994). The outcome remains to be evaluated.

Epidemiology

The DHS estimates that in Germany, about 17 million are dependent on nicotine, 3 million on alcohol, 1 million on psychoactive medicaments (principally tranquilizers and sleeping pills), and 120,000 on illicit drugs. Public interest in addiction is concentrated on illicit drugs.

Several research groups have carried out studies on lifetime prevalence of illicit drug use (e.g., Bundeszentrale für gesundheitliche Aufklärung [Federal Center for Health Information], 1994). Although the studies differed widely in sampling design and techniques, they revealed similar trends. In 1994, a telephone survey of 2,023 adults in former West Germany and 447 in former East Germany revealed,

Table 14.1 Lifetime Prevalence of Illicit Drug Use in Former West German States
(Länder), 1990 (in percentages)[a]

		Sex				Age Groups						
	Total	Male	Female	12-13	14-15	16-17	18-20	21-24	25-29	30-34	35-39
Cannabis	14.5	18.1	10.8	0.1	2.1	6.9	14.8	19.4	19.0	15.9	13.5
Amphetamines	2.7	3.0	2.5	—	0.3	1.0	2.0	3.4	3.6	3.0	3.5
LSD, mescaline	1.8	2.2	1.5	—	0.4	0.2	1.1	1.4	2.6	2.5	2.8
Heroin	0.4	0.4	0.3	—	0.1	0.1	0.3	0.3	0.4	0.7	0.3
Methadone	0.1	0.2	0.1	—	—	—	0.1	0.1	0.2	0.1	0.1
Other opiates	1.3	1.4	1.3	—	—	0.2	0.8	1.4	1.7	2.4	1.3
Cocaine	1.3	1.6	1.1	0.1	0.1	0.4	1.2	1.7	2.0	1.6	1.0
Others	3.5	3.6	3.5	—	0.8	2.0	2.7	3.6	4.6	4.4	4.5
Any illicit drug	16.0	19.3	12.6	0.2	2.5	7.7	16.1	20.6	20.7	17.6	15.8

SOURCE: Herbst, Schumann, and Wiblishauser (1993).
a. Age group 12 to 39 years; $N = 19,206$.

in the 18-to-39 age group, a lifetime prevalence of illicit drug use (including cannabis) of 19.6% in the West and 5.1% in the East (Herbst, Kraus, Scherer, & Schumann, 1995). The findings reflect differences between the two parts of the country in the evolution of drug use: Whereas experimenting with illicit drugs in the West is part of the youth culture, it is still uncommon in the East, even though prevalence rates increased in the East from 1.1% in 1990 to 5.1% in 1994. Table 14.1 summarizes lifetime prevalence data for 1990 in former West Germany.

It is well documented that men experiment with, and consume, illicit drugs much more than women. In 1990, the most popular illegal drug was cannabis, with lifetime prevalence rates of approximately 13% to 20% in the 18 to 39 age group. Young teenagers do not use many opiates. Today, it is later in life that drug users turn to heroin, a finding corroborated by the data on consumption patterns of street addicts. However, the 1990 data indicate that a substantial number of young people were interested in cocaine, amphetamines, and hallucinogens, a trend that persists today.

The number of drug offenses (violations of the Narcotics Law) doubled from 60,588 in 1984 to 122,240 in 1994, but tended to level off at the end of the period. Two thirds of all violations consisted of acquisition and possession of illicit drugs—typical crimes without a victim.

One study (Hartmann, Möller, Schmid, & Schu, 1994) found that more than 70% of the 566 subjects had been convicted at least once. On an average, drug addicts spent 2.3 years in prison, and 10% served more than 6 years. Drug addicts spend more time in prison than in residential treatment. The data raise a number of issues, primarily the social meaning of drug addiction; it is still seen much more as a crime than a sickness, regardless of the rhetoric on all sides.

In the autumn of 1991, the open drug scene in Frankfurt am Main was mainly in two areas: a park in the center of the city, and the central train station. The authorities more or less tolerated the gathering of drug addicts in the park, but not in or around the station. On an average, 300 gathered in the park daily to sell and buy illicit drugs; offer services (e.g., information about dealers or the best illicit offers, material to "shoot up," etc.); exchange needles; and meet friends. They ran a high risk of being arrested but still preferred the open drug scene as their meeting place. Of the 237 respondents to a questionnaire study of regulars at the open drug scene (Vogt, 1992), 70% were male and 30% were female, with a mean age of 28 years and 27 years, respectively. In 1991, 23% of young men and 14% of young females on the open drug scene were under 21 years of age. Of those interviewed, 90% were addicts, most preferring heroin to all other illicit drugs. Usually, however, they took a variety of substances, separately or in combination—some heroin, a fairly high amount of psychoactive drugs (preferably short-acting benzodiazepines), cocaine, cannabis, alcohol, and smoked cigarettes. Although their social and living conditions were mostly quite bad, only 27% judged their health as poor. About 90% reported having been tested for HIV infection, of whom 14% admitted to having tested positive (14% of the males and 14% of the females). The percentage of HIV infection was highest (43%) in the subgroup of homeless addicts (9% of all those interviewed).

Since 1991, the numbers on the open drug scene in Frankfurt am Main have decreased substantially because of the efforts of city officials and the police to reduce drug dealing and drug use in the streets. It is now rare to find 50 or more drug addicts together anywhere. Kemmesies (1995) studied 100 street addicts interviewed at seven different places and 50 at low-threshold counseling centers: 75% were male and 25% female, with a mean age of 31 years. Heroin was still the dominant drug, closely followed by cocaine. Other psychoactive substances were used when preferred drugs were in short supply. The patterns of drug use of street addicts have changed. Again, only 25% judged their health as poor, but now 26% admitted to being HIV positive, a much higher percentage than in 1991, and a finding not easily explained.

A study in 1991 of a representative sample of 1,194 drug users and addicts found a 20% rate of prevalence of HIV infection (Kleiber & Pant, 1991). In samples of people who had died of drug-related causes, 9% tested positive for HIV infection (8% men and 13% women; Heckmann et al., 1993), and 37% for hepatitis-B and 44% for hepatitis-C infection. In summary, then, drug addicts are at much higher risk of hepatitis (C more than B) than of HIV infection.

Since the beginning of the drug crisis in the 1970s, drug-related deaths increased slowly but progressively up to the late 1980s, then increased steeply to a peak in 1991, and decreased again in the following years (Table 14.2).

There is no simple explanation for the steep increase in the number of drug-related deaths around 1990. Of course, the misery of drug addicts had accumulated over the years, including ever-growing numbers of chronically sick people with hepatitis or HIV infection. Many of those who died of drug overdoses or from dangerous drug cocktails were indeed street addicts who were in bad health. Most of them had also given up looking for professional help in conventional counseling centers, which offered nothing but transfer support to enter into residential treatment. Over the years, a credibility gap had opened up between social workers at conventional treatment centers and addicts who needed help but did not get it at

Table 14.2 Drug-Related Deaths

Year	Total[a]	Male	Female	Average Age
1984	361	281	80	27
1985	324	235	89	27
1986	348	275	73	28
1987	442	356	86	28
1988	670	548	122	28
1989	991	815	176	28
1990	1,491	1,227	264	28
1991	2,125	1,770	329	29
1992	2,099	1,750	332	29
1993	1,738	1,419	298	30
1994	1,624	1,346	264	30

SOURCE: Bundeskriminalamt (1995).
NOTE: From 1991 on, this table includes drug-related deaths in the former East German Länder (1991: 1 death; 1992: 3 deaths; 1993: 2 deaths; 1994: 6 deaths).
a. Refers to all deaths, including those in which the sex is unknown.

those centers. In the end, addicts turned away from the centers regardless of their health. When the low-threshold centers opened their doors, street addicts came back, especially when there were also needle exchange programs and emergency medical support. The change in the treatment system probably influenced the living conditions of street addicts and their health conditions, but there is no clear-cut correlation. In Frankfurt am Main, a city with a more liberal drug policy and an abundance of low-threshold and methadone programs, the number of drug-related deaths declined from 183 in 1991 to 53 in 1994. However, in Hamburg, a state and a city with a similar drug policy and drug treatment system, the number of drug-related deaths stabilized at a high level only after a small decline in 1992. The indications are that other factors were mediating the effects of drug policies, drug politics, and drug treatment.

Drug Treatment

General Outline

The federal system in Germany permits considerable diversity in outpatient and inpatient drug treatment services. Regrettably, there is no federal monitoring system or database with respect to drug users, addicts, and the drug treatment system. The best available data come from health insurance agencies and nonprofit nongovernmental organizations. The interplay of the governmental and private sectors is complex and, at times, contentious, owing partly to conflicting financial and other interests. So far, despite efforts at all levels to reduce the costs of health care, the federal and the Länder governments, as well as local communities, have progressively increased their financial support of measures to deal with drug problems, but reductions are now likely.

Since 1976, residential treatment is covered in the first place by statutory health and pension insurance. In 1993, the statutory pension insurance covered the costs of 70% of all drug addicts notified, the health insurance companies covered 20%, and the welfare payments the last 10%, who had never joined any health or pension insurance plan (Verband der Fachkrankenhäuser für Suchtkranke e.V., 1994). The percentage of illicit drug addicts who have their inpatient costs paid by welfare is four times higher that that of all patients diagnosed as dependent on any psychotropic drugs (mostly alcohol). It is one of the many indicators of the higher level of social disintegration of illegal drug addicts.

The prescription of methadone by physicians is covered by health insurance or welfare payments, and physicians have to assess the degree of dependency of their patients and monitor their health status and drug use (by means of urine control). The addicts receiving methadone are expected to cooperate with counseling centers, but no more than about 10% of them attend counselors at the centers. Most of those who are prescribed codeine have to pay for it themselves.

Outpatient Drug Treatment

In 1993, Germany had about 1,220 outpatient counseling facilities for all addicts, with about 6,000 employees (Hüllinghorst, 1994). The average yearly budget of an outpatient center was estimated at DM 440,000 (US$300,000), and low-threshold centers had much higher budgets. Nongovernmental and nonprofit organizations ran 70% of the centers, and city councils ran 30%. Different institutions address different target groups. Of all institutions, 370 offer special services for women (mostly group counseling), and 16 institutions counsel women only.

About 300 counseling centers care for illicit drug addicts (Leune, 1994). They are concentrated in large towns and often advertise their services under the heading "Youth- and Drug Counseling Center." The ratio of drug counselors to clients is better than that for alcoholics, and much better than that for the mentally ill.

The high-threshold centers offer individual counseling and casework, case management, motivation and preparation for residential therapy, help with substitution therapy, and after-care. They mediate when there are problems with drug addicts in the community and pay special attention to community policies on drugs. They often arrange lectures on prevention for young people in schools or youth centers.

The low-threshold centers, which are mostly in large towns, provide day and night shelters for addicts, as well as a variety of services, such as alcohol-free drinks and cheap meals, laundry facilities, needle exchange, condoms, support in the case of homelessness or unemployment, and counseling if necessary. Many of them operate special services, such as methadone dispensaries, supervised housing, help for addicted prostitutes of both sexes, and job creation measures. All of these facilities and services are in constant use. In Frankfurt am Main in 1994, the city council approved the opening, at a few low-threshold centers, of rooms in which to "shoot up." The addicts bring their drugs to the rooms, where they can inject with clean equipment and use clean water. Dealing is forbidden at the centers and "shooting" rooms. Methadone clients are not allowed to use these facilities. With the opening of the "shooting" rooms, it is hoped to bring the intravenous users in from the streets and eventually to persuade them to apply for a substitution or other long-term therapeutic program (Kemmesies, 1995).

For drug addicts who have failed in methadone programs, there are plans to set up heroin prescription programs (Nimsch, 1993), but the federal authorities have not approved of them.

The estimated numbers in methadone programs increased from 150 in 1990 to 10,000 in 1993 (Arnold, Feldmeier-Thon, Frietsch, & Simmedinger, 1995). Another 20,000 to 30,000 are on codeine preparations. The data document impressively the change in drug politics in the past 10 years. Unlike most other programs, including outpatient and inpatient counseling and treatment, substitution programs have a high proportion (40%) of female clients. Addicts benefit from substitution programs in better health and living conditions and social integration.

The former East German states have no drug treatment system because there are so few illicit drug users. With the financial support of the Federal Ministry of Health, a combined treatment system for users of licit and illicit drugs has been set up as a pilot project by local nongovernmental and nonprofit organizations in a new effort to bring together again alcohol and drug counseling. Data on the success rate of the new centers are not yet available.

Inpatient Drug Treatment

Inpatient drug treatment usually begins with detoxification. In 1993, there were at least 1,500 beds exclusively for detoxification, mostly in psychiatric wards. A number of new projects admit drug addicts for detoxification without compulsion to accept long-term inpatient treatment afterward; they may return for detoxification when they need it. Although in the 1970s and 1980s, physicians and counselors regarded "cold turkey" as the best form of detoxification, medication-supported detoxification has become increasingly common in the 1990s.

In 1993-1994, for residential treatment, there were 4,000 beds in approximately 80 institutions, most of them therapeutic communities with 20 to 40 places, and a few with 60 to 100 places. A typical institution had the following staff: five social workers, one psychologist, one physician psychotherapist, three work therapists, two to four administrators (according to the numbers of beds), and one individual doing community service instead of military service (*Zivildienstleistender;* Küfner, Denis, Roch, Arzt, & Rug, 1994). In an institution of 40 places, the overall ratio of staff to patients was 1:2.6; without the administrators it was 1:3.3. Again, the ratio of staff to patients was higher than that for alcoholics in residential treatment and much higher than that for the mentally ill.

The numbers of inpatients covered by statutory pension insurance increased from 2,711 in 1984 to 5,528 in 1993 (VDR, 1994). In the past 10 years, the numbers in residential treatment have doubled; the rate of increase has changed little since the introduction of substitution programs in 1990.

For about 20 years, the normal duration of long-term residential treatment was set at 12 to 18 months, followed by a rehabilitation phase of 12 to 24 months. However, drop-out rates averaged 80% (Küfner et al., 1994). After much effort, with little success, to reduce the drop-out rate, and after long discussions on the usefulness of extending residential treatment to 18 months, the health insurance associations asked to have it reduced. Today, the average duration of residential treatment is set at 9 to 12 months. Some institutions offer short-term residential treatment, set at 3 to 6 months. Also, growing numbers of counseling facilities are offering outpatient casework and therapy.

A number of studies have evaluated the retention rate of inmates in residential treatment for 12 to 18 months (cf. Feuerlein, Bühringer, & Wille, 1989; Küfner, Feuerlein, & Flohrschütz, 1986). It is often argued that the length of stay in residential treatment correlates directly in the long run with success measured as abstinence from illicit drugs (Herbst, 1992; Kunz, Overbeck-Larisch, & Kampe, 1992). If this is so, dropping out and dismissal can be seen as negative factors in the evaluation of outcome of long-term treatment. Most of those who drop out decide to do so in the first 3 months (1991 drop-out rate: 50%; 1992-1993 drop-out rate: 39%), which appears to be a critical phase. Although the drop-out rate has fallen over the years, it was still around one third of all those entering residential treatment in 1993; 20% to 25% were being dismissed by the authorities, and about 40% of patients go on to regular discharge. The figures reveal discontent on the part of the inmates, many of whom drop out, and on the part of the staff, who dismiss about one fourth of their inmates.

Küfner et al. (1994) indicate why some institutions succeed in retaining 90% in residential treatment: They differ from other institutions in their selection of patients; their criteria stress acceptability of the newcomer by the group of residents, rather than personality and drug-related variables; they offer alternatives to confrontational group therapy, such as individual therapy, group therapy without confrontation, and group leisure activities; and they have a less complex system of rules and sanctions. In sum, their approach is, in a broad sense, more "democratic" or "humanistic" than that of other institutions and stresses the counselor-patient relationship (Lewin, Lippitt, & White, 1939; Rogers, 1991). There is a need to know more about institutions with democratic leadership and well-structured group rules, which seem to appeal to drug addicts much more than authoritarian settings and are represented by high success rates on a number of indicators.

Conclusion

In the past 20 years, and in the western part of the country, the drug treatment system has developed separately from the alcohol treatment system. There is still some overlap at counseling facilities in small cities and rural areas but not in large cities or residential treatment. The differentiation of the drug and alcohol treatment systems reflects the interests of all concerned, experts as well as clients. It signals as well the assumption that drug problems and addictions differ considerably from those of alcohol and need to be treated differently, an assumption that needs to be discussed further. Developments in the eastern part of the country and the comparison with other countries' treatment systems may spur the discussion.

REFERENCES

Arnold, T., Feldmeier-Thon, J., Frietsch, R., & Simmedinger, R. (1995). *Wem hilft Methadon? Daten, Fakten, Analysen: Ergebnisse der wissenschaftlichen Begleitung der Substitutionsbehandlung in Hessen* [Who needs methadone? Data, facts, analyses: Results of the evaluation of methadone treatment in Hesse]. Frankfurt am Main: ISS.

Bschor, F. (Ed.). (1979). *Langzeitstudien an Drogenabhängigen: Zwischenbilanz und Perspektiven* [Longitudinal studies of drug addicts: Interim report and perspectives]. *FU-Workshop Berlin, Diskussionsberichte Drogen, H.1.* Berlin.

Bschor, F. (1987). Erfahrungen bei der Wiederaufnahme von Kontakten zu ehemaligen Drogenpatienten [Experiences with new contacts to former drug patients]. In D. Kleiner (Ed.), *Langzeitverläufe bei Suchtkrankheiten* [Long-term developments of addicts] (pp. 211-313). Berlin: Springer.

Bundeskriminalamt. (1995). *Rauschgiftjahresbericht 1994* [1994 annual report on illegal drugs]. Wiesbaden: Author.

Bundeszentrale für gesundheitliche Aufklärung. (1994). *Die Drogenaffinität Jugendlicher in der Bundesrepublik Deutschland* [German youth and their affinity to drugs]. Cologne: Author.

Deutsche Hauptstelle gegen die Suchtgefahren (DHS). (Ed.). (1993). Positionspapier zur Drogenpolitik und Drogenhilfe [Positions on drug policies and drug treatment]. *Informationen zur Suchtkrankenhilfe, 1.*

Feuerlein, W., Bühringer, G., & Wille, R. (Ed.). (1989). *Therapieverläufe bei Drogenabhängigen* [Therapy development of drug addicts]. Berlin: Springer.

Franke, M. (1992). Drogenpolitik im Umbruch?—Gedanken und überlegungen [Are drug policies changing? Thoughts and reflections]. *Sucht, 38,* 43-47.

Gölz, J. (1994). Methadonsubstitution in der ärztlichen Praxis [Methadone substitution by general practitioners]. In J. Klee & H. Stöver (Eds.), *Drogen und AIDS* [Drugs and AIDS] (pp. 88-108). Berlin: DAH.

Hartmann, R., Möller, I., Schmid, R., & Schu, M. (1994). *Modellprogramm Verstärkung in der Drogenarbeit—Booster-Programm, Schriftenreihe des Bundesministeriums für Gesundheit, Bd. 35* [The pilot programme "Boosting Drug Aid"]. Baden-Baden: Nomos.

Heckmann, W. (Ed.). (1982). *Praxis der Drogentherapie* [Drug therapy in practice]. Weinheim: Beltz.

Heckmann, W., Püschel, K., Schmoldt, A., Schneider, V., Schulz-Schaeffer, W., Soellner, R., Zenker, C., & Zenker, J. (Eds.). (1993). *Drogennot- und -todesfälle. Eine differentielle Untersuchung der Prävalenz und Ätiologie der Drogenmortalität. Schriftenreihe des Bundesministeriums für Gesundheit, Bd. 28* [Drug-related emergencies and deaths. A differential study on prevalence and etiology of drug-related mortality]. Baden-Baden: Nomos.

Herbst, K. (1992). Verlaufsanalyse bei Drogenabhängigen nach stationärer Behandlung [Follow-up of drug addicts after residential treatment]. *Sucht, 38,* 147-154.

Herbst, K., Kraus, L., Scherer, K., & Schumann, J. (1995). *Repräsentativerhebung zum Gebrauch psychoaktiver Substanzen bei Erwachsenen in Deutschland—Telefonische Erhebung 1994* [Representative epidemiological study of adult consumption of psychoactive substances in Germany—Telephone survey in 1994]. Munich: Institut für Therapieforschung.

Herbst, K., Schumann, J., & Wiblishauser, P. M. (1993). *Repräsentativerhebung zum Konsum und Mißbrauch von illegalen Drogen, alkoholischen Getränken, Medikamenten und Tabakwaren* [A representative survey on use and abuse of illegal drugs, alcoholic beverages, and tobacco]. Bonn: Bundesministerium für Gesundheit.

Heuer, R., Prigann, H., Witecka, T., Lenz, R., Kranich, R., Struck, T., Höhne, D., Parow, E., Pachelke, L., Haberland, M., Meister, H., & Potraz, E. (1971). *Helft euch selbst! Der Release-Report gegen die Sucht* [Help yourselves! The release report against addiction]. Reinbek bei Hamburg: Rowohlt.

Hüllinghorst, R. (1994). Zur Versorgung Suchtkranker in Deutschland [Care for addicts in Germany]. In Deutsche Hauptstelle gegen die Suchtgefahren (Ed.), *Jahrbuch Sucht 1995* [1995 annual report on addiction] (pp. 153-162). Geesthacht: Neuland.

Kampe, H., & Kunz, D. (1983). *Was leistet Drogentherapie?* [What are the effects of drug therapy?]. Weinheim: Beltz.

Kemmesies, U. (1995). *Szenebefragung Frankfurt/Main 1995. Die "Offene Drogenszene" und das Gesundheitsraumangebot in Ffm. Ein erster Erfahrungsbericht* [A survey of the "open drug scene" and the "Gesundheitsräume" in Frankfurt. First experiences]. Unpublished typescript.

Kleiber, D., & Pant, A. (1991). *HIV-Prävalenz, Risikoverhalten und Verhaltensänderungen bei i.v. Drogenkonsumenten: Ergebnisse einer sozialepidemiologischen Studie* [HIV prevalence, risky behaviour, and changes of behaviour patterns. Results of a socio-epidemiological study]. Berlin: spi.

Küfner, H., Denis, A., Roch, I., Arzt, J., & Rug, U. (1994). *Stationäre Krisenintervention bei Drogenabhängigen. Schriftenreihe des Bundesministeriums für Gesundheit, Bd. 37* [Crisis intervention in the residential treatment of drug addicts]. Baden-Baden: Nomos.

Küfner, H., Feuerlein, W., & Flohrschütz, T. (1986). Die stationäre Behandlung von Alkoholabhängigen: Merkmale von Patienten und Behandlungseinrichtungen. Katamnestische Ergebnisse [Residential treatment of alcohol addicts]. *Suchtgefahren, 32,* 1-86.

Kunz, D., Overbeck-Larisch, M., & Kampe, H. (1992). Drogenfreiheit und soziale Integration Drogenabhängiger nach einer stationären Behandlung [Living without drugs and social integration after residential treatment]. *Sucht, 38,* 155-159.

Leune, J. (1994). Wege aus der Drogenabhängigkeit [Ways out of drug addiction]. In M. Nowak, R. Schifman, & R. Brinkmann (Eds.), *Drogensucht* [Drug addiction] (pp. 93-101). Stuttgart/New York: Schattauer.

Lewin, K., Lippitt, R., & White, R. K. (1939). Patterns of aggressive behaviour in experimentally created "social climates." *Journal of Social Psychology, 10,* 271-299.

Nimsch, M. (Ed.). (1993). *Heroin auf Krankenschein* [Heroin on prescription]. Basel, Frankfurt am Main: Stroemfeld/Nexus.

Raschke, P., & Schliehe, F. (1985). *Therapie und Rehabilitation bei Drogenkonsumenten* [Therapy and rehabilitation of drug users]. Düsseldorf: Ministerium für Arbeit, Gesundheit und Soziales des Landes Nordrhein-Westfalen.

Rogers, C. (1991). Rogers, Kohut und Erickson: Eine persönliche Betrachtung über einige Ähnlichkeiten und Unterschiede [Rogers, Kohut and Erickson: A personal reflection on some similarities and differences]. In J. K. Zeig (Ed.), *Psychotherapie* [Psychotherapy] (pp. 299-313). Tübingen: DGVT.

Scheerer, S. (1989). Die Heroinszene [The heroin scene]. In S. Scheerer & I. Vogt (Eds.), *Drogen und Drogenpolitik. Ein Handbuch* [Drugs, drug policies, and politics. A handbook]. Frankfurt am Main, New York: Campus.

Schmid, M. (1994). Drogenszene, Drogenpolitik und Drogenhilfe. Eine Betrachtung aus der Normalisierungs- und Entdramatisierungsperspektive [Drug scene, drug policies and drug treatment]. In H. Neubeck-Fischer (Ed.), *Sucht: Ein Versuch, zu überleben* [Addiction: An attempt to survive] (pp. 33-59). Munich: Fachhochschulschriften Sandmann.

Schmidtobreick, B. (1994). Drogenpolitik und Drogenhilfe—Die Position des Deutschen Caritasverbandes unter dem besonderen Aspekt der Heroinabgabe an Schwerstabhängige [Drug policies and drug treatment—the position of Caritas on heroin prescription for seriously ill addicts]. *Sucht, 40,* 267-270.

Schwoon, D., & Krausz, M. (1994). *Psychose und Sucht* [Psychosis and addiction]. Freiburg: Lambertus.

VDR (Verband Deutscher Rentenversicherungsträger). (1994). *VDR Statistik Rehabilitation* [VDR rehabilitation statistics]. Frankfurt am Main: Author.

Verband der Fachkrankenhäuser für Suchtkranke e.V. (1994). *Dokumentationssystem DOSY '93. Therapie— Daten der stationären Behandlung für Suchtkranke. Auswertung der Daten-Erhebungsbogen 1993* [The documentation system DOSY '93. Data on residential therapy of addicts]. Kassel: Eigendruck.

Vogt, I. (1989). Die Alkoholwirtschaft [The alcohol economy]. In S. Scheerer & I. Vogt (Eds.), *Drogen und Drogenpolitik. Ein Handbuch* [Drugs, drug policies, and politics. A handbook]. Frankfurt am Main, New York: Campus.

Vogt, I. (1992). *Abschlußbericht der Studie "Offene Drogenszene in Frankfurt/Main"* [Final report of the study "Open drug scene in Frankfurt/Main"]. Unpublished manuscript.

Vogt, I. (1995). Zum Selbstverständnis der Sozialarbeit in der Drogenhilfe [Social work in drug treatment]. *Akzept e.V. Rundbrief, 2,* 10-18.

Vogt, I. (1996, June). *Living on the open drug scene in Frankfurt/M.* Paper presented at the 22nd Annual Alcohol Epidemiology Symposium of the Kettil Bruun Society, Edinburgh.

Wanke, K., & Täschner, K.-L. (1985). *Rauschmittel. Drogen-Medikamente-Alkohol* [Narcotic substances. Drugs—pills—alcohol]. Stuttgart: Enke.

Chapter 15

The Development of Drug Treatment in the Shadow of the Narcotic Law: The Case of Austria

Irmgard Eisenbach-Stangl
Wilhelm Burian

A "Low-Profile" Drug Policy

Neither the Austro-Hungarian Monarchy nor the First (1918 to 1938) or the Second (since 1945) Republic of Austria has been eager to sign international treaties restricting the market in opiates, cocaine, or other psychoactive substances. The Austro-Hungarian Monarchy took part in the first international conference on narcotic drugs, but—like Germany or Great Britain—did not sign the Convention that was finally adopted in 1912. Eight years later, the Republic of Austria had to sign it—the International Opium Convention was part of the peace treaty of Versailles. But it took 8 years more before a law on the incriminated substances was enacted, and it dealt not only with narcotics but with toxic substances in general. Two other examples: Austria signed the Single Convention on Narcotic Drugs, 1961, as late as 1979, 1 year before the International Narcotics Control Board moved to Vienna, and has not yet signed the 1988 United Nations Convention Against Illicit Traffic in Narcotic Drugs and Psychotropic Substances, which entered into force in 1990. Thus, on policy regarding treatment responses to drug-related problems, Austria can be described as a country hesitating to adapt to international policies, as a country "muddling through," taking one piece of drug policy from one neighboring country and the next from another.

Drug Consumption After World War II: The Delayed "Drug Wave"

Since World War II, there have been two phases of drug consumption, distinguished by numbers and social characteristics of drug users, the drugs they used, and their sources; the first phase ended and the second began at the end of the 1960s.

Between 1948 and 1968, there were 744 convictions for drug-related offenses, an average of 35 a year. In 1968, Hans Grassberger, the leading criminologist of the time, who investigated these convictions, found that many individuals had been sentenced more than once, and he calculated that only about 320 in all had been sentenced. Almost one third (29%) were medical professionals (mostly physicians and a few nurses) or relatives (mostly wives of doctors). Most had begun to take drugs because of a physical disease (47%), an injury in war or at work (25%), or psychological distress (20%), and only 5% (the hippies) because of "hunger for experience." The average age at which they first took a drug was 32 years for men and 34 years for women (68% of the sample were male and 32% female). The most commonly used substances by far were heptadone, morphine, and products containing morphine. Only the so-called hippies preferred hashish. The source of supply was almost exclusively pharmacies, and the means of supply were prescriptions that were being misused or had been stolen or falsified (Grassberger, 1969).

According to official statistics and the reported characteristics of sentenced offenders, drug consumption during the first phase was quite uncommon, the consumers were middle-aged, the main reasons for taking drugs were diseases and injuries, the source of supply was the medical system itself, and the main drugs used were heptadone and morphine. Of course, these drugs were also prescribed legally, and an unknown number of even long-term consumers obtained their drugs officially by being registered at the Ministry for Social Affairs.

In 1969, the number of drug offenders and the proportion of adolescents among them began to increase. A new type of drug study emerged: the representative study of drug experience and drug use among youth. At least 13 such studies have been carried out—only a few representative for all of Austria—and their results can be summarized as follows (Eisenbach-Stangl, in press): During the past 24 years, between 2% and 15% of young Austrians (about 14 to 21 years old) have used illicit drugs, and there has been no obvious variation in the prevalence of drug use. More than half tried only one drug, once or a few times, and very few were regular users. Hashish has been by far the leading drug; only up to 3% also used heroin, cocaine, LSD, or other illicit substances (e.g., amphetamines or sleeping pills sold on the black market).

Since 1975, annual statistics on drug-related offenses have been published (*Suchtgiftstatistik*). Figure 15.1 presents the number of drug offenses becoming known to the police, the number of those related to opiates, and the number of drug-related deaths. Until 1989, the statistics referred only to the deaths of people known to the police in relation to illicit drugs; since then, they have also included hospital deaths of diagnosed drug addicts. Since 1990, the statistics on drug-related deaths are produced by the Ministry of Health.

The more than fourfold increase in drug offenses corresponds well to the findings of the epidemiological studies presented above. The sharp increase in reported drug-related deaths since the end of the 1980s is attributable largely to the greater availability and purity of heroin since the fall of the Iron Curtain, as

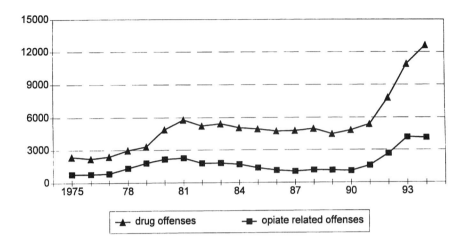

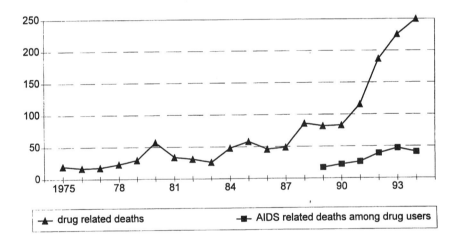

Figure 15.1 Number of Drug-Related Offenses, Opiate-Related Offenses, and
Drug-Related Deaths
SOURCE: Bundesministerium für Inneres (1975-1993).
NOTE: Opiates include poppy straw, raw opium for smoking, opium oil ("Opiumtinktur"), heroin, morphine, and
derivatives.

well as to a change in the method of taking opiates, from drinking infused opium
tea to intravenous injection of heroin, rather than to AIDS or the change in the
registration of drug deaths.

The second phase of drug use was characterized by a steady increase in the
number of young adults using illicit drugs fairly regularly. Their treatment needs
differed from those of the middle-aged addicts of the first phase, who had begun
to take drugs because of diseases and injuries; detoxification or custody in psychiatric hospitals or individual improvement by imprisonment did not seem sufficient.

The first impulse for the establishment of a special treatment system was an amendment of the narcotic law in 1971, and further amendments in the 1980s extended its scope, as we shall see below.

Punishment and Treatment:
The Development of the Narcotic Law After World War II

In 1946, for the first time, a special law on illicit drugs, the *Suchtgiftgesetz,* was enacted. Its German name recalls its history. In 1928, a *Giftgesetz* had been introduced—a law for the control of toxic substances as well as of substances defined as narcotics by international treaties. The 1946 law increased considerably the penalties laid down in the 1928 law: People intentionally producing, importing, or dealing in a quantity of illicit drugs that would endanger the life and health of others now committed a crime against public health and could be imprisoned between 1 and 10 years instead of the previous scale of 1 week to 6 months (*schwerer Kerker*). An amendment in 1948 declared unauthorized purchase and possession of an illicit drug an offense, whether or not the purchaser or possessor intended to deal in it. Thus, purchase and possession for personal use, and such use, became a crime. Austrian law had to be reestablished and updated according to the international treaties signed since 1928 (Erläuterungen, 1946). In 1948, Austria was an occupied country, and the most powerful of the occupying powers—the United States—had tightened up its narcotics laws during the 1930s and 1940s and continued to do so during the 1950s (Eisenbach-Stangl, 1980; Pilgram, 1992).

The law was next amended in 1971, after a contentious public debate on illicit drugs and the drug problem. The amendment represented a compromise (Schilder, 1980): The purchase or possession of drugs for personal use for 1 week was decriminalized, but the user had to undergo a medical examination, and anyone who was prescribed medical treatment or supervision and did not follow the advice for 1 year was reported to the legal authorities, and the criminal procedure was resumed. Thus, sociomedical measures, or, more precisely, enforcement of medical treatment and medical supervision of drug misusers, became part of the narcotic law. This stimulated the establishment of the first special facilities for drug addicts—for involuntary as well as voluntary patients. A further amendment, in 1980, compelled *all* drug users to accept medical treatment or supervision. The health authorities were required to examine every drug user who became known to them; order detoxification, medical treatment, or supervision if necessary; and inform the legal authorities. A third change was the introduction of a new type of institution: the *Anerkannte Einrichtungen* (approved institutions). The Federal Minister of Health has to approve institutions treating or advising drug users, and may subsidize them ("normal" medical institutions are financed by the *Länder,* or states). The approved institutions, together with probation officers, are authorized to carry out the treatment and supervision ordered by the health authorities or the courts. But federal approval and subsidies were linked to federal control; the 1980 amendment required public and private hospitals to inform the Ministry of Health of treated drug addicts. If the law had been strictly enforced, few drug users could have gotten treatment or advice without being penalized or at least risking penalties. General practitioners and psychiatrists or psychotherapists, who are not paid directly by the state and are not part of the control net, at this time refused to treat drug users or addicts.

An amendment in 1985 at last provided for the suspension of prison sentences of up to 2 years to permit convicted drug users to have treatment. The underlying principle may be called "effective therapy instead of imprisonment" (Eisenbach-Stangl & Pilgram, 1985, p. 5).

After 1985, the Ministry of Health issued two decrees on substitution treatment of drug addicts—probably the first purely medical regulations since the enactment of the first narcotic law in 1928. The first substitution decree was issued in 1987 and the second, an amendment of the first, in 1991. In Austria, unlike Germany (Bschor, 1984), the medical profession had never declared substitution—the prescription of opiates to opiate addicts—to be a nonmedical practice. Before 1987, a considerable number of people were permitted to use substances listed in the Suchtgiftgesetz. They had started drug use because of a medical condition—they had received their first drug within the medical system—and were never part of the drug scene. The first substitution decree, in 1987, ended this double standard; it also reflected a change in medical attitudes. This change had set in before the first drug addicts died of AIDS and was probably caused by the persistence of the drug scene—with increasing numbers of long-term users—and by its increasing marginalization, due to the failure of therapy to achieve abstention (Eisenbach-Stangl & Uhl, 1992). In 1991, on the basis of experiences with the decree and its enforcement, the decree was altered. The main changes were that methadone was defined to be the substitution substance of choice and that intravenous drug use no longer was defined as a precondition for substitution.

The Development of the Treatment System in the Shadow of the Narcotic Law: The 1970s

Before 1971, it was only in psychiatric hospitals that illicit drug users could get residential treatment. In 1971, 790 people, or 3% of all those admitted to psychiatric hospitals, were given the diagnosis "drug misuse" (Katschnig, Grumiller, & Strobl, 1975). This number was, no doubt, already influenced by the "drug wave" and exceeded annual admissions during the 1960s. Most were involuntary patients who were detoxified and soon discharged. On a fixed day in 1974, only 0.5%, or fewer than 55, of psychiatric inpatients were drug users (Katschnig et al., 1975).

After 1971, the first inpatient and outpatient centers for drug addicts were founded. The first facility, an outpatient center for drug users and their families, belonged to the Private Association for Probation, a vocational group that had played a key role in introducing treatment instead of punishment. Later, its task was restricted to after-care of released drug offenders who had been treated in prison (Pernhaupt, 1980). Therapy with a group of imprisoned drug offenders began in

1972. In 1975, an amendment to the penal code made it possible to establish institutions combining custodial and therapeutic aims ("treatment prisons"), and one, the so-called penal institution for offenders in need of withdrawal, opened in the same year. It accommodates 80 offenders whose sentences must not exceed 2 years.

The first free (i.e., outside of prison) inpatient facility for drug addicts was established in Vienna in 1972 as part of a psychiatric hospital for alcoholism. In 1975, a second was opened in Tyrol, in western Austria, with 20 beds and a small halfway house for after-care (Pernhaupt, 1980). It was founded by a private association, and its work was based on the self-help principles of Synanon. It was financed partly by private donations and partly by the social welfare authorities of Tyrol and of clients' home states. Treatment, or rather "care," was provided for about a year.

The first notable increase in the number of outpatient facilities occurred only at the end of the 1970s with the establishment of about 10 centers, mostly by health or social welfare authorities. The expansion of outpatient treatment reduced the power of treatment staff and increased the freedom of patients to choose therapists or advisers and the right to codetermine the time and place of treatment or advice. This gradual change in the treatment system was marked particularly by a pilot project of a new type of outpatient work: In September 1979, the first street workers began to work in Vienna, and in June 1980 their role was formally established (Nittmann, 1980).

Expansion and Emancipation: The First Half of the 1980s

In the early 1980s, three more inpatient facilities were founded: the first as a private association like that in the Tyrol, partly applying the principles of Synanon (Rittmannsberger & Ebner, 1988); the second as a department of the Psychiatric Hospital of Vienna; and the third as a department of a psychiatric hospital for alcoholics in the most western Austrian state (Hauser & Haller, 1988). The first free (i.e., outside of prison) inpatient facility in Vienna more than doubled its beds and founded a department for detoxification at a general hospital. This tripled the number of beds in free facilities (120), slightly exceeding the number in the treatment prison (110), which had also been increased.

The development of outpatient facilities for drug users since 1980 has been more complex. In 1981, the Ministry of Health issued a brochure on illicit drugs (BMfGuU, 1981), listing approved institutions, which numbered 36 outpatient facilities. However, only 27 of them treated drug users, and of these, only 11 were specialized—no more than in 1980. Also, most of the nonspecialized institutions had been established and worked with drug users before 1980 (Eisenbach-Stangl & Pilgram, 1983). In other words, after 1980, the Ministry of Health—which administered the narcotic law and the federal funds for the approved institutions—approved a large number of diverse outpatient facilities and probably subsidized all of the specialized facilities; but it also approved a large number of psychiatric outpatient facilities, a few health authorities, youth advisory centers, and other institutions. The most numerous professionals were medical, followed by social workers. The juridical system referred two thirds of the clients, and the approved outpatient facilities in 1982 treated 2,039 drug users, of whom one third were female (Erlacher, 1985).

Thus, it appears that in the first half of the 1980s, as 10 years earlier, the special inpatient facilities expanded more than the outpatient facilities. The narcotic law still played an important part, providing both inpatients and outpatients and defining the aims of treatment, which were almost exclusively withdrawal and abstinence. However, criticism of these aims defined by the penal system had begun. For instance, in 1980, the first public discussion on substitution therapy, with Swiss and German speakers, took place at the department of psychiatry of the University of Vienna, and an issue of the *Viennese Journal on Addiction Research* was devoted to the topic. A psychiatrist at the psychiatric clinic of the University of Vienna began to experiment with methadone treatment: At first, he prescribed it for pregnant women and, after a few years, also for long-term opiate addicts (Eisenbach-Stangl & Uhl, 1992). In 1984, a study of the attitudes of approved institutions for substitution therapy found that only 14% opposed it, compared with 66% in the 1982 study (Eisenbach-Stangl & Lingler, 1986). Also, in 1984, the first Austrian interest group of drug workers, founded at the end of the 1970s, announced its acceptance of substitution therapy under certain circumstances—for example, if it was accompanied by psychosocial care and was not compulsory (Österreichischer Arbeitskreis, 1984). Finally, in 1986, the faculty of medicine of the University of Vienna declared substitution therapy to be a scientific method. A medical doctor who was prosecuted for giving opiate addicts codeine and heptadone was acquitted (Fakultätsgutachten, 1986).

Attitudes toward substitution therapy in psychiatry and in the special treatment system for drug addicts had begun to change before the first drug users became infected with HIV. In 1983, two addicts were registered; in 1984, none; and in 1985, five. The change was influenced mainly by experience with drug work—the many relapses and the few "cures"—by the change in the drug scene, and by observing treatment policies in neighboring countries, especially in Switzerland.

Professionalization, Diversification, and Medicalization: The Second Half of the 1980s and the 1990s

This period began with upheavals in four of the six free inpatient facilities, unconnected with one another, and never investigated in detail. Patients went on strike, and three heads of institutions were replaced. Two were private facilities applying the principles of Synanon (one later became a department of the psychiatric hospital), and two were psychiatric institutions, one of which was the first inpatient clinic. The head of another inpatient facility offered the following explanation:

> It seems to us that the therapists who at first dominated therapy and the drug facilities by their personalities have been replaced by a generation of helpers with solid training, including training in psychotherapy, less pronounced personal engagement, more realistic expectations, and less identification with their clients. (Hauser & Haller, 1988, p. 43)

This description is accurate. Nevertheless, the replaced head of the first free psychiatric inpatient facility immediately founded another one in the countryside (*Grüner Kreis*), with about 100 beds, and by 1993 it had grown to 150 beds, or half of all beds in free inpatient facilities. It again applies Synanon principles and is the most closely connected with the juridical system. It is financed partly by the social welfare system and partly by the juridical system, which has paid for "cures" since 1985.

Also after 1985, two residential detoxification facilities and two small private facilities were established. Thus, by 1993, the free inpatient facilities provided more than three times as many beds (320) as the treatment prison, which had reduced the number of its beds to 90 to improve its living conditions.

The most remarkable development in outpatient care was the provision of a few low-threshold facilities offering a "bed for the night," medical care, syringe exchange, and sometimes street work. Also, of course, substitution therapy was promoted in 1987, although the police actively impeded it in at least one of the three *Länder* that took immediate advantage of the change in the regulations and extended methadone treatment to addicts other than those who were HIV-infected. From 1987, when 214 addicts were treated with methadone, until mid-1996, a total of 4,006 addicts were treated. Methadone prescription is controlled by the regional health authorities.

It can be concluded that offers of inpatient and outpatient treatment were remarkably diversified after 1985 and more closely met clients' needs than ever before. This diversification was due to the increasing professionalization of medical and nonmedical drug workers, as well as to the increasing acceptance by the medical-psychiatric system that addicts should be treated, owing to the new health risks posed by HIV infection and AIDS. Work with drug addicts was integrated in more psychiatric institutions and also in the general medical system (especially substitution therapy). However, drug addicts are still far from being treated like other patients, even in Vienna, which has the most extensive and diversified special treatment system.

The special treatment system is also more divided than ever. Professionalization, diversification, and medicalization concern only one part—the larger part if outpatient facilities are counted. The other part, which was also expanding strongly after 1985, is based on self-help principles, linked to the social welfare and juridical systems, and cheaper than the medical-psychiatric part. And because the daily rates of neither the health insurance nor the social welfare (for noninsured patients) system cover the expenses of the inpatient facilities, the medical-psychiatric and the social welfare, or cheaper, facilities are already competing acrimoniously for additional funding.

Discussion

Special treatment for drug addicts, other than detoxification and custody in psychiatric hospitals, was established only after the emergence of the first adolescent and young adult drug users at the end of the 1960s. The 1971 amendment of the narcotic law introduced medical controls and treatment instead of court sentences for minor drug offenses, reflecting largely the proposals of probation officers and teachers that medical supervision and treatment replace punishment, and that the possession and use of drugs be decriminalized. The amendments of 1980 and 1985 extended the process of substituting treatment for punishment, and since 1980, treatment facilities have been directly and increasingly promoted by federal financial support. Consequently, treatment was aimed at abstinence, and the courts monitored its effects.

Although the special treatment system remained closely linked to penal controls and was subordinate to them until 1985, it had already begun to change, though slowly, by about 1980. Its expansion enabled drug workers to form a stronger, more visible, and more influential interest group, whose members emphasized the health aspects of the drug problem and the need for therapeutic answers to it. Substitution was increasingly considered to be one answer, and the first experiments with methadone took place.

A more remarkable change occurred after the mid-1980s. The numbers of beds in free inpatient facilities for drug addicts began to exceed those of beds in the treatment prison; the Ministry of Health recommended substitution therapy, and it was increasingly applied; and low-threshold outpatient centers were opened. HIV and AIDS were only one reason for the change, but no doubt the only one that counted to the public. Others were the aging and marginalization of the drug scene, as well as the increasing number of long-term addicts who were not attracted by abstinence therapy or who could not be "cured" by it. The consolidation of the drug market, especially that of heroin, at the end of the 1980s and the associated increase of drug deaths may have supported the change. It became obvious that the police and the system of justice could not "solve" or even control the drug problem. And notably, the change was stimulated and supported by developments in neighboring countries, especially Switzerland.

References

BMfGuU. (Ed.). (1981). *Drogen, Sucht und Therapie. Das Drogenproblem in Österreich und die Wege zu seiner Lösung* [Drugs, addiction, and therapy. The drug problem in Austria and possible reactions to it] (Vol. 1). Vienna: Author.

Bschor, F. (1984). Permissive, repressive oder rehabilitative Strategie im Suchtgiftbereich [Permissive, repressive, or rehabilitative strategies against addiction]. In I. Eisenbach-Stangl & W. Stangl (Eds.), *Grenzen der Behandlung* [Limits to treatment] (pp. 173-182). Opladen: Westdeutscher Verlag.

Bundesministerium für Inneres. (1975-1993). *Jahresbericht über die Suchtgiftkriminalität in Österreich.* Vienna: Bundesministerium für Inneres, Abt. II/f, Zentralstelle für die Bekämpfung der Suchtgiftkriminalität.

Eisenbach-Stangl, I. (1980). Drogenpolitik und ihre Folgen—Ein internationaler Vergleich [Drug policies and their consequences—An international comparison]. In R. Mader & H. Strotzka (Eds.), *Drogenpolitik zwischen Therapie und Strafe* [Drug policy between therapy and punishment] (pp. 355-442). Vienna: Jugend und Volk.

Eisenbach-Stangl, I. (in press). Ausmaß und Entwicklung jugendlichen Alkohol- und Drogenkonsums [Extent and development of alcohol and drugs consumption by juveniles]. *Wiener Zeitschrift für Suchtforschung.*

Eisenbach-Stangl, I., & Lingler, F. (1986). Für und wider die pharmakologische Unterstützung Morphinabhängiger. Ergebnisse einer Befragung von Drogenbetreuern und Bewährungshelfern [Pro and contra substitution treatment of opiate addicts. Results of a study on the attitudes of drug workers and probation officers]. *Wiener Zeitschrift für Suchtforschung, 1/2,* 38-45.

Eisenbach-Stangl, I., & Pilgram, A. (1983). *Zum Behandlungsgedanken im Strafrecht—Folgen und Probleme der Suchtgiftgesetzesnovelle 1980* [Treatment and penal law. Consequences and problems of the amendment of the narcotic law of 1980] (Vol. 1). Vienna: L. Boltzmann-Institut für Suchtforschung und Institut für Rechts- und Kriminalsoziologie.

Eisenbach-Stangl, I., & Pilgram, A. (1985). Gift im Gesetz. Die 4. Novelle zum Suchtgiftgesetz trat am 1.9. in Kraft [Poison in the law. The 4th amendment of the narcotic law came into force on 1 September]. *Falter, 18,* 5-10.

Eisenbach-Stangl, I., & Uhl, A. (1992). Geschichte und Praxis der Substitutionsbehandlung in Österreich [The history and present state of substitution treatment in Austria]. In H. Bossong & H. Stöver (Eds.), *Methadonbehandlung* [Methadon treatment] (pp. 181-197). Frankfurt/Main: Campus.

Erlacher, I. (1985). Jahresstatistik 1982 der anerkannten Einrichtungen zur Betreuung von Suchtgiftmißbrauchern und -abhängigen [Data on approved institutions for the treatment of drug misusers and addicts in 1982]. *Mitteilungen der österreichischen Sanitätsverwaltung, 3,* 46-50.

Erläuterungen zum Entwurf eines Suchtgiftgesetzes [Comments on the draft of the narcotic law]. (1946). Bundesgesetzblatt.

Fakultätsgutachten [Expertise of faculty]. (1986). *Wiener Zeitschrift für Suchtforschung, 1/2,* 32-37.

Grassberger, R. (1969). Suchtgiftmißbrauch und Kriminalität [Drug misuse and crime]. In *Kriminalpolitische Schriftenreihe* (Vol. 2, Part 2, pp. 111-143). Vienna: Austrian Ministry of the Interior.

Hauser, W., & Haller, R. (1988). Drogenstation Krankenhaus Stiftung Maria Ebene [Drug clinic Krankenhaus Stiftung Maria Ebene]. *Wiener Zeitschrift für Suchtforschung, 2/3,* 41-50.

Katschnig, H., Grumiller, I., & Strobl, R. (1975). *Daten zur stationären psychiatrischen Versorgung Österreichs: Vol. 1, Inzidenz; Vol. 2, Prävalenz* [Data on psychiatric inpatient treatment in Austria: Vol. 1, Incidence; Vol. 2, Prevalence]. Vienna: Österreichisches Bundesinstitut für Gesundheitswesen.

Nittmann, G. (1980). Streetwork mit Drogenabhängigen [Street-work for drug addicts]. In R. Mader & H. Strotzka (Eds.), *Drogenpolitik zwischen Therapie und Strafe* [Drug policy between therapy and punishment] (pp. 307-314). Vienna: Jugend und Volk.

Österreichischer Arbeitskreis. (1984). 5. Arbeitstagung. *Wiener Zeitschrift für Suchtforschung, 1/2,* 85-86.

Pernhaupt, G. (1980). Behandlungsprogramme und -möglichkeiten für Drogenabhängige in Österreich [Treatment programs for drug addicts in Austria]. In R. Mader & H. Strotzka (Eds.), *Drogenpolitik zwischen Therapie und Strafe* [Drug policy between therapy and punishment] (pp. 227-306). Vienna: Jugend und Volk.

Pilgram, A. (1992). Mit dem Gesetz gegen Drogen—Zur Geschichte des österreichischen Suchtgiftgesetzes [With the law against drugs. The history of the Austrian narcotic law]. *Beiträge zur historischen Sozialkunde, 1,* 26-32.

Rittmannsberger, H., & Ebner, W. (1988). Entwicklung von Teamstruktur und Konzept: Die ersten fünf Jahre der Therapiestation Erlenhof [The development of the treatment team and the treatment program. The first five years of the drug clinic Erlenhof]. *Wiener Zeitschrift für Suchtforschung, 2/3,* 17-22.

Schilder, E. (1980). Zur Entstehung des § 9a Suchtgiftgesetz [History of the § 9a of the narcotic law]. In R. Mader & H. Strotzka (Eds.), *Drogenpolitik zwischen Therapie und Strafe* [Drug policy between therapy and punishment] (pp. 263-276). Wien: Jugend und Volk.

Chapter 16

German *Rechthaberei* and Its Contribution to a Modern Drug Abuse Treatment System

Gerhard Bühringer

Comment on Part 4

Austria, with 7 million inhabitants, and Germany after reunification, with 81 million, resemble each other in many respects and differ from other European states. Besides German as their common national language, they share commonalities in politics, society, and culture—in short, in how they understand important aspects of life and especially how they adapt to changing times. When change becomes inevitable and its direction and course have to be decided, they tend to manifest a characteristic attitude of *Prinzipientreue* (clinging to principles) or, with a more negative connotation, *Rechthaberei* (disputatiousness) or even *Verbissenheit* (doggedness). They do not adopt the future-oriented, trial-and-error attitude of Anglo-American culture, or the sophisticated French style of discussing the future, or the laissez-faire way of progress of the Mediterranean countries. Their stance is, rather, "Here I am and I am right; I did it yesterday in my way, and I do it today in the same way, and this is the perfect way for the future." The development of the drug abuse treatment system in the past 30 years in both countries is a good example. Germany is much more extreme than Austria in this respect; therefore, more examples in the following text are taken from that country.

A naive observer of the treatment service system in both countries today would note nothing striking, in comparison with European drug use prevalence figures and standards of treatment service:

— The prevalence of drug dependence is average to low, and the rate of cannabis users among young people is also inconspicuous.
— Negative consequences of drug abuse, as indicated, for example, by cases of drug-related death and rates of HIV-infected drug abusers, are average or even low by European standards.
— In Germany, over the past 25 years, federally funded demonstration projects with dozens of facilities and hundreds or thousands of clients in each program have shown improvements under field conditions in nearly all areas of drug abuse treatment, such as outreach work, outpatient and residential treatment, drop-out rates, treatment in prison, and after-care. Until about 1985, the Federal Department of Health was, surprisingly, the major source of new ideas for the treatment system and often challenged its conservative administrators.

Altogether, qualitatively and according to statistical figures, the position is much better than many experts and politicians inside and outside these countries would have the public believe. What is the reason, therefore, for the German *Rechthaberei*? We note this cultural trait when we try to understand why certain developments in the treatment system, clearly necessary for some time, simply have not materialized. Some of the reasons are the following:

— There are endless and pointless disputes among experts about the *true cause* of substance-induced dependence and the preference for oversimplified concepts such as "society," "family," or "heredity."
— There is a quest for the *best* and *only way* to treat drug abuse, and a rejection of individually tailored treatment.
— There is a need *to solve all facets of the drug problem* for good by developing a comprehensive theoretical framework, at the same time discrediting any kind of pragmatism.
— There is an assumption that only the *genuine motivation* of drug dependents is a valid basis for any kind of treatment; this motivation has to be carefully checked, and clients are expected to prove it constantly.
— Complete abstinence is the *only acceptable goal* of treatment.
— People are treated only if they swear on their knees that their true inner wish is to achieve complete abstinence; otherwise, they are not worth treating. Improving certain life conditions without abstinence is a waste of therapeutic effort and results in even more drug abuse.

There are many more instances of such attitudes, which have delayed improvements for years in the well-established and well-organized, predominantly inpatient and abstinence-oriented, drug treatment system, improvements that would move it in the direction of a modern public health-oriented system. However, the picture would be incomplete without mention of the structural factors that have long impeded change:

Federalism: Germany and, in part, Austria have an extensive form of federalism, which delegates to their states many rights and responsibilities, including health and social care. Therefore, there are differences in treatment rationales, service systems, density of services, and even the practice of court sentencing.

Subsidiarity: In the German drug abuse service system, except for detoxification in psychiatric hospitals, about 90% of the services are run by nonprofit organizations. They are locally organized and well financed by a complex system of city, regional, and state funding; health and pension insurance; and local and regional social security systems. Altogether, they amount to hundreds of responsible public and private agencies, an excellent basis for many committees, meetings, and discussions about the *right way.*

Belief in legal control: Until about 1985, the Austrian treatment system and rationale were heavily influenced by legal authorities; modifications were difficult.

Lack of competition: Given the excellent financing of drug treatment services compared with that of other health and social services, there was for years no need of competition, and therefore, there was enough time for discussing principles instead of improving details.

The conventional service system for drug dependence was not prepared for HIV infection or new concepts such as harm reduction. The advocates of a more public-health-oriented drug service system had new ideas but not a new way of thinking—dogmatism as usual. Again, they discussed principles instead of broadening the empirical basis of knowledge about the consequences of possible changes (e.g., codeine substitution and the advantages or disadvantages of public "shooting galleries").

The various elements of the drug treatment system need to be integrated. They include the ideologically separated treatment *service* systems, low-threshold activities, methadone maintenance, and residential treatment that is abstinence oriented and based on professional care as well as self-help. Such integration and a more coherent policy should be based on the following considerations:

— Some drug dependents, for whatever reason, seek treatment, and some do not; an effort should be made to reach those who do not. At the same time, it must be realized that some do not want to change their lifestyles and therefore will continue to be subject to a certain extent to health, social, and legal problems.

— Drug dependents cannot be treated as a homogeneous group. Therefore, in each case, it is necessary to do an individual problem analysis and to clarify for each individual and for treatment staff the goal of treatment and the values to be cultivated so as to design an individually tailored treatment plan.

— The problems, concepts, and needs of clients change over time. The treatment response has to be matched continuously with changing demands and client profiles.

— Abstinence is truly the ultimate goal in terms of social independence and freedom, but it has to be accepted that some clients do not want to, or cannot, reach this target at a given point, or for a given time period, or even in their lifetimes. But for ethical reasons, they must be given care; they need treatment to improve their health, and even for financial reasons, so as to avoid the expensive negative consequences of drug abuse.

Putting these principles into practice seems simple. It remains to be seen, however, whether *Rechthaberei* will prevail over healthy pragmatism and whether pragmatism will be backed by favorable structural and socioeconomic conditions.

Part V

The Latin American

Connection

Chapter 17

Drug Consumption and Drug Treatment in a Drug-Producing Country: Colombia Between Myth and Reality—A View From the Inside

Augusto Pérez-Gómez

Colombia has acquired notoriety in relation to the international trade in cocaine. In the past 15 years, most newspaper, magazine, or journal headlines with the word "Colombia" refer to narco-trafficking, narco-traffickers, money laundering, or methods of producing cocaine. Colombia is seen as a corrupt narco-democracy, and Colombia, in turn, labels the United States as an eager consumer of drugs, the demand for which is at the root of the problem. This stereotype of Colombia overlooks completely the existence of "homemade," domestic drug problems. They have consequently been widely ignored and even denied, although drug use inside the country mirrors the narco-trafficking and affects tens of thousands of adolescents and young people and their families. Official police reports show that the increase in rates of street crime (robberies, assaults, muggings, homicides) in the large cities—Bogotá, Medellín, Cali—is strongly associated with drug use and drug dealing (Policía Nacional de Colombia, 1990-1995). The government's countermeasures are insufficient. Domestic, drug-related social problems are ignored, and very little money is expended on prevention or rehabilitation. The police are poorly paid and understaffed (fewer than one policeman per 1,000 population) and not always well-equipped. In 1995 alone, 22 policemen were killed and 43 injured in combating drug activities. Nevertheless, police action was having some effect, according to statistics for 1996 presented by the Director of the National Police Drug Squadron. Moreover, Bolivia, Colombia, Ecuador, Peru, and Venezuela agreed in June 1996 to step up repressive measures;

they established an Andean antidrug intelligence unit, for example. Nevertheless, it can be assumed that 93% of the cocaine produced in Colombia can be readily exported.

Several years ago, the three main cocaine-producing/processing countries, Colombia, Peru, and Bolivia, adopted a collective policy of concealing the facts about internal drug abuse, on the basis of the widely publicized argument that "drug consumption is a problem of the rich countries"; in fact, they were avoiding conflict with the *cocaleros,* or peasants whose main crop is coca leaf. In 1996, this policy revealed its extremely negative long-term consequences: On one hand, the United States "decertified" Colombia (an official expression of its dissatisfaction at what it regarded as Colombia's inadequate cooperation in combating the drug trade), with serious economic implications; on the other hand, the *cocaleros* rioted, protesting violently against the government's commitment to finally destroy the crops. Colombia, Peru, and Bolivia have relied mainly on international cooperation (from the United Nations Drug Control Program or European Union programs) to deal with internal drug use, which is why almost all of the organizations that are engaged in primary prevention, treatment, and rehabilitation in those countries are nongovernmental and private, for-profit and nonprofit, organizations.

Drug consumption in Colombia can be regarded as a new problem if it is thought of as a social condition. Local native communities (the Paeces, Huitoto, or Kogi Indians) have taken psychoactive substances for centuries without any trouble, in the context of highly ritualized ceremonies.

Like other developing countries, Colombia has undergone rapid transformation in the past 30 years. The mid-1960s saw the onset of rural-to-urban migration: Today, 70% of the population lives in cities, and 30% in just four (Bogotá, Medellín, Cali, and Barranquilla). The history of violence in Colombia is closely connected with this modernization process (on the modernization theory, see Boulez & Vaughn, 1995); it was associated with not only economic difficulties but also guerrilla warfare and narco-trafficking, which particularly provoked the massive migration from rural areas and consequent explosive urban and periurban conditions of misery and bitterness.

The Epidemiology of Drug Use

The first epidemiological study of drug use in Colombia, published in 1987, estimated that there were 81,246 users of coca paste and 31,207 of cocaine (Torres de Galvis & Murrelle, 1987). Although the results of the Drug Use National Household Survey (Encuesta Nacional de Hogares sobre Uso de Drogas) conducted in 1992 showed a seeming increase (an estimated 343,218 lifetime users of coca paste and 338,419 of cocaine), this has to be interpreted very cautiously. The former study was carried out on a sample of 2,800 subjects, restricted to four major cities (700 in each), and the conclusions were generalized to the whole country. The latter study was more representative; it used data from the national census to construct a master sample from six areas (Rodriguez & Duque, 1992). All studies show a remarkable agreement on the principal substance of abuse: alcohol. The three main illicit substances are marijuana, cocaine, and *basuco* (coca paste). The abuse of opiates is limited; most of the heroin is smuggled out of the country, mainly to the United States, where heroin of Colombian origin has accounted for the bulk of the heroin seized. The amount of illicit opium production in 1995 was estimated at 65.5 tons (International Narcotics Control Board, 1997). The 1992 household survey showed the highest lifetime and past-month prevalence of use of cocaine and coca paste in the big cities, peaking at between 30 and 39 years (cocaine, 9.1% and 2.0%, respectively; coca paste, 13.2% and 2.0%, respectively; Torres de Galvis, 1993).

Epidemiological surveys have led to the establishment of monitoring systems in Colombia (Epidemiological Surveillance System of Drug Use and Abuse/VESPA) and also in Peru (Sistema de Registro del Uso y Abuso del Alcohol y Drogas). VESPA is based on data obtained from the High School Senior Students Survey and from treatment admissions, emergency room visits, household surveys, and forensic medicine autopsies. Its objective, to generate information for the assessment of drug abuse policies and programs (Torres de Galvis, 1993), should also provide a sound baseline for evaluating the treatment response—the major focus of this chapter. Finally, Montoya and Chilcoat (1996) note in their comparative analysis of the epidemiology of the use of coca derivatives in the Andean region that "in contrast to the decline of cocaine use observed in the United States, the use in Colombia shows a marked increase" (p. 1235). Again, this finding calls for appropriate preventive as well as treatment measures.

Treatment

We have seen that drug treatment is provided mainly by private, for-profit and nonprofit organizations. The government provides around 200 beds for drug dependents in several state hospitals around the country, but they are occupied mostly by psychiatric patients. No hospital or clinic, public or private, has yet published reliable information on the results of treatment, for various reasons: Follow-up is extremely difficult; it is not customary to evaluate health services; and there are no trained evaluators. Mainly, however, it is because the government has almost no interest in treatment for drug addicts: It maintains that Colombia has hundreds of other health priorities, which is consistent with its refusal to acknowledge that the country has a drug problem.

This reflects to some extent changing public opinion. In the late 1980s and early 1990s, drug use became the sixth source of worry for average Colombians, after street violence and insecurity, guerrillas, narco-trafficking, kidnapping, and unemployment. The serious political difficulties of 1995/1996 displaced drugs as a matter of public concern (Centro Nacional de Consultoría, 1989-1995).

Very few institutions have published detailed accounts of their procedures, which may vary with the interests of a new director or a new trend. Of course, this lack of information is also a reflection of governmental indifference to drugs. One must stress, however, that there are more than 150 treatment centers for drug addicts, a fertile but neglected field for research.

In summary, there is no reliable information on the evaluation of drug treatment in Colombia; there are no national and very few regional statistics on the subject. However, an estimated minimum of 20,000 drug users receive some kind of treatment every year, not including those who attend Alcoholics Anonymous or Narcotics Anonymous programs.

The influence of foreign models of treatment has been negative. In the 1970s and 1980s, the most popular were those influenced by Italian and North American therapeutic communities (CeIS, Daytop Village, Straight, Walden House, Phoenix House). Most were strongly confrontational, which proved unacceptable to most Colombian patients, who usually dropped out of treatment after a few days or weeks. The therapeutic communities that remain are "softer" versions of the original models, and a large proportion are managed by religious organizations (Protestant more than Catholic, although more than 90% of the population is Catholic).

Many clinicians reject treatment with substitution drugs (methadone for heroin, diamorphine for certain opiates, and licit for illicit amphetamines). Drug use is not seen as merely a personal matter, but one that involves the family and society as a whole. Typically, the public and the media ask how a developing country can employ its limited resources to perpetuate a problem (drug abuse) instead of solving it, and why people who choose to become drug addicts are given drugs when thousands of poor children and elderly people with serious health problems get no treatment.

It is of interest that addicts and former addicts were those who raised the loudest public outcry against the decision of the Constitutional Court in May 1994 on the definition of the "maximum amount of a given drug for personal use" and on the right to use drugs (see also Ambos, 1993, p. 178, art. 34). The Congress eventually modified the Constitution and, at the end of 1995, approved an amendment making prohibition the norm. Initiatives favoring legalization, recently supported by intellectual leaders such as García Márquez, are exceptional.

Types of Institutions

Several kinds of institutions treat drug users. Until the early 1980s, only conventional psychiatric clinics did so, but owing to their poor results, together with the rapid increase in numbers of users, different approaches had to be considered, including the use of 12-step models, of which there are many (about 75 Alcoholics Anonymous but only three Narcotics Anonymous groups). From the available information, despite its poor quality, some of these approaches can be considered successful, whereas others cannot. Surprisingly, there has been no systematic effort to establish a link between drug use and AIDS, probably because more than 80% of cases of HIV infection are still strongly related to male homosexual intercourse (Ministerio de Salud, 1996).

In principle, all drug treatment institutions are members of the Health Network, which is under the Ministry of Health. But it has never functioned properly because it lacks the expertise, the finances, and the operational capacity to exert adequate control over the large number of highly heterogeneous institutions.

Psychiatric Clinics and Mental Hospitals

Conventional psychiatric facilities have low credibility because their treatment, based mainly on neuroleptics, is highly inappropriate, and almost all patients relapse within a month of discharge. There are some exceptions, such as the Hospital Mental de Antioquia, where low-income patients receive group and occupational therapy and medication. Generally, however, this option is considered a last resort, and many would prefer no treatment at all.

Day Clinics and Nonresidential Hospital Wards

These became very popular a few years ago. Some are funded by the government (there are only six in Bogotá), and some are charities (such as Caminos, in Cali). Usually, they concentrate on physical recuperation, raising self-esteem, and adoption of new lifestyles. Most have an excellent reputation among patients in serious trouble from their drug use. Some of their staff are professionals (psychologists, psychiatrists, social workers), and others are former addicts who have received some training. Difficulties with the latter are not rare because of their high rates of relapse.

Therapeutic Communities

Influenced by European or North American models, therapeutic communities were the first alternative to psychiatric clinics during the 1980s, but they have several disadvantages: Colombians dislike their ideology and repressive style, and the prolonged reclusion (6 months to 3 years) that they impose complicates social reinsertion. Still, they suit particularly well users of hard drugs with long histories of drug abuse and criminal or delinquent behavior. In the past few years, they have modified substantially some of their original methods to reduce rising drop-out rates.

Short-Term Residential Clinics

Most of these are in large cities and follow the methods of Alcoholics Anonymous. Treatment is residential (30 to 90 days), confrontational, and, by Colombian standards, expensive. They suit intensive and compulsive users with no criminal background.

Outpatient Centers

Outpatient centers have a particular connotation in Colombia: Patients attend voluntarily and are treated intensively (as much as 24 therapy hours per week). La Casa, in Bogotá, exemplifies this modality. Typically, their patients are very young (90% between 13 and 25 years) and want to become abstinent, although this is not a prerequisite for entering treatment; they receive individual, family, and group therapy, and their parents are expected to take part in the process by attendance at special weekly meetings; the fees are low; motivational interview and relapse prevention strategies are routine; and social reinsertion programs are obligatory, because most patients are unskilled and unemployed and have nothing to do.

Mostly, the outpatient services are used by those still in education or in work and who are not compulsive users. For this reason, and because they are inexpensive and well adapted to circumstances in South America, where they were developed, they are described in general outline below.

Typical Client Profiles

Outpatient programs in general share many characteristics, some related to the patients, some to the interventions, and some to theoretical issues. For instance, most accept only volunteers of 14 to 45 years old; the typical patient is male, single, unemployed, and 18 to 30 years old; 85% of cases attend because of polydrug use, mainly in the "ABC pattern" (alcohol, *basuco,* coca paste), and cannabis, or alcohol, *baretta* (slang for cannabis), and cocaine hydrochloride. In the past 4 years, this pattern has been changing: There are now more very young adolescents (14 to 16 years old) and more girls. The kind of substance is also changing: Many more are using benzodiazepines, especially Rohypnol, and there is a small, though not negligible, number of heroin users.

As mentioned before, Colombia has no national comprehensive system of statistics for monitoring characteristics of patients. Institutions are not obliged to report data, and families pay for treatment, which is not covered by social security. However, there are regional VESPA statistics about some characteristics of 292 admissions to institutions in the period from October to December 1992. The primary drug was alcohol in 41% of cases; in 31% of cases, it was marijuana; in 20%, it was coca paste; and in 3%, it was cocaine. These data, from three drug abuse treatment centers in the Medellín area, showed also that most patients were male (86%), single (59%), and reasonably well educated (12% college or more), but mostly unemployed (46%). Even though 51% had been arrested previously, only 5% had been referred by the justice system, compared with 30% by the education system, and 25% were admitted because of family pressure. Lack of funding for involuntary treatment or committal is an obvious explanation of this finding. Another indicator of the low degree of integration and development of the treatment system is the high percentage of first admissions (76%). The revolving-door phenomenon, well known in other countries, does not occur in Colombia, it seems (Torres de Galvis, 1993, 1994; Torres de Galvis & Montoya, 1997).

Treatment Modalities and Treatment Rationale

The 92 nongovernmental outpatient treatment centers form a loose network that organizes training and shares experience in treatment methods and standards. In my capacity as Director of the La Casa treatment center, which is part of the network, I have found that certain principles are valid for successful treatment, and these and more general ideas on the treatment rationale of most of the centers are outlined below.

Treatment Strategies

Most centers would agree that therapeutic measures ought to combine individual, family, and group strategies as well as education. For almost a decade now, those in charge of these programs have been aware of the need for a combination of treatment methods in a multimodal pattern; individual therapy alone is rarely effective, but group therapy does not meet some patients' needs. Except when someone who is homeless or alone comes for treatment, which is unusual, the addict patient must be accompanied through the treatment process by a relative or close friend.

It is a golden rule in some of these centers that patients are never asked to do more than they can at any given moment: For example, to require total abstinence from the beginning is a most effective way to ensure early drop-out. It is only when change has definitely set in that therapists introduce specific demands as proof of commitment to treatment, such as looking for work, changing patterns of drug use, or refusing to see "dangerous" friends. Nevertheless, some organizations require abstinence from the outset.

The centers appreciate cooperation with self-help groups during after-care. Many such groups provide free training to those willing to organize self-help groups in their areas of residence; when this is not possible, the centers make the necessary contacts with one of the nearly 70 Alcoholics Anonymous or Narcotics Anonymous groups meeting in Bogotá or the nearly 200 in the whole country.

Treatment Models

Mostly, the medical model is rejected. In general, drug abuse is not considered a health hazard or a disease but a *social* problem; therefore, drug users are not "sick" people. Such a view is clearly consonant with the fact that drug treatment is not medically controlled. Paradoxically, several institutions, influenced by the 12-step model, base their treatment on the assumption of disease as the explanation of drug use.

In accordance with the previous point, in almost all treatment centers or institutions, patients are seen as being responsible for a large part of their behavior, and this is true particularly of drug use. Nobody has been forced to become an addict, and understanding the underlying reasons for the individual drug career does not rule out the notion of self-responsibility; at the same time, there is no connotation of guilt. The object of intervention is the development of self-control, including the avoidance of situations and circumstances that may trigger relapse. This is why voluntary attendance for treatment is required. It is assumed that any adult can decide to use or not use drugs, with all the implications and consequences of such a decision; in this context, compulsory treatment cannot be considered a legitimate option.

Some institutions require total abstinence; others, like La Casa, expect abstinence from illicit drugs and controlled use of licit substances (alcohol and tobacco). We are aware of the controversies surrounding this position, but (a) we have to function in the framework of current laws; (b) all current positions on the drug problem, except perhaps the more radical (total repression, total liberalization), are inconsistent and contradictory; (c) we work with compulsive users, in whom the damage resulting from drug use is undeniable (and this includes, of course, alcohol); and (d) this position may change if social and cultural conditions are modified.

Conclusions

Drug abuse in Colombia became a problem in the mid-1970s but was recognized as such only in the past decade. Today, the main efforts in prevention and treatment are supported by nongovernmental organizations; they are trying to develop intervention strategies suited to local conditions instead of merely replicating what has been done elsewhere. Despite the lack of evaluation, these programs are largely accepted by the population, and often the organizations cannot cope with the demand.

The growing use of heroin, even if still small, is a new threat. The relationship between drug use and AIDS is becoming clearer; so far, it is linked almost exclusively to sexual activity and not to intravenous use of psychoactive substances. However, this may change.

In the current conditions of South America, and of Colombia in particular, day clinics and outpatient intensive treatment centers seem to offer the best conditions for those abusing psychoactive substances.

It is not easy to be optimistic about the future. Colombia is experiencing one of the most difficult periods in its history, in many respects. The social, political, economic, and international dimensions of Colombia's situation are in permanent deterioration, and this may stimulate massive drug use and—given the government's priorities—a further deterioration of prevention and treatment.

References

Ambos, K. (1993). *Die Drogenkontrolle und ihre Probleme in Kolumbien, Peru und Bolivien* [Problems of drug control measures in Colombia, Peru, and Bolivia]. Freiburg: Max-Planck-Institut für ausländisches und internationales Strafrecht.

Boulez, E. E., & Vaughn, M. S. (1995). Violent crime and modernization in Colombia. *Crime, Law & Social Change, 23,* 17-40.

Centro Nacional de Consultoría [National Center of Consultancy]. (1989-1995). Encuesta anual: qué opinan los colombianos? [National survey: What do Colombians think?]. Santafé de Bogotá: Revista Semana.

International Narcotics Control Board—Vienna. (1997). *Report of the International Narcotics Control Board for 1996* (United Nations Publication no. E.97.XI.3). New York: United Nations.

Ministerio de Salud. (1996). *Boletín Epidemiológico Nacional* [National Epidemiological Bulletin]. Bogotá: MinSalud.

Montoya, I. D., & Chilcoat, H. D. (1996). Epidemiology of coca derivatives use in the Andean region: A tale of five countries. *Substance Use & Misuse, 31,* 1227-1240.

Policía Nacional de Colombia [National Colombian Police]. (1990-1995). *Revista de la Policía Nacional* [National Police Magazine]. Santafé de Bogotá: Author.

Rodriguez, E., & Duque, L. F. (1992). *Encuesto nacional sobre el consumo de sustancias psicoactivas en Colombia* [National survey on the consumption of psychoactive substances in Colombia]. Unpublished manuscript.

Torres de Galvis, Y. (1993). Epidemiologic surveillance system of drug use and abuse (VESPA) in Medellin, Colombia. In National Institute on Drug Abuse (Ed.), *Epidemiologic trends in drug abuse* (pp. 418-432). Rockville, MD: National Institute on Drug Abuse.

Torres de Galvis, Y. (1994). *Drug abuse epidemiological surveillance (VESPA).* Medellín: Luis Amigo University.

Torres de Galvis, Y., & Montoya, I. D. (1997). *National mental health survey.* Medellín: Luis Amigo University.

Torres de Galvis, Y., & Murrelle, L. (1987). *Estudio nacional sobre alcoholismo y consumo de sustancias que producen dependencia* [National study on alcohol and other substances that create dependency]. Medellín: Universidad de Antioquaia.

Chapter 18

Who Is to Blame? The Discovery of Domestic Drug Problems and the Quest for Recognition of Therapeutic Communities in Peru

Antonio Lara-Ponce

From Culturally Integrated Coca Cultivation to Drug Trafficking

Coca—A National Product

Peru is the world's first producer of coca leaf and has gained notoriety as a center of drug trafficking in spite of national and international countermeasures, such as support for crop substitution programs and alternative development. The cultivation and use of coca leaves goes back to Peru's ancient past. Because of its climate and soil, the country has always been a privileged place for coca growing. In its legislation, the State regards coca leaf as a natural heritage as well as a source of public wealth because of the tax revenue it generates. Cocaine is found in the leaves of *Erythroxilum coca* sp., which grows in the wilderness throughout South America. Coca is cultivated in great quantities in Bolivia, Peru, Colombia, and Ecuador. The chewing of coca leaves (*coqueo, acullicado, chacchado*) in these countries is an ancient custom as is evidenced by archeological remains, old chronicles, and pottery. The same Andean society regulated this cultural use. People who abuse the substance are considered *opas*, a Quechua word that means "worthless to the community." This word has strong emotional and control connotations.

The Rise of Narco-Business as a Branch of the Economy

The first case of addiction to the basic paste of cocaine (Cocaine sulphatum, PBC) was reported in 1970. It was rapidly shown to be a highly addictive substance, owing to its particular neurophysiological action. In the following substance, owing to its particular neurophysiological action. In the following decades, the illicit production and commercialization of coca derivatives increased considerably under the control of the *firmas* (organizations of drug traffickers).

Many sectors of society and groups are engaged in the production of cocaine; they include a growing labor force and a hierarchical system of farmers (landowners, day laborers); intermediate merchants (*traqueteros*—young people acting as assistants or small collectors); collecting traffickers (agents between the wholesalers and independent groups); wholesalers (including a network of occasional merchants, the sellers of "joints"); and the export firms, who are direct partners of international drug cartels (owners of airplanes, landing strips, laboratories).

The volume of drug trafficking in Peru can only be estimated. Satellite data for 1997 (INM-USA, 1997) indicate 94,400 hectares of coca cultivation in areas of illicit production of cocaine derivatives, which corresponds to a production of nearly 145,300 tonnes of coca leaf. This represents a reduction of 18% in comparison with 1995.

The production for licit demand—chewing of the leaf and exports of the Empresa Nacional de la Coca (ENACO, or National Coca Enterprise)—constituted only 5% of the total estimated production for 1995 (Ministry of Internal Affairs, 1996). This low proportion reflects the country's poor economic condition; narcobusiness, which meets the demand in many Western industrialized countries, brings, at least in the short term, substantial economic benefits: rapid and sustained growth; increasing involvement of new sectors of the population in the cultivation of coca, and its commercialization and associated services; and the influx of foreign currencies and capital.

One of the main reasons for the expansion of coca production has been the high income it generates: "It is estimated that the coca farmer earns US$1,500 by hectare annually, an amount reduced due to interdiction actions, while his income from legal crops, such as corn, rice, cacao, coffee or beans, averaged only US$220—that is, 6.8 times less than that from cultivating coca" (field-work estimates from the price of PBC in its growing areas in February 1998).

Consequences and Changes

In the long run, however, the prospering of drug trafficking undermined gradually the country's institutional structure, making a successful defense response from the society increasingly difficult. The impact of organized crime on the society, public health, ecology, lifestyle, and public order has been a high price to pay. The agreement between the drug traffickers and the terrorist group settled in the Huallaga river valley is seen as a threat to national and regional security on the continent because the group receives money from drug traffickers in exchange for security.

In the meantime, market forces led to lower prices for cocaine on the international drug markets. In October 1994, the price of the rough paste fell to US$400/kg and of coca paste to US$900 to $1,200/kg, although these prices are still attractive in the economy of the coca region of the Huallaga drainage basin.

Likewise, the opportunity to cultivate alternative crops caused many peasants to give up the coca crop. Also, their income had been reduced by a fall in the exchange rate of the currency, the liberalization of prices, and a reduction of subsidies. The high cost in violence through which they had lived led them to consider the cultivation of crops not associated with violence, tension with the law, and their being seen as suspects and criminals by the forces of order. The recession in the narco-business has also affected rural areas and people who initially found work in this "economic sector." By the end of 1996, many small towns in the jungle that had been involved in the coca trade were experiencing poverty and negative economic impact (inflation, loss of native crops, etc.)—a consequence of easily earned money, which not only subverted the economy but also changed the people's lifestyles because of the overproduction of coca.

Changing Markets

Are the *firmas* in this business cycle diversifying their production? So far, there are no reports of experimental cultivation of poppy plantations under the control of drug traffickers, and the latest epidemiological studies (Castro & Rojas, 1997) have not indicated a rising consumption of heroin or opium. However, in many zones near the inter-Andean valley of the central highlands and in the east, there are now people whom the local population associates with interests of Mexican and Colombian *firmas,* and this may be the first sign of an increase in the near future; in principle, the conditions are ideal for such a diversified production. Thus, the farmers in the production zones are experienced and skilled in the illicit production of coca leaf and its transformation into coca paste; they could become poppy growers and even producers of opium and heroin. The climate in certain zones (cold and humid at 800 m) favors the cultivation of the poppy and a high-quality, profitable product. Likewise, opium resin is more profitable than the by-products of cocaine, and this is a strong incentive for its production, particularly in view of the low prices of traditional crops and the distance of markets for these crops. Clearly, this combination of factors favors the cultivation of the poppy and trafficking in heroin.

Epidemiological Data—Drug-Related Consequences

The following rough outline of the epidemiological situation is based on surveys conducted in 1988 and 1995 by the Information and Education Center for the Prevention of Drug Abuse (CEDRO), a nongovernmental organization.

Drug consumption is mainly an urban phenomenon, but the increase in its lifetime prevalence between 1988 and 1995 (Table 18.1) points to a similar growth in the provinces. In Lima, lifetime prevalence even dropped from 3.6% in 1988 to 3.3% in 1995, whereas in the provinces, it increased from 1.5% to 2.8%. For other drugs, such as cocaine hydrochloride, the relative differences between the city and

Table 18.1 Lifetime Prevalence of Illicit Drug Use by Type of Substance and Region (in percentages)

Substance	1988		1992	
	Lima	Province	Lima	Province
Marijuana	6.2	3.9	7.6	4.4
Coca paste	3.6	1.5	3.3	2.8
Cocaine	1.8	0.5	2.6	0.7

SOURCE: Ferrando (1990), Rojas (1995).

the rural areas have changed little. Therefore, it would be premature to conclude that a general homogenization of consumption patterns is taking place.

Coca paste is smoked, cocaine hydrochloride is inhaled, and intravenous use is not common. Therefore, virus transmission by the use of needles is uncommon in Peru. No reliable statistics on drug users infected by HIV are available so far. Finally, Ferrando's (1991) study—the first of its kind in the country (sample size $N = 15,000$, 15-to-24-year-old population group, 52 cities)—points roughly to the following results: 16% of the male and 6% of the female population of the surveyed age group indicated they had used one or more of the following at least once: inhalants, coca leaf, marijuana, cocaine, or coca paste. Marijuana was the most consumed illicit drug; there are signs that coca paste (PBC) is becoming the most consumed. Coca leaf is a special case; it is part of the culture of wide sectors of the Andean farming population and of small groups of the rest of the coast and the highlands; 6% of the sample had "chewed" or "chacchado" coca leaves at least once.

Defining the Problem: Politicians and Public Opinion

Governmental Positions and Legal Provisions

Peruvian strategies in the fight against drugs are stated in Law 824, called "Law of the Fight Against Drug Trafficking," promulgated by the President of Peru in April 1996, which states as objectives of the government the strengthening of the fight against drug use, support of rehabilitation of drug addicts, and the substitution of other crops for coca leaf cultivation. It established the Commission for the Fight Against Drug Consumption, "Counter Drugs," to be responsible for the design, coordination, and execution of preventive action. The Commission's objectives are the following:

- Prevent the consumption of drugs in Peru by means of education, information, and the promotion of healthy lifestyles and behavior.
- Contribute to the creation and strengthening of rehabilitation programs for drug addicts.

  — Promote the substitution of other crops for coca leaf cultivation, and create a national
    consciousness of the dangers of illicit crops.
  — Promote educational programs on the risks of drug use and the traffic and trading in
    coca leaf by-products and other illicit substances.
  — Seek international cooperation in support of national efforts in the fight against drugs.

The 1996 law also provides for economic policies to promote in coca production zones and at consumption points those socioeconomic conditions that are favorable to national investment; this strategy is called "Fight Against Poverty."

At the same time, the government introduced changes in the law designed to combat the use of even licit drugs. Law 25357 prohibits smoking in closed public spaces: public transport, public buildings, and restaurants and recreation facilities, which should restrict smokers to special zones. In 1993, regulations on tobacco advertising were strengthened. They provide for fines of about US$200 for smokers who break the law and from US$2,000 for the proprietors of restaurants or other places if a "no smoking" sign is not properly displayed or if smokers are allowed in nonsmoking areas. These provisions were very well received by the whole population.

Public Opinion About Drugs and Adequate Measures

In April and May 1992, CEDRO carried out the Third Survey of Public Opinion on Drug Issues, a follow-up to an earlier survey in 1988. A main interest was to compare public perceptions of drug issues as a domestic or an international problem and to evaluate potential public support for policy measures and the treatment response. Drug problems ranked third on a list of the most pressing domestic issues; economic problems (e.g., unemployment, poverty, hunger, low wages, and lack of public welfare services) came in first place, followed by problems of violence, especially terrorism. More than half of the respondents (51%) assumed that drug trafficking had increased, mentioning increased use and higher production of drugs. Only 6.7% believed that economic problems were the main reason that people became involved with drugs.

A trend analysis, relating the data from the 1988 and 1992 studies, showed that the proportion of people who thought that the problem had decreased was constant (around 10%). Nevertheless, in 1992, the number of respondents who considered that the problem had increased was lower (51%) than in 1988 (66.2%); in 1992, one third of the respondents thought that the problem was unchanged, whereas in 1988, only one fifth were of this opinion. In any case, almost all respondents (92.2%) perceived a wide range of negative consequences of drug trafficking, in particular the harmful consequences for young people. This perception is based much more on personal daily experience than on the media: People live with small traffickers of PBC in the streets, and some have friends or relatives who are addicts. Therefore, it is not surprising that they underestimate the damage caused to the whole economy (acknowledged by only 8.4%) but rather perceive social harm such as violence, delinquency, prostitution, and corruption in the foreground (34.4%). People are also concerned about the country's loss of prestige and its stigmatization as a backward country.

These priorities are also reflected in people's recommendations: Not surprisingly, their tolerance of drug traffickers is low. Almost 60% consider that legal measures should be considered to prosecute and imprison them, 10% say they should be deported, and 31% suggest the death penalty. Respondents consider that addicts should receive adequate treatment but realize that this would be difficult because of its cost and duration.

As to the attitudes of young people, Ferrando's (1993) schoolchildren study, conducted in 1992 for the Ministry of Education (COPUID—Committee for the Prevention of Drug Abuse; sample size $N = 10,221$, first to fifth grades of high school), revealed some interesting results also with respect to the perceived usefulness of treatment.

The students do not condemn drug users but would try to persuade them to give up their use of drugs and inform and educate them on the issue. Also, they think that if the case is rather serious, the person should receive counseling or be hospitalized.

More precisely, 31% consider that drug addicts should receive advice and be rehabilitated, whereas 61% consider education only, 5% think they should be punished, 1% think they should be given the death penalty, and 2% do not care. Sixty percent of respondents consider that a friend who consumes drugs should be helped (with counselors or through a rehabilitation program) and advised, and 35% would stay away from and isolate the friend. Most, therefore, favor drug treatment: an excellent basis for encouraging people who seek treatment and a good reason to finance the expansion of the treatment system.

Half of the young people condemn coca cultivation altogether, whereas the others are more tolerant and claim that people have to receive help to enable them to substitute other crops for coca.

The Discovery of Drug Abuse as a Domestic Public Health Problem

The government did little about treatment and preventive services in spite of the public's views. Only in recent years has drug abuse been considered a public health problem. Consequently, outpatient programs in health care centers, massive public campaigns, and programs oriented to young people have been launched. The main preventive efforts have been undertaken by private institutions and nongovernmental organizations. Therapeutic communities as an alternative approach—described below—appeared because the health services did not provide a sufficient number of, or adequate, centers for hospitalization; they offer only outpatient services, which mostly fail to prevent patients from taking drugs.

Coordinating Bodies and Legislation

Primary prevention is largely the domain of the Center of Information and Education for the Prevention of Drug Abuse (CEDRO), a nongovernmental organization that has been very active, in cooperation with the government, in this field since 1986. It conducts preventive activities with high-risk populations, such as people from poor sectors and young people. It works through almost 2,500 institutions, public and private, throughout the country, coordinating educational activities and preparing and providing educational materials for different age groups and regions. A successful program for the substitution of other crops for coca cultivation is operating in the Peruvian jungle to educate the people to change the illicit subculture that has spread in the valley of the Huallaga river.

The Registry of Drug and Alcohol Abuse (RENAD)

In August 1978, the Pan-American Health Organization, at the request of the government of Peru, designed a study called Epidemiological Surveillance of Dependence in the Americas (VEDA), which was intended to help Peru and other Latin American countries interested in establishing a system to compile data about the harmful use of alcohol and other substances. VEDA is modeled on the American Drug Abuse Warning Network (DAWN) and was initiated in 1973 by the National Technical Information Service. Later DAWN versions have been the responsibility since 1975 of the National Institute of Drug Abuse (NIDA).

The DAWN system is designed for general hospital emergency services and to obtain information from forensic medical specialists about trends in episodes of drug abuse and deaths caused by drugs. So far, seven health institutions in metropolitan Lima—an emergency hospital, four general hospitals, and two specialist psychiatric units—have been included in the data collection system; they include Hermilio Valdizan, a public hospital that started out with 10 patients in 1972 (Valdizan Hospital statistics), as well as one of the most successful experiences in the field of rehabilitation since the 1970s, the Center of Treatment and Rehabilitation of Naña, which is also part of the system of public health. These institutions were designated collaborating centers.

To ensure reliability and cooperation, the medical staff of the collaborating centers followed an introductory training session. The fieldwork was done by senior students of the infirmary of the Universidad Nacional Mayor de San Marcos (UNMSM), who were also trained in workshop seminars. Finally, in 1990, a system to monitor both public and private treatment services was tested but did not meet expectations. In 1996, a national workshop on evaluation of treatment services for drug dependents was held in Lima, with the participation of experts in drug dependency from a number of organizations, both public and private. A new register was designed for a national survey that is now under way, and the results are expected soon. The primary model for the register was taken from documents

Table 18.2 Addiction Treatment and Rehabilitation in State Institutions in 1995

Facility	Inpatient Number of Beds	Outpatient Drug Care Service	Type of Treatment Modality
Hermilio Valdizan Hospital (specialized service)	70	X	Mixed[a]
Center of Naña (rehabilitation)	70	—	Behavioral[b]
Larco Herrera Hospital	25	X	Mixed
National Institute of Mental Health "H. Delgado-Hideyo Noguchi"	25	—	Mixed[a]
Rehabilitation Center of Iquitos	25	—	Mixed[a]
Nonspecialized service—psychiatric services in general hospitals of the Ministry of Health	—	X	Medical
Pharmacodependent service offered by Dos de Mayo hospital	—	—	Medical

SOURCE: Instituto Nacional de Salud Mental "Honorio Delgado—Hideyo Noguchi"; National Institute of Mental Health, pharmacology department; National Institute of Statistics and Computing.
a. The hospital gives integral programs of treatment and rehabilitation that make use of different techniques for pharmacodependent patients and their families.
b. It offers treatment and rehabilitation programs with cognitive behavioral techniques.

initially prepared by the United Nations International Drug Control Program and the Organization of American States (Interamerican Commission for the Control of Drug Abuse).

The Public Treatment Sector

The inhabitants of Peru are mainly concentrated in the cities (almost 30% of the population). Epidemiological studies show that users of illicit and licit drugs are also concentrated in urban areas. Therefore, treatment facilities are most frequently located in Lima and the larger cities. The best hospitals, which specialize in mental health services and belong to the Ministry of Health, are located in Lima (National Institute of Mental Health "Hideyo Noguchi," Hermilio Valdizan Hospital, and Victor Larco Herrera Hospital) and provide services for drug dependents.

Table 18.2 gives an overview of the treatment capacity according to RENAD statistics. Public and private services offer about 4,730 beds, almost 90% of them in Lima, for drug-dependent patients.

During the week of August 14-20, 1990, a total of 3,183 patients were admitted to the emergency room services of seven collaborating centers. Of these cases, 165 (5.2%) were related to alcohol and/or drug use (144 to alcohol, 27 to coca paste, 27 to tranquilizers, and 13 unspecified cases according to the *System of Register of Alcohol and Drugs Use and Abuse* [RENAD—Peru Agreement—AI]). The great importance of alcohol abuse emerges also from an analysis of the profiles of patients who attended outpatient services (slight decrease from 43% to 38%), with a slight increase of combined consumption patterns "coca paste and alcohol" over the period 1990-1992 (27% to 31%; Table 18.3).

Table 18.3 Outpatients by Type of Substance Abuse, 1990-1992

	1990		1991		1992	
	n	%	n	%	n	%
Alcohol	206	43	212	40	220	38
Alcohol and coca paste	126	26	155	29	179	31
Coca paste	105	22	115	22	123	21
Marijuana and coca paste	19	4	19	4	21	4
Pharmaceutical products	19	4	22	4	26	4
Marijuana	2	—	4	1	5	1
Nicotine	3	1	3	—	5	1
Total	480	100	530	100	579	100

Source. National Institute of Mental Health "Honorio Delgado—Hideyo Noguchi"; National Institute of Mental Health, pharmacology department; National Institute of Statistics and Computing.

Treatment Methods—
Minimal Intervention

In Peru, the treatment of drug dependence, until the appearance of the so-called therapeutic communities, had always been in the charge of psychiatrists, who used mainly pharmacotherapy. The early reports in the literature were on the treatment of alcoholism (Alva, 1976; Griebenow, 1969, 1974, 1984; Marconi, 1970). Alva, Fábrega, and Jerí (1979) published "Rules for Treatment and Rehabilitation Centers," and Jerí (1984) published "Coca and Derivates: Evidences, Fantasies and Fallacies"; both were based on experiences in developed countries.

Treatment of addiction from the beginning has included psychopharmacology— the prescription of drugs to control addiction symptoms, with consideration of the pharmacokinetics of PBC. Ambulatory therapy, which is based on the motivation of the addict, is the most commonly used model in the public health care services; family support is encouraged, but relapse rates are high, and the follow-up of cases is always difficult, if not impossible. Inpatient treatment begins with detoxification, continues for 3 months or more, and is usually in the hands of a multiprofessional team, including psychologists.

Crisis intervention measures were first introduced by CEDRO. In 1987, a special service of counseling and orientation was initiated, and in 1989, it became the program "Lugar de Escucha" (Place of Listening). It offers hot line services, psychological counseling, and brief therapy designed to motivate the addicts toward acceptance of their problem and their transferral to specialized services, either public or private. Until 1996, this program dealt with 8,020 phone calls (Castro & Rojas, 1997), and in the first month of 1997, it registered 111 cases, which indicates a slight increase in requests for services for this year. In the same way, the Peruvian Institute for Social Security, a public health agency, has implemented a hot line that is used mostly by cases of self-medication and users of pharmaceutical products.

Progetto Uomo and Therapeutic
Communities as Treatment Alternatives

Therapeutic communities emerged in the 1980s in Peru as a response to the lack of treatment alternatives accessible and affordable to marginal populations. They are located in suburban and deprived areas of the city, high-risk zones in which professional services are not usually available. The provinces have only a few specialized services, mainly in provincial capitals. The services of psychiatry and psychology undertake the treatment, sometimes with insufficient preparation. In the provinces, 81% of these services are undertaken by informal therapeutic communities, which generally lack adequate conditions and facilities (Ferrando, 1994). They were influenced by the Italian model of *Progetto Uomo* and were at first rejected by the professionals. Their directors, usually ex-addicts, were considered charlatans or even criminals. The rejection intensified as the number of communities increased, and their lack of adequate conditions was often considered a violation of basic human rights. Today, the situation has changed, and the initial apprehension is changing to acceptance.

The therapeutic communities use a variety of approaches, including Progetto Uomo, the 12 steps from Alcoholics Anonymous, cognitive therapy, and others, depending on the community's orientation. A recent report states that there are 130 such communities, most without an adequate legal constitution.

Most operate with insufficient resources and sometimes in precarious conditions. Some receive food from government sources because they are situated in zones of extreme poverty. Their nature makes it difficult for public bodies such as the Ministry of Health to supervise their performance and quality of treatment.

The following account of some of their characteristics is based on semistructured questionnaire interviews with therapeutic communities in the urban area of Lima in 1994-1995. This investigation was difficult, mainly because of their suspicious attitude toward the inquirers, for fear of being kept under observation or reported to the authorities. Some called themselves "resting houses" or "praying homes" in order to conceal their activities from the public and evade the regulations of the Ministry of Health for their functioning. Information was collected on 46 of the 80 institutions in the areas. Only 4.6% qualified as "professional." The number of therapeutic communities had increased from 1993 to 1994, a success due to the lack of treatment offered by the public health care system and to their low costs in many cases that are self-financed by the sale of different products as part of the therapy (its social reinsertion stage).

Types of Therapeutic Communities

There are four types of therapeutic communities. The professional types include on their staff social and mental health specialists such as psychologists, psychiatrists, and social workers, and they are usually managed by well-known professionals. They charge the highest fees and observe all public regulations and requirements. The semiprofessional types are directed and operated by former addicts and professionals. They aim at a balance between the life experience of the ex-addict and the knowledge and skills of the expert. The religious types are usually directed and operated by former addicts, evangelical ministers, pastors, or laypeople. Treatment is based on the strict observance of religious principles and follows spiritual or religious concepts rather than any formal treatment concepts. Traditional, nonprofessional communities are usually managed and owned by former addicts. In some, there have been serious instances of mistreatment and, in several cases, attempts on the lives of inpatients.

Regarding professional services, 74% of therapeutic communities provide psychological services, and 52% provide medical services; 10.8% are linked to hospital services, and 15% employ social workers. Other professionals employed include lawyers in 30% of communities, accountants in 24%, and managers in 24%.

Client Profiles of Therapeutic Communities

The 46 therapeutic communities had a capacity of 2,130 patients and reported a client load of 1,445. One fourth of these received some financial assistance, which generally covered 50% of the cost of residence and treatment. Some therapeutic communities waived treatment costs in exceptional cases.

Two thirds of the communities interviewed accepted patients who had court convictions; 24% refused such cases.

Treatment Methods

One of the professional therapeutic communities, called *Takiwasi,* in the Peruvian jungle, is known for its use of plants and shaman (medicine man) activities, along with scientific treatment, to enhance the process of physical detoxification and help patients gain insight into the reasons that led them to become addicted.

Inpatient treatment lasts 5 months. There is no systematic information on therapeutic outcome. All of the therapeutic communities interviewed, including those of the public services, consider their spiritual and religious aspects to be very important. Most follow the model denominated "Uomo Project," with certain variations. The professional approach refers to cognitive behavior and transactional analysis models.

First Data on Outcome Monitoring

Recent and systematic reports about follow-up programs are not available. Data from the Naña Rehabilitation Center (Navarro, 1988) show that, of a group of 223 patients, 93 abandoned treatment prematurely; 20 ran away; 20 were excluded for recurrence of drug use; 10 were excluded for dangerous behavior (mainly aggression); and 43 left at their own request, stating that they could not adapt to the rules of the center. The three stages of the program were completed by 130 patients. Of these, 24 (18.5%) resumed substance abuse and 106 (81.5%) remained abstinent for follow-up periods of up to 6 years. The most recent evaluation revealed that 42 were working in factories, 29 had independent work, 12 were continuing their studies, 10 were public employees, 6 were working in other countries, and 4 had become members of religious groups.

Folk Medicine

Folkloric medicine is being considered an option by the common people, especially in areas where it is difficult to obtain professional care. In these places, the *curandero,* or shaman, has knowledge of the use of different herbs with therapeutic potential. There have been no systematic studies of this practice or of the outcome of treatment or of attempts to rehabilitate drug users.

Changes and Professionalization in the Treatment System

The participation of professionals in therapeutic communities is basically assumed as a part of the whole treatment, which is why, in some cases, they are employed part-time, and it is not usual to find a resident physician.

A system of preprofessional practice developed by students completing their studies for careers in health care or social work is also very common and is sometimes accepted by educational institutions as a valid learning experience. This has generated a debate between those who seek the complete professionalization of the therapeutic communities and those who consider it necessary to be more flexible with them, to permit them to develop progressively toward a legal status.

At present, there is a lack of skilled therapists. The medical curricula of Peruvian universities do not include training in the treatment of drug dependency or in prevention. Efforts to establish specialized centers for professionals or public agencies and to regulate and supervise therapeutic communities have been undertaken only recently. Often, they represent isolated initiatives, such as the establishment by CEDRO of a network to support its constitutional obligation to provide information about treatment techniques and technical assistance: It is called the "Red Nacional" Program (National network) and is part of its service for treatment of drug dependents. However, an improvement in the country's economic state and a more efficient handling of the broad problem of drug trafficking are necessary conditions for accelerating professionalization of the treatment system and closer coordination of the efforts of private and public sectors.

References

Alva, J. (1976). Diseno para un programa de rehabilitación integral del alcoholismo cronico en asegurados obreros del Hospital Central No 1 [Design for a program of integral rehabilitation of chronic alcoholism in secured laborers of the Central Hospital No. 1]. In *Anales del Cuarto Congreso Nacional de Psiquiatria—Balance y perspetivas de la psiquiatria en el Peru* [Annals of the Fourth National Congress of Psychiatry in Peru] (pp. 194-198). Lima: Peruvian Psychiatric Association.

Alva, J., Fábrega, M., & Jerí, R. (1979). Normas para centros de tratamiento y rehabilitación de farmacodependientes [Norms for centers of treatment and rehabilitation of pharmacodependants]. *Revista de la Sanidad del Ministerio del Interior, 40,* 184-193.

Castro, R., & Rojas, M. (1997). *Epidemiología de drogas en la población urbana peruana—1995* [Drug epidemiology in Peruvian urban population—1995]. Lima: CEDRO, Research Area.

Ferrando, D. (1990). *Uso de drogas en ciudades peruanas* [Drug use in Peruvian cities]. Lima: CEDRO, Research Area.

Ferrando, D. (1991). *Adolescentes en Perú: Opiniones, actitudes y valores—Encuesta Nacional de Hogares* [Adolescents in Peru: Opinion, attitudes, and values—National Home Survey]. Lima: CEDRO, Research Area.

Ferrando, D. (1993). *Conocimiento y uso de drogas en escuelas secundarias. Encuesta Nacional* [Knowledge and use of drugs in high schools. National survey]. Lima: Ministry of Education—Technical committee for the prevention of drug abuse (COPUID)—Agency for international development (AID).

Ferrando, D. (1994, November). *Evaluación de estrategias de tratamiento, rehabilitación y reinserción social de drogadictos en Perú* [Evaluation of treatment, rehabilitation, and social reinsertion strategies of drug addicts in Perú]. Unpublished research. Lima: United Nations International Drug Control Programme (UNDCP).

Griebenow, W. (1969, July). *Sindrome maladaptivo en pacientes alcohólicos en proceso de rehabilitación* [Maladaptive syndrome in alcoholic patients in rehabilitation process]. Paper presented at the First National Congress of Psychiatry, Lima.

Griebenow, W. (1974, October). *Reflexiones sobre el tratamiento del alcoholismo* [Reflections about the treatment of alcoholism]. Unpublished dissertation presented at the 4th National Congress of Psychiatry, Lima.

Griebenow, W. (1984). *Contribución al concepto de curación social del alcoholismo* [Contribution to the concept of social healing of alcoholism in Perú]. Unpublished doctoral dissertation, National University of Saint Marcus, Lima.

INM-USA [International Narcotics Matters—Department of State]. (1997). Paper of internal circulation. Washington: Author.

Jerí, R. (1984). Cocy y derivados: Evidencias, fantasías y falacias [Coca and derivates: Evidences, fantasies, and fallacies]. *Police Enforcement Health Services Magazine, 45*(1), 27-34.

Marconi, J. (1970). *Modelos de valor epidemiológico para la investigación en Latino América* [Models of epidemiologic value for the investigation in Latin America, Epidemiology in Latin America]. Buenos Aires: Acta Psiquiátrica y Psicológica de América Latina (ACTA).

Ministry of Internal Affairs (OFECOD). (1996). *Narcotraffick control in Peru: Statistical information system* (Quarterly report, Vol. 3, No. 4). Lima: Author.

Navarro, R. (1988). Aspectos clínicos de la dependencia a la pasta básica de cocaína [Clinic aspects of the dependence to basic paste of cocaine]. In R. Castro & F. León (Eds.), *PBC: Un enfoque multidisciplinario* [Basic paste of cocaine (PBC): A multidisciplinary focus] (pp. 117-136). Lima: CEDRO.

Rojas, M. (1995). *Drug epidemiology in Peruvian urban population.* Lima: CEDRO, Research Area.

Chapter 19

Drug Policies and Tradition: Implications for the Care of Addictive Disorders in Two Andean Countries

Enrique Madrigal

Comment on Part 5

Bolivia, Colombia, and Peru, countries with a traditional drug culture going back five millennia, have been plagued for the past two decades by an aggressive international allegation that they are solely responsible for the increased supply of cocaine worldwide and partly for the supply of heroin and marijuana.

This new situation arose and developed during the late 1970s and early 1980s when an aggressive marketing scheme was devised by internationally operating dealer-entrepreneurs—later called "drug barons"—targeting a growing demand for illicit drugs in "consuming countries." Almost at the same time, Andean countries were labeled "producing countries" because of their cultivation of coca leaf and their profiting from its buoyant and illicit international market.

The ensuing debate about these issues attracted the attention of international organizations and governments, prompted in part by the pressure and scrutiny of zealous advocates of public opinion who were concerned about drug abuse and addiction and their social and political implications. In this context, most responses to solving the problem have been predominantly geared, by and large, to curtailing production of drugs and strengthening interdiction and law enforcement.

It may be argued that social acceptance of a certain controlled and moderate use of coca leaf products may contribute to hampering awareness of both the impact of cocaine dependence and consequent needs for appropriate levels of care, but this is, rather, most likely related to lack of resources and hampered capacity building across the board. Also, health and social priorities for stemming poverty and alleviating very degraded living conditions have obviously overridden a desirable improvement of mental health and addiction services. This particular pattern of consumption has affected socially marginal, mostly male, and very young populations. It is plausible that, other than alcohol and tobacco, the appearance and continuing dependence on coca paste in the mid-1970s has been the most prevailing factor in the increasing demand for services for drug-dependent individuals in the Andean subregion. The increasing use of services and serious social problems linked to the use of and dependence on coca paste have burdened the health care system, especially in such complex urban centers as Lima, Bogotá, and Medellín.

It has been argued that, until recently, there has been a dearth of appropriate responses from the health sector. There may also be a pervasive low awareness and commitment among providers of conventional services, prompting the emergence of concerned groups, such as social agencies, therapeutic communities, religious groups, and nongovernmental organizations, which have gradually increased in numbers during the past 15 years in those countries. In my opinion, aside from the vying for resources among health and social agencies, the most significant factors hampering appropriate governmental responses are a combination of underreporting of cases and a vague idea that addiction is a matter for law enforcement. At the same time, some country or local responses are motivated politically or, more simply, by the lobbying of some nongovernmental or governmental organizations seeking opportunities to set their programs in particular communities or to serve particular populations.

Given these conditions, it seems clear that both of the authors of these chapters on treatment and rehabilitation have had to depend on descriptive and anecdotal sources, obtained mostly from registers and the scarce literature on the subject.

Leading examples in both Peru and Colombia depict initial rudimentary conditions involving already overburdened psychiatric facilities. Later, more specialized efforts ensued, comprising a behaviorally structured center in Peru (Naña Rehabilitation Center), a treatment and rehabilitation unit at the Bello Psychiatric Hospital in Medellín, and Corporación Caminos in Colombia. These three leading institutions, as well as scores of nongovernmental organizations, therapeutic communities, and self-help groups, have responded to an increasing demand for treatment and have seriously attempted to systematize clinical approaches and contribute to the growth of knowledge.

Naturally, drug-abusing and -dependent young people at the school and university levels have had limited access to these services. This is what Pérez-Gómez depicts in his chapter, and it resulted in the creation of a unique facility at the University of the Andes in Bogotá. Elsewhere, the frequent involvement of drug dependents in unlawful activities and violent behavior has made necessary a compulsory system of alternative treatment rather than a purely repressive approach. This has been the case in Lima, Bogotá and Medellín, and consequently there is a trend to develop emergency room and detention center databases. Frequent violent behavior has also pointed to the need to explore the impact of substance abuse among forensic or coroner's centers.

Therapeutic communities and a diversity of private treatment centers have added to this complexity and, by and large, have provided badly needed coverage for this neglected condition, notwithstanding the efforts of conventional public health programs.

This is an extremely difficult area to explore because the unlawful and socially censored nature of the disorder still prevails in those countries. Underdiagnosing and lack of reporting systems, as pointed out above, go together with understaffed substance abuse and dependence programs in the public health sector.

The Pan American Health Organization and the World Health Organization are holding a series of country and regional workshops that convene responsible agencies and normative-level managers to seek consensus on standards of care, interorganizational coordination, and reporting systems to monitor the treatment and rehabilitation of addictive disorders.

Some schedules were developed through a multicenter study sponsored by the United Nations Drug Control Program and the World Health Organization in the mid-1980s. Chile, Venezuela, Panama, and Costa Rica have developed locally adjusted standards of care and monitoring programs, including accreditation requirements. The Andean Health Initiative carried out a regional workshop on this topic in 1997.

As a caveat for those engaged in decision making or the planning and management of treatment, it may seem convenient at times to accept at face value some technical support from both European and North American models. These packages are offered as part of more comprehensive agreements, such as law enforcement and crop eradication or substitution, inter alia. Some of these experiences, obviously, have the advantage of having been time-tested, and some have been positively evaluated. The major risk is that of proceeding without further local situation analysis and of adopting models that may not quite suit either local idiosyncracies or special care needs.

The two country reports may very well be telling a story applicable to many countries or areas across the region; it may also be a lesson in pointing to the need to strengthen mechanisms to assist treatment agencies in networking and, most of all, in developing a consensus-based system to deal with such pertinent issues as case registering, monitoring, and quality assurance.

Part VI

Wine and Illicit Drugs

Chapter 20

A System at Its Starting Blocks:
Drug Treatment in France

Philippe Mossé

Although French society has been grounded in the ideology of the French Revolution, according to which each individual belonged directly as a citizen to the nation, France is on the verge of a new form of societal structure that is founded on community identity rather than individual rights and duties. Being immigrant, young, homeless, and unemployed is considered less and less a transitory or secondary characteristic but, rather, a permanent social feature. Meanwhile, individualistic and competitive values are to the fore, and drug use is seen as one possible way of coping with the new economic climate (Ehrenberg, 1994).

Even if it is difficult to explain fully the multiple reasons for the increasing concern about drug problems since the beginning of the 1980s, interest in drugs and drug treatment has risen sharply among decision makers, physicians, and researchers. In a centralized country such as France, governmental and political decisions are significant in raising such increased social concern. The creation of government agencies such as Délégation Générale à la Lutte contre la Drogue et la Toxicomanie (General Delegation to the Campaign against Drugs and Addiction) and the publication of two major reports—a survey of the international literature (Lert & Fombonne, 1989) and a study of the accessibility and availability of information on drugs and drug treatment (Padieu, 1990)—are expressions of this concern.

Moreover, in 1991 and 1992, the Descartes Association, a private organization close to the Ministry of Research, organized a multidisciplinary seminar on

AUTHOR'S NOTE: The research for this chapter has been supported by the French Ministère de l'Emploi et de la Solidarité, Contract 41/94.

drug-related problems and published several books on the topic (Chambas, 1992; Ehrenberg & Schiray, 1992) with contributions from economists, ethnologists, psychoanalysts, sociologists, and others.[1] These saw the drug treatment system as a response to a growing social problem, an attempt to meet an emerging need for care, cure, and control. More recently, government agencies and individual experts have set up a French Observatory on Drug and Drug-Related Problems and a research group on this topic.

The debate does not take place in a social and economic vacuum, however. The French welfare state was established long before drugs became a national problem. The national security system is strongly centralized, costly, and rather inefficient. In view of the country's financial and economic difficulties, several reforms have been implemented since the early 1980s to lower the costs of services while maintaining their quality. The proportion of health care expenses in the French economy is the highest in the world except for the United States. Many reasons have been given for this, including the high degree of autonomy of French physicians.

The medical profession is not directly involved either in the heart of the regulation process, as in Germany, for example, or in strong competition, as in the United States. Physicians have no strong motives to lower costs (of consultations, prescriptions, or hospitalization; Mossé, 1994), and they are free to choose and organize the medical care submarket in which to practice. In these circumstances, it is clear that there can be no treatment system if physicians as a social group are unwilling to organize and build one. A so-called system is no more than a random scattering of spots ruled by individuals with little or no connection with one another and no organized health policy. This was the case during the first phase of drug treatment in France.

From today's perspective, the 1970s can be seen as an experimental phase. Enthusiastic physicians established some treatment facilities on the margin of mainstream medicine. They were generally against psychiatric confinement (*enfermement;* Foucault, 1963) and control, which was, in the main, the only form of treatment for the few patients treated as drug users. Few physicians were treating drug users until the early 1980s. Then, as the number of drug users increased, several hospital treatment units were created. Some were specialized in addiction treatment, and others were nonspecialized but admitted drug addicts for treatment. Soon after, many hospitals began to offer drug treatment services. This coincided with a shift in drug treatment ideology from social control to a more medically oriented approach (Morel, 1994).

As treatment developed from experimental to more or less standard forms, it became strengthened by improved statistical information. Since 1987, the Health Ministry's Service of Statistics, Studies, and Information Systems (Service des statistiques, des études et des systèmes d'information—SESI) has conducted an annual survey of all types of drug treatment units. Participation is voluntary, and the Ministry publishes an annual report itemizing the key characteristics of patients and services. The following discussion, although based on these reports, is intended to go beyond a mere description of the system to an account of its dynamic qualities in recent years; it focuses on two aspects—the development of the treatment system as a legitimate and professional part of the health care system, and the effects of the increasing national concern about drug-related issues.

Health Care for Problem Drug Users

The simplest way to estimate the importance of the drug problem in the health care system is to quantify its extent, but a purely quantitative approach is insufficient for assessing its scale or explaining its causes. Its effects on French society are far greater than merely the number of individuals involved, whether as drug users or as professionals. Nevertheless, quantitative information has its place.

Statistics of the Ministry of Health and specialist organizations for 1994 put the number of visits to physicians or hospitals related to abuse of drugs, excluding alcohol, at about 100,000, compared with around 250 million visits and consultations for all illnesses. Hospital statistics, also for 1994, show that 40,000 drug users received inpatient treatment, compared with a total of 15 million inpatients. Both of these ratios suggest that only a relatively small percentage of drug users are treated in the health care system.

The Treatment of Problem Drug Users

Statistics compiled by the Ministry of Health (Tables 20.1 and 20.2) show that almost half of all drug users admitted to treatment are treated in addiction-specialist facilities, and the rest either in health care establishments not concerned primarily with drug abuse (34%) or in social service institutions (21%).

Annual surveys show that different types of drug users may be found in different kinds of treatment centers. However, a multidimensional analysis of 1987 data showed that drug users were distributed within the health care system mainly according to age and type of substance used (SESI, 1989). It indicated also that cannabis users younger than 22 years were most likely to be in social treatment settings, heroin users of 22 to 29 years in specialist units, and psychotropic drug users over 30 years of age in psychiatric departments or clinics.

Heroin is the most frequent drug of dependency of drug users in treatment, which tends to contradict the dominant view about the ravages of cocaine. Although it is true that the use of cocaine is increasing, its users in France are still very few. According to a Ministry of Health study, specialist treatment is organized mainly around psychological help and follow-up care, whereas nonspecialized services provide detoxification and medical care. Social treatment is the responsibility of social workers, whose primary aim is the social reintegration of young, marginalized cannabis users.

Although in February 1994, only 77 patients were in methadone programs, compared with 40 in the early 1970s (Moore, 1978), the government has recently

Table 20.1 Profile of Problem Drug Users and Their Treatment in 1994

	%	n
Units		
Medical	14.7	3,991
Psychiatric	19.5	2,635
Specialized	44.9	9,282
Social	20.8	4,484
Substance		
Heroin	62	11,013
Cannabis	18	3,755
Psychotropics	11	1,545
Cocaine	2	374
Referral (1990)		
Self	50	2,867
Professional	22.5	660
Court injunction	5	323
Family	14	913

SOURCE: SESI (1996).
NOTE: Owing to missing data or varying participation of the facilities monitored by the Ministry, raw percentages presented here do not always add up to 100%.

Table 20.2 Sociodemographic Background Characteristics of Problem Drug Users Under Treatment in 1994

	%	n
Age		
< 20 years	7.3	1,471
20-29 years	57.2	11,556
30-39 years	31	6,250
> 39 years	4.5	913
Occupation		
Unemployed	57	14,402
Employed	30	5,001
Other (unknown)	13	502
Sex		
Male	76	13,968
Female	24	4,595

SOURCE: SESI (1996).

agreed to extend the number of authorized units. Some postcure centers are run on a community basis, as therapeutic communities on the borders of the official treatment system, financed by neither the social security system nor the state. There is little available information on these centers.

Nearly two thirds of problem drug users state that they sought help on their own or their families' initiative, and less than 10% are referred for treatment by professionals. This lack of professional encouragement of drug users to attend treatment and the reluctance of drug users to seek treatment indicate that there is still room for the system to expand.

Table 20.3 Growth of the French Drug Treatment System, 1987-1993

	1987	1990	1993
Number of units (specialized)	726 (149)	760 (186)	1,080 (206)
Number of patients in November	8,804	14,520[a]	19,300

SOURCE: SESI (1988-1994) and Antoine (1993).
a. Counted in 1989.

A Drug Treatment System Ready to Expand

Quantitative Growth

At first sight, figures indicate that the task of raising awareness is already under way, because the annual increase both in the number of establishments offering treatment and in the number of drug dependents being treated is around 15% (see Table 20.3).

However, this increase has two specific features. The first is the uneven development of the three types of treatment center. Since 1987, the number of drug users treated in a given month has increased regularly in specialist centers, whereas in the other two types the increase began in 1989. Between 1989 and 1991, the main growth was in the medical, nonpsychiatric services (30% per year), owing to an increase in HIV-infected patients treated in medical services. There is no explanation of why HIV-infected patients chose medical rather than more specialized services. Data from November 1994 showed that, of the 18,380 drug users under treatment, 13% of those in specialist units and 27% in general hospitals were HIV positive. This may reflect a shift in attitudes on the part of the medical profession: Physicians are now more willing to accept drug users as patients and not as "deviants" to be ignored.

The second feature is the growth of "patients treated each month," an item that demands careful examination. As the statistical service of the Ministry of Health noted:

> The increase in problem drug users being treated does not mean a rising incidence of drug dependence in France. In 1988 fewer people sought treatment for the first time than in 1987. Thus the increased activity of specialist treatment centers is due to their treating more drug users already known to the system. (SESI, 1989, p. 5)

The increasing average age of patients (from 25.6 to 28 years between 1987 and 1993) supports the view of researchers that the increase has been due primarily to a trend toward greater awareness and interest.

"Soft Coercion"

Unlike other European countries (such as the Netherlands, the United Kingdom, or Italy), which distinguish between soft and hard drugs, the French government has recently reaffirmed its belief in the "gateway" theory, that the use of soft drugs leads automatically to use of hard drugs. However, in general, and because of the gap between enforcement at the national and local levels, repression is less severe and less often used for cannabis users or dealers than for heroin users. The police have been officially instructed not to prosecute users caught with small quantities of cannabis, although the instruction is inconsistently applied. Figures on enforcement policy show that 75% of arrests are of users and only 10% are of dealers. Several official reports and parliamentary hearings support the view that penalization is less costly than treatment and that it is morally justifiable on the grounds that diminishing availability diminishes the number of drug users (Trautmann, 1990).

The growth of the AIDS epidemic and the increase in drug-related problems[2] gave rise to a social movement against penalization. Physicians as a group opposed the movement and instead advanced the concept of "therapeutic injunction" as an alternative to depenalization (Seguela, 1993). This gives the arrested drug user the choice of entering drug treatment instead of being charged. Regardless of the impact of this "soft coercion" ideology, it indicates that legal penalization is seen as a possible way of directing drug users toward the treatment system.

A Professional Issue

Looking for Professional Recognition

Since the end of the 1960s, the practice of custodial care of psychiatric patients has been abandoned. As we have seen, drug abuse raises acutely the problem of social control. However, until recently, outpatient drug treatment was unavailable. Until the 1980s, there was a contradiction between what problem drug users needed—strong medical and social control—and more open forms of medical practice. Problem drug users were generally treated in some form of custodial care, a practice that ran counter to the new and more open practices that the medical profession was espousing, for a variety of ethical, medical, and economic reasons.

A similar change had occurred earlier in alcohol treatment, when alcoholism began to be regarded as less of a social and more of a medical problem. The rise of alcohology as a medical specialty was accompanied by a theoretical and practical debate on the concept of supervision and the function of the medical profession in supervision. Today, the advance toward professionalization and specialization in alcohol treatment is virtually complete, and the indications are that these changes are occurring now in relation also to drug treatment.

Characterized by a large but defined mix of programs—technical, medical, psychiatric, and social—the drug treatment system is in search of a dominant and comprehensive theory and practice. Moreover, the designations of some drug treatment facilities, such as Centre d'Accueil (Reception center), Centre de réadaptation (Readaptation center), and "Prevention club" show that physicians are still unwilling to be regarded by their colleagues as specialists in the treatment of drug users. In the case of therapeutic communities, this practice is even more pronounced: They are called such names as Tremplin (Springboard), Maison des pins

(House of pines), and Le Patriarche (an extensive organization that owns several centers in Europe, is run on community lines, and uses mainly behavioral therapies inspired by the Synanon model). Even though physicians are playing a more important part in drug treatment in view of the AIDS epidemic, these facilities are often managed by former drug users. Their efficacy has yet to be demonstrated, however. A survey of international literature to assess program efficacy, carried out by the National Institute of Health and of Medical Research, is one of the rare attempts to compare several programs and outcomes (Lert & Fombonne, 1989). Its main conclusion, also supported by other researchers (Le Gales, 1992), is clear: "There is little or no difference in the outcomes of different drug treatment techniques and programs" (Lert & Fombonne, 1989, pp. 126-127). However, although the authors found no major differences between ambulatory and inpatient care and methadone maintenance, detoxification alone seemed the least effective.

A Public-Private Dualization

Whereas market segmentation—the distribution of problem drug users within the social security and health care systems—is already relatively advanced, the private and public sectors are split. The national social security system finances public and private care differently. Since 1983-1984, public hospitals are financed on a global budgeting basis, but private clinics continue to be funded on a per-diem basis. Most of the private clinics are small, nonprofit associations, a type of organization very common in economics, culture, and science. They have the advantage of a high degree of freedom in their financial management. For instance, they can obtain funds from either local or national sources. They are also ideal for voluntary participation, and their flexibility allows them to cross professional and institutional boundaries. In many respects, they can operate outside the controls of the centralized health care system. Some offer inpatient programs designed to reintegrate drug users (mainly 15 to 35 years old) into society after medical treatment in the public services.

Overall, the modes of care, as well as the patients themselves, are distributed on either side of a public/private divide. This distribution reflects not the various phases of the natural history of the disease, but rather the fact that one or another sector is the dominant provider of care at the beginning and during various phases of the process. Thus, the segmentation of the market is not based on the progression of the disease. For example, according to the Ministry of Health survey, assistance with reintegration into the economy or society in general is offered to about 12% of the drug abusers treated in the system. This kind of care is offered almost exclusively in private centers, which provide 93% of all reintegration programs. In contrast, the public sector provides 75% of withdrawal and detoxification services, and it is also where 75% of drug users with AIDS and 97% of those with other diseases are primarily treated.

Moreover, as the literature (Goffi, 1991; Ogien & Mignon, 1994) indicates, similarly designated programs are not necessarily identical in content regarding treatment sequences or even medicines. For instance, detoxification techniques may differ according to whether further treatment is to be mainly medical or mainly psychiatric. In general, detoxification follows several stages, beginning with 5 or 6 days without any drug substitution. Mainly in public hospitals, this phase may be shortened by medical intervention to accelerate the elimination of the drug; the patient is isolated, and many kinds of biological tests and medical examinations are performed. According to the seriousness of the withdrawal syndrome (état de manque), it may happen that a patient is given a placebo instead of a substitution drug.

Despite this diversity, based mainly on a public/private divide, some authors believe that continuity of care is maintained because patients may be referred from one sector to the other according to their diagnoses (Lert & Fombonne, 1989, p. 51), but there has been no systematic study to test this optimistic belief. This representation would also support the theory of a health care system adapting itself to the "natural evolution" of these illnesses, but this is not the case, and specialization does not run along these lines.

In the French drug treatment system, the severe and more medically serious cases (those of AIDS or heroin addiction) tend to be treated in the public sector, and the more "social" and less medically serious (cannabis postcure and follow-up) cases in private centers. For instance, in November 1989, of the 863 patients referred to the treatment system by social workers, 84% were sent to private services, and of the 695 referrals by general practitioners, 74% were to public services.

This points to a contradiction between the needs of patients and decisions made at the micro level. Given the current distribution of patients between private and public services, economic incentives favor cooperation between ambulatory care physicians and inpatient facilities that treat the more severely affected drug users, but no such cooperation is apparent when social treatment is indicated. Moreover, public hospitals, where the seriously ill are more likely to be treated, must have a high turnover of patients, whereas private facilities, which admit less severely affected patients and charge by the day, have an incentive to extend length of stay.

Conclusion

Despite the increasing concern about drug-related problems, the public/private division that characterizes the French drug treatment system is more the result of a large number of decisions made at the micro or local level than the outcome of a clear national policy. The public/private division of programs as a key characteristic of the system hampers the development of a coherent and organized system. It may equally well hamper the solution of an even greater problem—the small percentage of drug users actually seeking treatment. If only about 15% of those who need care enter the system, it is not so much that the others do not wish to do so, but that the type of care or support offered does not meet their needs. Global figures show that to enter a private facility, drug users have to be in good health and must need social and psychological support; after detoxification, an addict with a somatic disease is more likely to be sent to a public facility. In between are the majority of drug users.

Without a clear public health priority, the French situation will be characterized for a long time by corporate divisions, by partition, if not opposition, between the State and the departments and cities, between prevention and cure, and between social and medical action. Moreover, with the emergence of AIDS, some problem drug users now have the social status of patients, which may accelerate the professionalization of the treatment of drug dependence. This may be paradoxical at a time when the disease model is under severe criticism.

Notes

1. This paper benefits from those earlier works. Special thanks go to E. Belliard, P. Chambas, C. Le Gales, A. Letourmy, D. Reinosa, and M. Schiray. The helpful comments of other readers also are gratefully acknowledged.

2. In 1994, an estimated 30% of drug users were HIV infected, compared with less than 10% in the United Kingdom, for instance.

References

Antoine, D. (1993). *Les toxicomanes et le système sanitaire et social* [Drug addicts and the health and social system]. Paris: Service des Statistiques, des Etudes et des Systèmes d'Information.

Chambas, P. (1992). *Modes de consommation: mesures et démesures* [Consumption patterns]. Paris: Editions Descartes.

Ehrenberg, G. (1994). Les drogues: un multiplicateur d'individualités [Drugs, a multiplier of individualities]. *Futuribles, 3,* 73-76.

Ehrenberg, G., & Schiray, M. (Eds.). (1992). *Penser la drogue, penser les drogues* [Thinking addiction, thinking drugs] (Vols. 1-3). Paris: Editions Descartes.

Foucault, M. (1963). *Naissance de la clinique* [The birth of the clinic]. Paris: Presses Universitaires de France.

Goffi, S. (1991). *Les institutions de soins pour toxicomanes dans les Bouches du Rhône* [Health care units for drug addicts in a French county]. Unpublished manuscript, Université Aix-Marseille.

Le Gales, C. (1992). L'évaluation des politiques en matière de toxicomanie [Addiction policy assessment]. In G. Ehrenberg & M. Schiray (Eds.), *Penser la drogue, penser les drogues* [Thinking addiction, thinking drugs] (Vols. 1-3). Paris: Editions Descartes.

Lert, F., & Fombonne, E. (1989). *La toxicomanie* [Addiction]. Paris: Institut National de la Santé et de la Recherche Médicale, Documentation Française.

Moore, M. (1978). A feasibility study of a policy decision to extend methadone maintenance. *Public Policy, 26,* 285-303.

Morel, A. (1994). Entre santé publique, interdits et réponses cliniques [Between public health and clinical answers]. In A. Ogien & P. Mignon (Eds.), *La demande sociale de drogues* [Social demand for drugs] (pp. 109-115). Paris: Délégation Générale à la Lutte contre la Drogue et la Toxicomanie, Documentation Française.

Mossé, P. (1994). Towards a professional rationalization. *American Journal of Economics and Sociology, 53*(3), 129-146.

Ogien, A., & Mignon, P. (1994). *La demande sociale de drogues* [Social demand for drugs]. Paris: Délégation Générale à la Lutte contre la Drogue et la Toxicomanie, Documentation Française.

Padieu, J. (1990). *L'information statistique sur les drogues et la toxicomanie* [Statistical information on drugs and addiction]. Paris: Délégation Générale à la Lutte contre la Drogue et la Toxicomanie.

Seguela, J. P. (1993). Lutte contre la drogue [Campaign against drugs]. *Le Quotidien du Médecin, 7-8,* 24.

SESI (Service des Statistiques, des Etudes et des Systèmes d'Information). (1988-1994). *Notes statistiques. Notes d'informations rapides* [Statistical notes. Rapid information papers]. Paris: Ministère de la santé [Ministry of Health].

SESI (Service des Statistiques, des Etudes et des Systèmes d'Information). (1989). *La prise en charge sanitaire et sociale des toxicomanes* (No. 113). Paris: Ministère de la santé [Ministry of Health].

SESI (Service des Statistiques, des Etudes et des Systèmes d'Information). (1996). *La prise en charge des toxicomanes en novembre 1994* [Drug treatment population, November 1994]. Paris: Ministère de la santé [Ministry of Health].

Trautmann, C. (1990). *Rapport au 1er Ministre* [Report to the Prime Minister]. Paris: Documentation Française.

Chapter 21

The Spread of AIDS
and Drug Treatment in Spain

Juan-Luis Recio Adrados

After the death of Franco in 1975, Spain began to experience a pattern of illicit drug use similar to that already under way in other Western European countries. Earlier, the use of drugs and alcohol had become associated among some college students with an antiauthoritarian and antigovernment attitude. By the early 1980s, with the transition to a democratic system, and partly as a result of international tourism, the use of illicit drugs, especially heroin, had expanded. Trafficking in cannabis, heroin, and cocaine had also increased.

By the mid-1980s, with unemployment at 25% of the workforce and a long list of political and economic scandals contributing to a pervasive anomie, the drug problem reached its peak. The government was slow to respond to it, even when Spain topped all European countries in its prevalence rate of AIDS.

The National Drug Plan

In 1985, the government of Spain approved and introduced a National Plan on Drugs that was designed to provide a basis for a coherent and coordinated response. In its preparation, the government drew upon a Sectorial Conference of representatives of the government and of the autonomous communities and cities that constitute the Spanish State, as well as upon an interministerial task force. The Plan had three general aims: achieve consensus at political, institutional, and social levels, coordinating the activities of the various autonomous community departments and voluntary organizations dealing with drug problems; control illicit supply and reduce demand; and provide the resources needed to implement the policy, strengthening the public treatment network and encouraging reliable private initiative.

The Sectorial Conference and an Inter-Autonomous-Community Commission are responsible for coordination between the central administration and the 17 autonomous regions and two autonomous cities. An Advisory Joint Commission composed of representatives of the government delegation for the National Plan on Drugs and a Standing Nongovernmental-Organization Council determines priorities and sets up programs. The Plan urged horizontal coordination of the autonomous communities to further coherence and cooperation among them and with the central government. Each autonomous community developed its own plan on drugs, which was designed to coordinate the activities of its own departments and local administrations with those of private institutions and facilities. In the end, there has been little coordination in the public administration of drug treatment. A former counselor on drug issues of one of the autonomous communities has referred to the "enormous lack of coordination, at the Spanish State level, between the city government and the autonomous-community levels, and between the health and the educational systems" (Pérez de Arróspide, 1992, p. 181).

In 1986, the government began to allocate funds to the regions for drug treatment services. Detoxification beds were made available in the National Health System hospitals of the autonomous communities through agreements with the Ministry of Health. Methadone maintenance programs had been introduced in a number of autonomous communities in 1985 and were funded by the central administration. Although it was initially planned that the central government would match regional authority funding, in little more than 7 years, the latter had outstripped central funding. Drug policy making has been the province of the central government; the autonomous communities have had little or no input to drug legislation.

Spain increasingly aligned itself with the other countries of Western Europe in moving toward a policy of criminalization. In 1993, two new pieces of legislation were approved: a law for the Protection of Citizen Security and an amendment of the Penal Code of Criminal Procedure regarding drug trafficking. The former imposed new penalties for the possession and use of illicit drugs and drug paraphernalia in public. Personal use incurred a number of administrative penalties, and prison sentences for drug sales varied from 1 to 3 years for the less harmful substances, and up to 9 years for the more harmful. Courts could also encourage convicted drug users to seek treatment and thereby have their sentences suspended. The shift to more severe penalties can be seen partly as the effect of increasing public concern about the heroin epidemic and the spread of AIDS. Recent public opinion surveys have shown a wide range of support for this shift.

Drug Abuse Prevalence Data

In 1987, Spain established the State Information System on Drug Abuse, which collects national information in three areas: treatment demand, nonfatal hospital emergencies, and deaths from acute reactions to drug use. Until 1995, only opiates and cocaine were monitored, but in 1996 all illicit drugs were included.

A 1993 survey of a national representative sample revealed that 29.5% of youths and young adults (15 to 29 years old) had tried cannabis (37% males, 21.9% females; Comas, 1994). The overall use of cannabis, heroin, and inhalants had remained relatively steady, whereas cocaine use had increased in the second half of the 1980s to stabilize in the 1990s. The estimated figures for regular or current users in the 15-to-29-year-old age group were the following: 700,000 used canna-bis; 200,000 used cocaine; 40,000 used heroin; 125,000 used speed; 105,000 used designer drugs; and 30,000 used inhalants (Comas, 1994, p. 157).

However, the estimate of 40,000 current heroin users nationally is much the same as that for admissions to initial treatment in 1992 (Cadafalch & Casas, 1993), obviously only a fraction of those who needed treatment. The estimate must be doubted, therefore, as being too low. Moreover, a study commissioned by the Madrid Regional Plan on Drugs gave an estimate of 40,000 current heroin users in 1992 for the Madrid region alone (Comunidad Autónoma de Madrid, 1994).

Of 15- to 16-year-old schoolchildren, 19% admitted using cannabis, 3% used solvents, 3.4% used amphetamines, 3% used Ecstasy, and 4.5% used LSD. Less than 2% admitted having used cocaine, and less than 0.5% admitted using heroin (European Monitoring Centre for Drugs and Drug Addiction, 1996). Drug-related deaths increased from 143 in 1985 to 579 in 1991 and then declined to 388 in 1994. In 1993, for the first time since 1988, cases of ambulatory treatment for heroin and cocaine dependency hardly increased from the previous year (39,033 in 1993 vs. 38,831 in 1992). This was attributable primarily to the decline in admissions for heroin-related problems; admissions and emergency room episodes for cocaine-related problems increased from 1,345 to 1,695. In the six cities continuously monitored since 1983, deaths attributed to opiates or cocaine declined from 556 to 442 during the same period. The average age of users of opiates and cocaine and age at onset of use of the main drug continues to rise (20.4 years), and the percentage of males has remained high (84.3% of treatment admissions, 79.1% of emergency room episodes, and 89.6% of deaths).

According to national health officials in 1995, AIDS had become the number-one cause of death among young adults aged 25 to 35 years (El Mundo, 1995). Now, the epidemic seems to be reaching its peak, and the number of HIV-infected people is expected to fall. However, heterosexual AIDS is still on the increase. In 1994, of the total of 4,657 cases, 3,088 were intravenous users (2,532 males, 556 females); of the remainder, 587 were heterosexuals (341 males, 246 females), and 682 were homosexual males. The incidence of AIDS among intravenous users rose dramatically between 1985 and 1994, from 2.5 new cases per million population in 1985 to 38.1 in 1988 and 120.5 in 1994. This sharp rise could be ascribed partly to a slow response on the part of the administration in adopting a variety of harm reduction methods. Nearly 66% of all AIDS cases are drug injectors (European Monitoring Centre for Drugs and Drug Addiction, 1996). However, "slow response" is a euphemism for a mistaken policy that had dramatic consequences.

Two other factors among several played a part in the government's lack of response to the pandemic. First, in that decade, the National Plan on Drugs had five different government delegates (in America, "drug czars"), which, regardless of the reason for so many, could only add to the general disarray in policy making. Second, very little and poor-quality science was brought to bear on policy making. Thus, drug surveys made no contribution to an objective assessment of the situation. Whereas the cumulative total of AIDS cases diagnosed up to 1997 was 45,000, according to the WHO *Weekly Epidemiological Record,* the only two general population surveys of the Plan in that decade reported that lifetime use of heroin had dropped from 1.8% in 1984 to 0.8% in 1995—which was unlikely and in sharp contrast to the AIDS statistics of the decade. Also, no rigorous evaluation of prevention was organized; the symbolic amounts of funds allocated to research, and their direct allocation, were not subjected to formal peer review. However, injecting has declined since 1987, and smoking and sniffing are on the increase.

The Drug Treatment System

The drug treatment system can be divided into four levels. City governments administer the first level. For example, the Madrid City government spent 10 billion pesetas (about US$70 million) on drug addiction care in the past 6 years and administers seven first-level centers. Day centers form the second level and serve more severely addicted patients, who need a longer and more specialized course of treatment. Detoxification units and therapeutic communities make up the third level. These highly specialized centers are open only to addicts referred from one of the two prior levels. The fourth level consists of a series of support programs linked to the first three levels, such as provision of apartments or temporary residences, orientation programs, and hot-line services. The city government often contracts with private institutions, especially at the third and fourth levels.

The official policy of the central government has been to include addiction treatment in the regular public health care and social services systems in order to avoid the marginalization of addicts. The opposite effect was achieved, however. Because the primary care centers often lack the necessary expertise to treat addicts, addicts have increasingly been referred to specialized centers run by city governments. Also, addicts from middle- and upper-income strata preferred expensive private clinics and therapeutic communities to municipal centers; such patients are usually covered by private health insurance for regular medical treatment.

Drug treatment came to reflect the state of the National Health Service. The avoidance of marginalization of addicts was meant to go along with the public sector monopoly of resources of health and social services, which, it was thought, would bar any significant contribution by even regulated private initiative. Private initiative was always suspect because of its commercial nature, whereas the shortcomings of, and wide public dissatisfaction with, the National Health Service (as attested to by the Blendon survey[1] in 1990) were overlooked. In short, access of private medicine to a health market monopolized by an overpowering national health service was severely curtailed. Private drug treatment was similarly curtailed: Clinics and therapeutic communities were strictly regulated and largely excluded. Global funding by autonomous communities of various nongovernmental organizations concerned with drug addiction represented only 8.8% of the total expenditure in 1995. However, treatment is only one, and likely the last, of their many activities, which include training, prevention, publications, and others.

The new administration that came to power in 1996, although severely constrained by its small parliamentary majority, is trying to modify the public monopoly enjoyed by the National Health Service, in line with the various European models of reform of health service or social security systems, as in the United Kingdom, Germany, or Sweden. The nationalist governments of Catalonia and the Basque Country are already taking steps to permit private initiative a larger input to the still publicly owned and regulated health care market. Such reforms are likely to affect the drug addiction care system also (see Bengoa, Echebarria, Fernández, Via, & Camprubi, 1997; Comisión de Analisis, 1991; Elola, 1994).

Although postgraduate training programs were established to provide these centers with professional staff, such as psychiatrists, physicians, psychologists, and social workers, most of the professionals had to receive their specialist training on the job. Health care providers in municipal addiction centers were in a better position than their counterparts in the National Health Service in that they could carry out treatment in accordance with the model of the municipal services rather than with that of the bureaucratic and overburdened health service. They followed a biopsychosocial approach, designed to reintegrate addicts fully into social life.

By 1995, Spain had established 399 outpatient centers, 48 hospital units, 75 day centers, 91 therapeutic communities, and 506 methadone programs. Between 1986 and 1995, methadone programs increased more than 50-fold, therapeutic communities doubled, and hospital units and outpatient centers quadrupled. Detoxification units were initially created in the late 1970s, and today there are 46, with a total of 208 beds; all work with heroin addicts. In 1994, a total of 66,362 patients attended outpatient services, an increase from 59,958 in 1993; and 18,027 attended methadone maintenance programs, up from 15,398 in 1993. The numbers of programs and patients varied in different regions. In 1994, whereas Andalusia had 156 programs attended by 4,151 patients, the corresponding figures for Catalonia were 45 and 2,806, and for Madrid, only seven programs, which dealt with 668 patients. These variations, especially between Madrid and Andalusia, can be attributed to a number of factors. Andalusia has a well-integrated plan and easy access to its services, whereas the plan of Madrid City is poorly integrated with that of the Madrid autonomous community. Outreach programs and mobile dispensing units (methadone buses) have been particularly important in Andalusia in facilitating access to methadone maintenance.

The increase in methadone maintenance programs in recent years has occurred as a result of the poor outcome of drug-free programs and the increasing rates of AIDS. Although they are seen neither as a panacea nor as a unique solution for heroin addicts, they remain a valid harm reduction method. Official acceptance of harm reduction programs began in 1983, but it was not until much later that the number of programs increased.

The first syringe exchange programs were launched in Madrid and the Basque Country in 1991, and by 1995 seven were operating. Attempts at establishing such programs elsewhere have been only partly successful; pharmacists have strongly resisted their establishment because they have enjoyed an exclusive right to distribute drug paraphernalia. In Barcelona County between May 1, 1992, and March 1, 1993, about 1,200 users exchanged syringes at the Services for the Prevention, Orientation and Treatment of Drug Dependents.

Conclusion

Illicit drug use became prevalent in Spain later than in many other European countries. Heroin use, now the major drug problem, did not set in until the beginning of the 1980s, closely followed by cocaine in the latter part of the 1980s. Despite its late entry on the European drug scene, Spain now has a growing drug problem, especially with respect to HIV infection and AIDS. Indeed, Spain is in the unenviable position of having the highest European rate of AIDS cases per million people. Moreover, about two thirds of AIDS cases are drug injectors, and HIV infection in drug users is especially high.

Spain's ability to tackle these problems and develop an adequate treatment system has been hampered in two major ways. First, the ability of the national and the regional governments to fund an efficient treatment system was undermined by the country's deteriorating economic situation and rather pervasive anomic climate in the past decade. Second, despite the creation of a national drug plan, an efficient treatment system has been hindered by the multiplication of political bureaucracies in the regional and city treatment networks in each of the autonomous communities. Spain's ability to tackle adequately its drug problem will depend on its already growing economy but also on at least moderate liberalization of its monopolistic bureaucracy. The growing awareness of the need for overdue reform of its National Health Service, which is run by political appointees, is sure to have an impact on the drug treatment system. Regulated competition and evaluation of services by peer review organizations establishing higher management and professional standards seem to be necessary ingredients of the improvement of both the drug treatment and the general health care systems.

Note

1. The survey, conducted by Robert Blendon of the Harvard School of Public Health, was ordered by a parliamentary commission (Comisión Abril). The administration disregarded its recommendations, however. (See Comisión de Analisis, 1991, appendix pp. 31-33.)

References

Bengoa, R., Echebarria, K., Fernández, J. M., Via, J. M., & Camprubi, J. (1997). *Sanidad: La Reforma Posible*. Barcelona: ESADE.

Cadafalch, J., & Casas, M. (1993). *El paciente heroinómano en el hospital general* [The heroin-addicted patient in the general hospital]. Madrid: National Plan on Drugs.

Comas, D. (1994). *Los jóvenes y el uso de drogas en la España de los años 90* [Youths and drug use in the Spain of the 1990s]. Madrid: Ministerio de Asuntos Sociales, Instituto de la Juventud.

Comisión de Analisis y Evaluación del Sistema Nacional de Salud: Informe y Recomendaciones. (1991). Madrid: Ministerio de Sanidad y Consumo.

Comunidad Autónoma de Madrid. (1994). *Estimación de la prevalencia de la adicción a la heroína en la Comunidad de Madrid durante 1992* [An estimate of the prevalence of heroin addiction in Madrid Autonomous Community in 1992]. Madrid: Plan Regional sobre Drogas.

El Mundo. (1995, April 13). *El SIDA en España* [AIDS in Spain]. Suplemento "Salud," p. 3.

Elola, J. (1994). *Sistema Nacional de Salud: Evaluación de su Eficiencia.* [The National Health Care System: Evaluation of its efficiency.] Barcelona: SG Editores.

European Monitoring Centre for Drugs and Drug Addiction. (1996). *Annual report on the state of the drugs problem in the European Union.* Lisbon: Author.

Pérez de Arróspide, J. A. (1992). Esperanza o desesperanza [Hope or despair]. *Adicciones, 4*(3), 181.

Chapter 22

Building a Drug Treatment System in Postrevolutionary Portugal

José Manuel Gaspar de Almeida
Rosa Encarnação

The political, economic, social, and cultural changes that Portugal has undergone in the past three decades are reflected in how drug problems have been perceived. For 48 years (1926 to 1974), Portugal was ruled by Salazar, Europe's longest-ruling dictator. He believed that everything that emanated from outside Portugal was harmful. In the 1960s, when new ideas were sweeping other European countries, the Salazar regime attempted to, but could not, prevent the ideas of the "flower power generation" from seeping into Portuguese society. Although drug use did not become common among the general public, certain groups, including high school students, artists, and intellectuals, experimented with cannabis and, occasionally, acid.

Under the Salazar regime, the official approach was simple: Because trafficking and drug consumption were forbidden, the problem could not exist, and organizations for drug treatment and prevention were unnecessary. To prevent any possibility of drug trafficking, border security was intensified. Although internally, the government denied the existence of drug problems, externally, it presented a different image and participated in a number of international meetings. It signed the 1961 Single Convention on Narcotic Drugs, but although the Convention called for services for addiction treatment, none were ever implemented.

One effect of the Portuguese revolution in April 1974 was to open up relations and contacts between the people of Portugal and of other countries, and the consequent new ideas and changes included new attitudes toward drugs, especially cannabis. Other factors associated with the revolution played a part in the increasing use of cannabis: Returning exiles, colonial soldiers, and refugees from the former regime brought new attitudes and new ways of behaving. Also, large numbers of Brazilian students arrived, bringing new attitudes to drug use. Opiates did not gain the same popularity as cannabis, and their use was confined to those who were well-off.

Data Collection Systems

Before 1976, data on drug use and dependency were not systematically collected, for a number of reasons: the complexity of the problem, insufficient resources, difficulties in coordinating the various disciplines concerned, and issues of social and political sensitivity. In 1976, the State established three official agencies: the Office of the Coordinator of the Campaign against Drugs, directed by the President's Council of Ministers and charged with the supervision of the two other new agencies; the Centers for the Study and Prevention of Drug Use; and the Center for Drug Control and Research, which was responsible primarily for investigating drug trafficking and use. The Office of the Coordinator received information and statistical data from the other agencies, on the basis of which it developed new services for drug addicts.

At this time, drug use was classified as criminal behavior, and its control consisted essentially of social and legal action. In 1982, a new law reorganized the structure of the official drug agencies. The Office of the Coordinator became the Office of Planning and Coordination to Combat Drugs and was made responsible directly to the Minister of Justice. The Centers for Study and Prevention remained unchanged, and the Center for Drug Control and Research was abolished. All criminal information related to drugs was to be handled by the Office of Planning and Coordination.

The Office had a double mandate: to represent Portugal at all of the international agencies concerned with drug-related problems (e.g., the United Nations agencies and the Pompidou Group); and to conduct research into drug addiction and the extent of drug problems, on the basis of analysis of data collected from the Study and Prevention Centers or obtained directly from criminal justice agencies, including the courts, prisons, and forensic laboratories. The objective was no longer social control, but rather to develop a better system for dealing with drug addiction and drug addicts.

The new Drug Law of 1983 (430/83) ratified the 1971 Convention on Psychotropic Substances, which defined drug addiction as "a disease, and not only a criminal behavior." The Law also provided for court sentences to be suspended if the offender chose to undergo treatment. The government established a national drug plan—the Integrated Plan to Combat Drugs—which in 1987 resulted in the creation of Projecto VIDA (Vida Inteligente Droga Ausente—Intelligent Life

Without Drugs), controlled by an Inter-Ministerial National Commission presided over by the Prime Minister. The VIDA Project contained 30 measures that were based on the first draft of the national drug plan, and it specified the functions of the various government ministries in its execution and implementation—Defense, for coordinating drug prevention and treatment in the Armed Services; Internal Affairs, for law enforcement; Justice, for coordinating measures to reduce supply, collecting statistical information, and complying with the International Conventions; Education, for drug prevention programs in schools; Health, for reducing demand for drugs through treatment and rehabilitation; Welfare, for policies and strategies for social issues pertaining to drug problems; and Employment, for occupational training and rehabilitation of marginal groups and individuals. The VIDA Project was also given the task of mobilizing local communities to develop a series of prevention projects that would be supported and coordinated by nongovernmental organizations.

The VIDA Project system established two separate information units. The first, the Observatorio Vida (the Observatory), collects epidemiological and observational data on drug-using behavior, which it supplies to the different government departments to ensure greater cooperation and coordination between them in designing strategies for social intervention. It has three units: Statistics and Epidemiology, Technology, and Documentation. The second information unit has as its primary function to provide a listing of key indicators that need to be tackled to prevent drug problems. These two units together supply objective and comparative information on drug addiction and its consequences.

In 1992, the European Union assisted Portugal in its efforts to collect systematic data by establishing in Lisbon the European Observatory of Drugs and Drug Addiction. Its tasks are to collect, analyze, and provide information on national policies and strategies, international cooperation, and issues related to drug trafficking throughout the 15 member states of the Union. According to a 3-year plan, it centralizes all information on drug matters throughout the member states, mainly for politicians and policymakers. The VIDA Project Observatory complements the activities of the European Observatory at the national level. It is charged with providing scientific and technical information to politicians and professionals, assisting politicians to develop rational social policies, and providing professionals with an accurate picture of the drug problem.

The Development of the Treatment System

Public Sector Services

The Drug Prevention and Study Centers were the focal point of the government's attempt to provide drug treatment services. Three were set up, one each in Lisbon,

Oporto, and Coimbra. They offered addicts treatment and other health care services, and they collected data on their patients. Each had two divisions: a medico-psychological division, which attended to drug addicts by providing consultation and detoxification on an outpatient basis, and a psychosocial division, which was designed to improve prevention services.

As noted above, various government ministries were allocated particular responsibilities in combating the drug problem. The Health Ministry set up the Service for the Prevention and Treatment of Drug Addiction, which in 1987 established the first drug addiction treatment unit in Lisbon, the Unit of Specialized Treatment of Drug Addiction. In 1989, it opened two similar units, drug addiction support centers, at Oporto and Faro, for the treatment and social reintegration of addicts. Two years later, the VIDA Project was modified to permit private institutions to obtain government support to establish drug treatment services. In 1995, the Service for the Prevention and Treatment of Drug Addiction was reorganized to improve health care in other cities. Three regional organizations were created—north, center, and south—and two new kinds of facilities for addicts were established in each region: specialized hospital units and outpatient centers. The former, of which there are six, provide outpatient and inpatient services and therapeutic communities; the latter, of which there are 18, are specialized units operating in the smaller towns. Treatment is free. In each region, the units and centers are interconnected and work jointly. The changed structure of official agencies concerned with drug addiction has led to high priority being given to the treatment and social reintegration of the addicts.

The numbers attending the treatment units, both inpatients and outpatients, increased by 17% between 1990 and 1991. The percentage increase then fell between 1991 and 1993, but rose again dramatically in 1994 and 1995, by 29% and 42%, respectively.

The Service for the Prevention and Treatment of Addiction operates three types of service: drug addiction support centers, detoxification units, and therapeutic communities. Addiction support centers are found in each of the 32 principal cities in Portugal and are solely for outpatient treatment. A survey in 1995 found that, of a total of 980 user-attenders, 81% were male, 72% were single or separated, and the average age was 27 years. The vast majority were heroin users (95%), and 39% of these had used it regularly for 2 to 6 years.

There are three detoxification units (Lisbon, Oporto, and Coimbra), with a total of 30 beds. They are linked to the addiction support centers. Patients, after 1 week in residential treatment, attend outpatient services. Admissions to all three units in 1995 numbered 1,086, representing a progressive increase since 1990, when the first unit was opened in Lisbon.

There are only two therapeutic communities (Lisbon and Coimbra), with only 20 beds, and relatively few clients—an average of 20 per year in Lisbon and 43 in Coimbra.

Apart from a harm reduction program in the Oporto public sector unit, which operates a methadone maintenance program, abstinence is the dominant treatment rationale of the public sector services, which use biopsychosocial models of treatment.

Private Sector Services

Private sector institutions are of three kinds: (a) for-profit medical clinics that use a traditional medical model of detoxification and inpatient treatment services, and a medical follow-up for relapse prevention; (b) for-profit institutions linked to religious organizations, both Catholic and Protestant, offering detoxification services, therapeutic communities, halfway houses, and self-help groups, all designed to prepare the client for reintegration into society; and (c) nonprofit prevention institutions. Like the public sector services, the private treatment and rehabilitation institutions operate on the abstinence principle. The type of model adopted to ensure abstinence varies from one institution to another. Unlike the public sector, which uses biopsychosocial models exclusively, private institutions apply several psychotherapeutic models based on alcohol dependency treatment programs. For instance, the Projeto Homem (Project of Man), with its origins in Italy, is used in institutions associated with the Catholic Church. Institutions linked with Protestant churches use other modalities, such as the Minnesota model and Alcoholics Anonymous.

Self-help groups first appeared in 1985. Today, there are about 1,000 Narcotics Anonymous (NA) groups, which hold 120 weekly meetings throughout the country. NA has also organized "Narcotic Families" groups. In 1995, the media provided extensive coverage of the NA Convention, which provoked much interest from the public.

Drugs and AIDS

In 1990, as part of the VIDA Project, the government created the Combat AIDS Commission to coordinate all efforts related to HIV infection and AIDS. However, it was given no power to enforce any new measures and could only issue a series of advisory notices. Their implementation depends on the willingness of individual government departments to follow the Commission's advice. For example, in 1993, it recommended that all prisons issue free condoms and syringes to prisoners; the authorities countered the recommendation on the pretext that there were no intravenous drug user or homosexual prisoners. Fortunately, 2 years later, a new director of prisons admitted the existence of the problem and commenced the free distribution of condoms and syringes.

The Commission is charged not only with informing the general public about HIV/AIDS but also with making prevention materials available to particular high-risk groups, such as teenagers and pregnant women. For example, in 1993, a syringe exchange campaign was undertaken for intravenous drug users.

Conclusion

Drug addiction in Portugal has changed from being a legal problem to a health problem. The most significant development in drug treatment has been the creation of the Service for the Prevention and Treatment of Drug Addiction, which has improved both the organization of treatment and the quality of information collected on the sociodemographics of addicts. Because of limited government resources, private drug treatment has also been encouraged as a way of coping with the growing problem of drug addiction.

The government has attempted to raise awareness of the problem through the VIDA Project, which has conducted media campaigns to alert the general public to its extent and to the dangers of drug addiction. At the same time, increased measures have been taken to combat the illegal traffic and consumption of drugs, but with little effect. This has raised discussion in the media on how to deal with drug problems and illicit drug use. The Drug Law that was enacted in 1992 decriminalized drug use and promoted treatment as an alternative to imprisonment. Its enactment, with its orientation toward decriminalization, represented a discrepancy between the legislative level and the social values of the people. Vigilante groups have formed in the countryside to attack suspected drug dealers. Apparently, the general population still perceives the addict as primarily a criminal and not as someone in need of treatment. Government officials, especially in the Ministry of Health, are concerned about these popular developments and have increased their efforts to ensure that drug addicts are treated with understanding and support from the general population.

Chapter 23

Legal Changes, Political Pressure, and Drug Treatment in Italy: From a Hard-Line Approach to Decriminalization

Luigi M. Solivetti

Italy's position on the international drug scene is notable in two respects: its very firm approach to tackling the drug problem and, more particularly, drug trafficking; and its tolerance of addiction per se. This tolerance led to Italy being the first country to officially decriminalize the holding of drugs for personal use. Italy also sought alternative approaches in drug policy in other respects, such as treatment of addicts (e.g., developing an extensive network of therapeutic centers for their care and resocialization).

Punishment and Treatment in Early Italian Drug Legislation—The Alcohol Connection

The delayed onset of the spread of drugs in Italy was reflected in the criminal laws of the past. The 1889 Criminal Code made no mention of drugs. True, it was a liberal code that penalized the adulteration of food, drinks (especially wine), and other substances, but let people buy any sort of unadulterated drug, including poison (Andreoli, Maffei, & Tamburino, 1982, p. 201). Little more than 20 years later, the term *drugs* entered criminal law. Italy signed the 1912 Convention of The Hague, which introduced international control on illegal trafficking of drugs, and in 1923 passed an act penalizing drug trafficking. The penalties it imposed were mild, however: imprisonment for up to 6 months for drug trafficking by unauthorized persons, and a fine for organizing and participating in meetings intended for drug use; it did not penalize the holding of drugs for personal use. The legislators' scant interest in repressing drug use is shown also by the lack of any provision for the treatment of addicts (Delogu, 1973, p. 153).

The next legislation enacted on drug use, the 1930 Criminal Code—the so-called Rocco Code—which is still in force, was largely similar. Drug use was clearly not regarded as a serious threat to society. Certainly, it was not good for the "health of the race" (Manzini, 1950, vol. 6, p. 415)—an idea dear to the new nationalist regime. The Code provided for imprisonment for up to 3 years for unauthorized drug trafficking but did not penalize drug use itself. However, anyone caught "in a state of serious mental disorder" due to drug use could be imprisoned for up to 6 months.

The very concept of "state of serious mental disorder" was derived from that applied to alcohol abuse, and the penalty provided was the same as for the alcohol user caught in that state. Moreover, the new Criminal Code introduced the same indirect control on both alcohol and drug abuse, excluding consideration of extenuating circumstances when an offense was committed under the influence of drugs or alcohol, willingly or culpably taken. It seems that the provisions regarding drug use were uncritically derived from those pertaining to alcohol abuse. Although wine consumption is integral to Italian culture, legislators and experts in social problems were very well aware of its negative effects, and when they had to deal with the "new" issue of such drugs as opiates and cocaine, they had recourse to concepts and measures already in place to tackle the abuse of the best known legal drug, alcohol.

The law on drug use did not change again until the 1950s, nor, it seems, did drug use. Criminal statistics indicated a few dozen cases of drug trafficking in Italy at that time. There was no obvious need for more severe penalties. However, Italy agreed to the new drug policy internationally supported by the United States as an expression of that country's concern about the marked increase in the number of its addicts. They had increased from a few thousand in the 1940s to hundreds of thousands, peaking precisely in the early 1950s (Ball & Cottrell, 1965, pp. 471-472). The United States government was therefore urging allied nations to join it in a stricter control of drug use and drug trafficking. For these reasons, the Italian 1954 Drug Act introduced a change. It covered the entire field of drug-related behavior by a blanket provision imposing imprisonment, for 3 to 8 years, for both drug use and drug trafficking. Moreover, it did not distinguish between hard and soft drugs; all attracted the same penalties for both use and trafficking.

For many years after the 1954 Drug Act, the use of drugs in Italy remained quite limited; fewer than 100 people per year were charged with drug trafficking. A turning point occurred at the end of the 1960s. There was a clear increase in the consumption of drugs, both opiates and cannabis derivatives (Italy, Ministero dell'Interno, 1992, p. 9), and a corresponding increase in the number of people charged with drug trafficking (Table 23.1). Owing to the rigidity of the law, people

Table 23.1 People Charged With Drug Trafficking Offenses, and Deaths Due to Drug Abuse in Italy

Year	People Charged With Drug Trafficking Offenses		Deaths Due to Drug Abuse	
	N	*per 100,000 pop.*	*N*	*per 100,000 pop.*
1967	73	0.14	—	—
1968	149	0.28	—	—
1969	155	0.29	—	—
1970	697	1.30	—	—
1971	660	1.22	—	—
1972	912	1.68	—	—
1973	1,934	3.53	1	< 0.01
1974	2,388	4.33	8	0.01
1975	3,347	6.04	26	0.05
1976	2,387	4.28	31	0.06
1977	2,714	4.85	40	0.07
1978	4,159	7.41	62	0.11
1979	5,242	9.31	126	0.22
1980	7,783	13.79	206	0.36
1981	9,469	16.75	237	0.42
1982	12,982	22.95	252	0.44
1983	15,184	26.83	259	0.46
1984	17,876	31.58	397	0.70
1985	18,571	32.80	242	0.43
1986	18,040	31.85	292	0.51
1987	22,972	40.54	543	0.96
1988	28,688	50.61	809	1.43
1989	26,179	46.17	974	1.72
1990	24,647	43.45	1,161	2.05
1991	30,025	52.91	1,382	2.43
1992	38,351	67.46	1,217	2.14
1993	32,947	58.10	875	1.56
1994	36,061	63.04	867	1.52

SOURCE: ISTAT (1995 and previous years); Italy, Ministero dell'Interno, Osservatorio permanente sul fenomeno droga (1995).

charged with drug trafficking (even if they were usually only drug users) were regularly imprisoned. The beginning of the 1970s saw the first deaths from drug abuse (Table 23.1).

This spread of drug use caused deep concern in Italy. At the same time, people began to raise objections to the 1954 Drug Act. Various groups, mainly of the Left, attacked its severity and its failure to discriminate between various drugs or between different kinds of behavior, such as the simple holding of drugs for personal use and international trade. The radical groups launched a campaign to decriminalize light drugs (Blumir, 1973). The small but active Radical Party presented a bill proposing the legalization of the holding for personal use of any drug (Arnao, 1976, pp. 219-222). This movement was like other legalization movements in the United States and Britain at the time (Akers, 1992; Goode, 1970). As elsewhere, many Italians questioned the effectiveness of the repressive policy that originated in the United States, contrasting it with the policy followed in Britain, where a milder approach to drug use and the legal administration of opiates to addicts had been accompanied by a relatively limited spread of drug use. All of these movements ultimately came together in a demand for legislation that would regard the addict not as a dangerous criminal but as a victim of drugs who needed therapy and rehabilitation.

The Innovative 1975 Drug Act
and the Decriminalization of Drug Use

The eagerly awaited new Drug Act was passed in 1975. Its timing was significant. The same year was marked by the peaking of the Italian Communist Party and in general by the influence of the Left culture, which favored a mild, treatment-oriented approach to the problem of drug use. The new Act symbolized the climate of the time, resembling in this respect the radical 1978 Psychiatric Hospitals Reform.

The 1975 Drug Act did not disappoint those expecting radical change. It decriminalized the holding for personal use of a "limited amount" of any illicit drug and distinguished between soft and hard drugs. It was the first instance of formal decriminalization of personal use of drugs in the Western world in modern times, and it provided also for the establishment of a welfare network for the treatment of addicts. Its aim in establishing this network was twofold. First, any addict needing therapy and assistance could obtain it by contacting voluntarily the facilities of the network. Second, anyone known to be an addict (e.g., someone holding a small amount of drugs for personal use) and regarded as in need of care was to undertake treatment at one of these facilities, compulsorily if necessary. However, the authorities rapidly discovered how difficult it was to implement this provision against the addict's will; it was difficult also because the act excluded the use of closed institutions for the treatment of addicts, and there was no penalty for failure to take treatment. At the same time, the treatment facilities rejected compulsory treatment as inapplicable and, in any case, futile. In practice, therefore, compulsory treatment was not implemented.

Besides this network, the act authorized private institutions for the treatment of addicts and permitted local authorities to use and fund nonprofit, private institutions.

Another innovation was the treatment of addicts detained in prison. Prison wards were organized to provide suitable medical, psychological, and social treatment. Later legislation (in particular, the 1990 Drug Act) extended these provisions, with the result that specialized sections dedicated to the treatment of addicts have been opened in almost all prisons, for both men and women, and a few prisons have been completely dedicated to the treatment of addicts. Some sections have been organized to ensure "attenuated detention"—a "soft" regimen thought to be particularly suitable for treatment purposes.

Table 23.2 Addicts Under Treatment in Public and Private Institutions in Italy, on 15 June
(1984-1994)

Year	Addicts in Public Institutions		Addicts in Private Institutions		Addicts in Public and Private Institutions	
	n	per 100,000 pop.	n	per 100,000 pop.	N	per 100,000 pop.
1984	18,483	32.6	4,373	7.7	22,856	40.3
1985	18,429	32.5	4,930	8.7	23,359	41.2
1986	19,079	33.7	5,540	9.8	24,619	43.5
1987	21,895	38.6	6,114	10.8	28,009	49.4
1988	25,533	45.0	7,527	13.3	33,060	58.3
1989	31,568	55.7	8,792	15.5	40,360	71.2
1990	37,804	66.6	10,667	18.8	48,471	85.4
1991	43,650	76.9	12,426	21.9	56,076	98.8
1992	55,797	98.1	15,663	27.5	71,460	125.7
1993	59,646	104.6	16,133	28.3	75,779	132.8
1994	72,681	127.1	15,517	27.1	88,198	154.2

SOURCE: Italy, Ministero dell'Interno, Osservatorio permanente sul fenomeno droga (1995).

Moreover, addicts who are charged with or sentenced for any crime and who are under treatment or willing to be treated at any public or private institution are accorded special privileges. They are not liable to detention pending trial, except for serious security reasons; and if already sentenced, they can be given the alternative of an assignment to the social service or a stay of sentence. Underage addicts charged with or sentenced for any crime benefit from the special conditions already applicable to all minors, namely, treatment at a public or private facility instead of custody.

The Reintroduction of Sanctions for Drug Use
and Coercive Treatment Measures

The 1975 Drug Act aroused remarkable interest in Italy as well as abroad. However, the expectations it raised were at least partly frustrated. In the following years, drug abuse spread widely in Italy, by comparison with other European countries (Reuband, 1995, p. 36). Of particular interest is the figure for addicts under treatment at public and private institutions: From 1984 (when official records were instituted), the increase has been constant, reaching a rate of 154 per 100,000 population in 1994 (Table 23.2).

The growth in the number of addicts under treatment in all of the institutions exceeded the growth in the number of institutions (Table 23.3). However, public and private institutions differed in this respect. Public institutions, which are obliged to take care of anyone in need of treatment but are, at the same time, slow to respond to change because of their bureaucratic organization, showed a limited growth in their number but a much higher growth in the number of addicts treated (Tables 23.3 and 23.4). Private facilities evolved differently; because they are much readier to respond to change, but, being as a rule residential, rather inflexible

Table 23.3 Number of Public and Private Institutions for Treatment of Addicts in Italy, on 15 June (1984-1994)

Year	Public Institutions		Private Institutions		Public and Private Institutions	
	n	per 100,000 pop.	n	per 100,000 pop.	N	per 100,000 pop.
1984	382	0.67	207	0.37	589	1.04
1985	419	0.74	280	0.49	699	1.23
1986	456	0.80	323	0.57	779	1.37
1987	456	0.80	320	0.56	776	1.37
1988	476	0.84	345	0.61	821	1.45
1989	489	0.86	361	0.64	850	1.50
1990	505	0.89	422	0.74	927	1.63
1991	505	0.89	454	0.80	959	1.69
1992	533	0.94	570	1.00	1,103	1.94
1993	528	0.93	602	1.05	1,130	1.98
1994	548	0.96	681	1.19	1,229	2.15

SOURCE: Italy, Ministero dell'Interno, Osservatorio permanente sul fenomeno droga (1995).

Table 23.4 Addicts Under Treatment in Italy in Public and Private Institutions on Average, per Institution

Year	Addicts in Public Institutions	Addicts in Private Institutions	Addicts in Public and Private Institutions
1984	48	21	39
1985	44	18	33
1986	42	17	32
1987	48	19	36
1988	54	22	40
1989	65	24	47
1990	75	25	52
1991	86	27	58
1992	105	27	65
1993	113	27	67
1994	133	23	72

SOURCE: Italy, Ministero dell'Interno, Osservatorio permanente sul fenomeno droga (1995).

as to number of clients per unit, they increased considerably in number but very little in number of clients per unit. All this seems to suggest that behind the rapid increase globally in the numbers treated, there has been an increasing demand for treatment, not just an increasing offer of treatment.

Conspicuous also was the increase in deaths from drug abuse (see Table 23.1), a reliable indicator of, in particular, the spread of hard drugs. Deaths reached a peak of almost 1,400 per year (2.4 per 100,000 population) in the early 1990s. Addicts deceased were quite young on average; about 30% were under 26 years old, and only 3% were over 40 (Italy, Ministero dell'Interno, 1993).

Toward the end of the 1980s, the failure of the heavy penalties to restrain the increasing use of drugs prompted new demands for legalizing the drug market as the best means of disentangling the intertwined aspects of drug use, drug trafficking, drug-related crime against property, and the interests of the criminal cartels.

The Radical Party was at the forefront of this movement for drug legalization. Also in favor of legalization were the most liberal groups of the Right and the most antiauthoritarian of the Left. Against legalization stood the Church and the powerful private associations for the treatment of addicts; both also opposed, as a rule, any policy of harm reduction, such as free distribution of syringes, just as they opposed similar policies in closely related fields (such as the free distribution of condoms to check the spread of AIDS). Not surprisingly, therefore, the new proposals had rather limited impact.

Together with legalization, the issue of treatment was at the core of the debate. Hard-liners criticized the lack of measures to enforce the treatment of addicts. In 1990, a new Drug Act was introduced. It saw the victory of the hard-liners. It further increased penalties for trafficking (e.g., not less than 20 years in prison for the leaders of drug-trafficking gangs). At the same time, it again regarded addicts as socially dangerous and not only as victims of society. Consequently, to deter drug use and induce the addict to accept treatment, the act introduced a long series of administrative measures directed at those holding drugs for personal use (e.g., warning, withdrawal of passport or driving license, or, for foreigners, suspension of tourist residence permits). The addict who failed to undertake treatment at a public or private facility was subject to heavier penalties, now applied by the courts (terms of probation, community service, seizure of the addict's vehicle if used to carry drugs, etc.). The same penalties were applied to addicts repeatedly caught holding drugs for personal use. Ultimately, the repeatedly recalcitrant addict was subject to a heavy fine or prison sentence of up to 3 months.

The decriminalization and legalization groups scored a victory in 1993, when a national referendum led to the abrogation of any provision for custodial measures or for a fine for the addict who failed to undertake treatment or was repeatedly caught holding drugs for personal use, as the 1990 Drug Act laid down. The addict is now liable only to the noncustodial measures mentioned above. The referendum led also to the abrogation of the concept of "limited amount," as to the holding of drugs for personal use. In practice, this means that the judge has to determine, case by case, whether the drugs seized—whatever their amounts—were held for personal use or not. However, the debate between hard-liners and "soft-liners" is far from over.

Treatment Concepts: Public Institutions and the "Outpatients Department" Model

This treatment network, introduced by the 1975 act, steadily developed over the following years until it had almost 90,000 addicts (more than 150 per 100,000 population) in its charge in 1994 (Table 23.2). The public institutions of this network bear most of the burden, being responsible for about four fifths of all addicts under treatment. They provide treatment free of charge to anybody who needs it. They are organized mainly according to the "outpatients department" model, which means that, as a rule, they provide treatment for only a few hours per day. (A few also provide residential treatment.) Their staff is mainly permanent (on average, 72%), plus a certain number of consultants (21%) and a few voluntary workers (7%). It is a highly skilled staff (although often, not all are equally motivated): Medical practitioners represent on average 27%, nurses 19%, psychologists 17%, social workers 16%, and educators 10% (Italy, Labos and Ministero dell'Interno, 1993, p. 37). Their patients take heroin as the main illicit drug (91.4% of the cases); cocaine users represent only 1.6% and cannabis users 4% (Italy, Presidenza del Consiglio dei Ministri, 1993, p. 290ff.).

The treatment consists of medical, pharmacological, psychological, psychotherapeutic, social, and bureaucratic assistance. The use of methadone (and similar substances) is standard but has declined constantly over the past few years, from 57% of the cases in 1984, to 39% in 1989, and 34% in 1993. Roughly half of those treated with methadone receive it as long-term treatment. Methadone is mainly meant to help in coping with withdrawal and in rehabilitation. Methadone maintenance is usually not favored; however, because the institutions wish to help their patients avoid the health and criminal risks of a relapse into drug addiction, they often continue to provide some form of methadone maintenance on an informal basis (Italy, Presidenza del Consiglio dei Ministri, 1993, p. 290ff.).

Because all of these institutions are public, they might be expected to exhibit a high degree of homogeneity. However, they are run by many different local health authorities with diverse policies and practices, and the institutions are correspondingly diverse. Even what is perceived as their main function—the administering of pharmacological therapies—is much less homogeneous than one might expect: Many delegate this work to other facilities, such as first-aid centers, special hospital wards, and pharmacies.

An extensive survey of most of the country's institutions (Italy, Labos and Ministero dell'Interno, 1993) classified them into four groups. The first, consisting of 14.4% of the institutions, practices medical treatment (pharmacotherapy) and social control, managing the relations of the addicts with the police and the courts. The second (25.1%) practices personalized therapy that is programmed to the clients' needs, given by a professional team, and usually includes psychotherapy or other forms of treatment, such as psychiatric, pharmaceutical, and general medical therapy. The third (30%) provides generic support to the client, which typically goes along with burdensome bureaucratic requirements. The fourth (30.5%) practices a combination of approaches.

A general characteristic of the Italian public network for the treatment of addicts is its marked interaction with other public and private institutions. These include, first of all, the police and the judiciary authorities, and the importance of this interaction has, of course, grown since the 1990 Drug Act established administrative and penal sanctions for those addicts failing to undertake treatment. Another important group in this respect is that of other public social and health institutions, as well as commercial companies (private enterprises, cooperative societies) with which the treatment network interacts to facilitate the addict's vocational rehabilitation (Italy, Labos and Ministero dell'Interno, 1993, p. 135ff.). Also noteworthy is the interaction with public and private educational and cultural institutions, such as schools, sports and cultural associations, and voluntary helper groups.

Treatment Modalities: Private
Institutions and the Residential Model

Private institutions have developed rapidly over the past few years (Tables 23.2 and 23.3); in 1994, they had in their charge more than 15,000 addicts. Their expansion seems to be linked with the good image of their treatment approach, which is broad and community-oriented, and capable of offering steady, global, and around-the-clock support to the addict. The addict is expected to make a contribution to the institution, either in money or by work. Addicts' parents are usually encouraged to collaborate with the institutions. However, these institutions receive both private and public funds. Also, they enjoy a basic advantage over public institutions in that they are not obliged to accept any addict in need of treatment, despite their often substantial public funding. They can choose clients whom they consider most likely to overcome addiction. The rest will inevitably head for the unselective public institutions. Naturally, private institutions claim high rates of success, but these rates are usually calculated on the numbers of addicts completing the period of treatment, out of all those who were accepted after a preliminary phase. Most failures occur during this preliminary phase. Moreover, there are no follow-up surveys covering the period after the end of treatment.

In comparison with public institutions, the private ones are mainly residential. Only about 20% are nonresidential; consequently, on average, they have in their charge significantly fewer addicts than the public institutions. Moreover, being the outcome of private initiatives, they reflect the country's economic, social, and cultural characteristics and therefore are not evenly distributed, as are the public institutions. Most are in the Northern regions, 20% are in the Central regions, and about 20% also are in the South. Their staff is mainly voluntary (61%); a minority are permanent workers (25%); and a few are consultants (11%). Two thirds of the institutions (67%) employ former addicts; they amount on average to 50% of the entire staff. Not surprisingly, the staff is also low-skilled and tends much more toward social rather than health care specializations: Medical practitioners represent on average 7% of staff, nurses 2%, psychologists 7%, social workers 2%, educators 28%, social animators 8%, and workers without any specialized skill 20% (Italy, Labos and Ministero dell'Interno, 1993, p. 47ff.).

An official survey of a substantial sample of former addicts who completed residential programs of treatment between 1981 and 1990 (Italy, Logos Ricerche and Ministero dell'Interno, 1993) found that they were predominantly men (85%); their average age was 31; and they had usually taken more than one illicit drug (opiates, methadone, cocaine, amphetamines, etc.), but mainly heroin, because 81.5% of the cases used it regularly.

To better understand the picture of the private institutions for the treatment of addicts in Italy, it should be remembered that they were established in the late 1960s and early 1970s, often at the initiative of the Catholic Church and in response to the spread of drug abuse and its relative newness for Italian society. Treatment of drug abuse has always been their main concern by far, although they may also treat alcoholics. Many of them are influenced by the American experience of Synanon, in the later revised model of Daytop Lodge and Phoenix House. Therefore, as a rule, these Italian institutions share some key concepts, such as the marked interaction between the participants; the significance of community values; particular attention to the involvement of newcomers in groups; the banning of substitution treatment (methadone or similar substances); and the employment of former, recovered addicts to take charge of newcomers.

The influence of the American experience, however, did not necessarily bring about its uncritical reproduction in the Italian institutions. On the contrary, there were noteworthy early initiatives designed to improve the methods and adjust them to local needs. Centro Italiano di Solidarietà, for instance, promoted an international center for the development of treatment strategies, and its models are now applied by many institutions in Europe and Latin America. Its initiatives include, for instance, "short programs" limited to 6 months, as well as nonresidential programs for subjects who are well integrated in the occupational field. Other institutions, such as Gruppo Abele, tried alternatives to a residential community, such as day and semiresidential centers for therapy and vocational rehabilitation, also in close contact with public agencies. The Villa Maraini Foundation focused mainly on harm reduction, through a variety of initiatives that included first aid and "on the road" interventions. Other institutions, such as San Patrignano, went in from the beginning for a treatment model essentially centered on vocational rehabilitation.

Conclusions

All in all, the treatment problems that have emerged in Italy over the past few years underline a basic doubt about the value of legal sanctions in the fight against drug abuse. Simple suggestions, even an order, to attend treatment institutions are largely ineffective unless they have some attached sanctions. Penal sanctions do not sufficiently deter drug use; and even a substantial increase in the severity of penal sanctions seems to have little effect on the spread of drug use (Solivetti, 1994). At the same time, a series of sanctions—such as those introduced by the 1990 Drug Act—designed to get addicts into treatment may accomplish this aim but does not ensure a positive outcome. The Italian drug treatment experience, therefore, confirms the low levels of success of compulsory or threat-induced drug treatment recorded in other countries (Leukefeld & Tims, 1988). Hence, it seems likely that there will be new attempts soon at legalizing the drug market, attempts that may well succeed, at least for soft drugs. In any case, the enforcement of repressive measures is likely to be further reduced on addicts, first on those involved in drug trafficking, then on those charged with common offenses. It may also be assumed that harm reduction policies will expand in connection with the decline of repressive measures, and also because of the gap between Italy and other Western countries in the development of harm reduction strategies.

References

Akers, R. L. (1992). *Drugs, alcohol, and society: Social structure, process, and policy.* Belmont, CA: Wadsworth.

Andreoli, V., Maffei, F., & Tamburino, G. (1982). *Il ciclo della droga* [The drug cycle]. Milan: Mondadori.

Arnao, G. (1976). *Rapporto sulle droghe* [Report on drugs]. Milan: Feltrinelli.

Ball, J. C., & Cottrell, E. S. (1965). Admissions of narcotic drug addicts to public health service hospitals, 1935-63. *Public Health Reports, 80,* 471-475.

Blumir, G. (1973). *La marihuana fa bene* [Marihuana does you good]. Rome: Tattilo.

Delogu, T. (1973). La problematica giuridica delle tossicomanie [Juridical problems of addiction]. In Comune di Roma (Ed.), *Società d'oggi e droga: Le implicazioni sociali, giuridiche e mediche del problema della droga e i compiti degli enti locali* (pp. 147-190). Rome: Comune di Roma.

Goode, E. (1970). *The marijuana smokers.* New York: Basic Books.

ISTAT. (1995 and previous years). *Statistiche giudiziarie penali* [Criminal statistics]. Rome: Author.

Italy, Labos and Ministero dell'Interno. (1993). *Strategie operative nei servizi per le tossicodipendenze* [Operative strategies in the services for the treatment of addicts]. Rome: Tipografica Editrice Romana (T.E.R.).

Italy, Logos Ricerche and Ministero dell'Interno. (1993). *Il reinserimento sociale dei tossicodipendenti* [The social rehabilitation of addicts]. Rome: Ministero dell'Interno.

Italy, Ministero dell'Interno, Direzione Centrale per i Servizi Antidroga. (1992). *Attività antidroga svolta dalle Forze di Polizia in Italia* [Police action against drug diffusion]. Rome: Ministero dell'Interno.

Italy, Ministero dell'Interno, Osservatorio permanente sul fenomeno droga. (1993). *Andamento delle tossicodipendenze in Italia etc.* [Evolution of forms of addiction in Italy, etc.]. Rome: Ministero dell'Interno.

Italy, Ministero dell'Interno, Osservatorio permanente sul fenomeno droga. (1995). *Tossicomani in trattamento etc.* [Addicts under treatment etc.]. Rome: Ministero dell'Interno.

Italy, Presidenza del Consiglio dei Ministri. (1993). *Relazione sui dati relativi allo stato delle tossicodipendenze in Italia, etc.* [Report on the data relating to the situation of addiction in Italy, etc.]. Rome: Author.

Leukefeld, C. G., & Tims, F. M. (Eds.). (1988). *Compulsory treatment of drug abuse: Research and clinical practice.* Rockville, MD: National Institute on Drug Abuse.

Manzini, V. (1950). *Trattato di diritto penale italiano* [Italian criminal law treatise]. Turin: Unione Tipografica Editrice Torinese.

Reuband, K.-H. (1995). Drug use and drug policy in Western Europe. *European Addiction Research, 1,* 32-41.

Solivetti, L. M. (1994). Drug diffusion and social change: The illusion about a formal social control. *Howard Journal of Criminal Justice, 1,* 41-61.

Chapter 24

Dionysus Is Back

Kaj Noschis

Comment on Part 6

For a perspective on drug addiction and drug treatment in viticultural countries of southern Europe, I suggest that these countries can be typified by their attitude toward drinking. In France, Italy, Portugal, and Spain, wine is the customary table drink. The mythological connotations of wine are connected with Dionysus—the Greek god of wine—and the celebrations held in his honor in Greece from the 6th century BCE as the god of the Bacchanals. They are connected in particular with the Dionysian celebrations—the excitement brought about by wine, dancing, and music; the presence of "possessed" women; and the procession from Athens to Eleusis to celebrate the Mysteries. Such bacchanalian rites have long disappeared in southern Europe and have been replaced by more prosaic drinking activities. Drinking is commonplace in the viticultural countries of the south; it is deeply embedded in everyday village life. My own bacchanalian experiences have been in the north of Europe, in Finland, my home country. Here, drinking is an exceptional celebration, intended to affect and alter the drinker so that he or she may step outside him- or herself and outside everyday routines, a practice called "explosive" drinking. It is as though the Dionysian rites have left their origins and migrated from the Mediterranean[1] to other regions of the world where wine is not an everyday beverage.

Dionysus compromised with Christianity, and his nectar became the new religion's life-giving blood. In the first centuries of the Christian era, in representations of Dionysus and Christ, Dionysus occasionally overlapped with Christ. On the shores of the Mediterranean, this was not surprising. Christians adopted ancient rites with the mystery intact, and wine drinking became a symbolic act in the celebration of religious rites. The use of wine in a religious rite coincided with its adoption as an ordinary, everyday drink. Dionysian rites no longer played a part in organized societal life. Ironically, with the complicity of Christianity, Dionysus found new dwelling places. As the Western world spread outward to new territories and imposed Christianity and colonization, bacchanalian celebrations merged with local customs, and Dionysus lived on in the shadow of Christianity.

In countries where Dionysus lives on, people who lose control over drinking are cared for, and there are special procedures for dealing with those who have serious problems with alcohol. Excess is recognized as an unpleasant but unavoidable by-product of the Dionysian cult. However, countries where wine drinking has long been part of everyday life have been more hesitant in introducing means of caring for people with alcohol problems.

How are these attitudes toward drinking and drinking problems related to the development of a drug treatment system?

If Dionysus and, especially, his more euphoriant rites have migrated from Mediterranean shores, then drugs may be the guise under which he attempts to return. Such an idea may not be outlandish, given that there is some evidence that *kykeon*—the drink of the Eleusinian Mysteries—contained a hallucinogenic drug derived from ergot, a fungus that grows on rye and other cereals. Thus, a hallucinogenic wine drink was used to honor Dionysus. In this way, it can be argued that the "feel of Bacchus" (Euripides, quoted in Paris, 1990, p. 5) has transferred from wine to drugs. Moreover, whereas the grape is a Mediterranean fruit, most drugs come from plants grown outside Europe; then, our argument that Dionysus has returned to southern Europe with the arrival of drugs may have even greater validity. However, drug consumption has failed to find a place in everyday rites of ordinary life, and without such informal but ritual control, drug consumption has too easily led to drug dependency. Encounters with a Dionysus, who opens the chemical doors of perception, require a ritual check. As Paris (1990) has noted, "Adolescents who get stoned on drugs . . . are unaware of the true power of their substance. . . . What they are looking for is Dionysus. What they are offered is an overdose of all sorts of drugs in the absence of a guiding spirit" (p. 12).

According to the authors of the chapters on the four Mediterranean countries, those countries reacted to the drug scene at first by ignoring it, and later by a confusing mixture of tolerant and radical interventions. Only recently have they adopted a more coordinated approach. They had assumed that drug consumption would soon find its place in the everyday ritual customs—as wine drinking had done earlier. Today, the unexpected return of Dionysus is seen to have had dramatic consequences for a new, mainly young, group of people overcome by its own consumption of drugs. All four chapters reveal that drug policies are often inconsistent in their attitudes toward drug dealers and drug users. In addition, the measures taken differ in several respects from one country to another and are consequently difficult to summarize coherently. Yet all appear to share a common origin in the way that, in responding to drug problems, the countries have adapted and extended earlier views on alcohol use. Today, because all four countries are part of a united Europe, they will probably move toward a shared policy on dealing with the problems of drug abuse. Each country has acknowledged that without ritual means of containment, its citizens who lose control over drug use must be cared for. In seeking ways of handling such problems, these countries, like others before them, have chosen models of "successful" care (see the example of Projetto Uomo). A successful model is adopted even though it has developed in very different social conditions, from different conceptual starting points. However, once a model is defined as successful, it becomes fashionable to export it to other regions. The assumption behind such an idea, at least in the case of these Mediterranean countries, may somehow be connected with the belief that, if Dionysian ritual controls can be established outside their origins, so can means of caring for problem drug users.

Note

1. Dionysus—a very complex and multifaceted god who has masculine and feminine attributes—was celebrated in Greece. Bacchus is his "Romanized and degenerate version" (Sanford, 1995, p. 96). He remains a Mediterranean creation, associated with grapes, and consequently, in the present context, his native region is extended to encompass the four countries under consideration.

References

Paris, G. (1990). *Pagan grace.* Dallas, TX: Spring.
Sanford, J. A. (1995). *Fate, love and ecstasy: Wisdom from the lesser-known goddesses of the Greeks.* Wilmette, IL: Chiron.

Part VII

Economic Revolution and Cultural Transformation in the Far East

Chapter 25

Societal Control and the Model of Legal Drug Treatment: A Japanese Success Story?

Kyohei Konuma
Shinji Shimizu
Takeshi Koyanagi

Historical Aspects of Drug Problems in Japan

Generally speaking, Japan has never had either endemic or epidemic drug abuse, except for a limited period after World War II. If any, there has been just the simple type of drug use (Bejorot, 1969) and the rather limited epidemic of drug use in the military days of World War II. A brief review of the history of Japan's drug policy indicates that Japan learned much from China's experience of colonization after China's defeat in the historic Opium Wars. As Japan sought to establish a new, modern nation in the latter part of the 19th century, this lesson influenced its political choice as well as its drug policy. When forced to open commercial relations with the United States, Russia, the United Kingdom, and the Netherlands, Japan consistently exercised strict control of opiate imports. In addition, the newly established Meiji government, in its first year (1868), issued an administrative order to launch a strong campaign against opium, highlighting its harmful effects, and a strong law enforcement policy penalizing illegal traffickers.

Nevertheless, Japan was questioned at international drug conferences (in Geneva in 1925 and Bangkok in 1931) about the national trafficking of extremely large amounts of opiates. Eguchi (1988), for instance, notes that "Japan's average consumption of heroin per one million population during 1932 and 1933 was 9 to 10 kg, far ahead of the second consuming country, Finland, with approximately 6 kg; the corresponding figure for cocaine was 14 to 15 kg." It is considered now that this very high amount of opiates trafficked was not consumed either illegally or legally in Japan at that time; the matter is thus a historical mystery (Okada, 1986). Both Eguchi (1988) and Okada (1986) regard the war between Japan and China (1937 to 1945) as Japan's invasion of China with opiates and imply that

Japan had engaged in illegal as well as legal international trading in opiates after the Opium Wars.

As for domestic drug problems, however, the Japanese government has consistently and strictly exercised a restrictive, controlled drug policy since the end of the 19th century, except during World War II, when military action and substantially forced labor of civilians at military factories were associated with stimulant use (Kato, 1969; Vaughn, Huang, & Ramirez, 1995). However, at present, the very restrictive governmental stance against illicit drug use is closely reflected in the people's consciousness and behavior regarding drugs, as shown below.

Some Epidemiological Features of Drug Use in Japan

Arrests Under Control Laws

Figure 25.1 shows the number of arrests for violation of the Stimulants Control Law and the Poisonous and Deleterious Substance Control Law. For comparison, Figure 25.2 shows the number of arrests for violation of the Narcotics and Psychotropics Control Law, the Cannabis Control Law, and the Opium Law. In 1954, about 55,000 people were arrested for violation of the Stimulants Control Law. Yet in the same year, the Ministry of Health and Welfare estimated that the actual number of stimulant users was 550,000, or 10 times more.

A steep rise in methamphetamine abuse shortly after World War II was reflected in a sudden increase in the number of arrests for violation of the Stimulants Control Law. This has been generally attributed to an outflow of methamphetamines from the military to civilians, and to the release of a considerable amount of methamphetamines that the pharmaceutical industry had stocked for military use. The number of arrests peaked in 1954 and then rapidly declined to low levels from 1957 onward, as the initial period of methamphetamine abuse came to a close. The yearly figures, however, resumed their increase in 1971, and a second period of methamphetamine abuse set in, which peaked in 1984 and has since declined gradually.

This decline has been attributed to several factors. The public had become keenly aware of the dangers of methamphetamine abuse as a result of a series of brutal abuse-related incidents reported by the mass media, such as the 1981 "phantom killer" siege incident in Fukagawa, Tokyo. In addition, the courts were imposing severe penalties for offenses involving stimulants; more diverse means of dealing with methamphetamine-related mental illnesses became established, chiefly in community hospitals; and a campaign to prevent abuse of methamphetamines was launched.

About 30,000 people have been arrested annually in the past few years for violation of the Poisonous and Deleterious Substance Control Law. Volatile solvents are, at present, the most commonly used substances. The offenders are mainly adolescents and children, and there is clinical evidence that abuse is becoming more common and that it is occurring at younger ages.

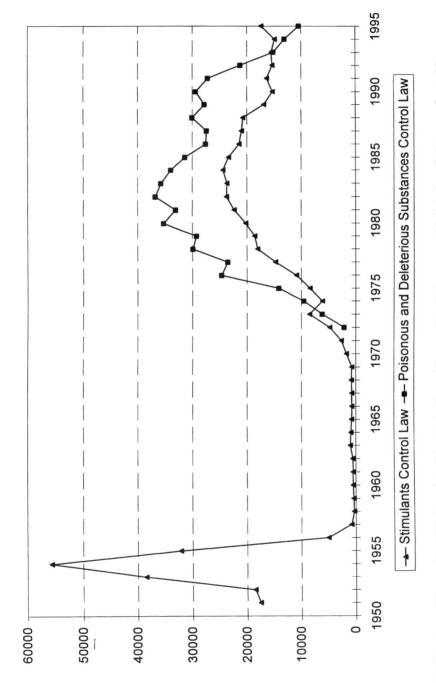

Figure 25.1 Numbers of Arrests for Violation of the Stimulants Control Law and the Poisonous and Deleterious Substances Control Law
SOURCE: Ministry of Justice (1996).

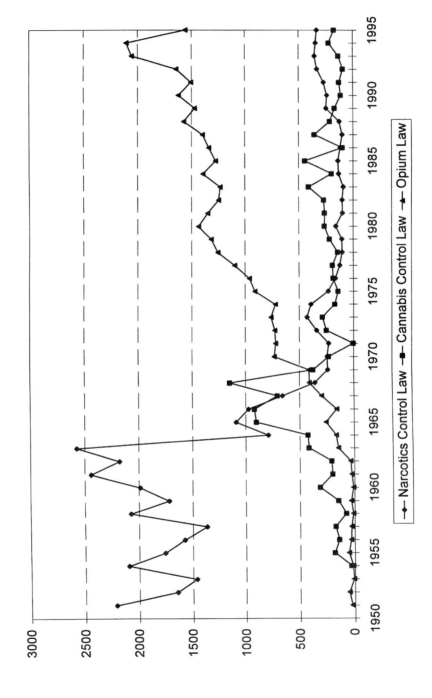

Figure 25.2 Numbers of Arrests for Violation of the Narcotics and Psychotropics Control Law, the Cannabis Control Law, and the Opium Law
SOURCE: Office of Pharmacy Affairs (1996).

There was sporadic narcotic abuse before World War II, but afterward, heroin abuse became more prevalent, reaching a peak in the early 1960s (Figure 25.2), mainly in the large cities, and thus becoming a social problem. In 1963, major revisions of the Narcotics Control Law and other changes successfully counteracted this trend: Surveillance of all forms of access to narcotics was intensified; legislation was enacted to set up a system of diagnosis and inpatient treatment of narcotic addicts, as well as a counseling system; and markedly more severe penal provisions were introduced. Heroin abuse has remained well under control ever since.

The number of people arrested under the Cannabis Control Law has increased steadily in association with the rising numbers of Japanese overseas travelers in recent years.

Although some volatile-solvent abusers are known to have switched to methamphetamines, few people took two or more drugs at the same time. Recently, however, there have been frequent simultaneous seizures of cannabis, methamphetamines, heroin, cocaine, and other drugs from the same site, indications of a trend of increasing numbers of multiple-drug abusers. This pattern is known to occur in the West, and it will be necessary to monitor carefully the direction of future changes in Japan.

Survey Data

So far, there is very little empirical documentation of drug use among the general population. A national household survey by Fukui (1996) of a representative random sample of 3,946 inhabitants over 15 years of age found the lifetime prevalence rate of use of volatile solvents to be 1.5%, of methamphetamines 0.4%, of cannabis 0.5%, of cocaine 0.05%, and of heroin 0%. The rates of respondents who indicated that they knew users of methamphetamines was 1.7%, of volatile solvents 5.2%, of cannabis 1.1%, of cocaine 0.4%, and of heroin 0.1%. Solvent use is most frequently observed among teenagers; a junior high school self-reported survey covering Tokyo and five other surrounding prefectures indicated that lifetime prevalence among 7,166 pupils was 1.6% for males and 0.7% for females (Wada, 1994).

Consequences of Substance Abuse

Drug-Related Crime

Illicit methamphetamine use is Japan's most serious drug problem. In 1980, of 851 people arrested for methamphetamine-related crimes, 553 (65%) had committed them while under the influence of the drug, and 205 (24%) had committed crimes to obtain it. The corresponding figures for 1990 were 154 and 108. Arrests for methamphetamine-related crimes were 208 in 1993, 143 in 1994 and 151 in 1995. Of the 59 methamphetamine users who became casualties in 1995, 20 were responsible for traffic accidents, 22 took overdoses, 9 committed suicide, and 8 died from miscellaneous causes (Ministry of Justice, 1996a).

Mortality

Reported deaths in relation to the use of either licit or illicit drugs numbered 491 (316 males and 175 females) in 1993. No death was recorded from drug-related psychosis or dependence. Solvent abuse among teenagers was responsible for 16 deaths or suicides in 1990 and 16 again in 1995 (National Police Agency, 1996).

HIV Infection and AIDS

As of April 30, 1996, reported cases of HIV infection and AIDS survivors numbered 1,836 and 645, respectively, not counting those caused by antihemophilic products. Of the total of 2,481, 61.5% were males and 38.5% females. Only 17 people were intravenous drug users. However, because illicit drug use is strongly opposed in Japan, infected intravenous users may have avoided inclusion in the official statistics. Indeed, a survey of patients with drug-related psychiatric disorders revealed that 22.2% of methamphetamine users were positive for hepatitis B antibodies and 47.2% for hepatitis C (Wada, Konuma, & Hirai, 1994). In view of the high prevalence rate of injection (83.3%) and shared needle use (38.9%), an increase in drug-related HIV infections is likely. The trend statistics show that the reported numbers of new cases of AIDS and HIV infection combined for each year from 1985 through 1989 grew from 6 in 1985 and 5 in 1986 to 69, 51, and 87, respectively, in the following 3 years. The next year (1990) began with 97 new cases, and then there was a marked increase to 493 in 1992, 434 in 1994, and 610 in 1996.

The Treatment Response to Drug Problems

The Legal Framework

The trafficking, manufacture, cultivation, import and export, possession, and use of illicit drugs and their raw materials are regulated under the following laws: the Stimulant Control Law (1951), the Opium Law (1951), the Cannabis Control Law (1948), the Narcotics and Psychotropics Control Law (1953), and the Poisonous and Deleterious Substance Control Law (1972). Abusers of the drugs covered by the 1971 Convention on Psychotropic Substance have begun to be treated recently, after the ratification of the Convention.

The Mental Health Act, on its introduction in 1950, did not provide for the treatment of patients with drug-related disorders other than psychoses, but a 1954 amendment extended its provisions to those found or suspected to be chronically dependent on methamphetamines, narcotics, and opiates. The amendment required the reporting of cases to prefectural governors, as well as compulsory hospitalization when governors considered it necessary. In 1963, these requirements were incorporated in the Narcotics and Psychotropics Control Law, and prefectural governors were authorized to impose compulsory hospitalization on drug dependents highly likely to continue to use narcotics and cannabis. The same holds true under the Mental Health Act for the methamphetamine users who endanger themselves or others. The maximum period of compulsory hospitalization is fixed at 6 months for users of narcotics and cannabis; no specific period is set for users of methamphetamines. When the conditions for compulsory hospitalization no longer apply, this enforcement is suspended. Requests to extend enforcement must be approved by a special inquiry committee set up in each prefecture.

Very limited use of these drugs and of methadone is permitted for medical treatment of addiction; otherwise, medical treatment consistently uses the "cold turkey" method. Methadone may be prescribed for foreigners under treatment as inpatients; they have to provide the methadone, which they may import for this purpose by permission of the Minister of Health and Welfare. For Japanese drug users, methadone is used for detoxification (overcoming withdrawal symptoms) in involuntary treatment only. There are no heroin prescription or other harm reduction programs, such as needle exchange.

The Organization of Outpatient and Inpatient Treatment:
Primacy of the "Legal Model"

There are three treatment models—the legal, the medical, and the social. The legal, which involves a judicial process, is the most developed. The medical has been in use under the Narcotics Control Law since 1963, specifically for narcotics addicts, and only recently and gradually for people dependent on other drugs. The social model, which is the least developed, offers drug abusers and drug-dependent people care and protection in the community, largely for their social rehabilitation. The legal model is applied in institutions daily to roughly 15,000 drug users; the medical to 1,500; and the social to only 150.

The Legal Model

The legal model treats people differently according to age. Medical and nonmedical treatment of drug abusers and drug-dependent people takes the form of a "protective approach" for children under 14 years, the age of legal responsibility; an "educational approach," calling for human growth through education, for adolescents of 14 to 20 years; and a "correctional approach," requiring imprisonment as a criminal correction, for adults. Although the legal model incorporates special educational programs on the harmfulness of drugs, drug abusers are not assembled for special treatment in drug prisons; rather, they are incarcerated in the same institutions as those who commit ordinary crimes, such as larceny or burglary.

The Protective Approach

Japan has 57 child welfare institutions (reform schools) that house children, mostly from poor families, who have committed delinquent acts. According to a survey of 700 of 2,000 inmates (Abe, Senoo, & Syoji, 1994), 198 (40.6%) of the 488 males and 147 (69.3%) of the 212 females had used volatile solvents, and 20 (4.1%) of the males and 48 (22.6%) of the females had used other drugs, including amphetamines, marijuana, and psychotropic drugs. Clearly, drug abuse by children as young as 13 to 15 years is a matter of concern.

Guidance at these reform schools incorporates living, scholastic, and vocational guidance within a single program. As a rule, they are structured on a cottage system, where the staff (guidance teacher and teacher/housemother) live with the pupils in an attempt to improve their character in an open and liberal environment.

The Educational Approach

According to the Annual Statistics on Corrections (Ministry of Justice, 1996b), the average daily number of residents in juvenile classification homes in 1995 was 915 (792 males, 123 females). Of the 13,844 new admissions in 1995, 873 (6.3%) had violated the Stimulants Control Law and 770 (5.6%) the Poisonous and Deleterious Substance Control Law. Residents with experience of some form of drug abuse numbered 3,464 (25.0%). By contrast, the average daily number of residents in juvenile training schools was only 2,847 (2,494 males and 353 females). Of the 3,828 newly admitted juveniles to these facilities in the same year, 366 (188 males and 178 females) had violated the Stimulants Control Law and 163 (120 males and 43 females) the Poisonous and Deleterious Substance Control Law; 1,237 (32.3%) admitted some form of drug abuse. At these schools, juvenile delinquents have either short-term or long-term treatment. Long term is defined as a residence period of less than 2 years (the average is 1 year). To ensure that needs of correction and social adaptation are smoothly met, five treatment approaches are provided: guidance on living, vocational training, academic education, special education, and medical treatment.

The Correctional Approach

At the end of 1995, correctional institutions held 38,585 prisoners (36,919 males and 1,666 females). They included 224 violators (203 males, 21 females) of the Narcotics Control Law and 10,331 (9,560 males, 771 females) of the Stimulants Control Law. Of newly admitted prisoners for drug offenses in 1995, 119 (107 males, 12 females) had violated the Narcotics Control Law and 6,152 (5,635 males, 517 females) the Stimulants Control Law; the latter accounted for 28.2% of all new prisoners. In all, 21,266 new prisoners were admitted that year: 20,311 males and 955 females. In terms of age, 25.3% of the males and 37.3% of the females were under 30 years; 31.9% and 29.6%, respectively, were between 30 and 39 years;

26.1% and 18.0% were between 40 and 49 years; and 16.6% and 15.1% were 50 years or older. The proportion of females in their 20s has tended to rise over the past several years. Some 26.0% of all newly admitted males imprisoned for violations of the Stimulants Control Law were members of organized crime groups. This percentage drops to only 14.1% when "stimulant" prisoners are excluded.

Since about 1980, penal institutions have conducted special antidrug educational programs in association with the increase in offenders abusing stimulants. They use audiovisual materials, lectures by specialists, group discussions, and individual guidance sessions. In addition, ordinary prisoners are educated on the harmfulness of stimulants.

The Medical Model

Under the medical model, patients who are dependent on alcohol and drugs are subject to psychiatric treatment. As of June 30, 1993, of the 343,926 inpatients in mental hospitals nationwide, 20,071 (5.8%) had drug-related mental illnesses. In 18,444 cases, the drug was alcohol; of the remaining 1,627 cases, 588 had methamphetamine-related illness (271 methamphetamine dependence and 317 methamphetamine psychosis), and in 1,039 cases, the illness was related to other drugs, including volatile solvents.

Japan has about 1,630 psychiatric hospitals. A survey by Konuma and Ohta (1994) of 1,028 responding hospitals found that 106 (10.3%) provided a total of 4,370 beds reserved for alcohol-related mental diseases, and 40 hospitals (3.9%) had 2,153 beds for drug-related mental diseases, including alcoholism. Psychiatric hospitals without such reserved beds treated alcohol- and drug-related patients without distinction. Another survey, reported in a guidebook of treatment for alcohol and drug dependence (ASK, 1995), found that 62 of the featured psychiatric hospitals that treated alcohol and drug addicts reserved 2,795 beds in either specific wards or specific rooms, and 64 of the hospitals had 2,865 beds in alcohol-specific wards or rooms; 61 hospitals had no specific wards or rooms, and no beds other than in mixed wards. In addition, 71 outpatient-only hospitals and clinics were counted.

The Social Model

Although, under the National Assistance Act, Tokyo and Osaka provide a few shelters for alcohol-dependent single people, there are no such facilities for drug dependents. The National Assistance Act provides only for subsidies to private institutions for rehabilitation of drug users. However, a 1988 amendment of the Mental Health Act permitted the establishment of several types of rehabilitation institutes, of which the shared working homes are open to not only patients with general mental disorders but also partly to a few cases of alcoholism and hardly at all to drug abusers or dependents.

Alternatives to Professional Treatment

Self-Help Groups

The official social care services make hardly any provision for drug dependents, but some informal social services have developed gradually, although sporadically. As of March 1995, 62 Narcotics Anonymous meetings per week were being held all over Japan. In addition to these community self-help activities, the Drug Addiction Rehabilitation Center (DARC) was established in Tokyo in 1985 and is run by former drug abusers, who serve as counselors. This movement had been extended to seven other cities by 1994. These eight centers have a total of 65 residents—61 males and 4 females—who, as a rule, participate in the meetings held at the centers, as well as at Narcotics Anonymous or Alcoholics Anonymous meetings in the community, because they primarily emphasize the principle of peer healing. DARC activities are not limited to posthospital functions; they also provide a full range of prehospital functions. A survey by Nagano (1994) found that 221 of 528 drug-dependent people who had been admitted to the Tokyo DARC during a period of 5.5 years completed the 3-month residential program.

Naikan Therapy

Naikan therapy originated in the Japanese therapeutic approach to neurosis in general; it emphasizes the significance of self-examination in relation to patients' past and present and to others in the patients' everyday lives (Suwaki, 1980). This approach has been in use since about 1955 in some prisons and juvenile training schools for correctional education or general high school education. Private institutions are gradually adopting naikan; they include some psychiatric institutions that use it for patients with drug-related disorders. The method is now used in a number of other countries, and the second international congress of naikan therapy was held in Vienna, Austria, in September 1994.

Private Educational Institutions

A few private-sector institutions that educate mainly children with asocial problem behavior have dared to take pupils with antisocial behavior, such as drug abuse or delinquency. They are mostly hostel-type institutions, where children apart from their parents and delinquent peers can share their own lives in nature. In this sense, they are very similar to a therapeutic community.

Public Opinion on Drug Problems

To what extent is the treatment response based on values shared by the general population? A national opinion survey on methamphetamines, the dominant illicit drug in Japan, was conducted with a representative sample of 2,320 people over

20 years old (Prime Minister's Department, 1988). Of almost all the respondents (97.9%) who answered "I know methamphetamine," 92.3% chose the response, "it is very horrible"; 6.4% chose "rather horrible," and only 0.5% the "not horrible" answer, combining both "not at all" and "rather." Information about this drug was widely obtained through the mass media (more than 90%). The statistical mode (43.5%) of their consequent opinions on the effective prevention of social contamination by methamphetamines was to significantly activate the mass media.

Another interesting result from the same survey shows the significance of informal control and intervention. The great majority of the respondents (88.4%) knew no methamphetamine users among them. But when asked "what would you do if you knew someone who uses this drug?" 50.9% replied "persuade him to quit it," 22.0% said "report him to a police station," and only 4.7% would "report him to a community health station." The figures suggest that people consider methamphetamine use from a legal rather than a medical or health perspective. The very small minority who responded "let them do it" (3.4%) and "watch for a while" (7.9%) may be regarded as advocates of "benign neglect" or "judicious non-intervention" (Lemert, 1967).

Arrests of members of organized crime groups for methamphetamine trafficking have shown a continuous decrease (e.g., from 64.0% of methamphetamine-related arrests in 1972 to 43.8% in 1990 and 42.0% in 1993), although they still constitute nearly half of all such arrests. Also, along with the internationalization of Japanese society, some Japanese tourists abroad and illegal foreign residents have begun to use and traffic in cannabis and opium. This situation seems to be reflected in the survey results mentioned above (Prime Minister's Department, 1988). When asked which of seven listed measures was the most effective, 31.6% of the respondents indicated "strengthened control of illegal imports," and 24% said "strengthened control of illegal trafficking by organized crime groups." "Strengthened awareness and educational activity" also was chosen by 24%. Thus, the attitude of the general population toward the drug issue may be characterized as moralistic; more specifically, it is seen as criminal behavior on the part of outsiders of the society.

Evaluation Studies on Treatment Outcomes

Outcomes by Type of Drug

The outcome of treatment of drug abusers in Japan has never been evaluated consistently. Among several general evaluation studies, a national survey conducted in 1966 (Takizawa, Henmi, & Higuchi, 1971) found that the time of the most active narcotics abuse in the life course of abusers was before 1963, the year in which the law was amended to increase penalties. Specifically, of 1,934 narcotics dependents living in the communities under the protective guidance prescribed by the Narcotics and Psychotropics Control Law at the end of 1966, 85.8% were found to be most active in their narcotics abuse before 1963, whereas 13.7% were most active after 1963. Among those who before 1963 had most actively used narcotics, 60.1% had used illicit narcotics and 35.7% had used medical narcotics. Conversely, after 1963, the overwhelming majority, 79.2%, used medical narcotics, and 14.10% used illicit drugs. Moreover, the rate of recurrence of drug abuse was much higher, 36.4%, in the pre- than in the post-1963 group: 14.0%. These results indicate a very substantial decrease in the availability of illicit narcotics on the black market after the judicial intervention in 1963.

In a psychiatric outcome study of stimulant abusers, Konuma (1993) reported on 110 methamphetamine-dependent patients who had been discharged 3 to 8 years earlier; the study indicated a fairly stable outcome. A minority were using methamphetamines, and the majority, 63.3%, excluding 12 deaths, had not used any during the previous year. This nonrelapse rate compares fairly well with the findings of alcohol studies, which showed the nonrelapse rate leveling off at around 20% 2 years after discharge from hospital (Suzuki, 1984). The conditions of social adaptation of the 110 subjects were judged as "adaptive" for 46.4%, and "poorly adaptive" for 26.6%; 16.4% were "missing," and 10.9% were "dead."

Meanwhile, an interinstitutional study of the outcome of psychiatric treatment of 291 solvent abusers (Fukui, Wada, & Iyo, 1992) evaluated only 29.2% as "successful," but another hospital survey (Ohta, Simura, & Ishizu, 1982) reported 46.3% as "employed." The wide range of the percentages of good outcome evaluations resulted partly from detailed differences in evaluation criteria and partly from sample differences. The study by Fukui et al. also confirmed a poor outcome in the group that had been using solvents for more than 5 years; the sample included subjects with much longer periods of volatile-solvent inhalation than the samples of other studies.

Conclusion

For a comprehensive understanding of the drug situation and drug treatment system in Japan, one should know how the general public as well as experts and policymakers have perceived the drug problem over time. A recent anecdote reflects much of this perception: Japan's Ministry of Health and Welfare had to make an announcement to encourage doctors to make more use of morphine to improve the quality of life of patients in terminal care, because doctors were afraid to use it even for medical purposes.

Given this cultural background, it may be said that Japan's two principal strategies—management of medicinal drugs and very strict control of the use and trafficking of illicit drugs—have been relatively successful. A drug "control system" rather than a drug "treatment system" has been the primary means of preventing illicit drug use. Consequently, Japan has a less-developed medical and social treatment system than European and North American countries, and this has resulted in serious defects in the secondary and tertiary prevention systems. However, this situation can be interpreted in different ways. The medical treatment system for drug addicts remains underdeveloped partly because relatively few patients with drug dependency or drug psychosis have required psychiatric treatment. At the same time, the dominance of the legal and correctional control effectively deters the relapse of addicts. The most serious deficiency of Japan's drug treatment system is its lack of a care system for recovering addicts.

We are convinced that the Japanese treatment system for drug abusers and dependents will never be effective without strong and strict control measures; nor will it be complete without many more medical and social services for addicts as well as rehabilitation for recovered addicts. Self-help groups such as DARC have introduced a few small community care programs in the past 10 years, but we are still at the gray dawn of the development of a social model for drug abusers. One of the most significant future directions and tasks must be the development of more social or community treatment programs and coordination among the relevant professionals and respective models, which function now almost independently of each other.

References

Abe, K., Senoo, E., & Syoji, M. (1994, March). *Current situation of volatile-solvents-abusing adolescents at child welfare institutions.* Paper presented at the Symposium on The Situation and Treatment of Drug Abuse and Dependence, Tokyo. (in Japanese)

ASK. (1995). *Addiction.* Tokyo: ASK Human Care.

Bejorot, N. (1969). Social medical classification of addiction. *International Journal of the Addictions, 4,* 391-405.

Eguchi, K. (1988). *Japan-China opium war.* Tokyo: Iwanami Syoten. (in Japanese)

Fukui, S. (1996). Household survey of drug abuse and dependence. In S. Fukui (Ed.), *Epidemiological research report on drug abuse and dependence* (pp. 5-36). Tokyo: Ministry of Health and Welfare. (in Japanese)

Fukui, S., Wada, K., & Iyo, M. (1992). A study on the long-term prognosis of volatile solvent dependents. *Journal of Mental Health, 38,* 39-45. (in Japanese)

Kato, N. (1969). An epidemiological analysis of the fluctuation of drug dependence in Japan. *International Journal of the Addictions, 4,* 591-621.

Konuma, K. (1993). A follow-up survey on the outcome of treatment for methamphetamine-related mental disorders: Relationship between the treatment outcomes and various factors on hospitalization. *Proceedings of Japan-U.S. Workshop on Drug Abuse Research,* 46-49. Tokyo: Ministry of Health and Welfare.

Konuma, K., & Ohta, K. (1994). A research project on treatment of drug abuse and dependence at psychiatric institutions. In K. Konuma (Ed.), *A research project on counseling, therapy, treatment and after-care for drug dependents* (pp. 73-104). Tokyo: Ministry of Health and Welfare. (in Japanese)

Lemert, E. (1967). The juvenile court—Quest and realities. In C. Bersani (Ed.), *Crime and delinquency* (pp. 424-435). New York: Macmillan.

Ministry of Justice. (1996a). *Annual report of statistics on correction (1980-1996).* Tokyo: Ministry of Justice. (in Japanese)

Ministry of Justice. (1996b). *White paper on crime 1996.* Tokyo: Ministry of Justice. (in Japanese)

Nagano, K. (1994). Comprehensive treatment and after-care for drug dependents of rehabilitation hostels: DARC of Japan. In K. Konuma (Ed.), *A research project on counseling, therapy, treatment and after-care for drug dependents* (pp. 125-135). Tokyo: Ministry of Health and Welfare. (in Japanese)

National Police Agency. (1996). *White paper on police.* Tokyo: Department of Printing, Ministry of Finance.

Office of Pharmacy Affairs, MHW. (1996). *Administrative abstracts of narcotics and stimulants.* Tokyo: Mental Health and Welfare.

Ohta, K., Simura, K., & Ishizu, F. (1982). The current condition and treatment of volatile-solvent abusers. *Japan's Medicine Newsletter,* 3049. (in Japanese)

Okada, Y. (Ed.). (1986). *Opium problems: Modern history* (Vol. 12). Tokyo: Misuzu Syobou.

Prime Minister's Department. (1988). *Public opinion poll on counter measures for the prevention of drug abuse.* Tokyo: Author. (in Japanese)

Suwaki, H. (1980). Japan: Culturally based treatment of alcoholism. In G. Edwards & A. Arif (Eds.), *Drug problems in the sociocultural context: A basis for policies and programme planning* (pp. 139-143). Geneva: World Health Organization.

Suzuki, Y. (1984). Prognosis and aftercare of alcohol dependents. In K. Ohara & S. Tadokoro (Eds.), *Alcohol and drug dependency: Biology and clinical therapy* (pp. 369-374). Tokyo: Kanehara Syuppan. (in Japanese)

Takizawa, K., Henmi, T., & Higuchi, K. (1971). A comparison study between opiate dependents in prison and in the community. In A. Kasamatu, T. Henmi, & K. Takizawa (Eds.), *A clinical epidemiology of drug abuse* (pp. 102-121). Tokyo: Ishiyaku Syuppan. (in Japanese)

Vaughn, M., Huang, F., & Ramirez, C. (1995). Drug abuse and anti-drug policy in Japan: Past history and future directions. *British Journal of Criminology, 35,* 491-524.

Wada, K. (1994). A survey of solvent-, tobacco- and alcohol-use among junior high school students. In S. Fukui (Ed.), *Research report on drug dependence and its socio-psychiatric features* (pp. 27-54). Tokyo: Ministry of Health and Welfare. (in Japanese)

Wada, K., Konuma, K., & Hirai, S. (1994, August). *HIV infection and STD among methamphetamine abusers and solvent abusers in Japan.* Paper presented to the Tenth International Conference on AIDS, Yokohama, Japan.

Chapter 26

Drug Treatment and Public Security in the People's Republic of China

Wang Zhengyan
Gérald Béroud
Cheng Maojin
Chen Shirong

Historical Background

Drug consumption in China is still a very sensitive issue. In the 19th century, the drug traffic imposed by outside forces caused two opium wars between the Qing dynasty and some Western countries and led to strong control of China by those powers. Opium addiction reached epidemic proportions, much more prevalent than today, and the Imperial Court, and afterwards the Republic of China, could not act effectively on what was a disastrous situation. Opium consumption was one of the main causes of the country's poverty, weakness, and backwardness. Before the constitution of the People's Republic of China in 1949, there were about 20 million drug addicts (Z. Wang, 1995a, 1995b). The new government introduced new laws to stop the production, traffic, sale, and consumption of drugs and, within 3 years, almost completely stamped out these practices. However, drug abuse has been rising steadily since the late 1970s, owing to the economic reform and the open-door policy of the Chinese government, social and cultural changes, and the large amount of opium and heroin produced in the Golden Triangle (Myanmar, Thailand, Laos) and smuggled into the Chinese territory. Excluding industrial and agricultural loss, the annual cost of the drug problem is estimated to be more than 10 billion yuan (US$1.4 billion; Beijing Information, 1996). Today, the drug problem is one of the country's most important social and political issues.

Drug Abuse at Present

Seemingly restricted at first to the southern provinces (Yunnan, Guangdong, Guizhou), the traffic, commerce, and consumption of drugs have spread throughout most of the country, mainly to the provinces of Sichuan, Shaanxi, Gansu, and Inner Mongolia. The trend is clear: from border areas to the inner regions, from the countryside to the cities. Except for some particular cases in border regions (such as Yunnan province), where many peasants were addicted to drugs (Dehong Anti-Epidemic Station, 1991; Li Jianhua et al., 1993), drug addiction has progressively become an urban question.

In 1990, the National Drug Prohibition Committee published the first figures on the number of drug addicts: 70,000 had been registered. This had increased to 148,000 in 1992 and to 300,000 in 1993 (Wang, Cheng, & Chen, 1993). By the end of 1995, the total had risen to 520,000. This increase reflected not only the extension of drug consumption but also growing awareness of the problem on the part of the political system, increased police work, and improved statistical data.

Epidemiological Characteristics of Drug Abusers

There are as yet no precise national data on drug abuse in China, but provincial studies or city epidemiological surveys have been conducted since 1990. Although these are not fully comparable because they use different categories of classification and sociodemographic features, they do permit a characterization of drug abusers. They are male and mainly 20 to 30 years old (e.g., see Wang & Shi, 1994; Wang et al., 1993; Wu, 1995). In Inner Mongolia and some other provinces (Li & Li, 1994; Liu et al., 1992; Lu, Liu, Li, Zhang, & Cai, 1994), the proportion of addicts older than 50 is surprisingly high, associated with different substances and methods of consumption. Educational level is rather low; most addicts have a lower than "middle" level of schooling. Occupational status is varied, but a high percentage are unemployed (30% to more than 50%, according to different studies; for a comparison and discussion on these sociodemographic data, see Béroud, 1995).

Heroin and opium are the two most frequently used drugs (mainly nasally inhaled, smoked, or intravenously injected), though with notable regional and cultural differences. Increased cost and reduced availability are reasons given by addicts for changing to injection (Wu et al., 1996). Others have already begun to reinject blood, which can be done 4 to 20 times. Cannabis and solvents are rarely used (Lu et al., 1995), and methamphetamine ("ice") use is not reported in the collected studies. The International Narcotics Control Board (1996) has reported that methamphetamine "represents a major drug problem" in the region (p. 48). In addition to the illicit manufacture of "ice" in mainland China, "increasing amounts of ephedrine, the most important precursor of methamphetamine production, are reportedly being seized in mainland China, as well in Taiwan Province of China" (p. 48). The International Narcotics Board (1995) has also reported on the smuggling of chemical precursors into China. A trend toward polydrug abuse has also been noted, typically involving analgesic drugs, alcohol, and sedative hypnotics (Lu et al., 1994).

In recent years, there have been reports of iatrogenic drug abuse, so-called legal drug abuse, manifested in dependence on benzodiazepines, analgesics, and other drugs, usually given as painkillers after surgery or to relieve pain of chronic diseases.

Drug Abuse and AIDS

At the end of 1995, there were 3,341 cases of HIV infection, of whom 117 had developed AIDS-related diseases; 1,400 were due to drug injection (Beijing Information, 1996). A study for the Yunnan province in 1994 showed that 78% of those who were infected with HIV were drug dependent. Intravenous drug use and the sharing of equipment are the most important causes of HIV infection among addicts, especially when drug injection is related to ethnic and cultural characteristics (Wu et al., 1996).

The Legal Framework of the Drug Treatment System

The government of China has introduced a series of laws and decrees in recent years: the Drug Administration Law of the People's Republic of China (1984), the New Drug Examination and Approval Law (1985), the Narcotics Administration Law (1987), and the Psychotropic Drugs Administration Law (1988). On December 28, 1990, the National People's Assembly issued a *Decision About the Prohibition of Drugs,* which provided inter alia for life imprisonment or the death penalty for drug traffickers (more than 50 g of heroin, 1 kg of opium), and detention for up to 15 days and fines for drug users. In addition, drug addicts must follow compulsory treatment, and if they resume drug use they are sent to work-education centers, where they begin compulsory treatment again.

A new regulation on the *Method of Compulsory Treatment* was issued in December 1995. It defines the competence of the Public Security, how the drug addict and his or her family and work unit are informed, and the procedure of recourse to appeal proceedings. The limits of the treatment period are 3 to 6 months, but it may be extended to 1 year. The addicts or their families must pay everyday expenses and the cost of medical treatment.

At the administrative level, a Coordinating Committee for Narcotics Administration and the Prohibition of Drug Traffic and Abuse was set up in 1989 with members from the Ministries of Health, Foreign Affairs, and Public Security and the Customs Head Office. Its tasks are to strengthen coordination between the concerned departments and promote bilateral or multilateral cooperation with foreign countries and international narcotics control organizations. To meet the new needs of a continuously and rapidly changing situation, a National Drug Prohibition Committee, led by the Ministry of Public Security, has been established.

The Drug Treatment System

With the growth of drug problems, more than 500 detoxification and rehabilitation centers have been established in areas where drug abuse is prevalent (232 in 1992, 252 in 1993; Beijing Information, 1995). There are 65 detoxification centers in detention centers (Beijing Information, 1996), and every general hospital has a specific ward for detoxification.

The structure of the Chinese drug abuse treatment system is shown in Figure 26.1.

The National Drug Prohibition Committee lays down laws and regulations on drug abuse, devises the appropriate measures, and coordinates the work of the different government ministries. Provincial authorities have similar tasks besides implementing the defined policy and encouraging research, but with a specific focus on the work to be done at the county or city level. The county or city is the third of the three levels of the network. It concentrates on the effective application of the drug prohibition policy (control, treatment, education, counseling), collects information and data, and has responsibility for scientific research. Under pressure from the county or city, rural administrative areas, the second level of prevention, execute the measures and policy defined by the upper level, which include the early tracing of risk factors and high-risk groups. At the first level, the village has to promote social prevention programs, provide general information on drug problems and health education, and prevent early drug use and risk factors.

Detoxification and Therapy

Between 1991 and 1995, about 180,000 addicts were sent to compulsory treatment centers; today, this number is more than 50,000 a year; in the same period, 10,000 went to voluntary treatment centers (Beijing Information, 1996). National policy gives addicts the choice of either seeking help at voluntary centers connected to health departments or being detained at compulsory detoxification centers if caught. They may be sent for treatment by sections of the Public Security, or else village leaders or heads of work units, parents, spouses, or family members may ask Public Security offices to take in addicts for compulsory treatment.

The Voluntary Treatment System

In general, a therapeutic period is 3 weeks—1 week for medical treatment and 2 weeks for rehabilitation, which consists of physical exercise and psychological counseling. These centers work with general hospitals in order to make doctors and nurses responsible for therapy and medical treatment. The drug users or their relatives or employers pay the treatment fees. Although this system treats addicts, it cannot prevent relapse, often brought about by lack of necessary long-term psychological support and after-care. Therefore, the actual therapeutic effect is very difficult to evaluate.

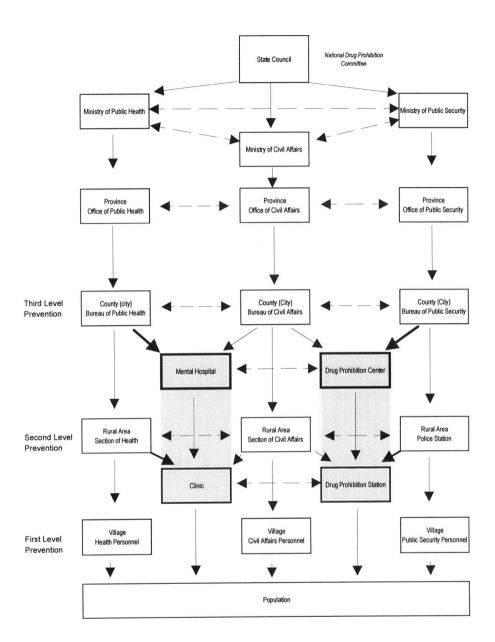

Figure 26.1 Political, Judicial, and Medical Organization of the Drug Abuse Treatment System in China: An Overview

The Compulsory Treatment System

Compulsory treatment centers are run by the Public Security, and they use a "cold turkey" approach, sometimes with the help of traditional Chinese medicine.

They impose a military-style discipline, associating physical exercise, manual labor, and education. There are also centers for involuntary clinical treatment that are not run by the Public Security. In this case, the addicts pay daily and medical expenses, but other expenses are covered by the government and work units. Those who are sent by Public Security offices for treatment are detoxified in closed wards. They are isolated from their drugs and given medical therapy for the first 10 days. Then they undergo rehabilitation, including mainly physical therapy, general education, and counseling. Medicines used for detoxification are discontinued during rehabilitation. When the treatment is over, addicts are evaluated by a special committee of doctors, social workers, and lawyers. They may leave only when the committee signs a recovery certificate and when the addicts pledge to abstain from taking drugs.

Private Detoxification Centers

More and more private rehabilitation centers have been established to serve addicts who seek treatment voluntarily. They are loosely regulated and extremely diverse in their methods, funding, and administration. They are not permitted to use methadone, other substitution drugs, or opioid antagonists; therefore, they use mainly traditional Chinese medicine and acupuncture. Although the State must approve the centers' medical and administrative background, the Department of Health remarked in 1993 that some were only profit-oriented and had deceived their patients. Because of the high cost of a 2-week course of treatment (sometimes up to US$700), its brevity, and its neglect of the mental aspects of withdrawal, these centers are unlikely to promote long-term rehabilitation. There are no national statistics on the outcome of treatment at these centers or at compulsory treatment institutions.

Treatment Methods

The major detoxification methods used in compulsory institutions and voluntary treatment centers are the following:

- *Substitution and decreasing dose therapy:* The principal substitution drugs are methadone and buprenorphine, which are used in decreasing doses. Dihydroetorphine hydrochloride (DHE) was tried for opioid addicts, but its action seemed temporary, it quickly produced resistance, and it had a strong addiction potential. As increasing numbers of cases of DHE abuse and intoxication have been reported in the past 2 years, government offices have recognized it as a particular problem.
- *Use of other drugs to inhibit or relieve the detoxification syndrome:* One of the complications of treatment is the detoxification syndrome. Nondependence drugs, such as clonidine, propanolol, antipsychotics, antidepressives, and drugs with immune active substances are employed in detoxification. In some treatment centers, mostly voluntary institutions, large doses of chlorpromazine were used to maintain the addicts

in a lethargic state—"hibernation therapy" or "narcolepsy"—designed to lessen the pain of withdrawal.

- *Ceasing drugs or using antagonist substances:* For those with a short period of drug abuse, it is effective to stop the drug use directly, coupled with supporting treatment and psychotherapy. Antagonists such as naltrexone are also sometimes used.

- *Traditional Chinese medicine:* Chinese herbal medicine, acupuncture, and qigong are widely used in treatment centers. Many Chinese herbal medicines are used in detoxification, but their effects are not satisfactory. Recently, experiments have been carried out with a compound of Chinese herbs called *fukang pian* for alleviating opiate withdrawal symptoms (Guo et al., 1995; Hu & Huang, 1995).

Acupuncture therapy is simple and economical. Somatic acupoints such as *zhusanli* (*He*-Sea point) and *hoku* (*Yuan*-Source point) are those preferred by practitioners of traditional Chinese medicine. Electric needles, massage, and other apparatus have also been used in the detoxification clinical treatment.

- *Comprehensive therapy:* Because treatment of drug abuse consists of not only detoxification therapy but also medical support, psychotherapy, and psychological counseling, doctors in detoxification centers often offer comprehensive therapy, such as adding other medicines that can inhibit withdrawal symptoms during dose reduction, combining antagonists with inhibitors, and coupling acupuncture with pharmacotherapy. When addicts have stopped drug consumption, rehabilitative measures are immediately taken to consolidate the effects of detoxification therapy. They are then sent to general hospitals for psychotherapy and psychological counseling. Usually, hospitals provide outpatient counseling for drug abuse.

Nowadays, some treatment programs put more emphasis on an individual's needs, the psychological aspects of withdrawal, and after-care support. Relapse in drug abuse is very high (e.g., about 90% within 1 month of finishing treatment; Wu, 1995; see also Y. Wang, 1995), so it is believed that a better follow-up of patients will improve the results of the treatment system.

Research and Education

Since the late 1980s, the Ministry of Public Health has been setting up a range of public institutions, committees, and working groups to study the drug situation and to diffuse scientific knowledge: the National Institute on Drug Dependence (1988), the National Drug Dependence Therapeutic Center (1988), the National Narcotics Laboratory (1990), and others. Since 1992, a professional quarterly, the *Chinese Bulletin on Drug Dependence,* has been published by the National Institute on Drug Dependence; it presents scientific research and surveys (in Chinese with short abstracts in English). Other publications are now available: the *Chinese Review on Drug Abuse Prevention* and the *Chinese Journal of Epidemiology.*

For a better understanding of drug dependence and health problems, general studies have progressively been carried out among the population and specific groups in order to analyze the attitude toward drug use among middle school students (Zhao et al., 1994) and women (Chen & Yao, 1994) or to investigate the relationship to volatile solvents (Lu et al., 1995).

Drug abuse surveillance centers and treatment and rehabilitation institutions have also been established by provinces and cities to strengthen detoxification and preventive work. Academic bodies—the China Toxicological Association and the Drug Dependence Professional Committee—have been set up, as well as a non-governmental mass organization, the Chinese Drug Abuse Prevention Association, composed of doctors, scientists, teachers, students, journalists, and others. This organization has a large network and provides professional training, education, and counseling; also, it contributes to academic journals and magazines. Besides holding a biennial academic conference to promote research, it organizes extensive public activities related to the prevention of drug problems.

Perception of Drug Problems and Treatment

For the past 20 years, as drug problems and the number of drug addicts have been increasing, the government has been more and more concerned about this evolution. Whereas at first, the drug problem was not discussed openly by the official world, this attitude has changed radically. The Chinese Central Television has broadcast a series of eight films on drug consumption and smuggling and on the risks and prevention of drug abuse. Other major events, such as Drug Prohibition Day (June 26), are also used to make the people aware of the strong measures taken against drug traffic and consumption.

Thanks to progressive improvement in legislation and organization, the State has begun to face the problem of drug addiction; to fight production, smuggling, and the transport of illicit drugs; and to establish treatment facilities and a national monitoring system, which is still under way. The attitude toward drug addiction is changing gradually from a perception of drug users as criminals to that of patients in need of medical, social, and psychological support.

In recent years, information on drug-related problems has been more and more widely disseminated by means of radio, television, and newspapers in order to expose the risks and the background of drug use, make the people aware of the laws and measures introduced by the government, and help them understand the policy of drug prevention and repression.

Problems and Prospects of the Therapy System

Although the Chinese government has adopted many measures in legislation, medical care, and organization, there are still serious problems related to drug abuse treatment and administration. The relapse rate is very high, owing to lack of essential rehabilitative facilities and psychological counseling. Health and preventive education for high-risk groups is deficient, especially in remote or backward areas. People need to be made more aware of the risks of drug abuse. The management of detoxification institutions is confused, control over private centers needs strengthening, and results of therapy are not evaluated. Also necessary are more means of prohibiting drug traffic, blocking drug supplies, and further improving the system of surveillance of narcotics and psychotropic drugs.

Research is needed to discover new treatment drugs that would be more effective, cheaper, and without side effects when used in detoxification. The various treatment and rehabilitation services need to be coordinated.

The People's Republic of China has a relatively short experience of "modern" but still very sensitive drug problems. Besides having to cope with a fast-growing economy and a changing society, the Chinese government has been trying to control drug abuse. Although the results as yet are insufficient, the recent progressive improvement should be recognized, and further help and information sought from foreign countries. Especially for a large country with such diverse living conditions as China, international collaboration is necessary for a better understanding of the problems of drug abuse, of new ways of treatment, and of other countries' experience in running treatment and rehabilitation services.

References

Beijing Information. (1995). French ed., *33,* 50.

Beijing Information. (1996). French ed., *34,* 19, 31, 36.

Béroud, G. (1995). Problèmes de toxicomanie en République populaire de Chine: situation actuelle. *Sciences Sociales et Santé, 13*(2), 65-89.

Cai Zhiji. (1994). *Drug dependence and drug abuse.* Beijing: National Institute on Drug Dependence, Beijing Medical University. (in Chinese)

Chen Jing, & Yao Yulian. (1994). A psychological survey and analysis of sixty cases of female opioid addicts. *Chinese Bulletin on Drug Dependence, 3*(1), 37-39. (in Chinese)

Dehong Anti-Epidemic Station and Yunnan Health Education Institute. (1991). *Veneral disease, AIDS, drug abuse.* Kunming: Dehong Popular Press. (in Chinese)

Guo Song, Jiang Zuoning, Wang Youde, Hu Guangcai, Wu Yammei, & Huang Mingsheng. (1995). A comparative study on Chinese herbal medicine Fukang Pian with clonidine hydrochloride on opiate withdrawal symptoms. *Chinese Bulletin on Drug Dependence, 4,* 210-216. (in Chinese)

Hu Guangcai, & Huang Mingsheng. (1995). Preliminary control study of detoxicated effect of Fukang Pian on heroin addicts—Clinical investigations of 40 cases. *Chinese Bulletin on Drug Dependence, 4,* 217-222. (in Chinese)

International Narcotics Control Board. (1995). *Report of the International Narcotics Control Board for 1994.* New York: United Nations Publications.

International Narcotics Control Board. (1996). *Report of the International Narcotics Control Board for 1995.* New York: United Nations Publications.

Li Genyuan, & Li De. (1994). An epidemiological survey of 100 heroin addicts in Baotou city. *Chinese Bulletin on Drug Dependence, 3*(1), 35-36. (in Chinese)

Li Jianhua, Zhu Hua, Fang Wenpeng, Shi Qing, Liu Dequan, Emerich, K., & Kroll, C. J. (1993). Study on substance abuse in Ruili, Yunnan Province. *Chinese Review on Mental Health, 9,* 217-218. (in Chinese)

Liu Zhimin, Li Mi, Cao Jiaqi, Sun Wenlin, Sun Guiduan, Lu Xianxiang, Zhao Chengzheng, Zhao Dong, & Cai Zhiji (1992). An epidemiological survey on opium abusers in some regions of Chifeng city. *Chinese Bulletin on Drug Dependence, 1*(2), 83-87. (in Chinese)

Lu Xianxiang, Liu Zhimin, Li Mi, Zhang Jie, & Cai Zhiji. (1994). Analysis of a surveillance data of drug abuse in Guizhou and Gansu Provinces. *Chinese Bulletin on Drug Dependence, 3*(2), 113-117. (in Chinese)

Lu Xianxiang, Zhao Chengzheng, Zhao Dong, Zeng Lan, Wang Huilan, Zhang Jie, Liu Yanhong, Cao Jiaqi, & Cai Zhiji. (1995). Investigation on volatile organic solvents liked in varying degrees in some primary school and middle school students in Beijing. *Chinese Bulletin on Drug Dependence, 4*(1), 34-39. (in Chinese)

Wang Youde. (1995). An analysis of psychological factors of opioid addicts. *Chinese Bulletin on Drug Dependence, 4*(1), 50-52. (in Chinese)

Wang Youde, & Shi Guobi. (1994). Analysis of an epidemiological survey on 568 drug abusers, *Chinese Bulletin on Drug Dependence, 3*(1), 50-52. (in Chinese)

Wang Zhengyan, Cheng Maojin, & Chen Shirong. (1993, October). *The prevalent characteristics of drug abuse and the strategies of drug abstinence in China.* Paper presented at the International Conference on Alcohol and Drug Treatment Systems Research, Toronto, Canada.

Wang Zhiqing. (1995a). Chinese administration on narcotics and psychotropic drugs. *Chinese Review on Drug Abuse Prevention, 1*(1), 32-33. (in Chinese)

Wang Zhiqing. (1995b). Chinese administration on narcotics and psychotropic drugs. *Chinese Review on Drug Abuse Prevention, 1*(2), 43-46. (in Chinese)

Wu Xiaowen. (1995). Analysis of heroin consumers' relapse. *Chinese Review on Mental Health, 9,* 217-218. (in Chinese)

Wu Zunyou, Detels, R., Zhang Jiapeng, Duan Song, Cheng Hehe, Li Zhirong, Dong Lelong, Huang Sufen, Jia Manhong, & Bi Xiuqiong. (1996). Risk factors for intravenous drug use and sharing equipment among young male drug users in Longchuan County, south-west China. *AIDS, 10,* 1017-1024.

Yang Dali L. (1993). Illegal drugs, policy change and state power: The case of contemporary China. *The Journal of Contemporary China, 4,* 14-34.

Zhao Dong, Zhao Chengzheng, Ge Yun, Liu Zhimin, Liu Yanhong, & Cai Zhiji. (1994). Analysis of the attitude to drug abuse in some middle school students in Beijing. *Chinese Bulletin on Drug Dependence, 3*(2), 120-124. (in Chinese)

Chapter 27

From the Opium Wars to Strict Drug Policies in East Asia

Michael S. Vaughn

Comment on Part 7

Both China and Japan learned indelible lessons from the 19th-century Opium Wars, structuring strict enforcement-oriented drug control policies and blaming external forces for modern drug problems. In China, for example, Wang, Béroud, Cheng, and Chen argue in "Drug Treatment and Public Security in the People's Republic of China" that economic liberalization and global trade increased drug problems in urban, coastal, and border areas. Likewise, Konuma, Shimizu, and Koyanagi contend in "Societal Control and the Model of Legal Drug Treatment: A Japanese Success Story?" that a recent increase in cannabis arrests in Japan are attributable to overseas travel of Japanese citizens, ostensibly importing the drug and desiring to smoke it.

In many countries, drug problems have evolved from a criminal activity and a criminal justice priority to a treatable disease within the realm of health care professionals. Where this transformation in thinking has occurred, substance abuse is perceived as a "disease to be cured by the health care system or as a social problem to be cared for by social welfare facilities" (Klingemann, Takala, & Hunt, 1993, p. 222). For the most part, however, Wang et al. and Konuma et al. inform us that China and Japan have not adopted this philosophy; rather, drug offenders are viewed as a legal problem that deserves attention by the criminal justice system. Like China, Japan has involuntary hospitalization of drug addicts, including psychiatric hospitals that treat drug-induced mental illness. Like the involuntary treatment imposed by China's Public Security Ministry, involuntary hospitalization in Japan is suspended when a committee determines that the conditions that necessitated treatment are no longer present.

Although responses to drug problems are harsh, Japan does recognize the role of prevention in the war on drugs. Methamphetamine arrests in Japan have declined since the early 1980s because of prevention campaigns and more mental health treatment in community hospitals; inpatient and counseling systems have also helped control heroin addiction. On balance, however, because Japan associates drug use with poor self-control, it offers more treatment options to drug-abusing juveniles than to adults. It is indeed perplexing that, in a communitarian society like Japan, no governmental shelters are operational for the treatment of drug addicts.

Like Japan, China views drug abuse as a serious social problem within the purview of both the criminal justice and the public health systems. Individuals who show remorse, admit addiction, and enter treatment programs voluntarily have their addiction treated from a health perspective. Having its roots in reliance on informal social control and personal responsibility, the voluntary treatment system views addiction as an illness to be treated by the medical establishment and private rehabilitation centers, although the private centers have been criticized by the government as ineffective and primarily concerned with profits, not treatment. Conversely, when addicts do not seek drug treatment voluntarily, addiction is viewed as a crime and a public security threat to be handled by the compulsory treatment system within the criminal justice apparatus.

As regards prevention, public health agencies conduct research and provide educational programs to enhance deterrence. Newly created organizations regularly hold conferences and publish materials that highlight preventive efforts, and community organizations investigate the health problems and public attitudes associated with drug use. Like Japan, however, China has few health departments and rehabilitation centers. As a result, the bulk of "treatment" occurs in compulsory detoxification settings.

Because punishment as opposed to treatment is emphasized, it is accurate to characterize Chinese and Japanese drug policy as efforts in drug control rather than drug treatment. Wang et al. and Konuma et al. remind us that citizens as well as policymakers demand harsh punishment and compulsory treatment because of residual memories of the deleterious effects of the Opium Wars. Moreover, evolution from a legal to a medical model has been slowed by a lack of rehabilitative infrastructure in China and Japan. Although both countries lack psychological and rehabilitative facilities; trained, publicly employed counselors; and accurate public information on addiction, some academics, public health figures, and intellectuals regard drug addiction as an illness, deserving medical attention and treatment. These individuals are in a minority, however, and it may take generations for the treatment approach to become manifest in public opinion and government policy; only then will there be less reliance on the punitive criminal justice approach that dominates drug policy in China and Japan.

Reference

Klingemann, H., Takala, J. P., & Hunt, G. (1993). The development of alcohol treatment systems: An international perspective. *Alcohol Health and Research World, 17,* 221-227.

Part VIII

Gender, Finance,

and System Integration:

Findings From 20 Countries

Chapter 28

Equal Access With Optimum Costs: Issues of Financing and Managing Drug Treatment

Juhani Lehto

How to reduce the inequality in access to services between people of different socioeconomic groups and regions has long been an issue in the financing and management of health care. More recently, the steep rise in the cost of health care has also become a prominent issue, and its containment is considered more and more a matter of economic incentives in health care systems. The same issues are discussed in relation to drug treatment. Even countries that have achieved equal access to general health services find it very difficult to do so for high-quality drug treatment. Also, drug treatment has been considered even less cost-effective than health services in general.

In this chapter, theoretical approaches and concepts of financing and management of health services in general are considered against actual drug treatment policies and systems on the basis of the information both contained in the draft country chapters of this book and received separately from the authors of the 18 chapters. The empirical approach is descriptive; the available data do not permit an empirical analysis whereby countries could be rated with regard to degrees of equality in access or effectiveness attained in their drug treatment systems.

First discussed are the financing and management of drug treatment systems in the 18 countries. These functions are seen to be much more fragmented than are the corresponding functions in general health services; the reasons for this fragmentation and its impact on access to treatment are analyzed. Next, the cost-effectiveness of drug treatment is considered: The countries differ in the signifi-

AUTHOR'S NOTE: The author gratefully acknowledges the cooperation of the authors of the country chapters in responding to a short questionnaire with additional information.

cance they accord to analysis of cost-effectiveness and in the criteria against which they evaluate treatment for its impact. The analogy of the market is then used for an analysis of incentives for effectiveness in treatment systems. The final section discusses the conclusions on equality of access to, and cost-effectiveness of, treatment and the difficulty of ensuring access and cost-effectiveness.

Equality in Access to Drug Treatment

Equality in access to appropriate health care for everyone with equal need is an application of the principle of equity, or justice. The right of everyone to the enjoyment of the highest attainable standard of health and of access to necessary health care services is laid down in international conventions and covenants on human rights and other statements on health policy (Whitehead, 1990). Not only is equality in access to health care a principle of health care ethics, but also it is claimed that inequality in access reduces the health impact of public health policy (e.g., Blaxter, 1996).

Some question whether the principle of equal access should apply to so-called self-inflicted health problems, such as alcoholism and drug addiction. At the level of principles, however, it has proved too difficult to exclude them. Most of the diseases of modern societies are at least partially linked to unhealthy diet, smoking and drinking, lack of physical activity, or the physical and social environment. Thus, the exclusion of self-inflicted health conditions would represent a basic change in public health policies. In practice, self-infliction is occasionally advanced as a reason for dealing with drug addicts differently from, say, patients with heart disease. However, the argument cannot be used to deny all drug addicts with equal needs equal access to drug treatment. Improving access in general and promoting equality in access are rationales of public financing and management of drug treatment. Often, this seems so self-evident that it is not felt necessary to draw attention to it. It is only when marked inequality in access is perceived as a policy issue that it comes to attention.

There are two principal public policy approaches to promoting equality in access to health services. A *selective* approach assumes that most people can pay either directly or by insurance for the services they and their families use, and that the responsibility of public policy is to fund or organize services only for those who are not insured by employers or who cannot afford the services or insurance they need. In a *universal* approach, public financing or universal compulsory insurance covers the services for the whole population. After World War II, there was a long period of development toward universal coverage of health care in most industrialized Western countries. The selective system of the United States became almost an exception in international comparisons between those countries.

Both the universal and the selective systems have particular arrangements for some population groups to ensure their use of certain services. For instance, the public funding of certain health services for children or the elderly may provide more complete coverage than does funding for people of working age. Certain communicable diseases, such as tuberculosis or sexually transmitted diseases, may be treated free in health care systems that charge patients for other services. Also, patients with serious mental disorders, addiction, or, in some countries, serious communicable diseases may be given compulsory treatment without charge.

The differences between the privately and publicly funded drug treatment sectors in the United States (see the U.S. chapter) illustrate the difficulties in ensuring equal access to services by a selective policy. Although selective funding arrangements cover access to services also for uninsured and poor drug dependents, the services they receive are not the same or of the same quality as those for the insured and the well-off. Significant differences in quality associated with different funding arrangements are reported also from a number of other countries, such as Switzerland, England, Italy, Japan, Russia, and Colombia. However, countries with extensive but less-than-universal coverage for general health services, such as Austria, Canada, Finland, France, Germany, the Netherlands, and Sweden, have particular arrangements for the financing and management of drug treatment (see Table 28.1). Reasons for not covering drug treatment under general health care vary:

- Universal coverage may exclude all or part of drug treatment.
- Drug users may tend to drop out of treatment if coverage is not complete.
- Even if universal funding does not formally exclude drug treatment, service authorities are not prepared to provide adequate or the favored kind of drug treatment on the general terms of universal funding.
- Equal or satisfactory access to drug treatment is not perceived as a guarantee for sufficient use of treatment services.
- Drug addicts, particularly when they are imprisoned, are separated from the general health care arrangements by the criminal justice system, which may finance and manage their treatment.

Universal Coverage May Exclude Certain Kinds of Treatment

The chapters on the countries with generally universal but incomplete coverage indicate that all cover at least some part of drug treatment. In most, for instance, serious acute drug problems such as poisoning and injuries are treated by the general emergency services and financed from general health care funds. Under universal health care funding, less serious and longer term problems, particularly those not usually treated medically, may not be covered or may have very restricted coverage, and certain kinds of treatment may be excluded (Table 28.1).

Quite often, advocates of drug treatment have contended that drug problems and drug dependence are diseases and that they should be dealt with by the health services rather than the criminal justice system. However, this does not seem to be enough. In most countries, at least in the northern hemisphere, conditions such as drug poisoning, drug withdrawal, and drug dependence are categorized as diseases, in accordance with the International Classification of Diseases (World Health Organization, 1992). However, even fully universal funding systems do not cover all forms of treatment for problems recognized as diseases. Not only must a

Table 28.1 Examples of Different Arrangements for the Funding of Drug Treatment

Characteristics of Drug Treatment Funding	*Examples Among ISDRUTS Countries*
Main source of funding	
Drug treatment funded in the same way as treatment of "normal diseases," or only one source of funding	None
General health care budget clearly the most significant source of funding	Austria, France, Germany, Italy, Portugal, England, the Netherlands
General social welfare budget clearly the most significant source of funding	Sweden, Finland
Criminal justice budget clearly the most significant source of funding	Japan
Funds earmarked for drug treatment; separate from general-health, social-welfare, and criminal-justice funding the most significant source of funding	Spain, Canada
Private funding (client fees, charities, etc.) main source	Colombia
No main source; funding from criminal justice, health, social welfare, private sources, and others	Russia
Other aspects	
Criminal justice budget a significant source (more than 15% of total funding)	Japan, Russia
Two main sources: health budget and particular drug treatment budgets	Poland
Two main sources: social welfare and health care budgets	Finland, Germany, Peru
Three or more main sources of funding	England, Japan, Russia
Three or more sources of funding mentioned	Most ISDRUTS countries
Significant variation among regions	Switzerland, Canada, England

problem be recognized as a disease, but also the treatment to be covered must be a recognized treatment. Coverage is assured if the treatment in question has been developed within medicine and applied by the medical profession. Coverage is much less likely if the treatment is outside the scope of conventional medicine and the authority of the medical profession.

Because various types and phases of drug treatment may encompass social work and social and vocational rehabilitation, and provide for even such basic needs as housing, hygiene, and nutrition, coverage by general health care funds is not assured. Responsibility for caring for a drug addict may move from one adminis-trative sector to another according to the type of drug problem or the mixture of drug problems as well as to the addict's socioeconomic background and social environment (see Table 28.2).

The position of drug treatment at the margin of general health care funding also explains the considerable regional variation in the availability of, and access to, drug treatment, and in federal countries as well as in such countries as England and Finland.

Drop-Outs in Fairly Universal Systems

Some countries, particularly in continental Western Europe, have extensive but not fully universal coverage by sickness insurance. Their insurance systems were

Table 28.2 Examples of Division of Responsibility for Three Major Segments of Drug
Treatment

Responsibility for Providing Drug Treatment	Examples Among ISDRUTS Countries
Treatment for drug addiction	
Health care administration has major responsibility	Canada, Germany, France, Italy, the Netherlands, Portugal
Social welfare administration has major responsibility	Finland, Sweden
Criminal justice system is the most significant provider of addiction treatment	Japan, Russia, China
Divided between several administrative sectors; no major sector	England, Russia, Austria, Peru
Private nonprofit or for-profit organizations have a very significant role	Colombia, Switzerland
Treatment of acute drug poisoning, injuries, and other acute conditions of addicts	
Health care administration has almost 100% responsibility	Austria, Canada, England, Germany, France, Finland, Italy, Japan, Sweden, and many others
Criminal justice system has a significant role, although health care administration is the most significant	Russia
Private nonprofit or for-profit organizations have a significant role	Colombia, Switzerland
Services for meeting basic needs of drug addicts, such as shelter, hygiene, nutrition	
Social welfare administration has major responsibility	Austria, Canada, China, England, Finland, Germany, Italy, Japan, Poland, Spain, Sweden
Private organizations very significant	Switzerland, England, Colombia
Private organizations rather significant	Finland, France, Russia

built up from separate arrangements for different groups (e.g., workers on normal
wages in the private sector, public employees, pensioners, private entrepreneurs).
Although most countries' systems have progressed to universal coverage and equal
rights for all, certain categories may drop out of coverage: They include people
who are not employed, entrepreneurs, pensioners, or young people who are not
covered through their families but live socially delinquent and marginalized lives.
This loss of coverage may not matter much in, for instance, the treatment of cancer,
coronary heart disease, or most communicable diseases or injuries, but it may be
significant in drug treatment because drug problems are often linked with social
marginalization, and methods of treating them are often outside the scope of
mainstream medicine. Thus, a significant proportion of drug dependents may need
separate funding for their treatment, and it may have to come from social welfare
or particular drug treatment funding programs.

The practice in Scandinavian countries whereby much of drug treatment is
provided by the social welfare and social services sector (see the Finland and
Sweden chapters) does not necessarily indicate a serious departure from the
universal coverage of their health care systems. Rather, it reflects their extensive
public social service system and their less medicalized perception of alcohol and
drug problems. Their public social services, particularly child day care, are much

more extensive than those of any other part of Western Europe and, like health care, may even be said to have universal coverage (Anttonen & Sipilä, 1996). Therefore, drug treatment as a social service is not, in principle, different from the same treatment in countries where it is a health service, but its social service basis reflects and promotes in it the higher status of social work.

Disliked Patients: Treatment Responding to Other Interests Than User Demand

Even if drug dependents have equal access to all necessary treatment, legally and financially, in the same way as, say, patients with coronary heart disease, they may still be treated very differently in practice. Informal professional, institutional, and other norms may lead to unequal access to treatment as well as to unequal treatment. Many studies have shown that in general health services, drug users are often discriminated against, or at least less favored than other kinds of patients. If a service unit can select which patients to serve and which to serve better, drug users tend to be excluded from some services (Lehto, 1991). Many chapters in this book give instances of such exclusion from general health services. One funding alternative used to try to change such attitudes and informal norms is to arrange special funding for drug treatment and thus to create an incentive for establishing separate drug treatment programs or units, responding to other interests besides user demand. Such special funding may also indicate that provision of treatment is not so much a response to user demand as a means of controlling drug-related problems perceived by others. Such countries as Russia, France, Poland, Sweden, the United States, and Austria have special funding for drug treatment provided by the criminal justice system or as an alternative to punishment. Many countries have increased general or special funding for drug treatment in the interests of preventing HIV/AIDS. Special funding may also be designed to prevent crime, youth problems, inner-city problems, suburban social problems, and others. At least in some Latin American countries, it comes also from international and foreign sources as part of their war on drugs. Presumably, if drug treatment were generously funded from general health care sources, there would be less need for special funding, but this cannot be proved from available data. It is also quite difficult to determine whether countries with more universal funding of general health or social care have fewer arrangements for special funding than do other countries, but this seems to be the case in Scandinavia.

It might also be assumed that drug policies that emphasize prohibition would differ from more liberal policies with regard to funding of treatment. A liberal policy would be thought to favor normalization of funding of drug treatment, with no need of particular arrangements. However, in practice, liberalization may also be promoted by particular funding for "soft" drug policies (see the England chapter). At the same time, a tight policy on drugs may be complemented by universal coverage of health and social care services and generous general funding of drug treatment, with less need for particular funding arrangements (see the Sweden chapter).

Table 28.3 Cost-Effectiveness Analysis in Drug Treatment Policy, According to Responses
       of 17 Country Authors

Statement on the State of the Art in the Reported Country	Number of Countries to Which the Statement Applies
Cost-effectiveness is discussed, but it is not a central topic	14
Cost-effectiveness is a central topic in discussing drug treatment, but the discussion has had little impact in practice	8
There is a significant increase in cost-effectiveness analyses of different treatment programs	5
Cost-effectiveness analysis or quality measurement is often a prerequisite of funding or is significant in determining which treatment programs receive funding and those for which funding is reduced or ended	3
Broad consensus on the rating of different treatment programs	2
General dissatisfaction on the part of national experts with the validity and reliability of cost-effectiveness analysis	9
Different treatment programs, treatment systems, and chains of different treatment programs are evaluated for cost-effectiveness, and decision makers are informed of the outcome	3

Cost-Effectiveness of Drug Treatment

Parallel to the increase in universal coverage of health care in industrialized Western countries after World War II, its costs have also increased. Had there been no exceptional countries, such as the United States, which remained selective but nevertheless experienced a rapid rise in health care costs, it might be assumed that universal coverage was its main cause. But because costs increased also, and even more highly, in selective systems, there must have been other reasons.

One, although not the main, reason has been the weakness of the structures and practices of financing and management. The first wave of efforts to improve them was based on more effective budgeting and planning, including information systems to support rational planning. Being under permanent political pressure for change and having to obtain funds from fragments of the plans and budgets of different sectors of public administration made it difficult for those responsible for managing drug treatment systems as a whole to implement the ideology of rational budgeting and planning. Rather, different parts of the system were under the pressure of different budgeting and planning practices. Probably the most visible result of efforts to improve budgeting and planning has been an increase in requests for evaluation studies of the cost-effectiveness of different drug treatments (see Table 28.3). There is a growing number of such studies, based mostly on data from North America. However, this has not led to a stable consensus, even among experts, on how to rate different treatment programs.

A major obstacle to reaching consensus is that different interest groups and funding sources set different objectives for drug treatment. The objectives may be abstinence, reduction in HIV risk, reduction in crime or public disorder, reduction in the social exclusion of drug users, or improvement in the health of drug users.

Table 28.4 Significance Accorded by Decision Makers to Different Indicators of
Treatment Outcome, According to Estimates of 16 Country Authors

Outcome Indicator	Sum of Ratings Given by 16 Respondents
Permanent abstinence from drugs	35
Reduction of crime	33
Reduction of risk-taking with drugs	28
Reduction of risk of HIV/AIDS	28
Resocialization into wage labor	28
At least temporary abstinence from drugs	28
Resocialization into other areas of "normal" life	27
Reduction of need of health and social services	13

NOTE: The significance of each outcome indicator was rated on a scale from 0 (*insignificant*) to 3 (*very significant*).

With such varied objectives, the outcome criteria for evaluating effectiveness of treatment will also be quite different, if not contradictory. Also, countries differ in the significance they accord to different outcome measures. In most ISDRUTS countries, abstinence seems to rate as the most significant measure, but others, such as France, the Netherlands, Portugal, Switzerland, and Spain, give higher ratings to reduced risk-taking with drugs and reduced risk of HIV/AIDS. In both groups of countries, reduction of crime is rated high (see Table 28.4).

The evaluation of different treatment programs, and particularly a comparison of their costs, may also be difficult, because the structure of costs and the mixture of funding sources differ from one to another. Analysis of cost-effectiveness is also complex because drug dependence is seldom cured by one short treatment period provided by a single treatment program. The outcome may depend on a patient's background, previous courses of treatment, the parallel use of the other services or programs, or after-care and subsequent living circumstances. Thus, it is difficult to determine the cost-effectiveness or cost-benefit of single courses of treatment, and even highly reliable findings may not be helpful for reaching consensus on policy or rational decision making with regard to a drug treatment system as a whole.

These are not reasons for pessimism, however. One general conclusion seems to be that no treatment program is superior to other programs across the range of drug problems or drug users. Reported outcomes of treatment tend to depend more upon the type of addict treated and the types of outcome criteria applied than on the type of treatment program. For instance, there is much evidence about the impact of various harm reduction programs on the incidence of HIV infection and crime related to drug use. Treatment may have a rather limited outcome if it is measured by the proportion of totally abstinent, treated individuals some time after the completion of a course of treatment. However, if the outcome measure is a reduction in costs of health care (including the cost of drug treatment), most treatment programs show a significant outcome and economic benefit. Thus, the difficulties of rating the effectiveness of treatment programs should not obscure the general conclusion that expenditure on drug treatment produces many positive results and even significant economic benefits (World Health Organization, 1993).

There is evidence also that, at least in the case of many groups of less severely addicted patients, the outcome of low-cost outpatient treatment does not differ significantly from that of long and expensive inpatient treatment. However, certain groups of severely addicted people may benefit more from expensive intensive or long-term inpatient treatment.

The ideal contribution to the formulation of drug treatment policy would be a competent analysis of individual-level cost-effectiveness of different treatment careers in addition to analysis of single episodes of treatment. This could also be the first stage of an evaluation of whole treatment systems for cost-effectiveness, in addition to an evaluation of single programs. For instance, the costs and the outcome of separate drug treatment compared with those of drug treatment integrated with general health services, or of fragmented compared with well-coordinated treatment systems, could then be determined.

Drug Treatment Systems as Markets

At present, reformers of health care systems in general seem to be pessimistic regarding rational, centralized budgeting and planning (World Health Organization, 1996). If the earlier fiction guiding discussions on reform was that of one central agency rationally planning and guiding the system, the present fiction seems to be the "market." However, the actual relationships that constitute health care systems are far from the ideal of a free market. For example, there are providing and purchasing monopolies; information asymmetries exist between actors; funding arrangements and regulations distort the relations between supply, demand, and price; regulations prevent competition; providers of services may have public responsibilities; and so on. However, this has not prevented the market fiction from being a powerful influence on health care reform. Thus, management ideologies are borrowed from the private sector, there are efforts to create market relationships by separating the functions of purchasing and providing services, and the image of service users is changed by calling patients customers.

A dominant theme of the market fiction is the use of incentives. A criticism of the rational planning and budgeting model was that everyone had an incentive to increase costs, but no one had a clear incentive to be more effective. A major objective of health care reform should be to rearrange relationships in such a way that everyone in the system has an incentive to act cost-effectively. The earlier fiction of rational budgeting and planning depended largely on visible guidelines from above, but the market fiction requires that relationships within the system guide its behavior, leaving—fictively—guiding from above to the "invisible hand" of market discipline.

The managing and financing of the drug treatment systems described in this book may also be analyzed on the market analogy. Indeed, it may be that, particularly from the point of view of service providers, the fragmented and weakly coordinated field of drug treatment may better fit the market fiction than many other parts of health and social services.

The Providers' Perspective

Many of the countries described in this book have no stable monopoly of one service provider of drug treatment. Competition between different treatment providers, public and private, may be quite sharp. It is fed by the multiplicity of sources of financing of treatment and the continuously changing opportunities for obtaining funds from different sources, as many chapters indicate. Often, however, the competition is about attracting funding agencies, not customers. Because there are a limited number of funding agencies in any case, the market is less an ideal "free market" than an arena of monopolistic competition.

Competition between providers could be an incentive for them to act cost-effectively if cost-effectiveness were a major asset in competition. However, cost-effectiveness actually does not matter too much, for various reasons: There are many different objectives of treatment; different "purchasers"—financing sources—expect or emphasize different outcomes; and cost-effectiveness is technically difficult and expensive to measure. Sometimes, the symbolic meanings of drug treatment programs may be more important than their actual performance to the politicians who allocate funds to them. Thus, the public perception of treatment—for instance, whether a treatment ideology is regarded as "prohibitionist" or "liberal"—may be more important than whether it has a good outcome at reasonable cost (see the Sweden chapter). The image of the "product" may be "treating young drug abusers," even though the actual clients may be middle-aged, with long drug-use careers (see the Finland chapter). The treatment units may be tempted to cheat, to promise better results—in terms of ending drug use—than they can achieve (see the Poland chapter).

Those examples of competing with images, ideologies, and false promises show that competition as such ensures no strong incentives for cost-effectiveness in the health care and social care market. What it needed is for those who work and use the system to be well-informed and motivated for cost-effectiveness, and for competition rules and arrangements to make cost-effectiveness a major asset in competition. The drug treatment market does not necessarily meet these conditions.

Although the actual conditions in drug treatment markets seem to leave providers some room for maneuvering, and even for a kind of deception, they are, in practice, unfavorable to providers. For instance, because the market is rather small and purchasers' expectations are fragmented, treatment units and numbers of clients for different programs often tend to be too small; it is difficult to reach optimum cost-effectiveness through economies of scale. A second factor may be high transaction costs: Market conditions are continuously changing; different purchasers set different product specifications; and political decision makers have to be convinced of the benefits of funding drug treatment in general and treatment by every competing provider in particular.

The Customers' Perspective

Customers—service users—are described in standard health care market schemata as poorly informed and with almost limitless capacity to use services.

Hence, an agency is needed between customers and providers to assess customers' needs, prevent "unnecessary" use of expensive services, and make better-informed choices of service providers for customers. The functions of assessing the needs of customers and choosing providers for them may be united, but in many health care financing and management arrangements they are separated as purchasing and gatekeeping agencies. Purchasing agencies represent, for instance, the insurance company of the public authority funding the service. Gatekeepers are normally professionals, responsible for deciding who is to be served in a particular facility and who is to be sent elsewhere. Disagreement between the customer and the purchasing/gatekeeping agency is not rare in general health services but is much more likely in the drug treatment market. First, there are not only gatekeepers but also barkers, whose function is to tout treatment services to drug abusers. Methods vary from outreach activities and methadone distribution to economic pressures, threat of punishment, or compulsion. Second, the drug treatment system rarely follows the model of general health services, where one function of primary medical care or the general practitioner is to act as gatekeeper to more expensive hospital and specialist treatment. The gatekeeping and barking functions may be much more dispersed and vary from one type of treatment to another. Third, what the purchasing agencies expect as the outcome of treatment may differ much more from customers' expectations than is the case in general health services.

The particularities of the customer role in the drug treatment market may contribute to some ineffectiveness in the use of scarce resources. For instance, where barkers are needed for some services and gatekeepers for others, inefficiency in allocation of resources is likely; programs needing barkers may be allocated too many resources and those needing gatekeepers too few. Publicly funded drug treatment may be available in the criminal justice system free of charge, but there may be high fees for high-quality treatment elsewhere. This may be an extreme example but, more generally, fragmentation of treatment systems creates quite different incentives for customers in different parts of the systems. This may complicate long-term treatment—for instance, when customers move through several treatment programs that use different incentives, thus contributing to fragmentation or interruption of the long-term process.

Discussion

Equal access to appropriate care is a broadly accepted principle of health policy. If it is interpreted as equal access to care for people with equally severe health problems, it is applied almost nowhere in the case of drug addicts. They are at risk of exclusion from normal health care for many reasons: Their condition may not be recognized as a health problem; the kinds of treatment they need may not be recognized as proper health care; they may not have acquired the same degree of health insurance coverage as other people; they may suffer discrimination in the everyday practice of services; and the link between drug use and criminality may prevent their equal access.

Exclusion from normal health care funding is partly balanced by funding of drug treatment from other sources. In most countries, this has led to rather fragmented financing and management of drug treatment systems. Different funding sources may also have different and at least partly contradictory goals of drug treatment. Apparently, equal access is not a main objective of policy. Although fragmented drug treatment systems may be a consequence of the need to compensate for the exclusion of drug treatment from normal financing and management of health care, they do not ensure equal access for people with equal needs of drug treatment, either. Fragmentation has resulted in drug treatment systems that can be analyzed on the basis of the analogy of the market. However, actual drug treatment markets differ considerably from the theoretical "free market." Their conditions and incentives do not ensure effectiveness of treatment or the allocation of treatment resources according to the needs of addicts. On the contrary, the fragmentation of their financing and management can be expected to cause ineffectiveness.

Economic analysis of health care systems in general is a complex exercise (Ashmore, Mulkay, & Pinch, 1989), but in regard to drug treatment it is even more difficult. Why is it more difficult to organize a drug treatment system that provides equal access with optimum costs? One reason could be the different way in which drug treatment is provided. Another may be that drug dependence is so different from usual medical conditions that general methods of financing and general approaches to improving cost-effectiveness are not applicable to it. Still another may be that it is not appropriate to apply to drug treatment the general approach of mainstream health economics, in view of the difficulties encountered in trying to do so. There is likely to be some truth in each of these propositions.

References

Anttonen, A., & Sipilä, J. (1996). European social care services: Is it possible to identify models? *Journal of European Social Policy, 2,* 87-100.

Ashmore, M., Mulkay, M., & Pinch, T. (1989). *Health and efficiency: A sociology of health economics.* Milton Keynes, UK, & Philadelphia: Open University Press.

Blaxter, M. (1996). The significance of socioeconomic factors in health for medical care and the National Health Service. In D. Blane, E. Brunner, & R. Wilkinson (Eds.), *Health and social organization* (pp. 26-48). London & New York: Routledge.

Lehto, J. (1991). *Juoppojen professionaalinen auttaminen* [Professional help for drunkards]. Helsinki: VAPK-Publishing.

Whitehead, M. (1990). *The concepts and principles of equity and health.* Copenhagen: WHO Regional Office for Europe.

World Health Organization. (1992). *The ICD-10 classification of mental and behavioural disorders.* Geneva: Author.

World Health Organization. (1993). *WHO expert committee on drug dependence, twenty-eighth report.* Geneva: Author.

World Health Organization. (1996). *European health care reforms: Analysis of current strategies.* Copenhagen: WHO Regional Office for Europe.

Chapter 29

Gender and Drug Treatment Systems

Irmgard Vogt

This chapter tries to synthesize research studies on gender issues, and more precisely on female drug addicts in treatment, from most of the countries represented in this book. This is not an easy task, because countries differ in all possible dimensions: their political systems, their health care systems, and their justice systems, to name only a few that are relevant to illicit drugs. It is beyond the scope of this chapter to consider the differences in the make-up of countries and discuss them in relation to drug problems. Its aim is modest; it is descriptive rather than analytic, comparing as much as possible what has been published so far in different countries on drug addiction and gender and on gender-specific drug treatment.

The literature on gender-specific drug treatment differs from the more elaborate studies on gender issues in alcohol treatment (cf. Institute of Medicine, 1990; Schmidt & Weisner, 1993). Overall, it is a much less well-studied research field, and methods of exploring different trends and outcome variables are less well established and agreed upon. Besides, the issues seem to be even more complex than those in alcohol research because they are embedded in broader political issues headlined as "Wars on Drugs." Politicians of all levels of society are exerting much pressure on the formal and informal treatment fields to react to drug problems at once, produce "success," and help effectively to make the world "drug free." In such a political setting, gender issues tend to disappear; they seem less important than the demand for success.

Small wonder that the women's movement and feminist activists were the first to draw attention to gender issues in drug treatment, often demanding gender-specific treatment settings and making it a political issue. At first, however, they were much more interested in the provision of gender-specific treatment facilities than in research. It took some time before the first well-designed, gender-specific treatment and evaluation studies were carried out and published. Indeed, the exploration of the drug treatment field from a gender-specific perspective is only at its beginning.

The first section of this chapter presents gender-specific epidemiological data on illicit drug use and drug addiction. The second consists of a short review of some of the main topics in publications on gender and illicit drugs, with little reference to socialization and gender roles as possible risks (cf. Thom, 1994) or protective factors with regard to drug addiction in women. The third gives an overview of gender-specific treatment settings in North America and Western Europe, women's preferences with regard to treatment settings, and, if possible, outcomes of evaluation research.

Women and Illicit Drugs: An Epidemiological Overview

In many studies in different countries, epidemiological data on use and abuse of illicit drugs are not classified by sex. It is not easy to collect data across countries on lifetime, previous-year, or previous-30-day prevalence rates for women and men separately; estimates of female and male drug dependents; or the sex ratios of addicts. Table 29.1 presents these data for a number of European and North American countries. The category "illegal drugs" refers mainly to cannabis, heroin, and cocaine/crack, and the category "drug dependents" refers to regular and compulsive users of heroin and cocaine/crack.

Women everywhere use illicit drugs much less than men do. In Sweden, Finland, Poland, England, the Netherlands, the former West Germany, Switzerland, Austria, Spain, the United States, and Canada, a much higher percentage of women than of men, of all age groups, never experiment with such drugs. Female-to-male ratios of lifetime prevalence rates vary around 1:2 in Europe and 1:1.5 in North America. These differences are primarily the result of different methods of measuring use. The U.S. figures include data on users of illegally acquired psychoactive substances. The overall lifetime prevalence rates of women legally using tranquilizers, analgesics, and related substances are about twice those of men (Riska, Kühlhorn, Nordlund, & Skinhoj, 1993; Vogt, 1985); also, women are more willing than men to buy these substances illegally when they are offered on the black market. If these categories are combined, as in the household survey data of the United States, the rates for women are higher than for men, which in turn influences the sex ratio. In short, the gender effect is more pronounced with respect to prevalence rates for the classic illicit drugs, such as cannabis, heroin, and cocaine/crack; it becomes less obvious when illegally acquired psychoactive substances are included.

In Western European and North American countries, cannabis is the most popular illicit drug, mostly smoked as either marijuana in North America or hashish in Europe, and often irregularly; and lifetime prevalence data on illicit drug

Table 29.1 Data on Lifetime Illegal Drug Use by Sex, Estimates of Drug Dependents per Country, and Sex Ratio of Dependents

Country	% Users of Illegal Drugs (lifetime)			Estimates of Drug Dependents (total N)	Ratio of Drug Dependents (female to male)
	Female	F + M	Male		
Sweden	6		11	17,000	1:3
Finland	4		6	500	1:4
Poland	—		—	25,000	1:3
United Kingdom	5	5		21,000	—
Netherlands	12	12		24,000	1:2.5
Germany[a]	9		18	125,000	1:2.5
Switzerland	12		22	30,000	1:3
Austria	12		17[b]	10,000	1:3.5
France	19	19		100,000	1:5
Spain	19	19		100,000	1:5
USA	32		42[c]	—	1:2
Canada	18		29[b]	—	1:3

SOURCE: Adrian, Lundy, and Eliany (1996); Driessen (1990); Eisenbach-Stangl (1995); Health & Welfare Canada (1990); Herbst, Kraus, Scherer, and Schumann (1995); Kinnunen (1996); Kontula (1995); Ministère de l'Intérieur (1991); Rehm (1994); Reuband (1995); Schweizerische Fachstelle für Alkohol- und andere Drogenprobleme (1993); Swedish Council for Information on Alcohol and Other Drugs (CAN) (1991).
a. Data for former West Germany only; for details, see the chapter by Vogt and Schmid in this volume.
b. Data on hashish/marijuana consumption only.
c. Data include those on consumers of marijuana, heroin, cocaine, inhalants, hallucinogens, PCP, illegal stimulants/sedatives/tranquilizers (cf. NIDA, 1987).

use refer primarily to cannabis. Many young people experiment with it, but most do so only a few times before giving it up; relatively few become habitual users or addicts.

The most commonly used drugs vary among cultures and regions. In some South American countries such as Bolivia, Peru, and now also Colombia, the most common drugs are coca leaves, cocaine, and other coca-paste preparations. China and some other Asian countries have a long tradition of opium use, and in some regions it is still common, either smoked or eaten as raw or processed forms of opium. It is not used as heroin there, nor is it injected.

There are differences also in regard to quantity and frequency of use: On average, women of all age groups use illicit drugs much less, and much less frequently, than do men, and they stop after even fewer experiences. Still, some become dependent.

Estimates of numbers of drug dependents vary widely between the countries. They indicate quite different levels of problems with illicit drugs and drug dependents. The female-to-male ratio varies between 1:3 and 1:5. Table 29.2 gives estimates of drug dependents in a few European countries as raw data and per 100,000 inhabitants by sex.

Once again, the data illustrate the place of women among drug addicts. Regardless of the drug policies of the different countries (Reuband, 1995), women are a minority, but their minority status changes between countries. In those with very few female addicts, such as Spain, there is little discussion on gender and drug addiction or the need for gender-specific treatment institutions. In others with relatively higher numbers of female addicts, and especially in those where female

Table 29.2 Estimates of Drug Dependents in Some European Countries per 100,000
Inhabitants by Sex

Country	Estimates of Drug Dependents (total N)	Drug Dependents per 100,000 Inhabitants	
		Female	Male
Sweden	17,000	51	154
Netherlands	24,000	47	117
Germany[a]	125,000	59	146
Switzerland	30,000	115	346
France	100,000	30	151
Spain	100,000	43	215

a. Data for former West Germany only.

addicts are highly visible in open drug scenes, such as the Netherlands, Germany, and Switzerland, gender-specific issues are now prominent and often discussed, a result of the many activities of the women's movement since the 1970s.

Background Variables of Drug-Dependent Women and Treatment Options

Drug treatment options for women are said to be the same as for men. However, in all of the countries covered in this book, the drug treatment systems were designed originally for drug-dependent men, to cure them and to reintegrate them into society (Musto, 1973; Rush, 1996; Takala, Klingemann, & Hunt, 1992); this is seldom mentioned explicitly with regard to women's treatment options. For many years, there has been little critical discussion of treatment systems as a complex set of institutions for addicted, deviant, or sick men. On admitting women to treatment institutions in the United States in the 1960s and in some Western European countries in the 1970s, the institutions did not change their structure or methods; they simply offered women the same professional treatment as men. This led to confusion on all sides. The men experienced some excitement at having women in the institutions but could not show it, the women were offered the same treatment as men but no more, and the professionals often did not know how to deal with the situation (Solomon, 1982).

At that time, drug treatment addressed first the needs of male addicts; women were assumed to have more or less the same needs, and this justified "gender-neutral" treatment. This assumption resulted in difficulties for both female drug dependents and those who treated them. It implied that drug dependence was not gender-specific and treatment therefore gender-neutral, but it disregarded psychological and biological gender differences, gender roles, and role expectations that were built into the future life perspectives of men and women regardless of their addiction. This changed when, in the 1970s and more so in the 1980s, ever more research studies were published stressing gender differences in addiction (cf. Beschner, Reed, & Mondanaro, 1981). There is now abundant evidence that the background of women who become drug addicts differs from that of men; that addicted women behave differently from addicted men, even in their efforts to quit; and that they have different needs when in treatment, needs that refer to treatment settings and methods that appeal more to them than to men. A selection of those background variables are discussed here, with special reference to violence and prostitution, which often arise in the literature on female drug addicts (cf. Ernst, Rottenmanner, & Spreyermann, 1995).

Male and female drug dependents differ in many ways, such as by age at onset of use of illicit drugs (women are, on the average, younger) and how long they use drugs before seeking professional help (women do so, on the average, a shorter time), but there are vast differences when it comes to help-seeking behavior in different countries, owing partly to differences between the health care systems and partly to the societal discourse on addiction. They differ in their preferred drug cocktails (which change over time and place), their method of use (on the average, fewer women inject drugs, and they inject less frequently and in smaller amounts), and their living arrangements (Powis, Griffiths, Gossop, & Strang, 1996; Vogt, 1995). They often live with drug-dependent men, whom they look after and with whom they share money and drugs. Their position within the subculture of drug dependents is inferior to that of men, but there are subgroups that seem to overcome traditional hierarchical patterns (Morgan & Joe, 1996).

A significant background variable in female drug addiction is women's subjection to violence, most often as sexual exploitation. The younger they are when sexual exploitation begins, and the more severe and long-lasting it is, the greater the risk of addiction. The risk also increases with the closeness in family relations of the exploiter; females who have been sexually abused in early childhood by members of their families are the most vulnerable to drug abuse and addiction in their teens (Ireland & Widom, 1994; Pedersen & Skrondal, 1996). The risk of sexual violence does not stop after childhood, however; it may hang over women all their lives. Victims of sexual abuse, whether as rape or as other forms of sexual violence, often undergo traumatic experiences with such long-lasting effects as chronic psychosomatic illnesses or behavioral disorders. Drugs offer a means of dealing with traumatizing experiences, memories of cruelty, and learned helplessness, and this paves the way to eventual addiction (Ladwig & Andersen, 1989).

Research into violence, sexual exploitation, and drug dependence is still at its beginning. More studies are needed to clarify the association between women's experience of violence and drug dependence, and to determine how the sexes differ in their reaction to violence and in beginning drug abuse.

Violence often precedes or accompanies drug dependence, but dependence also breeds violence, particularly in the case of street addicts; this has been described extensively for inner-city, crack-dependent women in the United States (Bourgois, 1989; Fagan, 1992). Swiss and German studies support these findings for groups of women who are in the open drug scene but are not dependent on crack. For street addicts, violence has two sides: An addict may assault any passer-by, whether a stranger or another addict; hence, anyone may become a victim. To be a street addict is to be a potential assailant and a victim, to accept violence as a way of succeeding or surviving, and to tolerate violence. Men are somewhat more aggressive than women; they profit more from the street life; and they exploit women, especially as prostitutes.

The findings on violence raise a number of questions about gender roles in drug subcultures. Without going deeply into a discussion of gender roles, it is obvious that women who display a certain amount of violence in the streets deviate strongly from the traditional role pattern as it has been described originally (e.g., Parsons, Bales, Olds, Zelditch, & Slater, 1955). In fact, it can be seen as a redefinition of the female role, which seems to merge more and more with that of the male role with respect to violent behavior. It is open to speculation whether this makes drug subcultures more attractive to particular groups of women.

Data on the percentage of addicted women in the sex business vary greatly between studies, from 20% (Erickson & Watson, 1990; Fagan, 1994; Vogt, 1997) to 100%, partly because of differences among subgroups studied but more because of faulty study designs, and sometimes also prejudice on the part of researchers (Inciardi, Lockwood, & Pottieger, 1993). Also, cross-cultural comparisons are difficult because of differences in laws on prostitution. Prostitution is legal in a number of central European countries but illegal in, for instance, England and the United States, and it is close to being illegal in Canada. It is condemned as immoral in all countries, but it is a crime only in some, which increases the attached stigma.

In countries in which prostitution is legal, women can run a legal business to pay for drugs. The police arrest them for drug offenses, not for prostitution. In these countries, women have lower rates of crime; consequently, they spend less time than men in the criminal justice system and are less often committed to compulsory residential treatment, and many have a negligible criminal record. This is often helpful when they stop drugs and try to become reintegrated into everyday life.

Sex work has its own hazards, however, notably its health risks. Addicted prostitutes do not always practice safe sex, for their customers often ask for unsafe sex and are willing to pay more for it. Indeed, the percentage of addicted women with chronic illnesses such as depression with attempted suicide; hepatitis A, B, or C; and HIV infection is quite high in some countries. In the case of street addicts, it is highest.

Women and men also differ in how they stop drug use. Many more women than might be expected are subjects of research studies on "natural recovery," for instance, and such studies reveal significant gender differences in ways of quitting. Many women who live through episodes of drug dependence—some lasting years—mature out naturally, sometimes with the help of professionals, although not necessarily expert drug counselors, but mostly with the help of friends and families. After long years of drug abuse, including prostitution to pay for drugs, many women still have an extended and well-functioning social network on which they can rely when they are ready to give up drugs. In the European countries, unlike alcoholics, women who want to quit do not rely on self-help groups such as

Alcoholics Anonymous (AA) or Narcotics Anonymous (NA). Rather, they activate their own, very private social networks, which often have no relationship at all to self-help organizations for alcohol or drug dependents (Biernacki, 1986; Happel, Fischer, & Wittfeld, 1993; Klingemann, 1990; Zurhold, 1993).

A strong motive to stop drug use, besides shame and sheer tiredness with street life, is pregnancy. In Western European countries, more young female addicts than ever before want to be mothers, and many of those who become pregnant give up drugs; enter a methadone program; or find a private doctor who prescribes a drug substitute, such as codeine. They try hard to change their lifestyle to qualify as future mothers, to convince officials of child and youth welfare services of their ability to care for a new baby. Many succeed in stopping drug use or in stabilizing their lives on methadone or codeine therapy. Some fail and return to the streets, even leaving children behind. Still, for many addicted women, the prospect of having a child is an incentive to quit or at least to transform their lifestyles. In this, they have an advantage over drug-dependent men, most of whom do not care much about becoming fathers. As always, there are exceptions, and for some men the prospect of fatherhood is similarly motivating.

Cross-cultural comparisons are difficult because of ecological and socio-economic differences. For instance, in inner cities of the United States, women often begin having children in their teens, which has little to do with experimenting with illicit drugs, although there is some association between the two behavior patterns (cf. Jessor & Jessor, 1977). They may become dependent on drugs later, when they are already mothers. Alternatively, motherhood in inner cities in the United States may be so demanding that some teenage mothers may turn to illicit drugs to escape their daily misery. Then, another pregnancy may add to their stress and even trigger drug dependence. In the United States, women who are arrested when on drugs and pregnant have to expect to be sentenced and may be imprisoned during pregnancy for the sake of the unborn child (Paone, 1997; Weber, 1992). After delivery, they have little chance of taking the baby home. They have little to expect from another pregnancy, and pregnancy may open up no new hopes or prospects but, rather, add to the stress of daily life.

In all countries, when drug-dependent pregnant women and mothers with young children are known to the authorities, they are scrutinized for their mothering qualities, whereas the absence of the father goes unnoticed. Both reactions tend to stereotype women and men in their traditional gender roles, which may not be helpful. Single case studies reveal that addicted or formerly addicted mothers who live with their children often manage with the help of relatives and friends to organize a fairly well-structured family life. In the absence of most fathers, however, the children's prospects depend in the first place on their mothers' abilities as parents and breadwinners. With dwindling welfare payments in many countries, this is an ever-demanding responsibility. Today, a growing network of services addresses the needs of these mothers and their children, thus expanding familiar treatment settings (cf. Kandall, 1995; Leopold & Steffan, in press; Mitchell, 1993).

Drug-Dependent Women
and Treatment Systems

Treatment systems of different countries vary widely as to types of institution and treatment, density of treatment networks, background of service providers, and financial regulations. The following description draws on gender-specific treatment facilities and preferred settings of female addicts and service providers, but not on the organization or structures of treatment systems or on financing in the different countries.

In Asian countries such as Japan and China, the use of illicit drugs is a crime, and it is the criminal justice system that "treats" drug dependents in the first place. The stern handling of drug dependents, mostly men, in correctional institutions is one reason given for their very low numbers. There are very few female addicts and therefore little demand for special facilities. Psychiatric hospitals provide some counseling and treatment, and there are a few self-help groups, such as Alcoholics Anonymous and Narcotics Anonymous, that welcome women if they find their way to the meetings. Also, Japan has set up its first residential center for female addicts and is planning day-care counseling services for alcohol and drug problems for women who have small children.

In Latin American countries, the production and export of illicit drugs are eminently political issues. For some decades, the United States has been intervening in the production of illicit drugs in Bolivia, Peru, and Colombia (Lee, 1991). At the same time, this production has also affected these countries' consumption patterns. More men than ever before are using inexpensive and low-quality coca products and becoming addicts. However, these countries have many more pressing needs than the provision of services for addicted men and a few women, and therefore, there are only a few institutions in metropolitan areas. More effective are self-help organizations such as AA (and NA), which have become established in large cities as a comparatively cheap alternative to a formal treatment system. There is little information on gender-specific self-help groups or on discussion of the specific treatment needs of women.

The picture is totally different in North America and Western Europe. Most countries have dense networks of treatment services for addicts and their families. They differ in a number of respects, such as generic or specialized treatment settings; the attractiveness of facilities, such as those for outpatients or inpatients or for women only; the training of service providers; and gender-neutral or gender-specific treatment programs. The following section gives a very brief description of these aspects, either separately for some countries (Canada and the United States) or for groups of countries (the Nordic countries of Norway, Sweden, and Finland, and the Western European countries of the Netherlands, Switzerland, and Germany).

Unlike most countries, Canada has built up it own generic treatment networks for addicts (Popham, DeLint, & Schmidt, 1968) and is now the country with the most experience in treating women and men together who are addicted to alcohol and drugs (Adrian, Lundy, & Eliany, 1996). Dense networks have been established in metropolitan areas, offering a variety of services. In some regions, alcohol and drug treatment services cooperate with community health centers, and this provides the opportunity to integrate diverse activities, including, eventually, political action programs. In generic treatment institutions for addicts, women make up about 30% of the clients, and the percentage corresponds well with population estimates of addicted women in Canada. Besides other services, they are offered assessment, outpatient counseling, short- and long-term residential treatment, and after-care. Most institutions offer their services to women and men, but there is a growing network of institutions for women only (for a summary, see Lightfoot, Adrian, Leigh, & Thompson, 1996a), concentrated in metropolitan areas. In the countryside, women (and men) have a much narrower choice of services. AA-type self-help groups are the backbone of noninstitutionalized services, and AA ideology has shaped treatment procedures in many residential settings. In a number of inpatient institutions, most of the staff are recovered alcoholics, but not in clinical care or professional counseling. On the average, women prefer outpatient counseling services and self-help groups to residential services, but this is once again better documented for women with alcohol problems than for drug addicts (Lightfoot, Adrian, Leigh, & Thompson, 1996b). Specialty services for drug-dependent women, such as low-threshold centers, harm reduction services, and counseling of pregnant women or mothers of young children, are lacking, and there are efforts to set up programs specifically for these groups (Erickson, Riley, Cheung, & O'Hare, in press).

Although there is much experimenting with treatment concepts and programs designed for drug-dependent women, this is not reflected adequately in addiction research. Brett, Graham, and Smythe (1995) monitored biased sampling and misleading interpretations in addiction research, and they concluded that "gender-sensitive research practices are needed in the addictions field not only to remedy the relative lack of knowledge regarding women, but also to contribute to our knowledge of humans and addictive behaviors in general" (p. 33; Ferrence et al., 1994). Biased research, however, may very well reflect biased practice, with more and better services designed for addicted men, whereas women go more or less unnoticed.

The Canadian model of generic services for addicts has proved quite successful. A number of countries that advocated multiple treatment systems for different types of addiction in the 1960s and 1970s are now considering the benefits of merging the systems, not only to cut costs but also to broaden the range of services and specializations. In the United States and some European countries, a number of organizations are experimenting with generic services, some quite successfully and others much less so.

In the United States, separate specialized facilities for alcohol and drug addicts have developed over the years and have been challenged only lately. One of the many reasons for reconsidering the arrangement is the imposition of budget cuts and the consequent financial difficulties of drug treatment and rehabilitation organizations. Also, addiction is being conceptualized as addictive behavior (cf. Baer, Marlatt, & McMahon, 1993), on the assumption that all kinds of addiction are fairly similar physiologically and psychologically. To implement this in practice, however, is difficult after so many years of working with two largely separate service systems. Besides, drug-dependent men and—to a lesser degree—women run a high risk of ending up in the criminal justice system. There, they are treated first as criminals and consigned to correctional institutions, where they are on their own when it comes to dealing with their drug problems.

Addicted women in the United States have a strong tendency to use informal rather than formal service networks, to prefer outpatient to inpatient services, and to prefer those services with mixed-gender rather than single-gender patients (for a summary, see Harrison, Hoffmann, & Streed, 1991). Whereas many formal service organizations offer different forms of treatment to alcohol- and drug-dependent women, especially in therapeutic communities (De Leon, 1995), informal service networks such as AA and other self-help groups related to its ideologies (e.g., Women for Sobriety) integrate all types of addiction when needed. Many addicts prefer to attend NA groups, however. Today, women can choose between mixed and women-only AA and NA groups. The network of such groups is much more dense in cities than in rural areas, and women who live in large cities have many opportunities to deal with drug problems within the informal service sector.

Since the late 1960s, there has been discussion about gender differences in addiction, and their significance and consequences. The discussion began in relation to alcohol but soon extended to drugs, and it is documented in a report sponsored by the National Institute of Drug Abuse (NIDA; Beschner et al., 1981; Reed, Beschner, & Mondanaro, 1982). In 1981, Lowinson (1981), in the introduction to the first volume of the report, stated:

> The women's movement has made those responsible for treating drug abusers more sensitive to women's issues. What has been lacking, up until now, is practical advice on how to provide basic services which will be acceptable and meaningful to female clients. (p. v)

Reed (1987), who coedited the report, took up the line 6 years later, complaining that

> the purpose of this article is to examine the reasons why so little progress has been made in reaching out to and providing gender-sensitive treatment services for women experiencing problems with alcohol and other drugs. . . . Women are far less likely to be able to find treatment programs that offer many key services that they need. In fact, in many programs, a woman's experience there may increase her difficulties. (p. 151)

From Reed's point of view, progress in drug treatment for women has been slow, a view that not everyone shares.

Progress may have been slow for drug-dependent women in general, but not for pregnant women or mothers of young children. As already mentioned, there is not only an ever-growing body of literature relating to substance use and misuse during and after pregnancy but also an increasing number of services for these women (cf. Finkelstein, 1990; Mitchell, 1993). This fits into the pattern of demand for more residential services for mothers and their children and for more outpatient family services (Soman, Brindis, & Dunn-Malhotra, 1996). Gender differences trouble the treatment sector, even if they are often neglected. It is remarkably conservative, however, to react to gender differences on the basis of the biopsychological states of pregnancy and motherhood. It signifies little enthusiasm on the part of those who treat and do research on drug dependency for looking seriously at the social implications of gender differences. Also, this is not what the women's movement had in mind when they demanded gender-sensitive treatment for addicts.

In North America, gender-specific outcome evaluation studies of drug treatment have produced contradictory results. Some researchers argue (cf. Toneatto, Sobell, & Sobell, 1992) that there is no sex bias, no underrepresentation of women, and no underreporting in evaluation studies. Women, they claim, do as well as men in conventional drug treatment facilities, which they do not consider male dominated. However, their data do not refer to gender-specific treatment outcomes, for researchers have not provided such data, a fact utterly at odds with their arguments. Other researchers have been much less positive about women's place in drug treatment systems and their long-term treatment outcomes (cf. Blume, 1991; Copeland & Hall, 1992; Swift, Copeland, & Hall, 1996). Without doubt, there are too few well-designed comparative evaluation studies of residential and nonresidential mixed-gender and single-gender facilities with respect to process and outcome of treatment, topics of individual and group counseling, the structuring of everyday life and the atmosphere in the institutions, and retention rates. However, most of the studies support one remarkable result. In contrast to former assumptions, women do fairly well in drug treatment. Regardless of setting, they do either as well as men or even better. This does not answer the question of what treatment best suits women addicts, but it strongly encourages efforts to explore the matter in more detail and with better-designed evaluation studies.

The European countries differ widely regarding illicit drug use; nevertheless, it is perceived everywhere as a serious social problem. Because addicted men outnumber women in all countries, and most in the south of Europe, discussions on treatment of drug problems relate mainly to men. However, sensitivity to gender differences in treatment has increased considerably during the past 15 years. As in the United States, it has been stimulated by the women's movement, and in the late 1970s, feminist groups began to offer special programs for female addicts. They focused the discussion on violence and sexual exploitation in the development of addiction in women, neglecting other explanations and such background variables as parental addiction and the behavioral and personality problems of the women themselves. They tended to see female addicts as victims and to overlook aggressive outbursts on their part. Also, they neglected issues of research and evaluation. Whatever the shortcomings of the feminist pioneers, they helped get women-sensitive programs in addiction off the ground and even into conventional treatment settings.

Western European, including the Nordic, countries have different treatment systems for alcohol and drug addicts, with partial overlaps within subsystems such as prisons, psychiatric wards, and a few other settings. For many years, generic treatment settings were rarely discussed; generic treatment of addiction was seen as unprofessional and was expected to fail. Only recently has the possibility of bringing the systems together and closing the gap between them been discussed. A few newly set-up institutions are already experimenting with generic services, opening their doors to alcoholics as well to drug addicts. Reports of evaluation studies of the new generic services have not yet been published.

In the Nordic countries, the first approach to the control of illicit drug problems is criminalization (Stangeland, 1987), and compulsory treatment is common in Sweden and Norway but not in Finland or Denmark. If caught with illicit drugs, women have to expect the same treatment from the criminal justice system as men. Besides prisons and specially designated psychiatric wards, there is a network of private facilities for addicts, some of which are for-profit. Self-help AA and NA groups dominate the informal sector, which is used by proportionately more women than men.

Drug problems in the Nordic countries vary greatly between them, with Denmark on top, Finland at the bottom, and the other two countries in the middle. Finland has an estimated 50 to 100 female addicts and no serious management problem; yet there is some discussion on women's special needs (cf. Ettorre, 1994), which some say are inadequately met. Sweden, with an estimated 3,500 female addicts, has much more difficulty in providing enough formal and informal services for them. All Nordic countries have by now built into their treatment systems special services for women, including a small number of facilities for women only (Andersson, 1995; Middelthon, 1995). Staff receive some training to deal with women's issues. Counselors with a professional background have more gender-specific training than do recovered addicts. All Nordic-country data support the Canadian and U.S. findings that women, on the average, have a better chance of rehabilitation after treatment than do men (Berglund et al., 1991; Björling, 1993), but that women with strong ties to the drug subculture are at higher risk of relapse.

The Nordic countries also have a few specialized counseling and treatment centers for pregnant addicts and mothers of young children (Olofsson, 1993). Ten years ago, Denmark opened a clinical care facility for HIV-positive addicts who are pregnant or have other severe chronic illnesses, such as hepatitis C. The services offered include supervision during pregnancy, substitution of methadone or buprenorphine for illicit drugs, assistance during delivery, management of the neonatal abstinence syndrome, training in child care and strengthening of mothering abilities, and long-term assistance for mother and child.

Some Western European countries, such as the Netherlands, Switzerland, and Germany, have their own problems with highly visible drug scenes and drug addicts in inner cities. Internationally well-known were the Zürich drug scenes (Platzspitz and Letten), which have been closed down successfully. Less well-known are the drug scenes of Amsterdam, Hamburg, and Frankfurt, and least well-known is that of Madrid. Wherever there is an open drug scene, women take part. They hang around the meeting places just like men but are much less represented. The visibility of women in open drug scenes has spurred discussions in most countries on the nature of women-sensitive services and how to attract women to treatment.

Since the 1970s, a very small network of outpatient and inpatient drug treatment facilities for female addicts only has been built up, especially in the Netherlands (Hurkmans, 1995, 1996), Germany (Vogt, 1996), and Switzerland (Ernst et al., 1995). In the past 10 years, harm reduction approaches have predominated, and with them came low-threshold centers and experiments with outpatient treatment. Women attend the low-threshold centers but in smaller numbers than expected, and they prefer outpatient to residential services. With the institutionalization of outpatient and residential treatment facilities for female addicts only, specialty services for women have flourished in conventional institutions. Most centers now offer special group meetings for women, and a few even offer men's groups. In therapeutic communities and other residential institutions, 80% to 90% of the clients are male and 10% to 20% are female; consequently, men outnumber women by 4:1 in group meetings and thus play a dominating role. It took a long time to set up women's groups in therapeutic communities. Undoubtedly, there is an awareness that gender matters in the treatment of addiction and that it is sometimes easier to work with same-sex than with mixed-sex groups.

In those countries, informal networks such as NA or other self-help groups are weak. Help-seekers who do not want to enter the formal drug treatment systems have to go to other service centers, such as psychosomatic clinics or outpatient nonspecific counseling centers, or else receive individual psychotherapy. There are some indications that a fairly large group of addicted women chooses to avoid the drug treatment system, but reliable data are lacking.

Staff training (social workers, psychologists, physicians) in gender-specific treatment differs between countries and is rare in some (as in Germany and Switzerland). It is still up to the women's movement and to feminists to advance women's issues and demand gender-sensitive facilities and programs.

At the same time, as residential facilities began to be provided for women only, fewer women were admitted to conventional facilities, although probably not for that reason. There are so few residential facilities exclusively for women that they cannot account for the decrease in conventional admissions. It is probably due to an increase of hidden forms of compulsory treatment, which were introduced in the 1980s. For instance, in Germany, men in ever greater numbers were transferred directly from prison into residential treatment. With fewer women than men sentenced for drug offenses, ever fewer could be compelled to have residential treatment. As the numbers of women diminished, the atmosphere in the institutions changed for the worse. In turn, the increasing unpleasantness made the residential centers less attractive for voluntary patients, especially women, and those who ran the centers did little to offer women-sensitive services. Instead, they often complained that the demands of female social workers and feminists were unjustified and unnecessary.

Meanwhile, addicted women have several attractive alternatives to conventional residential centers. Given the choice, women prefer outpatient counseling centers that offer them special services, as well as medical treatment provided by general practitioners. In the 1970s, the Netherlands and Switzerland introduced methadone treatment for heroin addicts; Germany followed in the late 1980s and France in the 1990s. There has been a strong demand from women for admission to substitution programs, and they are relatively overrepresented. They often make up 40% to 50% of the patients, much higher than their proportion of drug addicts. Overall, they comply fairly well with the medical rules, and most do well on the medication. Many have changed their lifestyles, settled down, built up families, and become mothers who are now rearing their own children, often with the help of specialized social workers. This pattern is likely to be repeated when women can enter in larger numbers into heroin prescription programs for long-term treatment models for addicts, which have been set up experimentally in Switzerland (ARUD, 1994).

With more alternatives available, female addicts are more willing to fulfill their wishes of having children. Many more become pregnant or have children than in the 1970s. The services have reacted to the trend and opened up new branches for pregnant women or mothers of young children, including one center in France, which is remarkable, given that country's rather oppressive drug politics. Nevertheless, the efforts lag behind the needs. In the future, service programs have to focus more on families and mothers with children to help them break with old habits for their children's sake.

In summary, in a number of Western European countries, women have acceptable alternatives to conventional male-dominated residential treatment, such as outpatient counseling, often combined with medication, substitution therapy, and treatment exclusively for women. However, because of their ability to maintain their social networks and to use them when they are ready for natural recovery, they have taught professionals a lesson that is not often well received.

References

Adrian, M., Lundy, C., & Eliany, M. (1996). *Women's use of alcohol, tobacco and other drugs in Canada.* Toronto: Addiction Research Foundation.

Andersson, M. (1995). Women, drug abuse and treatment. In Council of Europe (Ed.), *Women and drugs* (pp. 63-74). Strasbourg: Council of Europe.

ARUD (Arbeitsgemeinschaft für risikoarmen Umgang mit Drogen). (1994). *DDD-F, Diversifizierte Drogenverschreibung und Drogenabgabe an drogenabhängige Frauen in Zürich in der ARUD Poliklinik ZOKL2* [Diversified drug-prescription for addicted women in Zürich; Preliminary Report]. 1. Bericht über die Zeit vom 29.11.1993 bis 31.5.1994 (Unpublished report). Zürich: Author.

Baer, J. S., Marlatt, G. A., & McMahon, R. J. (Eds.). (1993). *Addictive behaviors across the life span.* London: Sage.

Berglund, G. W., Bergmark, A., Björling, B., Frönbladh, L., Lindberg, S., Oscarsson, L., Olsson, B., Segraeus, V., & Stensom, C. (1991). The SWEDATE project: Interaction between treatment, client background, and outcome in a one-year follow-up. *Journal of Substance Abuse, 8,* 161-169.

Beschner, G. M., Reed, B. G., & Mondanaro, J. (1981). *Treatment services for drug dependent women, Vol. 1.* Rockville, MD: National Institute on Drug Abuse.

Biernacki, P. (1986). *Pathways from heroin addiction: Recovery without treatment.* Philadelphia: Temple University Press.

Björling, B. (1993). Female and male addicts before, during, and after treatment. In Council of Europe (Ed.), *Women and drugs* (pp. 106-118). Strasbourg: Council of Europe.

Blume, S. B. (1991). Women, alcohol, and drugs. In N. S. Miller (Ed.), *Comprehensive handbook of drug and alcohol addiction* (pp. 147-178). New York: Marcel Dekker.

Bourgois, P. (1989). In search of Horatio Alger: Culture and ideology in the crack economy. *Contemporary Drug Problems, 16,* 619-650.

Brett, P. J., Graham, K., & Smythe, C. (1995). An analysis of speciality journals on alcohol, drugs and addictive behaviors for sex bias in research methods and reporting. *Journal of Studies on Alcohol, 56,* 24-34.

Copeland, J., & Hall, W. (1992). A comparison of women seeking drug and alcohol treatment in a specialist women's and two traditional mixed-sex treatment services. *British Journal of Addiction, 87,* 1293-1327.

De Leon, G. (1995). Therapeutic communities for addictions: A theoretical framework. *International Journal of the Addictions, 30,* 1603-1646.

Driessen, F. M. H. M. (1990). *Mathodonverstrekking in Nederland* [Methadone distribution in the Netherlands]. Utrecht: Rijswijk.

Eisenbach-Stangl, I. (1995). *Geschlechtsspezifischer Umgang mit dem Körper, mit Gesundheit und Krankheit* [Gender-specific body and health care]. Bericht über die Situation der Frauen in Österreich. Frauenbericht 1995. Vienna: Bundesministerium für Frauenangelegenheiten/Bundeskanzleramt.

Erickson, P. G., Riley, D., Cheung, Y., & O'Hare, P. (Eds.). (in press). *Harm reduction: A new direction for drug policies and programs.* Toronto: University of Toronto Press.

Erickson, P. G., & Watson, V. A. (1990). Women, illicit drugs, and crime. In L. T. Kozlowski, H. M. Annis, H. D. Cappell, F. B. Glaser, M. S. Goodstadt, Y. Israel, H. Kalant, E. M. Sellers, & E. R. Vingilis (Eds.), *Research advances in alcohol and drug problems, Vol. 10* (pp. 251-272). New York: Plenum.

Ernst, M.-L., Rottenmanner, I., & Spreyermann, C. (1995). *Frauen-Sucht-Perspektiven* [Women and addictions]. Bern: Bundesamt für Gesundheitswesen.

Ettorre, E. (1994). Women and drug abuse with special reference to Finland. *Women's Studies International Forum, 17,* 83-94.

Fagan, J. (1992). Drug selling and licit income in distressed neighborhoods: The economic lives of street-level drug users and dealers, In A. Harell & G. E. Petersen (Eds.), *Drugs, crime, and social isolation: Barriers to urban opportunity* (pp. 99-146). Washington, DC: Urban Institute Press.

Fagan, J. (1994). Women and drugs revisited: Female participation in the cocaine economy. *Journal of Drug Issues, 24,* 179-225.

Ferrence, R., Annis, H., Graham, K., Harrison, S., Kalant, H., & Room, R. (1994). *Gender issues in addictions research. The report of the task group on gender-focused research.* Toronto: Addiction Research Foundation.

Finkelstein, N. (1990). *Pregnancy and exposure to alcohol and other drug use: CSAP Technical Report—7.* Rockville, MD: U.S. Department of Health and Human Services.

Happel, V.-H., Fischer, R., & Wittfeld, I. (1993). *Selbstorganisierter Ausstieg. Überwindung der Drogenabhängigkeit ohne professionelle Hilfe* [Maturing out of drug dependence] (Unpublished report). Frankfurt: Fachhochschule Frankfurt am Main, Fachbereich Sozialpädagogik.

Harrison, P. A., Hoffmann, N. G., & Streed, S. G. (1991). Drug and alcohol addiction treatment outcome. In N. S. Miller (Ed.), *Comprehensive handbook of drug and alcohol addiction* (pp. 1163-1197). New York: Marcel Dekker.

Health and Welfare Canada. (1990). *National alcohol and other drugs survey: Highlights report.* Ottawa: Minister of Supply and Services.

Herbst, K., Kraus, L., Scherer, L., & Schumann, J. (1995). *Repräsentativerhebung zum Gebrauch psychoaktiver Substanzen bei Erwachsenen in Deutschland—Telefonische Erhebung 1994* [Representative epidemiological study of adult consumption of psychoactive substances in Germany—Telephone survey in 1994]. Munich: Institut für Therapieforschung.

Hurkmans, I. (1995). Clinic for addicted women of all kinds. *Jellinek Quarterly, 2,* 6-7.

Hurkmans, I. (1996). Power to cope with the clean world. *Jellinek Quarterly, 3,* 6.

Inciardi, J. A., Lockwood, D., & Pottieger, A. E. (1993). *Women and crack cocaine.* New York: Macmillan.

Institute of Medicine. (1990). *Broadening the base of treatment for alcohol problems.* Washington, DC: National Academy Press.

Ireland, T., & Widom, C. S. (1994). Childhood victimization and risk for alcohol and drug arrests. *International Journal of the Addictions, 29,* 235-274.

Jessor, R., & Jessor, S. L. (1977). *Problem behavior and psychosocial development.* New York: Academic Press.

Kandall, S. R. (1995). *Improving treatment for drug-exposed infants.* Rockville, MD: Center for Substance Abuse Treatment.

Kinnunen, A. (1996). *Isännät, rengit ja pokat. Huumemarkkinat ja oheisrikollisuus Helsingissä* [Drug markets and drug related crime in Helsinki]. Helsinki: Oikeuspoliittisen tutkimuslaitoksen julkaisuja 133.

Klingemann, H. (1990). "Der Freitag wo alles kaputt war" oder "die Macht des Positiven"? Eine dimensionale Analyse "natürlicher Heilungen" bei kritischem Alkohol- und Heroinkonsum ["The Friday when I was hitting bottom" or "the power of the positive." Dimensions of natural recoveries from problem alcohol- and heroin use]. *Zeitschrift für Soziologie, 19,* 444-457.

Kontula, O. (1995). The prevalence of drug use with reference to problem use in Finland. *International Journal of the Addictions, 30,* 1053-1066.

Ladwig, G. B., & Andersen, M. D. (1989). Substance abuse in women: Relationship between chemical dependency of women and past reports of physical and/or sexual abuse. *International Journal of the Addictions, 24,* 739-754.

Lee, R. W. (1991). *The white labyrinth.* London: Sage.

Leopold, B., & Steffan, E. (in press). *Special needs of children of drug misusers.* Strasbourg: Council of Europe.

Lightfoot, L., Adrian, M., Leigh, G., & Thompson, J. (1996a). Substance abuse: Prevention and treatment for women. In M. Adrian, C. Lundy, & M. Eliany (Eds.), *Women's use of alcohol, tobacco and other drugs in Canada* (pp. 186-207). Toronto: Addiction Research Foundation.

Lightfoot, L., Adrian, M., Leigh, G., & Thompson, J. (1996b). Women's use of and views of substance abuse treatment. In M. Adrian, C. Lundy, & M. Eliany (Eds.), *Women's use of alcohol, tobacco and other drugs in Canada* (pp. 208-227). Toronto: Addiction Research Foundation.

Lowinson, J. E. (1981). Foreword. In G. M. Beschner, G. Reed, & J. Mondanaro (Eds.), *Treatment services for drug dependent women, Vol. 1* (pp. v-vi). Rockville, MD: National Institute on Drug Abuse.

Middelthon, A.-L. (1995). Development of services for women drug users in Norway. In Council of Europe (Ed.), *Women and drugs* (pp. 29-38). Strasbourg: Council of Europe.

Ministère de l'Intérieur. (1991). *Infraction à la législation sur les stupéfiants. Usage de drogues en France. Les statistiques de l'année 1991* [Crimes against drug laws. Use of drugs in France. Statistics of the year 1991]. Paris: Author.

Mitchell, J. L. (1993). *Pregnant, substance-using women: Treatment improvement protocol (TIP) series.* Rockville, MD: Center for Substance Abuse Treatment.

Morgan, P., & Joe, K. A. (1996). Citizens and outlaws: The private lives and public lifestyles of women in the illicit drug economy. *Journal of Drug Issues, 26,* 125-142.

Musto, D. F. (1973). *The American disease.* New Haven, CT: Yale University Press.

NIDA (National Institute on Drug Abuse). (1987). *National household survey on drug abuse: Population estimates 1985.* Rockville, MD: Author.

Olofsson, M. (1993). The care of pregnant drug users and those with babies/small children: The well-being of the mother and the child. In Council of Europe (Ed.), *Women and drugs* (pp. 63-76). Strasbourg: Council of Europe.

Paone, D. (1997, April). *Reframing the debate: Effective treatment for crack using women.* Paper presented at the 8th International Conference on the Reduction of Drug Related Harm, Paris.

Parsons, T., Bales, R. F., Olds, J., Zelditch, M., & Slater, P. E. (1955). *Family, socialization, and interaction process.* New York: Free Press.

Pedersen, W., & Skrondal, A. (1996). Alcohol and sexual victimization: A longitudinal study of Norwegian girls. *Addiction, 91,* 565-581.

Popham, R. E., DeLint, J. E. E., & Schmidt, W. (1968). Some comments on Pittman's "rush to combine." *British Journal of Addiction, 63,* 25-27.

Powis, B., Griffiths, P., Gossop, M., & Strang, J. (1996). The differences between male and female drug users: Community samples of heroin and cocaine users compared. *International Journal of the Addictions, 31,* 529-544.

Reed, B. G. (1987). Developing women-sensitive drug dependence treatment services: Why so difficult? *Journal of Psychoactive Drugs, 19,* 151-164.

Reed, B. G., Beschner, G. M., & Mondanaro, J. (1982). *Treatment services for drug dependent women, Vol. 2.* Rockville, MD: National Institute on Drug Abuse.

Rehm, J. (1994). Aktuelle Prävelanz des Konsums illegaler Drogen in der Schweiz. Neue Daten aus der Schweizerischen Gesundheitsbefragung 1992/93 [Brand-new prevalence data of consumption pattern of illegal drugs in Switzerland, 1992/93]. *Drogalkohol, 18,* 85-94.

Reuband, K.-H. (1995). Drug use and drug policy in Western Europe. *European Addiction Research, 1,* 32-41.

Riska, E., Kühlhorn, E., Nordlund, S., & Skinhoj, K. T. (Eds.). (1993). *Minor tranquilizers in the Nordic countries.* Helsinki: Nordic Council for Alcohol and Drug Research.

Rush, B. (1996). Editorial: Alcohol and other drug problems and treatment systems: A framework for research and development. *Addiction, 91,* 629-642.

Schmidt, L., & Weisner, C. (1993). Developments in alcoholism treatment. In M. Galanter (Ed.), *Recent developments in alcoholism* (pp. 369-396). New York: Plenum.

Schweizerische Fachstelle für Alkohol- und andere Drogenprobleme (SFA). (1993). *Zahlen und Fakten zu Alkohol und anderen Drogen 1993* [Facts and figures on alcohol and other drugs]. Lausanne: Author.

Solomon, K. (1982). Counselling the drug dependent women: Special issues for men. In B. G. Reed, G. M. Beschner, & J. Mondanaro (Eds.), *Treatment services for drug dependent women, Vol. II* (pp. 572-612). Washington, DC: Government Printing Office.

Soman, L. A., Brindis, C., & Dunn-Malhotra, E. (1996). The interplay of national, state, and local policy in financing care for drug-affected women and children in California. *Journal of Psychoactive Drugs, 28,* 3-15.

Stangeland, P. (1987). *Drugs and drug control: The Scandinavian experience.* Oslo: Norwegian University Press.

Swedish Council for Information on Alcohol and Other Drugs (CAN). (1991). *Report 91, trends in alcohol and drug use in Sweden.* Stockholm: Author.

Swift, W., Copeland, J., & Hall, W. (1996). Characteristics of women with alcohol and other drug problems: Findings of an Australian national survey. *Addiction, 91,* 1141-1150.

Takala, J.-P., Klingemann, H., & Hunt, G. (1992). Afterword: Common directions and remaining divergences. In H. Klingemann, J.-P. Takala, & G. Hunt (Eds.), *Cure, care, or control: Alcoholism treatment in sixteen countries* (pp. 285-304). Albany: State University of New York Press.

Thom, B. (1994). Women and alcohol: The emergence of a risk group. In M. McDonald (Ed.), *Gender, drink and drugs* (pp. 33-54). Oxford, UK: Berg.

Toneatto, A., Sobell, L. C., & Sobell, M. B. (1992). Gender issues in the treatment of abusers of alcohol, nicotine, and other drugs. *Journal of Substance Abuse, 4,* 209-218.

Vogt, I. (1985). *Für alle Leiden gibt es eine Pille* [A pill for all seasons]. Opladen, Germany: Westdeutscher Verlag.

Vogt, I. (1995). Women and addiction: A frame of reference for theory and practice. In Council of Europe (Ed.), *Women and drugs* (pp. 3-28). Strasbourg: Council of Europe.

Vogt, I. (1996). Frauen und psychotrope Substanzen: Konsummuster, Abhängigkeiten und die Suchtkrankenhilfe [Women and psychotropic substances: Their consumption patterns, addictions, and the helping services]. *Zeitschrift für Frauenforschung, 14,* 117-128.

Vogt, I. (1997). *"BELLA DONNA"—die Frauendrogenberatungsstelle im Ruhrgebiet* ["BELLA DONNA"—The drug counseling center for women in the Ruhr region]. Berlin: Verlag für Wissenschaft und Bildung.

Weber, E. L. (1992). Alcohol- and drug-dependent pregnant women: Laws and public policies that promote and inhibit research and the delivery of services. In M. M. Kilbey & K. Asghar (Eds.), *Methodological issues in epidemiological, prevention, and treatment research on drug-exposed women and their children* (pp. 349-365). Rockville, MD: National Institute on Drug Abuse.

Zurhold, H. (1993). *Drogenkarrieren von Frauen im Spiegel ihrer Lebensgeschichte.* Berlin: Verlag für Wissenschaft und Bildung.

Chapter 30

The Relationship Between
Alcohol and Drug Treatment Systems

Anders Bergmark

In some countries, drug treatment systems—in their financing, methods of treatment, dominant professional control, and legal framework—directly follow the model of a larger and preexisting alcohol treatment system; in other countries, the systems are organized and function very differently. To be unclear about or to disregard the degree to which alcohol and drug treatment systems are integrated or overlap (or indeed are identical) is to risk having a distorted view of the resources allotted to drug treatment as well as of the numbers of drug users treated.

This chapter describes and discusses the relationship between the alcohol and drug treatment systems in the countries covered in this book on the basis of the material contained in the country chapters or of information obtained from an unpretentious survey of the relationship between the two systems in each country. Because the chapters are not standardized and the survey questionnaire was basic and completed only by the authors of the country chapters, the information available may not be sufficiently representative to permit valid conclusions to be drawn.

Perspectives on Integration

To determine the extent to which drug and alcohol treatment systems are integrated, it is first necessary to know how the terms and concepts concerned, namely "system," "integration," and "drug and alcohol treatment," are defined. It is beyond the scope of this chapter to analyze these concepts in any depth; instead, this chapter deals with some of the associated issues.

The ad hoc definition of "drug treatment system," for the purposes of the ISDRUTS study, refers to treatment measures and to the organizations that explicitly offer drug users treatment or help. Although the definition is reasonable, it assumes that a country's drug and alcohol treatment systems are identical, as if both systems were included under "substance abuse treatment" or "dependency care," which is largely the case in the Netherlands. In other places, the systems may be identical in that drug treatment is, in effect, part of the alcohol treatment system, as in Finland, although the Finnish system differs in certain respects from that of the Netherlands. An amalgamation of alcohol and drug treatment under "dependency" or "substance abuse" represents an integration different in type from that in which drug treatment is provided by a predominantly alcohol treatment system.

Degree of integration may also be assessed with reference to a number of features shared by both systems, such as sources of financing, treatment methods, and dominant type of profession; these features may be regarded as indicators of degree of integration.

In many cases, the categorizations in Table 30.1 oversimplify the actual circumstances. For example, the "no" concerning domination of the same type of professions within alcohol and drug treatment in Germany covers the fact that the same professions (social workers, physicians, and psychologists) are the dominant professions in both alcohol and drug treatment, but the relative weights of these professions are different within each system; in drug treatment, social workers are more important than physicians, whereas the relationship is the opposite within alcohol treatment (the decision of whether or not this type of situation should be interpreted/truncated into a "yes" or a "no" has been made by the authors of the chapter on Germany).

Table 30.1 indicates that the prevailing pattern is one of common source of financing and same type of profession dominating both alcohol and drug treatment; similarity in treatment methods is somewhat less prevalent. The exceptions to correspondence between financing and professional domination are Germany, the United States, and Switzerland; this may be attributable in Germany and the United States to their complex financing arrangements. In the United States, a distinct division between privately and publicly funded treatment is common to both alcohol and drug treatment. In Germany, the division is between public and semipublic sources of funding.

Similarities or differences between methods of alcohol and drug treatment in any country are not simple and direct indicators of integration or the degree of, or lack of, integration of the two systems. In Japan, both systems have common methods of treatment but differ regarding source of funding and professional dominance, and, as indicated below, there is a very low degree of integration. The treatment methods are similar apparently because drug treatment methods were modeled on those of the previously established alcohol system, but the systems are kept apart because society attaches very different symbolic meanings to alcohol

Table 30.1 Presence of Same Type of Major Source of Financing of Alcohol and Drug
Treatment, Same Type of Profession Dominating Both Alcohol and Drug
Treatment, and Domination of the Same Type of Treatment Methods in
Alcohol and Drug Treatment

Country	Same Type of Financing	Same Type of Dominant Profession	Same Types of Treatment Method
Austria	Yes	Yes	Yes
Canada	Yes	Yes	Yes
China	Yes	Yes	No
Colombia	No	No	No
England	Yes	Yes	No
Finland	Yes	Yes	Yes
France	Yes	Yes	No
Germany	Yes	No	No
Hungary	Yes	Yes	Yes
Japan	No	No	Yes
Netherlands	Yes	Yes	Yes
Peru	Yes	Yes	No
Poland	Yes	Yes	No
Portugal	Yes	Yes	Yes
Russia	Yes	Yes	No
Spain	No	No	No
Sweden	Yes	Yes	Yes
Switzerland	Yes	No	No
United States	Yes	No	No

and drugs and has instituted very different arrangements for dealing with alcohol
and drug problems. In line with the observation of Roizen (1993) that the "alcoholism paradigm emphasizes treatment whereas the illicit-drug paradigm emphasizes enforcing the taboo" (p. 4), Japan's drug treatment methods seem to be
determined largely by its strategies for controlling drug abuse.

The degree of integration of the alcohol and drug treatment systems in each
country has also been expressed by a comprehensive measure in the country
survey, namely, a straightforward estimation of degree of integration (on an analog
scale with the endpoints "No integration" and "Completely integrated"). By and
large, this estimation confirms that common financing sources, dominant profession, and treatment methods are valid indicators of degree of integration.

To determine whether integration, both as a general characteristic and in more
particular respects, is associated with the extent to which the public considers
alcohol and drug problems to be serious, questions on the issue were included in
the country survey. The responses did not support an a priori assumption that a
relatively high degree of integration could be expected in countries with a "temperance culture," where alcohol consumption is viewed as a serious problem.

The relationship between degree of integration of the treatment systems and
whether the public sees alcohol or drugs as the greater problem is shown in Figure
30.1, although neither variable is displayed in "direct" form. Instead, Figure 30.1
represents an output from a statistical computation that is commonly labeled an
"optimal scaling" procedure. More specifically, it is an output from a PRINCALS

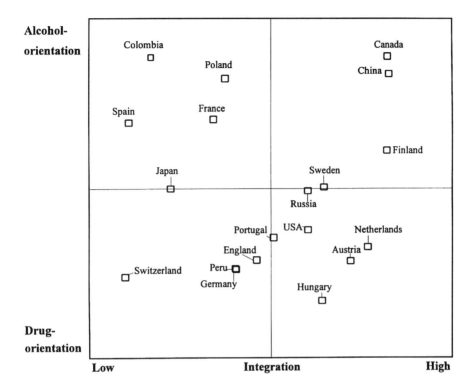

Figure 30.1 The Degree of Integration Between Alcohol and Drug Treatment Systems, and the Relative Degree to Which the Public Sees Drugs or Alcohol as the More Serious Problem in the Different ISDRUTS Countries

NOTE: By inspecting "component loadings" and "categories quantifications," one can judge the extent to which the solution reflects a clear separation between the variables connected with integration (e.g., degree of integration, same type of financing sources, same type of dominant profession, and same types of treatment method) and the variable of the extent to which the public sees drugs or alcohol as the more serious problem. The configuration of component loadings and categories quantifications indicates that the latter variable is almost perfectly parallel with the *y* axis, and the other variables are closely connected to the *x* axis.

(principal components analysis by means of alternating least squares) procedure in the statistical package SPSS. Like classical principal components analysis, PRINCALS can be a method of data reduction. The two types of analysis differ mainly in that PRINCALS can perform nonlinear analysis and deal with variables at different levels of measurement (nominal, ordinal, interval, and ratio).

Figure 30.1 represents a two-dimensional solution of a five-variable data set, namely degree of integration, relative intensity of the drug problem vis-à-vis the alcohol problem, same type of financing source (presence/absence), same type of dominant profession (presence/absence), and same type of treatment method (presence/absence). It is not the solution in itself that is of chief interest here but, rather, the distribution of the different countries within the two-dimensional space: The analysis can be expected to show integration as the first dimension and drug or alcohol orientation as the second. In the interpretation of the positions of different countries in Figure 30.1, two factors must be kept in mind: one is that the analysis in itself should not be compared with results from techniques that have a confirmatory purpose—PRINCALS is mainly an exploratory technique that provides opportunities for graphic presentations of relations between objects (observations) as well as variables; the other is that the variable that substantiates the dimension of drug or alcohol orientation is a construct that reflects a relative level of seriousness of the drug or alcohol problem—this is because the variable in question is the product of a calculation whereby the perception of the seriousness of the alcohol problem has been subtracted from a corresponding measure of the drug problem. Hence, the position of any given country on the dimension of drug or alcohol orientation does not necessarily reflect the absolute magnitude of an alcohol or drug problem.

In general, in most countries, drugs tend to constitute the more serious problem.[1] In absolute (raw) figures, only five countries exhibit a negative total. Figure 30.1 shows that the origin does not represent a zero for the absolute values. Instead, the countries arranged along the x axis—Japan, Sweden, and Russia—have positive (absolute) values between 2 and 3. Sweden, where both alcohol and drug abuse are considered to be serious social problems, holds a middle position, because the difference in public perception of alcohol and drugs as serious problems is less than in Hungary, for example, where drugs score high and alcohol scores low. Hence, the position of Hungary in the lower right corner of Figure 30.1 is attributable to the substantial difference between the public perception of the seriousness of alcohol problems and that of drug problems. However, the absolute values for the perception of the seriousness of the drug problem are slightly higher in Sweden than in Hungary.

The distribution on the second dimension—degree of integration between the treatment systems—is less complicated in that the countries' varying combinations of financing sources, dominant profession, treatment methods, and degree of integration determine their different positions.

As Figure 30.1 shows, Switzerland and the Netherlands, which are usually described as "experimental" or liberal in their social responses to drug problems, are similar in their drug orientation but very dissimilar in degree of integration of their treatment systems.[2] This may be attributable to the distinction made in the Netherlands between hard and soft drugs; the corresponding erosion of the institutional borders between alcohol and drug use; and the consequent likely integration of alcohol and drug treatment, which (in the form of a substance-dependence rubric) may be seen as a manifestation of such erosion. In the case of Switzerland, there is no clear tendency to abolish the borders between alcohol and drugs; instead, we might interpret the present situation—the seriousness of the drug problem in the public view, the low degree of integration, and the use of a harm reduction approach—as indications that the Swiss drug treatment system is "walking on a tightrope." Minor changes in public opinion could possibly turn the system upside down, and Switzerland could become one of the control-oriented countries instead of one of the most liberal.

Of the countries in the top left corner in Figure 30.1—those characterized by an alcohol orientation and a low degree of integration—some are more or less without any real possibilities for integration for the simple reason that there are no systems to integrate. In the case of Colombia, both alcohol and drug treatment, to a certain extent, seem to lack system characteristics. Drug treatment in France is by and large controlled by the medical profession, but the treatment approaches have not been institutionalized. It is a field characterized by a lack of constraints concerning medical practice, and hence the organization of drug treatment is not complex enough to identify an interaction with alcohol treatment—it is still "a system in its starting blocks" (see Mossé in this volume).

Of the countries that combine an alcohol orientation with a high degree of integration—the countries in the top right corner in Figure 30.1—Canada (Ontario) exhibits an "addiction" or "substance abuse" type of integration, whereas the situation in China seems to be related mainly to the dominance of the medical profession. Canada's public health approach has partly succeeded in creating a professional and public acceptance of addiction as a complex psychosocial phenomenon requiring medical and psychological treatment and not simply as the indulgence of social outcasts who deserve punishment. But unlike the Netherlands, which also has integration of the dependence/addiction type, the situation in Canada, to a certain extent, seems to be a product of professional efforts rather than to a prevailing liberal attitude (see Derks, Hoekstra, and Kaplan in this volume). The alcohol orientation in Canada can be attributed to professionals having successfully maintained the profiles of alcohol and tobacco as the drugs of greatest concern (see Ogborne, Smart, and Rush in this volume).

Polydrug Users: A Reason for Combined Treatment?

Now and then, integration between alcohol and drug treatment is advocated and justified with reference to the existence of a profound misconception concerning individual drug consumption—it is maintained that the classic addict, characterized by the relation to the specific properties of his or her (single) drug, is an illusion that should be replaced by the observation that a majority of drug users are polydrug users.

It is clear that this type of claim has a bearing on the situation of the drug problem in many of the ISDRUTS countries. Between 20% and 90% of the populations within each different drug treatment system are identified as polydrug users (median 55%). But it is not entirely clear, however, what type of empirical phenomenon these polydrug users represent.

The different terms that can be found in relation to this topic reflect some of the difficulties that are involved. Whereas concepts such as "multihabituation," multiple drug abuse, and polyvalent abuse are mainly related to patterns of consumption, concepts such as "polytoximania" and "multiple dependence" represent efforts to connect with different notions of addiction (Cohen, 1981; Keup, 1990). Yet if the empirical approach focusing on drug consumption patterns/combinations a priori can be considered the most attractive option for polydrug definition, description, and classification (because it makes it possible to avoid many of the theoretical problems connected to the concepts of dependency, compulsion, and addiction), this might not always be true in practice. A major reason for the shortcomings of the empirical approach is the difficulty of getting a sufficient amount of information concerning the consumption pattern. In 1992, a country-wide case-finding study in Sweden reported that 77% of "heavy drug abusers" used two or more substances (not including alcohol), but it yielded no systematic information on the intensity and stability of the drug use; this undermined its purpose, which was to determine the prevalence of "heavy drug abuse."

The alternative approach, to try to estimate the prevalence of what Keup (1990) designates as monopolar, bipolar, or "multipolar" drug dependence is beset by the difficulties of establishing criteria for the diagnosis of dependence.[3] In practice, however, the use of dependence as a point of reference has resulted in more detailed information than could be obtained from the use of other points of reference, and hence a more solid empirical base for studies on polydrug use.

The term "polydrug" gives no indication of the high number of possible combinations of different substances. In practice, however, two main types of combination can be distinguished. Keup (1990) has characterized the "hard core" of polydrug users as consisting of "alcohol dependents who are also dependent upon medical drugs and illegal drug users who also are dependent upon alcohol and/or medical drugs" (p. 126).

The variation in the estimated proportion of polydrug users in the different countries is likely to be related both to differences in the interpretation of the term polydrug and to the demarcation of the population concerned. Also, polydrug use is likely to have developed for different reasons in different countries. In some cases—the United States, for example—it is possible that some erosion of the institutional border between alcohol and illicit drugs may have occurred in that a larger proportion of individuals with alcohol problems also develops problems with substances such as cannabis and cocaine. In other cases, an increase of reported/identified polydrug abuse could be due to a more careful study of consumption patterns of alcohol and different types of drugs among individuals identified as drug users.

Some claim that the discovery that polydrug use is widespread has made it possible to give up classifications based on specific types of drug use for more complex and accurate classifications of drug use problems. This is not necessarily the case, however. Polydrug use can be regarded as a variant of terms employed to designate use of different specified substances, either in combinations or singly; designations based on single drugs are merely replaced by others indicating different blends of drug use. A different perspective on classification of drug problems may be obtained from the empirical configuration of polydrug abuse, which indicates two basic forms: alcohol and "medical drugs"; and alcohol, medical drugs, and illicit drugs (Keup, 1990). That is to say, the institutional division between alcohol and drugs may largely determine how we perceive and handle problems connected with polydrug use. In line with the suggestions put forward by Fingarette (1988), a conceptualization that reorganizes polydrug problems as different types of "way-of-life" problems might be fruitful, because such an approach can incorporate all of the problems that are connected with the fact that the illegality of certain drugs has major consequences for the drug users' way of life.

Perspectives on the Future of Integration

Clearly, the material presented in this chapter can reveal no systematic pattern of the interrelationships of alcohol treatment and drug treatment systems. Instead, it indicates more or less unique national configurations. The ways in which the specific configurations of professional dominance, financing structures, control policy, and relative magnitude of drug and alcohol problems came about in each country have determined the present position. Nevertheless, there are certain features that characterize the relation between alcohol and drug treatment systems in general. Roizen (1993) has suggested four possible developments, any of which could favor the merging of alcohol and drug systems:

> (1) a shift toward the "drug-ification" of alcohol; (2) a shift toward the "alcoholization" of drug problems; (3) the emergence of some sort of moral/pragmatic middle ground, defined by melding the two domains' social paradigms; or (4) the development of a new social paradigm whose structure somehow redefined and accommodated the requirements of both formerly distinct problem areas. (p. 8)

Although Roizen's analysis refers mainly to the United States, it is generally applicable.

The "drug-ification" of alcohol problems should be understood as an increase in the degree to which the public views alcohol consumption as a serious problem. This is occurring, and the rationale for such "drug-ification" is articulated in different types of discourses. The new health awareness constitutes a different motive than, for example, the reasoning advanced by the Mothers Against Drunk Driving organization in the United States, which has set out to increase public awareness of the problems caused by alcohol and motor vehicles.

The "alcoholization" of drugs would then comprise efforts to diminish the seriousness of drug use in the public's view, not primarily to do with legalization of drugs but with a less punitive approach and with such alternatives as reduction of demand and harm reduction. In many instances, it seems as if this type of development is fueled by arguments that refer to the failures, or economical consequences, of alternative tough approaches. Hence, it seems possible to claim that countries such as Germany, Switzerland, and the Netherlands exhibit tendencies of this form.

An emphasis on "technical" measures, such as primary prevention for both alcohol and drug problems, can be regarded as an exponent for a pragmatic middle ground. To some extent, a development associated with this scenario can be found in Sweden. Mäkelä (1983) has pointed out that the management of the alcohol issue in Sweden gradually has been drifting away from the temperance movement toward a small group of bureaucrats/researchers that mainly embrace a technical—not a moral—perspective on the alcohol issue. This technical perspective has, over time, expanded in such a fashion that it now also is an important doctrine in the formation of drug problem strategies, as well as actions directed toward both alcohol and drug consumption.

Even if a public health approach to alcohol and drug problems cannot be considered to represent a paradigm with clearly defined characteristics,[4] Roizen (1993) identifies it as the only serious candidate for his fourth option—the new social paradigm. The relative "fuzziness" of this paradigm is illustrated by the fact that it can be seen as a summation of the first three options; that is, a public health approach comprises a reproblematization of alcohol use, a deproblematization of drug use, and a technical (i.e., nonmoralistic) approach when it comes to problem interventions. In this book, Canada provides the most distinctive example of the public health approach. Canadian health professionals have successfully maintained the profiles of alcohol and tobacco as the substances of greatest concern (see Ogborne, Smart, and Rush in this volume). Their objective, expert advice has become established as the rule for society, and it explicitly gives alcohol (and tobacco) use the status of a public health problem, thus implicitly "downgrading" drugs as a problem. However, the French experience (see Mossé in this volume) shows that when the public health model of alcohol and drug treatment is incorporated into medical specialization, the two systems are less likely to be merged than to remain separate.

It is not altogether unrealistic that an expansion of the public health approach also could bring about more integration between alcohol and drug treatment systems. At the same time, it might be wise to remember that such a development does not necessarily represent "progress." Thirty years ago, Pittman (1967) criticized the Addiction Research Foundation (ARF) in Toronto, Canada, for their "rush to combine." Pittman identified the combination of alcoholism and drug abuse programs as based on the oversimplified rationale that both phenomena involved dependence. Thus, neither the practice of treatment integration nor the criticism of such activities represents something totally new. Moreover, Pittman's challenge cannot be considered entirely outdated. We do not know for sure that it is better to organize our treatment systems with the dependence concept as the bedrock, instead of placing focus on the sociocultural aspects put forward by Pittman.

Notes

1. The public view on whether alcohol or drugs is the more serious problem has been measured on scales ranging from 1 to 13, and accordingly, the possible variation can be found between −12 to 12; the actual variation is −4 to 8.

2. However, there is a recent trend in Switzerland to merge outpatient-specific services with drug counseling services, and both were possible with the even more unspecific social services.

3. The term *monopolar polydrug dependence* refers to dependence upon a main substance plus simple abuse of additional substances; *bipolar polydrug dependence* refers to dependence upon two substances, in different main substance groups, and possibly simple abuse of other substances; *multipolar polydrug dependence* refers to dependence on three or more substances, and possibly simple abuse of other substances (Keup, 1990).

4. Roizen (1993) provides the following list of possible public health species: classic agent-host-environment model, risk factor model, demand reduction model, single distribution model, and community organization model, but he also notes that such complexity might be a necessary property of a paradigm that should serve to integrate many different purposes.

References

Cohen, S. (1981). *Substance abuse problems.* New York: Haworth.

Fingarette, H. (1988). *Heavy drinking: The myth of alcoholism as a disease.* Berkeley: University of California Press.

Keup, W. (1990). Polydrug abuse: Standards for comparative measures. In M. Plant, C. Goos, W. Keup, & E. Österberg (Eds.), *Alcohol and drugs—Research and policy* (pp. 125-141). Edinburgh: Edinburgh University Press.

Mäkelä, K. (1983). Alkoholkonsumtionens vågrörelser och alkoholfrågans historiska former [The waves of alcohol consumption, and the historical configurations of the alcohol issue]. *Sociologisk Forskning, 20*(1), 11-19.

Pittman, D. (1967). The rush to combine. *British Journal of Addiction, 63,* 337-343.

Roizen, R. (1993, October). *Merging alcohol and illicit drugs: A brief commentary on the search for symbolic middle ground.* Paper presented at the International Conference on Alcohol and Drug Treatment Systems Research, Toronto, Canada.

Appendix: Summary Table

Country	Size of Population[a]	Political Economy[b]	Surface Area (sq. km)[c]	Urban/Rural Area (%)[d]	GNP 1993 (current dollars)[e]	Unemployment Rate 1995 (%)[f]
Austria	7,995,000	Left-Catholic corporatist[g]	83,858	65/35	180	4.6
Canada	28,114,000	Least corporatist	9,971,000	76.2/23.8	526	9.5
China	1,190,431,000	Democracy in transition	9,600,000	60/40	2,047	5.2 in urban areas; substanial under-employment
Colombia	35,578,000	Democracy in transition	1,138,910	NA	47	9.5
England	48,707,000	Least corporatist	128,632	56/44	938	8.6
Finland	5,069,000	Left corporatist	338,145	81.6/18.4	78	17.0
France	57,840,000	Corporatist without labor	550,000	81/19	1,239	11.7
Germany	81,088,000	Catholic corporatist	356,978	63/37	1,698	West, 8.7; East, 14.9
Hungary	10,319,000	Democracy in transition	93,030	62.2/37.8	64	10.4
Italy	58,138,000	Catholic corporatist	301,000	35.6/64.4	975	12.2
Japan	125,107,000	Corporatist without labor	377,800	24/76	4,260	3.1
Netherlands	15,368,000	Left-Catholic corporatist	34,000	68/32	299	7.1
Peru	23,465,000	Democracy in transition	11,285,216	NA	39	15; extensive under-employment
Poland	38,655,000	Catholic corporatist	321,000	NA	193	14.9
Russia	149,609,000	Democracy in transition	17,075,000	73/27	777	8.2; extensive under-employment
Spain	39,600,000	Least corporatist	504,782	75.5/24.5	472	22.8
Sweden	8,778,000	Left corporatist	449,964	NA	179	7.8
Switzerland	7,207,060	Corporatist without labor	41,290	NA	244	3.3
United States	258,245,000	Least corporatist	9,628,382	75.2/24.8	6,348	5.6

a. Taken from U.S. Bureau of the Census, *World Population Profiles, 1994.*
b. Taken from H. L. Wilensky, *Tax and spend: The political economy and performance of rich democracies* (forthcoming).
c. Taken from Central Intelligence Agency, *The World Factbook 1996.*
d. Authors' estimates.
e. Taken from Organization for Economic Cooperation and Development, *Annual growth rates of real gross domestic product, 1995* (annual).
f. Taken from Central Intelligence Agency, *The World Factbook 1996.*
g. *Corporatism* is a highly institutionalized method of aggregating interests of key actors in the political economy such that labor, industry, and the state bargain together to create policy and work together to ensure its implementation.

Glossary

Alcohol tithe/*Alkoholzehntel* *(Switzerland):* The Swiss Constitution (art. 32, paragraph 9) provides for the net income of the Alcohol Administration to be set aside for social purposes, a provision unique in the world. The income is divided equally between the federal government, for the Old Age and Widows and Orphans Pension Scheme and the Invalid Insurance, and the cantons, according to their populations. The cantons receive 10% of it (US$8.2 million for the budget year 1996-1997) earmarked to combat the causes and effects of alcoholism, drug dependency, and the abuse of generic drugs.

Approved institutions/*Anerkannte Einrichtungen* *(Austria):* A category of inpatient and outpatient facilities introduced by the amendment of the narcotic law in 1980. Since then, the Ministry of Health has to "approve" institutions, which then become the designated institutions for the treatment of those who are on probation under the narcotic law.

Autonomous communities/*Comunidades Autónomas* *(Spain):* The autonomous communities are the 19 political and administrative divisions that make up the Spanish State. They enjoy various degrees of political and fiscal autonomy. Most have set up their own (regional) plans on drugs.

Basuco* (coca paste) *(Colombia): A compound obtained from mixing coca leaf with benzoic acid, methanol, kerosene or leaded gasoline, cocaine sulfate, sulfuric acid, and other alkaloids. The mixture yields coca paste, also known as *basuco* in Colombia. When smoked, its combustion is rich in fumes of freebase cocaine.

Canada Health Act *(Canada):* A federal law that guarantees federal health funding to provinces that support universally accessible health services.

Chacchar/Chacchado* *(Peru): A Quechuan word for the traditional use of coca leaves by Andean people; it represents the act of chewing the leaves and swallowing the juices produced.

Coffee shop *(Netherlands):* The most prominent feature of the "separation-of-markets policy" in the Netherlands and a mainstay of Dutch drug policy. It represents a distinction in the marketing of illicit drugs between hard drugs (heroin, cocaine, amphetamines)—which are treated as black-market commodities and in which trafficking incurs severe penalties—and soft drugs (cannabis), which may be marketed in the open in a system of so-called coffee shops ("hash cafes"). The logic of this distinction is that drugs of unacceptable risk (hard drugs) are to be marketed differently from drugs of acceptable risk (cannabis) and that the markets should be separated so as to prevent soft drug users from being exposed to hard drugs.

Community drug team (CDT) *(England):* A community-based team comprising community psychiatric nurses and social workers that provides training and support functions for generic health services and acts as a link between generalist and specialist services; its members also carry a client caseload.

Consultation Center for Alcohol and Drugs/Consultatiebureau voor Alcohol en Drugs—CAD; Categorical care *(Netherlands):* This is the main service center within the "categorical care system" for addicts: a nationwide network of institutions for outpatient treatment, care, and advice for addicts (alcohol, drugs, prescribed medicines, gambling). The system is called *categorical* because it serves addicts only, not nonaddicted psychiatric patients. Therefore, to be eligible for CAD services, individuals must be addicted to, or at least manifest problem behavior related to abuse of, psychotropic substances or gambling. CADs are members of the Dutch Association of Addiction Treatment and Care Centres.

D'66 *(Netherlands):* A left-wing political party (Democratic Liberal) founded in 1966, with its intellectual core mainly in Amsterdam. In 1984, the Amsterdam department of D'66 proposed legalizing "all substances that could be used for pleasure," including such hard drugs as heroin and cocaine. In 1997, D'66 is the country's fourth-largest political party and part of the ruling coalition, together with social democrats and right-wing liberals.

Drug dependence unit *(England):* A facility staffed by a specialist multidisciplinary team clinically directed by a consultant psychiatrist and offering assessment and treatment of drug misusers. The team is designed to deal with complex and difficult cases.

Deutsche Hauptstelle gegen die Suchtgefahren (DHS)/(German Council on Addiction Problems) *(Germany):* An umbrella organization of all nonprofit organizations concerned with addiction to alcohol or drugs. It includes government agencies and temperance groups. It organizes an annual congress and publishes a journal.

Drug and Drug-Addiction European Observatory/Observatório Euripeu das Drogas e Toxicodependência (OEDT) *(Portugal):* A European Union agency, decentralized to Lisbon, whose task is to collect, analyze, and disseminate data on the search for drugs, strategic and national policies, international cooperation, and other aspects of drug traffic throughout the 15 member states of the Union.

The National Coca Enterprise (Empresa Nacional de la Coca; ENACO) *(Peru):* A government enterprise permitted to buy and trade in coca leaf and its derivatives for multiple uses (medicinal, infusions, cosmetic, etc.). It keeps a record of farmers legally permitted to grow coca.

Firma *(Peru):* A cartel or local mafia in coca-growing zones that controls the production and commercialization of basic paste of cocaine (PBC), an intermediate substance in the production of cocaine chlorhydrate.

Harm reduction approach *(Netherlands, England, Switzerland):* Harm reduction was appropriated from the safety and insurance industries. These industries try to minimize the consequences and probabilities of accidents and costly illnesses by providing incentives for behavior such as wearing safety belts, not smoking, and avoiding high-risk sports. This business philosophy has been transferred to drug-related public policy and basically aims at the minimization of adverse effects of both drug use and drug prohibition. Specific policy measures include the promotion of sterile syringes for injection drug users, methadone and other opioids for opiate-dependent people, adequate treatment for individuals suffering from chronic pain, noncoercive drug treatment programs for substance abusers, and medical marijuana for seriously ill people whom it might benefit. Harm reduction programs as prominent alternatives to use-reduction have been developed in many countries, such as Australia, Switzerland, and the Netherlands, as a very successful response to the threat of AIDS. However, the definition of types of harm reduction remains difficult when referring to the reduction of net total harm (i.e., total harm minus benefits of use to users), the reduction of total harm, or the reduction of harm to nonusers without considering the harm to users (e.g., see Caulkins, J. P., & Reuter, P. (1997). Setting goals for drug policy: Harm reduction or use reduction? *Addiction, 92,* 1143-1150).

The harm reduction approach is not limited to the case of illicit drugs only. The term also refers to those policies and programs that attempt to reduce the harm associated with alcohol consumption without the drinker necessarily giving up his or her drinking at the present time. Examples of such measures include server intervention programs, creating safer bars, standard unit labeling of alcohol containers and warning labels, as well as local regulations and enforcement strategies for licensed premises (e.g., see Plant, M., Single, E., & Stockwell, T. (1997). *Alcohol: Minimising the harm—What works?* London, New York: Free Association Books).

Health maintenance organization (HMO) *(USA):* HMOs are health insurance systems developed as a response to rising health care costs in the United States. They are health insurance organizations that admit those insured to medical care only within a designated provider group. In some states, such as California and Oregon, they account for a large market share of the health care system.

Junkie organizations *(Netherlands):* In the Netherlands, there is an organization called the National Platform of Drug Users. The Netherlands' health system has always provided for continuity of care between the official care and treatment system and the community, the informal sector. This general principle has been applied uniquely to heroin users. Over the years, the government has supported a number of "user organizations" that advocate policy changes and protect the human rights of patients in the official system. These organizations are akin to support groups with respect to other chronic disease categories of patients in the Dutch system. Today, the former Junkie Unions have been reorganized into a national platform organization for policy advocacy for drug users.

Kotanski, Marek *(Poland):* A psychologist concerned with drug treatment for more than 20 years. In the late 1970s, he introduced therapeutic communities into drug treatment. He is founder and charismatic leader of Monar, the first nongovernmental organization in the drug field in Poland. Monar runs a network of counseling and residential rehabilitation centers as well as preventive activities. Kotanski, as its leader, has undertaken many initiatives in such different fields as drug prevention, environmental issues, AIDS, homelessness, and prisons. He also competed in Poland's first presidential election.

LTP *(Russia):* The Russian prophylactic labor treatment center for alcohol and drug addicts with a stern regime (as in prison).

NDATUS (National Drug and Alcohol Treatment Utilization Survey) *(USA):* NDATUS is cosponsored by NIDA and NIAAA, and it represents the only national data system on public and private alcohol and drug programs in the United States. Point prevalence surveys have been conducted between 1979 and 1996. The data refer to agencies rather than clients.

NIDA (National Institute on Drug Abuse) *(USA):* Originally the Division of Narcotics Addiction and Drug Abuse within the Department of Health, Education and Welfare, NIDA was established in 1973 or 1974 (there appears to be some discrepancy as to when NIDA began). In addition to continuing the research programs, one of its major tasks is to oversee the national network of treatment programs.

NIAAA (National Institute on Alcohol Abuse and Alcoholism) *(USA):* The federal agency mandated by the U.S. Congress to fund alcohol research and provide policy direction.

Parents' organizations against drugs *(Finland):* These are voluntary organizations that help and support young drug users and their parents and promote a search for effective means of combating the dangers of drugs in society. The first such organization in Finland, *Vapaaksi Huumeista ry* (Freed from drugs), was set up in 1983. Similar organizations had been created in Sweden and Norway at the end of the 1960s. One organization, *Irti Huumeista ry* (Free from drugs), has 18 sections throughout the country and 300 trained volunteers.

Progetto Uomo *(Italy, Spain):* An organization founded in Rome in 1979 by a militant Catholic group and "exported" to Spain and many other countries. Progetto Uomo adopted the American Daytop Village mixed model of therapeutic community, including professionals and former addicts on its training staff. Its therapy is socioeducational in nature and based on the principles of discipline and self-help, leading to behavior modification.

SAMHSA (Substance Abuse and Mental Health Services Administration) *(USA):* In 1992, a reorganization of the original Alcohol, Drug Abuse and Mental Health Administration (ADAMHA) took place. NIDA, NIAAA, and NIMH (National Institute for Mental Health) were transferred to NIH (National Institutes of Health), and the remaining agencies—CSAP (Center for Substance Abuse Prevention), CSAT (Center for Substance Abuse Treatment), and the Center for Mental Health Services were left in the restructured organization, whose key mission was to improve service delivery nationwide.

Sectorisation (France): Organization of mental health services introduced in the 1960s. It allocates to every mental hospital unit the care of a defined geographical area. Its effect has been to develop outpatient care.

Service des Statistiques, des Études et des Systèmes d'Information (SESI) *(France):* A service of the French Ministry of Health and Social Affairs. It collects data on the whole social security system in a broad sense, and it studies and analyzes financial, demographic, and health information. It conducts an annual survey (*enquête toxicomanies*) of medical and social units that declare themselves as taking drug addicts in charge.

Traditional Chinese medicine *(China):* The study of the physiology and pathology of the human body and the diagnosis and control of diseases. It has a unique theory system and rich clinical experience. The theory system of traditional Chinese medicine was deeply influenced by ancient materialism and dialectic thought—the theory of yin and yang (the two opposing, yet uniting, forces in nature)—and the five elements—wood, fire, earth, metal, and water. Its medical theory system is characterized by taking the concept of the human body as a whole as the dominant idea; the physiology and pathology of the organs, bowels, channels, and collaterals as the basis; and the determination of treatment on the basis of the differentiation of symptoms and signs as the main method of diagnosis and treatment.

Traqueteros *(Peru):* Usually, young people involved with the *firmas* in zones where coca leaf is transformed into PBC; their task is to buy PBC in small amounts and send it in bulk to places where it will be further processed into cocaine chlorhydrate.

Treatment prison (Behandlungsvollzug) *(Austria):* A category of prisons introduced by the amendment of the penal code in 1975 and designed to both prevent prisoner addicts from taking drugs and treat their addiction. The treatment prison for alcohol and drug addicts in Vienna—the so-called penal institution for offenders in need of withdrawal—was the first such treatment prison.

Volunteer probation officer *(Japan):* Volunteer probation officers, commissioned by the Minister of Justice, are a unique feature of Japan's community-based treatment. Their most important tasks are to supervise and assist probationers and parolees in their efforts to rehabilitate themselves in the community.

War on Drugs *(USA):* President Reagan first used the term in 1982, but it was not until the emergence of crack cocaine in 1986 and the passing of the Anti-Drug Abuse Act that the term was taken up by the media and politicians in general. However, in the 1997 White House National Drug Control Strategy report, the War on Drugs metaphor was considered, for the first time, "misleading." According to the White House report, "A more appropriate analogy for the drug problem is cancer." Under this new rhetoric, the task is "to reduce the cancer of drugs in America."

Wohlfahrtsverbände **(Welfare organizations)** *(Germany):* Six large, national, nonprofit welfare organizations dominate the nongovernmental social sector in Germany: Caritas, a Catholic organization; Diakonisches Werk (DW), run by the Protestant Church; Zentralwohlfahrtsstelle der Juden in Deutschland, which represents Jewish institutions in Germany; Arbeiter Wohlfahrt (AW), which has strong ties to the labor unions; Rotes Kreuz, the German Red Cross organization; and Deutscher Paritätischer Wohlfahrts-Verband (DPWV), a conglomerate of nonreligious groups. They differ in numbers of members, influence, focus, and realization of their goals. Up to 90% of their budgets come from the federal government, the states, and local communities.

Index

About the Editors

Harald Klingemann, *Switzerland,* studied at Cologne University (Germany), where he received the degree of Doctor of Economics and Social Science. He has taught at the University of Bonn, where he was a senior researcher in criminology, and at the Fachhochschule of Cologne. Currently, he is director of research at the Swiss Institute for the Prevention of Alcohol and Drug Problems (Lausanne). His main research interests include the cross-cultural analysis of treatment systems, deviant careers, and the natural recovery process. He has coedited *Cure, Care, or Control* (State University of New York Press, 1992). Recent journal and book chapters include "Drug Treatment in Switzerland: Harm Reduction, Decentralization and Community Response" (*Addiction,* 1996); "Coping and Maintenance Strategies of Spontaneous Remitters From Problem Use of Alcohol and Heroin in Switzerland" (*International Journal of the Addictions,* 1992); and "Environmental Influences Which Support or Impede Change in Substance Behaviour" (Oxford University Press, 1994).

Geoffrey Hunt, *USA,* PhD, is principal investigator of a research project on street groups, alcohol, and violence that is sponsored by the National Institute on Alcohol Abuse and Alcoholism at the Institute for Scientific Analysis, Alameda, California. His previous research, in the United States and England, has been on drinking practices and behavior, community substance abuse prevention programs, and the culture of drug and alcohol treatment systems. He has published on alcohol and drug use, alcohol and drug treatment systems, ethnographic evaluation, youth gangs, and international migration.

About the Contributors

José Manuel Gaspar de Almeida, *Portugal,* a medical graduate of Oporto University, trained in psychiatry and specialized in alcohol-related problems. He is a member of a multidisciplinary team engaged in prevention programs in alcohology and is in charge of inpatient treatment at the Oporto Regional Alcohology Centre for the prevention and treatment of alcohol-related problems in the north of Portugal. He is an associate member of the Portuguese Family Therapy Society, the Portuguese Behavioral Therapy Society, and the Kettil Bruun Society, and he has Direction Membership of the Portuguese Alcohology Society.

Gabriele Bammer, *USA,* PhD, is a Fellow at the National Centre for Epidemiology and Population Health at the Australian National University. Her primary area of interest is multidisciplinary research into complex social problems. She has directed a 5-year feasibility study into an Australian trial of heroin prescription, the implementation of which is awaiting a political decision.

Judith C. Barker, *USA,* PhD, is an associate professor in the Medical Anthropology Program, Department of Epidemiology & Biostatistics, University of California, San Francisco. Trained in medical sociology and medical anthropology in New Zealand, Great Britain, and the United States, she has done field research for over 10 years in Australasia, the Southwest Pacific, and the United States. This research, primarily qualitative, has examined the recognition, day-to-day management, and expression of a variety of health conditions (especially chronic illnesses) and health-related behavior, particularly with respect to the frail elderly in community living. She has a long-standing interest in gender and ethnic differences in the experience and expression of illness. She is widely published in gerontology and in anthropological sources.

Anders Bergmark, *Sweden,* is a professor in the Department of Social Work at Stockholm University. He is director of the Addiction Research Group, which is engaged in several extensive research projects on alcohol and drug treatment in

Sweden. His published work includes *Drug Abuse and Treatment, The Concept of Control and Alcoholism, The Limits of Phenomenology and Objectivity, Long-Term Follow-up of Residentially Treated Drug Abusers,* and *Swedish Alcohol Treatment in Transition? Social Conditions of Treatment Programs.*

Gérald Béroud, *China,* is a graduate in sociology and has done further study in sinology. He is the Director of SinOptic—Services and Studies on the Chinese World, in Lausanne, Switzerland. For many years, he was on the staff of the Swiss Institute for the Prevention of Alcohol and Drug Problems. He has conducted research on drug problems in mainland China as well as Taiwan and Hong Kong.

Gerhard Bühringer, *Germany,* PhD, is the Director, IFT Institut für Therapieforschung (Institute for Therapy Research), Munich. Formerly, he was director of the Addiction Research Group of the Max Planck Institute of Psychiatry in Munich. His research, mainly federally funded, has been in epidemiology; prevention and treatment of addictive behavior (alcohol, illicit drugs, pharmaceuticals); pathological gambling; and the evaluation of treatment programs and facilities in behavioral medicine and psychosocial health care. He is author or coauthor of many publications on substance abuse research. He is a member of the scientific advisory boards of a number of German and international associations and editor or a member of the editorial boards of several German and international scientific journals.

Wilhelm Burian, *Austria,* Dr.med., is a psychiatrist and Director of the Department for the Treatment of Drug Addicts, Anton Proksch Institute, Vienna. He is also a Member of the Vienna Psychoanalytic Society (IPA). Since 1972, he has published papers and three books on the treatment of alcoholism and drug addiction, psychoanalytical treatment, and sociology and the addictions.

Cheng Maojin, *China,* is Deputy Director of the Institute of Social Medicine, Tongji Medical University in Wuhan; Vice-Dean of the School of Public Health; and Director of the Department of Health Education. He has conducted a project supported by the World Bank on health facilities in some medium-size cities.

Chen Shirong, *China,* is Director of the Institute of Social Medicine, Tongji Medical University in Wuhan, where he teaches health education, social medicine, and mental health.

Jack T. M. Derks, *Netherlands,* PhD, is adjunct professor at the International Institute for Psycho-Social and Socio-Ecological Research, University of Limburg. He was with the Netherlands Institute of Mental Health from 1980 to 1996 and was founder and director of the drugs and gambling research unit of the Amsterdam Institute for Addiction Research, 1993-1995. He is on the executive board of the European Methadone Association; vice-president of the COST A-6 program (Evaluation of action against drug abuse in Europe) of the European Commission; co-coordinator of working group 1 of COST A-6 (Evaluation of drug policies, drug policy changes, and societal responses to drug policies); and scientific coordinator and vice-principal-investigator of the IPTRP/BIOMED 2 program of the European Commission.

Irmgard Eisenbach-Stangl, *Austria,* Dr.phil., Univ.Doz., is a researcher at the Ludwig Boltzmann Institute for Addiction Research and a lecturer at the Institute of Sociology of the University of Vienna. Her main research interests are the social history of alcohol and illicit drugs, especially in Austria; gender-specific consump-tion patterns of psychotropic substances; development and structure of profes-sional treatment of addiction (institutions, programs, methods, especially psycho-therapy); and nonprofessional mutual aid. Her publications include *A Social History of Alcohol: Consumption, Production and Social Control of Alcoholic Beverages in Austria, 1918-1984; Haschisch: Prohibition or Legalization* (with W. Burian, ed.); and *Alcoholics Anonymous as a Mutual-Help Movement: A Study in Eight Societies* (with K. Mäkelä et al.).

Zsuzsanna Elekes, *Hungary,* is a sociologist and associate professor in the Department of Sociology of Budapest University of Economic Sciences. Her main field of study is the sociological analysis of deviant behavior, with special emphasis on drug epidemiology. She has published numerous articles in Hungarian and international journals. She has participated in a number of international research projects, the most recent a European project on drug consumption and attitudes toward drugs, reported in *Alcohol- and Drug-Consumption Among Secondary-School Students in Hungary* (1996).

Rosa Encarnaçáo, *Portugal,* is a medical graduate of Oporto University and a specialist in psychiatry. In 1994, she instituted the multidisciplinary team of the Oporto Regional Alcohology Center and is in charge of its day hospital. She works in prevention of alcohol-related problems in schools, municipalities, and prisons. Her interests are group therapies, alcohol-related problems of young people and women, rehabilitation programs, and epilepsy. She is co-author and author of papers on alcohology, epilepsy, and group therapies, and she is an associate member of the Portuguese Family Therapy Society, the Portuguese Association of Mental and Psychiatric Problems, and the Portuguese Epilepsy League.

Yakov Gilinskiy, *Russia,* PhD and Doctor of Science in Law, Leningrad State University, is professor at the Institute of Sociology of the Russian Academy of Sciences in St. Petersburg, as well as Head of the Department of Sociology of Deviant Behavior. His current research is in criminology, the sociology of deviant behavior, and social control. He has published more than 210 works, mostly on sociology and criminology.

Marten J. Hoekstra, *Netherlands,* is managing director of the Dutch Association of Addiction Treatment and Care Centers. He has a degree in sociology and has worked in several umbrella organizations and institutes of mental health, primary health, and addiction. Topics on which he has written include alcohol and drug policy and organization of treatment. He is on the board of directors of the International Council on Alcohol and Addictions.

Charles D. Kaplan, *Netherlands,* PhD, is Director of the Division of Drug Use and Abuse, International Institute for Psychosocial and Socio-Ecological Research, University of Limburg, Maastricht, and adjunct professor, Division of Social and Policy Sciences, University of Texas, San Antonio. He was visiting professor at the Johann Wolfgang Goethe Universität, Frankfurt, 1977-1984, and held the Tinbergen Chair at the Institute for Preventive and Social Psychiatry, Erasmus University, Rotterdam, 1984-1992. In addition, he founded the European Addiction Research Institute in Rotterdam. He is on the advisory board of the *Journal of Psychoactive Drugs* and on the editorial board of the *Scandinavian Journal of Social Welfare.* He is principal investigator of the IPTRP/BIOMED 2 program of the European Commission.

Éva Katona, *Hungary,* is a psychiatrist and was a founder of Hungary's first crisis intervention center. From the late 1980s, she was active in setting up the national drug program, and she became a member of the planning and executive board of the National Health Promotion Council and of the National Education, Training and Research Board on Drugs while she continued to practice. She helped to establish the first outpatient clinic for drug addicts in Budapest and another in the country. She is a senior lecturer at the Budapest Postgraduate Medical School/ Institute of Public Health. She has done collaborative research with American counterparts on drug epidemiology and has represented Hungary in the Multi-City Network of the Pompidou Group/Council of Europe in 1995-1996.

Aarne Kinnunen, *Finland,* is a criminologist at Finland's National Research Institute of Legal Policy. He has published books and articles on pretrial investigation, victim surveys, credit card fraud, violence in workplaces, drug use patterns, and drug markets. He is now studying criminal careers and socioeconomic background factors of drug offenders at Statistics Finland. He is also Secretary of the Finnish Commission on National Drug Policy.

Hans-Dieter Klingemann, *Germany,* PhD, is Professor of Political Science at the Free University of Berlin; director of the Research Unit on Social Institutions and Social Change at the Science Center for Social Research, Berlin; and permanent Research Fellow in Politics and Society at the University of California, Irvine. He has authored, coauthored, or edited 21 books, two book series, and numerous journal articles and book chapters. Recent coauthored publications include *A New Handbook of Political Science* and *Citizens and the State* (Oxford University Press); and *Parties, Policies and Democracy* (Westview Press). His current research is on democratic transition and consolidation in Central and Eastern Europe.

Kyohei Konuma, *Japan,* MD, is a psychiatrist and Director of the Department of Drug Dependence Treatment and Research at the National Psychiatric Institute of Shimousa. He has long been engaged in treatment and clinical research and is leading a national epidemiological survey on drug dependence and psychiatric services for drug dependents. His most recent work is on the use and abuse of amphetamines in Japan.

Takeshi Koyanagi, *Japan,* is a psychologist and director of the Kushiro Juvenile Classification Home of the Ministry of Justice. He has been engaged in treatment of offenders and research on mainly drug-related offenses. At present, he is a professor at the United Nations Asia and Far East Institute for the Prevention of Crime and the Treatment of Offenders. He has published several works, most recently *Current Trends of Foreign Prisoners in Japan* (Gyosei Press, 1995).

Antonio Lara-Ponce, *Peru,* is a graduate in psychology of St. Mark's National Major University and a member of the Peruvian College of Psychologists and the Committee of Community Psychology Consultants. He coordinates the fieldwork and heads the Jungle Program of the Center of Information and Education for Prevention of Drug Abuse. He is designing a community preventive program for zones at high risk of production and use of drugs, jungle territories exposed to terrorism, and shantytowns. He is the national representative of the local chapter of social psychology of the Interamerican Society of Psychology, a member of the Regional Office of Health Education for Latin America, and a volunteer for the Andean area at the European Center against Drugs.

Juhani Lehto, *Finland,* is professor of social and health care management at Tampere University and head of the Services and Quality Unit at the National Research and Development Centre for Welfare and Health in Helsinki. He has been a consultant at the Regional Office for Europe of the World Health Organization and a researcher at the Finnish Foundation for Alcohol Studies. Recent publications include studies on evaluation of alcohol and drug policies, economic aspects of alcohol policy, and financing and management of social and health care.

Susanne MacGregor, *England,* MA, PhD, is Professor of Sociology and Social Policy at Middlesex University. Recent books of which she has been coauthor or coeditor are *The Drugs Treatment Services in England, The Other City People and Politics in New York and London, Activating Local Networks: A Comparison of Two Community Development Approaches to Drugs Prevention,* and *Transforming Cities: Contested Governance and New Spatial Divisions.* She has been scientific advisor to the Department of Health and is the London Co-Coordinator of the Mega-Cities Project, an international action-research project on issues of poverty, environment, women, and governance. Her research interests include drug treatment and prevention, urban regeneration, and poverty. Current work includes research on community development and drug prevention, contributing to the

REITOX program of the European Monitoring Centre for Drugs and Drug Addiction, and directing an evaluation of drug action teams.

Enrique Madrigal, *USA,* is Doctor of Medicine and Surgery, University of Costa
Rica, and a specialist in adult and child psychiatry, Columbia University, New York
City. He is also Regional Advisor, Prevention and Control of Addictive Behaviors,
Pan American Health Organization/World Health Organization Regional Office for
the Americas, Washington, DC. Former appointments have been Medical Director,
Department of Community Psychiatry, Saint Luke's Roosevelt Hospital Center,
Columbia University, New York; Clinical Director, Children's Aid Society, New
York City; and Director General, National Institute on Alcoholism, Costa Rica.

Jacek Moskalewicz, *Poland,* PhD, is a researcher at the Institute of Psychiatry and
Neurology, Warsaw. His major interests are alcohol and drug policy and the
sociology of social problems. He is a member of the WHO Expert Committee on
Drug Dependence and Alcohol Problems. He has coauthored the chapter "Changing Definitions of the Drug Problem" in an international report from the Baltica
Study, *Social Problems in Newspapers: Studies Around the Baltic Sea;* a chapter
on Poland in *International Handbook on Alcohol and Culture;* and an international
report from the WHO study on community response to alcohol-related problems,
Alcohol and the Community.

Philippe Mossé, *France,* is a research economist at the Laboratory for the Study
of the Economics and Sociology of Work at the National Center for Scientific
Research, Aix-en-Provence, and a board member of the French Social Economics
Association. His studies are mainly on reforms of the French social security system
and hospital management. His current studies are on hospital industrial relations
and financing reforms (in Germany, Italy, and France), and on the working-time
issue in several industrial and services sectors in France and Great Britain. He
teaches postgraduate courses in work economics and health economics and
assesses the local impact of social policies. Recent publications in English are
"Towards a Professional Rationalization: Lessons From the French Health Care
System" (*American Journal of Economics and Sociology*); *Private Markets in
Health and Welfare, France* (N. Johnson, ed.); and *Industrial Relations in Health
Care.*

Kaj Noschis, *Switzerland,* PhD, has worked as a Jungian analyst in private practice
in Lausanne, Switzerland, for the past 12 years. He has also taken part in research
projects on alcohol-related problems.

Alan C. Ogborne, *Canada,* PhD, is a senior scientist at the Department of Social
and Evaluation Research of the Addiction Research Foundation of Ontario. He has
conducted research on many aspects of substance use and abuse and addiction,
including many studies of treatment systems and services. His recent research has

concerned the characteristics, beliefs, and training needs of specialists in addiction services.

Borbála Paksi, *Hungary,* is a sociologist who has been engaged over the past 10 years in sociological analysis of various forms of deviant behavior, with special emphasis on suicide and drug consumption. She has published numerous articles on the topic, and several articles and studies have cited the results of her research. She is coauthor of *Alcohol- and Drug-Consumption Among Secondary-School Students in Hungary* (1996).

Augusto Pérez-Gómez, *Colombia,* PhD, is Full Professor at the Department of Psychology, University of the Andes, Bogotá. He founded the La Casa Program in 1986, a center for prevention and treatment of, and research into, drug-related problems, AIDS and suicide, and, more recently, social violence, mainly kidnapping and extortion. In 1994, he was visiting professor at the Chelsea and Westminster Medical School, London, and consultant to the Riverside Mental Health Trust. He has published five books and more than 100 papers and book chapters in Spanish, English, and French. He is vice president for Latin America of the International Federation of NGO Against Drugs, and a representative of SOS Drogue International for Latin America and the Caribbean.

Juan-Luis Recio Adrados, *Spain,* PhD, is Professor of Sociology at the Madrid Universidad Complutense and a member of the editorial staff of the journal *Adicciones,* of the Technical Commission of the Foundation for Help Against Drug Addiction, and of the Complutense Institute for Drug Dependencies. He is scientific advisor to the Spanish National Plan on Drugs. He was project director of the first population survey of drug misuse in Spain (1980). In 1988-1989, he directed a longitudinal study on the role of the family in adolescent drug misuse among Madrid high school students. He was visiting scientist at the United States National Institute on Drug Abuse (NIDA) in 1991-1992 and coedited NIDA Research Monograph No. 130 on the theoretical and methodological issues of drug misuse among U.S. minorities.

Brian R. Rush, *Canada,* PhD, is a senior scientist with the Addiction Research Foundation of Ontario. His research interests include the evolution of Ontario's addiction treatment system, the cost-effectiveness of treatment, and forecasting models for addressing the need for treatment services.

Martin Schmid, *Germany,* is a graduate of the University of Frankfurt am Main and a sociologist at the Institute for Social Work and Social Pedagogics (*Institut für Sozialarbeit und Sozialpädagogik*), Addiction Research Group, in Frankfurt am Main. He has worked for 5 years for a drug-counseling institution. His main areas of research are the evaluation of pilot programs for drug addicts and the development of the drug treatment system. His publications include articles on low-threshold centers, drug scenes, and drug policies. He also takes part in the training of drug counselors.

Shinji Shimizu, *Japan,* MS, is head of the Mental Health Planning Section, National Institute of Mental Health, Tokyo, and one of the few sociologists who studies alcohol and drug problems in Japan. He is also a family sociologist who deals with clinical issues, specifically in family health and addiction. He has been associate professor at Osaka City University and is a member of the Expert Committee on Alcohol-Related Problems at the Ministry of Health and Welfare. He has published several books, most recently *Hungarian Society and Health/ Alcohol Problems.*

Janusz Sierosɬawski, *Poland,* is a sociologist at the Institute of Psychiatry and Neurology, Warsaw. His main areas of interest are social problems related to alcohol and drug consumption, the epidemiology of alcohol and drug dependence, international comparability of epidemiological indicators, social response to alcohol and drug problems at the local and national level, and prevention and policy issues. He is an epidemiology expert of the Pompidou Group at the Council of Europe, as well as coordinator of the Warsaw Multi-City Study and the Polish part of the European School Survey Project on Alcohol and Drugs.

Reginald G. Smart, *Canada,* PhD, is Director of Social Evaluation and Principal of the Addiction Research Foundation of Ontario. His interests include the epidemiology of substance use and abuse, alcohol policy, and studies of prevention and treatment programs.

Lynne Smith, *England,* MSc, is research officer at the Social Policy Research Centre at Middlesex University. As a senior manager in the voluntary sector for many years, she was responsible for developing and managing welfare services. She was coauthor of *The Drugs Treatment Services in England* (1994) and *Activating Local Networks* (1996). Recent work has included an antipoverty audit for a London borough and research into young people's attitudes toward drugs and the law. Her research interests include women and community development, drug treatment, and drug prevention. Current research is on community development and drug prevention, evaluation of drug action teams, and a typology of drug treatment systems for the REITOX project of the European Monitoring Centre for Drugs and Drug Addiction.

Luigi M. Solivetti, *Italy,* is a graduate in law (criminology) and psychology, and he is permanent research fellow and lecturer in sociology at the Faculty of Statistical Sciences, University of Rome "La Sapienza." He has been research fellow with Italy's National Research Council and visiting professor at the London School of Economics and Political Science, and he has done research and teaching in Africa (University of Sokoto, Nigeria). He is a consultant in crime issues to the Ministry of Justice, Italy and a referee for several international journals. He has been extensively published, mainly on deviance and social control, in such international journals as *The Howard Journal of Criminal Justice, Africa* (International African Institute, London), *Revue Internationale de Sociologie—International Review of Sociology,* and *Sociologia del Diritto.*

Grażyna Świątkiewicz, *Poland,* MA, is a researcher at the Institute of Psychiatry and Neurology, Warsaw, mainly in social research on licit and illicit drugs. She has been a consultant to a Pompidou Group project on drug use in pregnancy. She coauthored a two-volume publication, *Alcoholics Anonymous as a Mutual Self-Help Movement: A Study in Eight Societies,* and a chapter on "Changing Definitions of the Drug Problems" in an international report from the Baltica Study, *Social Problems in Newspapers: Studies Around the Baltic Sea.* She contributed an article on "Using Drugs to Ease the Pain of Transition" to a special issue of *Women and Pharmaceuticals* prepared for the Fourth World Conference on Women in 1995.

Michael S. Vaughn, *USA,* is an assistant professor at the Department of Criminal Justice, Georgia State University. He received his PhD in 1993 from the College of Criminal Justice at Sam Houston State University. He writes on legal issues in criminal justice and cross-cultural crime and social control.

Irmgard Vogt, *Germany,* PhD, is a social psychologist and professor at the Department of Social Work of the Fachhochschule Frankfurt-am-Main. Her main research areas are sociological and psychological aspects of alcohol and other psychoactive drug use and abuse in the past and at present; prevention of addiction and addictive behavior; health problems in the female life cycle and family violence; counseling institutions, counselors, and the counseling process for addicts; and sexual abuse in counseling and therapy. Her published books include *Für alle Leiden gibt es eine Pille* [For all suffering there is a chemical cure]; *Alkoholikerinnen* [Female alcoholics]; *Drogen und Drogenpolitik. Ein Handbuch* [Drugs, drug policies and politics: A handbook] (coauthored with Sebastian Scheerer); *Beratung süchtiger Frauen: Konzepte und Methoden* [Counseling female addicts: concepts and methods] (coauthored with Klaudia Winkler).

Wang Zhengyan, *China,* MD, is a senior scientist at the Institute of Social Medicine of Tongji Medical University. Her research interests include the epidemiology of substance use and abuse and studies of prevention and treatment systems.

Anna Xiao Dong Sun, *USA,* is a research assistant at the Institute for Scientific Analysis. A Chinese national, she is an undergraduate student in sociology at the University of California, Berkeley. Her research interests are social policy and addiction. She also conducts research into the formation of taste among American art collectors, a project funded by the University of California President's Fellowship. Her publications include a paper on Ezra Pound (Paideuma, forthcoming) and a number of short stories.

Vladimir Zobnev, *Russia,* PhD, is a senior research worker at St. Petersburg's Psychological Research Institute. His current research is in medical psychology and narcology. He has published more than 50 works.